Devotional literature in South Asia

Current research, 1985–1988

Papers of the Fourth Conference on Devotional Literature
in New Indo-Aryan Languages, held at
Wolfson College, Cambridge, 1–4 September 1988

edited by

R. S. McGREGOR

CAMBRIDGE
UNIVERSITY PRESS

University of Cambridge Oriental publications
published for the Faculty of Oriental Studies
For a complete list see the end of this volume.

Published by the Press Syndicate of the University of Cambridge
The Pitt Building, Trumpington Street, Cambridge CB2 1RP
40 West 20th Street, New York, NY 10011-4211, USA
10 Stamford Road, Oakleigh, Victoria 3166, Australia

First published 1992

Printed in Great Britain at the University Press, Cambridge

A catalogue record for this book is available from the British Library

Library of Congress cataloguing in publication data

Conference on Devotional Literature in New Indo-Aryan Languages (4th:
1988: Wolfson College, Cambridge)
Devotional literature in South Asia: papers of the Fourth
Conference on Devotional Literature in New Indo-Aryan Languages,
held at Wolfson College, Cambridge, 1–4 September 1988 / edited by
R. S. McGregor.
p. cm. – (University of Cambridge oriental publications)
Includes bibliographical references and index.
ISBN 0 521 41311 7
1. Hindu literature – History and criticism – Congresses.
2. Islamic literature – History and criticism – Congresses. 3. Bhakti
in literature – Congresses. I. McGregor, Ronald Stuart. II. Title.
III. Series.
BL1147,C66 1988
294.5'92 – dc20 91-13833 CIP

ISBN 0 521 41311 7

UP

CONTENTS

CONFERENCE MEMBERS

Papers were read by, or on behalf of, those Conference members whose names are marked with an asterisk.

* **Dr Ali S. Asani**, Department of Near Eastern Languages and Civilizations, 6 Divinity Avenue, Cambridge, Mass. 02138, USA.

* **Dr H. T. Bakker**, Instituut voor Indische Talen en Culturen, Oude Kijk in 'tJatstraat 26, Postbus 716, 9700 AS Groningen, Netherlands.

* **Dr R. K. Barz**, Faculty of Asian Studies, Australian National University, Canberra ACT 2601, Australia.

* **Dr K. E. Bryant**, University of British Columbia, Department of Asian Studies, 1871 Westbrook Mall, Vancouver, BC, Canada V6T 1W5.

* **Dr Maya Burger**, Section des langues et civilisations orientales, Université de Lausanne, BFSH 11, CH-1015 Dorigny/Lausanne, Switzerland.

* **Dr W. N. Callewaert**, Departement Orientalistiek, Katholieke Universiteit Leuven, Blijde Inkomststraat 21, B-3000 Leuven, Belgium.

Mr D. J. F. Clinch, St John's College, Cambridge, UK.

* **Mrs Vasudha Dalmia-Lüderitz**, Seminar für Indologie u. Vergl. Religionswissenschaft, Universität Tübingen, Münzgasse 30, 7400 Tübingen, Germany.

Dr Françoise Delvoye 'Nalini', 64 rue Vieille du Temple, 75003 Paris, France.

Dr A. W. Entwistle, Department of Asian Languages and Literature, Do-21 University of Washington, Seattle, Wash. 98195, USA.

Mr P. Friedlander, School of Oriental and African Studies, University of London, Malet Street, London WC1E 7HP, UK.

* **Professor P. Gaeffke**, 815 Williams Hall/CV, University of Pennsylvania, Philadelphia, Pa., USA.

* **Dr G. Gopinathan**, Head of the Department of Hindi, Calicut University, Calicut, Kerala 673635, India.

Dr John S. Hawley, Department of Religion, Barnard College, Columbia University, 3009 Broadway, New York, NY 10027-6598, USA.

* **Professor Jin Dinghan**, Hindi Section, Department of Asian Languages and Literature, Beijing University, Beijing, China.

* **Dr Catharina Kiehnle**, Mümmelmannsberg 69, D-2000 Hamburg 74, Germany.

Miss Sagaree Sengupta Korom, South Asia Regional Studies, 820 Williams Hall, University of Pennsylvania, Philadelphia, Pa. 19104-6305, USA.

* **Professor V. D. Kulkarni**, 'Jogawa' 1–11, Saraswati Colony, Uppal, Hyderabad 500039, India.

* **Dr R. S. McGregor**, Faculty of Oriental Studies, Sidgwick Avenue, Cambridge CB3 9DA, UK.

* **Dr Françoise Mallison**, Les Montèzes, F-30170 St Hippolyte-du-Fort, France.

* **Dr Denis Matringe**, Flandre 2, Lormoy, 91240 Saint-Michel-sur-Orge, France.

* **Dr G. N. Morje**, Ahmednagar College, Ahmednagar 414001, India.

* **Dr S. M. Pandey**, Istituto Universitario Orientale, Piazza Giovanni Maggiore 30, 80134 Napoli, Italy.

Mrs I. Patel, 83 Blinco Grove, Cambridge, UK.

Miss K. Pauwels, Departement Orientalistiek, Katholieke Universiteit Leuven, Blijde Inkomststraat 21, B-3000 Leuven, Belgium.

* **Dr G. Pollet**, Department Orientalistiek, Katholieke Universiteit Leuven, Blijde Inkomststraat 21, B-3000 Leuven, Belgium.

* **Mr Erik Reenberg Sand**, Københavns Universitet, Institut for Religions-historie, Købmagergade 44–46, København, Denmark.

Dr G. H. Schokker, Instituut Kern, Arsenaalstraat 1, 2311 VV Leiden, Netherlands.

* **Dr C. Shelke, SJ**, Snehsadan, Institute for Research in Religion, Poona 411014, India.

* **Dr W. L. Smith**, Institutionen för orientaliska språk, Avdelningen för indologi, Stockholms Universitet, Stockholm, Sweden.

* **Dr R. Snell**, School of Oriental and African Studies, University of London, Malet Street, London WC1E 7HP, UK.

Dr S. N. Srivastava, Faculty of Oriental Studies, Sidgwick Avenue, Cambridge CB3 9DA, UK.

Mrs S. Srivastava, High Commission of India, Aldwych, London WC2, UK.

* **Professor Dr Monika Thiel-Horstmann**, Indologisches Seminar der Universität Bonn, Regina-pacis-Weg 7, D-5300 Bonn 1, Germany.

* **Professor S. G. Tulpule**, 952 Sadashiv Peth, Poona 30, India.

Dr E. Turbiani, Vico Pescatori 1/11, 18039 Ventimiglia, Italy.

* **Dr H. van Skyhawk**, Abteilung für Religionsgeschichte und Philosophie, Südasien-Institut der Universität Heidelberg, INF 330, 6900 Heidelberg, Germany.

* **Professor Charlotte Vaudeville**, 191 rue d'Alésia, 75014 Paris, France.

* **Mr S. C. R. Weightman**, School of Oriental and African Studies, University of London, Malet Street, London WC1E 7HP, UK.

PREFACE

Following the earlier Conferences on Devotional Literature in New Indo-Aryan Languages held at Leuven (1979), Bonn (1982), and Leiden (1985), the fourth Conference in this series was held at Wolfson College, Cambridge, from 1 to 4 September 1988. It was agreed that the papers read to the Cambridge Conference should, like those of the preceding Conferences, be published. Of the twenty-nine papers read at, or promised to, the Conference all but two are presented here.

The papers deal with recent research interests of the Conference participants: topics from within the wide field of 'bhakti literature'. This term has gained some currency to refer to the devotional poetry and other compositions of devotional character found in the earlier literature of the modern South Asian languages. The Conference has restricted itself to the field of the Indo-Aryan languages. The study of modern South Asian languages and their literatures has in recent years made the above material much more accessible to scholarly study than in the past, and this has opened the way towards improved knowledge of the history of Indian religions in the last millennium: a field largely beyond the reach of India's classical languages and one of interest both for its own sake, and as throwing light on aspects of modern life in the subcontinent. The topics discussed in the present papers range, in time, from roots of the bhakti tradition to its adaptation in the modern age: from aspects of the early history of Kṛṣṇaism to the emergence of modern religious and cultural attitudes in the nineteenth century and of new religious movements in the twentieth. Geographically, the South Asian range of these topics is from Bengal to Sind, and from the Panjab to Maharashtra. The papers deal with materials in some six modern Asian languages, viz. Bengali, Gujarati, Hindi in its main literary forms, Marathi, Panjabi, and Sindhi; as well as with materials in Sanskrit, Arabic, and also Chinese. Many papers are studies of literary works or bodies of originally orally transmitted material belonging to the Kṛṣṇa or Rāma traditions of north and west India and of Bengal, or of particular topics connected with such works and materials. Others treat particular Ṣūfī compositions and aspects of their interpretation. Other papers again, however, are less directly oriented to the study of language materials. Topics dealt with in these include the early history of sacred places and sites; the emergence, around the beginning of our period, of the religion of Rāma; the formulation of later religious attitudes in different parts of the subcontinent, and their transmission with greater or less change; aspects of the interaction between Islamic and Indian religious attitudes, and of the Ṣūfī presence in north and west India; and features of organisation and practice in particular religious communities. Two papers deal specifically with regions of the world beyond South Asia as well as with South Asian regions, while several raise relevant questions about affinities between Indian and non-Indian religious attitudes.

Because the South Asian regions concerned in these papers share so much in cultural terms, for all their cultural distinctiveness (a situation well reflected in their languages), the present papers have much in common in intention and approach. They have lent themselves readily to thematic arrangement despite their individual differences in subject-matter, as well as in length and scope. They may be allowed to speak for themselves, however, in these respects. Those who have worked in any aspect of Indian devotional literature will find much of interest in the information, analysis, and conclusions which they present.

Devanāgarī script has been used, rather than a roman transcription, for free-standing quotations from Hindi, Marathi, and Sanskrit sources, and likewise Arabic script for quotations from Arabic and Dakkhinī Hindī sources, in the text of articles and in the notes; but only exceptionally for items embedded in the text of sentences in English. As to roman transcription, it was impossible using any one system to do equal justice to the varied forms of modern South Asian languages involved, while to have rendered all these forms according to the system used for the Indian classical languages would often have misrepresented their non-classical character. Consistency of practice in individual papers seemed the right thing to aim at in these circumstances, except in some cases where its demands conflicted with established conventions of usage, and very occasionally where a variation was desirable for some contextual reason.

I would like to express my thanks to Wolfson College, Cambridge, and to the members of the College staff for their contribution to the organisation of the Conference. The Conference was supported, and the present publication assisted, by awards from the Smuts Memorial Fund of Cambridge University.

R. S. McG.
February 1990

ABBREVIATIONS

AH	*Hijra* year
BE	Bengali era
NIA	New Indo-Aryan
VS	Vikramāditya era
AA	*Arts Asiatiques*, Paris
ABORI	*Annals of the Bhandarkar Oriental Research Institute*, Poona
AION	*Annali, Istituto Universitario Orientale di Napoli*, Naples
BCR 1979–1982	M. Thiel-Horstmann, ed., *Bhakti in Current Research (1979–1982)*, Berlin, 1983
BCR 1982–1985	G. H. Schokker, ed., *Bhakti in Current Research (1982–1985)*, Lucknow and New Delhi, forthcoming
BhP	*Bhāgavata Purāṇa*
BLP	*Śrī bayālīs līlā tathā padyāvalī*, ed. Lalitā Caraṇ Gosvāmī, 2nd edn., Vrindaban, VS 2028.
BSK	*Bhāratīya saṃskṛti koś*, ed. Mahādev Śāstrī Jośī, Poona, 1974.
BSOAS	*Bulletin of the School of Oriental and African Studies*, London
CII	*Corpus Inscriptionum Indicarum*
CSSH	*Comparative Studies in Society and History*, *The Hague and London*
DLCR	W. M. Callewaert, ed., *Early Hindi Devotional Literature in Current Research*, Leuven, 1980
DP	Dādūpanth
DPī	Dādūpanthī
EBh	*Ekanāthī-bhāgavat*
HR	*History of Religions*, Chicago
IAR	B. K. Thapar, ed., *Indian Archaeology*, New Delhi
IIJ	*Indo-Iranian Journal*, Dordrecht
JAAR	*Journal of the American Academy of Religion*, Philadelphia

JAOS	*Journal of the American Oriental Society*, New York
JAS	*Journal of Asian Studies*, Ann Arbor
JASB	*Journal of the Asiatic Society of Bengal*, Calcutta
JBRAS	*Journal of the Bombay Branch of the Royal Asiatic Society*, Bombay
JCSR	*Journal of Comparative Sociology and Religion*, Ottawa
JIH	*Journal of Indian History*, Calcutta
JOIB	*Journal of the Oriental Institute*, Baroda
JRAS	*Journal of the Royal Asiatic Society*, London
KBS	*Kulliyāt-i-Bullhe Śāh*, ed. Dr Faqīr Muḥammad Faqīr, Lahore, 1963
MSP	*Mahārāṣṭra sāhitya patrikā*, Poona
OLP	*Orientalia Lovaniensia Periodica*, Leuven
PL	*Premāvalī-līlā*
QI	*Qānūn-i 'iśq*
RL	*Rasānand-līlā*
RML	*Rahasya-mañjarī-līlā*
RMM	*Revue du Monde Musulman*, Paris
SEI	H. A. R. Gibb and J. H. Kramers, eds., *Shorter Encyclopedia of Islam*, Leiden, 1961
SS	*Sūr-sāgar*, ed. Jagannāthdās 'Ratnākar', Munśī Ajmerī, and Nanddulāre Vājpeyī, 4th edn., Varanasi, 1972
SVL	*Siddhānt-vicār-līlā*
TU	*Taittirīya Upaniṣad*
VJL	*Vaidyak-jñān-līlā*
WZKSA	*Wiener Zeitschrift für die Kunde Südasiens*, Vienna

Sacred places and sites

Govardhan, the Eater hill

CHARLOTTE VAUDEVILLE

Already in the early Upaniṣads, such as the *Chāṇḍogya* and the *Bṛhadāraṇyaka*, dependent on pre-Upaniṣadic Vedic ritual, an extraordinary importance attaches to food, *anna*. In the *Taittirīya Upaniṣad* (*TU* iii. 1, 2), when the sage Bhṛgu[1] approaches his father, the god Varuṇa, and asks about the nature of Brahman, Varuṇa defines Brahman as 'Food, Breath, Sight, Hearing, Mind and Speech' – in that order – and Bhṛgu himself finally understands that 'Brahman is food':

> The man who knows this about the nature of food roams at will, eating what he will, changing form at will. *TU* iii. 9

> He who knows that food depends [and is firmly based] on food has himself a firm basis: he becomes an owner of food, and eater of food, rich in offspring, cattle and the vital form of Brahman, rich in fame. *TU* iii. 9

> I am food! I am food! I am food!
> I am an eater of food! I am an eater of food! I am an eater of food! *TU* iii. 10

The mountain and the hero

Mountains, associated with *Nāgas*, divine cobras, on the one hand, and with milchcows on the other, are among the most ancient objects of cult in India.[2] In the *Ṛg-Veda* (1. 544, 2), Viṣṇu is *girikṣit*, 'mountain-dwelling'; the Lord of waters is Varuṇa, of plants, Soma, and of cattle, Rudra.[3] In later literature, Rudra himself is the Lord of mountains, *girīśa*. As Mountain-Dweller and Lord of cattle, Kṛṣṇa-Gopāl also relates to Rudra, thus assuming a Śaivite background.

As a cowherd hero, Kṛṣṇa assumes the dark hue of the mountain deity Govardhan, as well as the activity of the pastoral castes. Under his human form, Kṛṣṇa controls the dangerous world of mountains and *Nāgas* on the one hand, and the life-giving food of the milchcows on the other. He is the Lord of cows and dispenser of the divine food, which is milk. His relation to milk is a unique one, making him the Food-Eater, as well as the Food-Giver *par excellence*.

In *Ancient Folk Cults*,[4] Vasudeva Agrawala gives several lists of archaic folk deities whose cult is in the form of *maha* ('festival') celebrations, as found in early Jaina and Buddhist literature. In all the lists *girimaha* ('mountain festival') and the closely associated *nāgamaha* ('*Nāga* festival') figure prominently. The same author notes that *girimaha* (or *pārvata-yātrā*) was connected with pastoral life 'in which people subsisted mostly on cattle-breeding'.

The supreme importance of worshipping hills, forests, and cattle is expressed in a well-known passage of the Harivaṁśa, in which Kṛṣṇa, as hero and leader of the cowherd tribe, undertakes to wean away his companions from other folk festivals and to impress on them the extreme importance of worshipping Govardhan Hill:

> We are milkmen and we live in forests and hills. Hills, forests and cattle, these are our supreme benefactors ... From hills we derive the greatest of benefits. We should therefore start sacrifices in honour of the hills. Let cows and bulls decorated with autumnal flowers go round yonder hill.[5]

The *govardhanadharaṇa* episode

Characteristic of the Govardhan myth is the interlocking of the cult of the divine mountain with the cult of the divine hero, Kṛṣna-Gopāl, leader of the cowherd tribe. The latter is first represented as *govardhanadhārī*, i.e. in the act of lifting Govardhan Hill itself on his raised left arm.

In the earliest representation of the famed *govardhanadharaṇa* episode, belonging to the Kuṣāna period,[6] the Lord of the sacred hill is represented in his human form: that of a young hero, possibly a *yakṣa*, standing within a mountain cave which looks like a subterranean cow-pen, surrounded by cows and cowherds. The hero's right arm rests on his right thigh, while his left arm is held aloft, effortlessly supporting the top of the rock cave, represented by five conical stones standing in a row. The hero's gesture is traditionally interpreted as a challenge to the rain-god, Indra, though the latter is not represented in the icon itself. The young hero's expression is benign and peaceful: the figure can be interpreted as an epiphany of the hill deity residing in the hill cave, together with his cows and cowherds.

As Lord of the hill and resident of the subterranean cave, the hill deity is the Eater of the food offerings supplied by his cowherd devotees. The deity's own form, however, remains somewhat uncertain, since it is said to be 'changing form at will'. In the Vaiṣṇava purāṇas, the deity of the rock cave is identified with Lord Kṛṣṇa, the deified leader of the cowherd tribe, and none else, in spite of his double appearance: sometimes cowherd, sometimes mountain, or even both at the same time:

> Accordingly, the inhabitants of Vraja worshipped the mountain, presenting to it curds, milk and flesh ... Upon the summit of Govardhan, Kṛṣṇa presented himself, saying: I am the Mountain' – and he partook of much food presented by the Gopas,

whilst in his own form as Kṛṣṇa he ascended the hill along with the cowherds and worshipped his other self. Having promised them many blessings, *the mountain person of Kṛṣṇa vanished* and, the ceremony being completed, the cowherds returned to their station.[7]

Kṛṣṇa is made to assume a dual personality: as leader of the Gopā tribe, and as Lord of the hill and Eater of food offerings. As Kṛṣṇa-Gopāl, in his human form, the hero does not consume the food: when he does so, it is in his 'mountain form'. Once the offerings are consumed, we are told that 'the mountain person of Kṛṣṇa vanishes' and the deity resumes his cowherd status. Although at the time of the festival Kṛṣṇa assumes the role of the 'Eater' (*bhogī*), his true nature does not change: as soon as the eating rite is accomplished, the phantasmagoria is over.

The Maharashtrian tradition

While the north Indian tradition as a whole assumes that Kṛṣṇa-Gopāl, in his mountain form, plays the part of the *bhogī* at the time of the *govardhana-pūjā* festival, the southern Maharashtrian tradition proposes a different interpretation, according to which the role of the *bhogī* is attributed to Kṛṣṇa-Gopāl in the form of a bull.

The earliest evidence in this matter is to be found in the *Śrīkṛṣṇacaritra*, a work in simple Marathi prose written in 1280 by Mhāīṁbhaṭṭa, an adept of the heterodox Manbhau (*mahānubhāva*) sect. In Manbhau belief, Lord Cakradhara, the founder of the sect, is identified with 'Śrī Kṛṣṇa'. In *līlā* 14 of the *Śrīkṛṣṇacaritra*, Mahādaīsā, a female disciple of Cakradhara, asks the Master about the *govardhanadharaṇa* episode: The Gopās had offered *pūjā* to Govardhan on Cakradhara's order, yet the *pūjā* was found fruitless (*abhāva*). So Śrī Kṛṣṇa himself came out of the mountain *in the form of a bull* and ate the offerings.[8]

In the Maharashtrian account, the crucial point is the denial that Kṛṣṇa, in his mountain form, could actually stand as the *bhogī* and consume the offerings: for this purpose, the divine hero should assume an animal form, here a bull. The Manbhau authors, however, are not very clear about the way the bull Kṛṣṇa eats the offerings. It should be presumed that he eats them straight from the Gopās' hands, as in the *govardhana-pūjā* ritual. As to the nature of the food offerings, the Maharashtrian accounts give no precise information: the bull being a pure, vegetarian animal, we must infer that flesh offerings (*bali*) are excluded: a position which agrees with the *Bhāgavata Purāṇa* account, but contradicts all the other sources, according to which flesh is an essential part of the *bhog* offering at the time of the *govardhana-pūjā*.

The Harivaṁśa account

According to the *Harivaṁśa* account, in the middle of Govardhan Hill, a Nyagrodha tree (*Ficus indica*) is seen 'as high as a yojana': it is called 'Bhaṇḍīra' and said to resemble a black cloud in the sky. That Bhaṇḍīra tree is also compared to a high mountain, which suggests another divine form assumed by the Lord of the hill: no longer human or animal, but vegetal. The Bhaṇḍīra tree is the archetypal image of the World Tree, with its branches expanding to the heavens and its roots plunging below into the subterranean waters – which is the primary image of the World Axis. The resemblance of the gigantic Bhaṇḍīra tree to a black cloud also suggests an identification with the dark-hued hero Kṛṣṇa-Gopāl. But the Nyagrodha tree cannot eat the offerings (any more than the mountain itself) for want of a mouth or mouths: to consume the offerings, what is wanted is a wild, flesh-eating animal, residing within the hill itself.

The anthill pattern

A close look at Govardhan Hill reveals that its southern part strongly suggests the shape of a snake, with its mouth at the Mānasī Gaṅgā pond in the north and its tail at the Puchrī village in the south. The word *puchrī* itself means 'tail'.[9] This resemblance, reflected in the names given to such *loci*, accounts for the identification of the strangely shaped Govardhan hillock with an anthill, known as a place frequented by snakes. Such a resemblance must have been behind the sneering remark found in a late passage of the *Mahābhārata* about the insignificant height of the famed Govardhan Hill:

O Bhīṣma, what is remarkable in that one Kṛṣṇa having lifted the mount Govardhan, which is but like an anthill? *Mbh.* ii. 38

Günther Sontheimer remarks that the popular deity Khandobā (alias Murugan), a wrestler god like Kṛṣṇa, itself has its origins in an anthill inhabited by snakes:

'The cows of a certain Gomuni used to spend milk into the holes of an anthill ... Gomuni changed the hill into the form of Mārtaṇḍa Bhairava': again a case of a hill deity changing form and assuming a human shape. In the Maharashtrian account, the merging *mūrti* is god Mallāri, 'the Enemy of [the wrestler] Malla'.[10]

The latter story may be taken as a variant of the Manifestation of Śrī Nāthjī on top of Govardhan Hill on a Nāg Pañcamī day, as narrated at length in the *Śrī nāthjī prākaṭya vārtā* by the Vallabhite Harirāy. In the Vallabhite story, the emerging snake-hood on top of Govardhan is interpreted as the very arm of the Lord Śrī Nāthjī, the Dweller in the hill cave: here the arm is a substitute for the snake-hood of the Nāga deity, long worshipped by local Braj people with oblations of milk.[11]

Actually the *rapprochement* between the Nāga's hood and the hand of Kṛṣṇa is already found at a much earlier date, in the *Riṭṭhanemi-cariu* of the Jaina poet Svayambhū (ninth century AD), describing the *Kāliya-damana* episode of the Kṛṣṇa legend:

There were five fingers with five shining nails and the Hand of Kṛṣṇa *was appearing like a serpent-hood* decorated with jewels; with his hand, he [Kṛṣṇa] caught hold of the hoods of the serpent Kāliya: at that moment, it could not be made out which was the serpent and which was the hand of Kṛṣṇa.[12]

In India, termite mounds derive an important part of their sanctity from the fact that they are conceived as entrances to the nether world and as sources of fertility. The residing Nāga of the anthill is the Eater, the *bhogī*; the feeders are his human devotees, whose duty it is to bring the food offerings at the appointed time. Those offerings consist of milk *and* flesh (*bali*): the anthill Nāga is no vegetarian and he is ever thirsty for blood. John Irwing notes that, at some sites, 'there are unmistakable signs of animal sacrifice, so much blood having been poured into the ventilation shafts that the mound is now defunct.'[13]

Sūrdās' testimony

Several poems in the *Sūr-sāgar* (*SS*)[14] throw an interesting light on the Ahīrs' way of celebrating the *Annakūṭ* or *govardhana-pūja* festival; and also on the unsolved mystery of the 'Eater hill':

1. In *SS* (811) 1429 ff., Sūrdās gives a fairly detailed account of the festival, as celebrated in his time.
2. In *SS* (819) 1437, Kṛṣṇa trells the Gopās about his own dream: how he has seen a 'big man' (*baḍa puruṣa*) who ordered him to worship 'Giri Govardhan' and to offer *bhog* to him.
3. In *SS* (823) 1441, 'Śrī Giridhar Lāl', i.e. Kṛṣṇa himself, is said to be the *kuladevatā*, the ancestral deity of the Braj people: *pūjā* is due to the sacred hill 'which is the living Gopāl' (*giri govardhana pūjiyai, jīvana gopāla*).
4. In *SS* (825) 1443, it is said that Sūrdās' Lord (i.e. Kṛṣṇa-Gopāl) is himself the *bhogī* taking on the *svarūpa* (own form) of the hill. This view does coincide with the purāṇic tradition, which supports the theory of Kṛṣṇa's dual form:

Kṛṣṇa ascended the hill and partook of much food . . . Along with the cowherds, He worshipped His other self. *Viṣṇu Purāṇa*.[15]

This Form which was Himself, He Himself worshipped, together with the people of Braj. *Bhāgavata Purāṇa*, ślo. 36

That same Form [Govardhan], changing form at will, kills the mortals who haunt these woods. Let us honour in It the Power which protects us and our cows. Ibid., ślo. 37.

Both the *Harivaṁśa* and the *Viṣṇu Purāṇa* mention flesh (*bali*) as part of the offerings. This is not mentioned in the *Bhāgavata Purāṇa*, a later, more Vaiṣṇavized text. Yet the line quoted above (ślo. 37) does imply that the Lord of Govardhan Hill is a dangerous personality – actually a potential killer – which of course fits the nature of a cobra or *Nāga*.

The *Sūr-sāgar* accounts

In the *Sūr-sāgar*, we find two distinct accounts concerning the mode of celebration of the Annakūṭ festival. The first concerns the ceremony performed by orthodox (presumably Vallabhite) brāhmans; the second account, much more developed, concerns the Braj people's traditional celebration of the Annakūṭ festival.

In the first account (*SS* (832) 1450), the local brāhmaṇs are in charge: they call the leader of the tribe, Nanda, to preside over the ceremony. They themselves perform the 'sacrifice' (*yajña*) and put the *tilak* on Govardhan's forehead – i.e. on the sacred effigy at Jatipura called *Mukhārvind*. So doing, Indra's sovereignty (his so-called *ṭhākurāī*) is abolished. Then the brāhmaṇs fashion a heap of food grains into the shape of the traditional *annakūṭ*, which is a figuration of the holy hill itself, and they worship it. So far will the brāhmaṇs go and no further: they will not put a foot on the hill itself.

In contrast with the first account, the second (*SS* (836) 1454 ff.)) allows us a deeper insight into the popular festival as performed by the Ahīrs themselves. In this account, the Gopās scramble all over the sacred hill, bringing the *bhog* in their *thālīs*: the deity itself seizes the *bhog* offered by the Gopās and even snatches it from their hands, 'spreading a thousand arms' (*sahasa bhujā pasāra*):

The Ahīrs in a crowd drench Govardhan with milk,
Closing their eyes, they offer Him the *bhog*
And the God spreads a thousand arms to snatch it.

The same formula, *sahasra bhujā pasāra*, is repeated again and again in the following *padas*: (837) 1455, 838 (1456) and (840) 1458, yielding a touch of magic to the whole episode.

An interpretation

How are we to interpret those thousand arms weirdly stretching out from the Govardhan rock? We somehow believe that the phantasmagoria can only be understood by reference to the anthill pattern mentioned above. If the Lord of the hill is the resident *Nāga*, his multiple arms must refer to the multiple shafts built into the hill itself, i.e. the channels through which the anthill snakes move, and the shafts' openings can only be the mouths through which the devout Ahīrs manage to feed their Lord with their naked hands.

In Sūrdās' version, the multiplication of the arms of the deity is a mystery of love: the merciful Lord multiplies his arms in order to bestow the supreme joy of his contact on each and every one of his devotees. Moreover, by himself tasting the food offerings, the Lord makes them *jūṭhā*, thus turning each morsel into *prasād*, for his devotees' greatest benefit. That mystery of love is explained in the last song, in which the Lord of the hill blesses his faithful:

You have done my *pūjā* very well!
With great devotion you have fed Me!
Stretching a thousand arms, I ate under your very eyes.
Yet, from now on, you should only know me as 'Kuṁvar-Kanhaiya' and none else.
With that *pūjā*, I have done away with all your pride: now go home, all of you, people of Braj!
Sūrdās: Śyām, taking it with his own hands, distributes the *jūṭhā bhog* to all of them.
SS (844) 1462

The Lord of the hill is the true *bhogī*, Eater of food – but, according to Sūrdās, he wants to conceal his identity from all but his loving bhaktas: *they* alone can grasp the mystery, fondly feeding Him with naked hands, as a mother does. For Sūrdās, at least, the popular Annakūṭ festival is a mystery of love, symbolized by the gift of an impure, yet divine, food. From that mystery, orthodox brāhmaṇs and Vallabhites are excluded. Happily transgressing orthodoxy, Sūrdās sides with the Ahīrs, humble devotees of the 'Eater hill'.

NOTES

1. The sage Bhṛgu, son or descendant of god Varuṇa, is supposed to be the author of the *Ṛg-Veda.*
2. See Vasudeva Agrawala, *Ancient Indian Folk Cults*, Varanasi, 1970; introduction, pp. 7 ff. and 42–5: *girimaha.*
3. Cf. J. Gonda, *Aspects of Early Viṣṇuism*, Utrecht, 1954.
4. Op. cit.
5. C. Vaudeville, 'The Govardhan Myth in Northern India', *IIJ* 23 (1980).
6. Located in the Mathura Museum; dated *c.* 3rd cent. AD.
7. *The Vishnu Purana*, ed. H. H. Wilson, 3rd edn., Calcutta, 1961, p. 419.
8. See Vaudeville, art. cit., p. 7 n. 20.
9. Ibid., p. 7, §2.
10. See G. D. Sontheimer, 'Some Incidents in the History of God Khaṇḍobā', *Colloque International du CNRS*, no. 582, p. 112, repr.
11. Vaudeville, art. cit., §2, pp. 19–20.
12. H. C. Bhāyāṇī, in *Apabhraṁśa sāhitya mã kṛṣṇa-kāvya*, quotes Svayambhū, *sandhya* 6, *kaḍavaka* 3, lines 5–6.

13. See John Irwing, 'The Sacred Anthill and the Cult of the Primordial Mound' in *HR* 1982, 339–60.
14. *Sūr-sāgar*, ed. Jagannāthdās 'Ratnākar', Munśī Ajmerī, and Nanddulāre Vājpeyī, 4th edn., Varanasi, 1972.
15. Ed. H. H. Wilson, p. 419.

The Manbhaus' seat on Ramtek Hill

HANS BAKKER

Two Old Marathi texts, the *Līḷācaritra* and the *Sthānapothī*, describe the place on Ramtek Hill where Cakradhara lived for ten months during the first part of his spiritual career as a lonely samnyasin. The *oṭā* (dais or raised platform) on which he sat, was within a 'Rāma temple' (*Rāmācāṃ deuḷīṃ*)[1] named Bhogarāma. 'Rāma' in this context may stand for Viṣṇu in general as I have argued at length elsewhere. Why did Cakradhara travel to Ramtek, and in which sort of temple did he stay?

The answer to the first question might be the easiest. In the thirteenth century under the regime of the Yadava kings of Devagiri Ramtek had risen to an important Visnuite, that is to say Ramaite, centre of pilgrimage. The *Śrīgovindaprabhucaritra* tells us that several pilgrims pass through Rddhipur (modern Ritpur) on their way to Ramtek. Among them were the prostitute from Alajpur and Akosem from the capital (i.e. Devagiri),[2] who both decided to stay in Rddhipur once they had met with the Gosāvī (Govindaprabhu).[3] Inscriptions in one of the Narasiṃha temples on the hill testify to the pilgrimages of the philosopher Śārṅgadeva (son of Kāmadeva) and the poet Trivikrama with his brother Rāghava.[4] The lengthy Yadava inscription of Rāghavadeva, the proxy of the Yadava king Rāmacandra, which is found in the Lakṣmaṇa temple on Ramtek Hill, eulogizes Ramtek or Rāmagiri and surroundings as an important holy place dedicated to Rāma, and this is endorsed by the monumental temple constructions including the Lakṣmaṇa temple itself, which may date from the thirteenth century.[5]

The *Līḷācaritra* informs us that when Cakradhara arrived in the Bhogarāma temple, he met with a female devotee, Boṇebāi, who lived in a nearby arbour or cell (*guphā*).[6] Cakradhara was invited by her to come to the *guphā* every day to take his meal. The *Sthānapothī* locates this *guphā* in the western part of the Bhogarāma compound, behind the temple (*maḍh*), near the porch of a Bhairava temple.[7] The Bhairava temple is also known from the abovementioned Yadava inscription which reads:

> And what about the Place of Sport of Kālikā, Lord Mahābhairava, who has a dreadful face with gaping mouth framed in large flames, who devours the entire universe at the end of time and who, when he came to see the Sindūra Mountain (i.e. Ramtek) out of desire for Rāma, immediately lost his appetite to live anywhere else?[8]

This temple of Bhairava is no longer extant, but Cakradhara's stay in the neighbourhood of a Bhairava temple does not come as a surprise in view of the ascetic, i.e. Nāthyogī, background of the Mahānubhāvas. Within their *devatācakra* the eight Bhairavas rank very high, above Viṣṇu and the other gods of Hinduism. Thus the eight Bhairavas is a group of deities most frequently referred to in the *Sūtrapāṭha* where they are explicitly connected with the Nātha sampradāya.[9] Yet he did not make his residence in the Bhairava temple but in a Vaiṣṇava sanctuary. As is well known, the only deity of the Vaiṣṇava pantheon that was accepted to some extent by the Manbhaus was Kṛṣṇa, the expounder of the *Bhagavadgītā*, who is considered the pre-eminent incarnation of Parameśvara.[10] Hence it would be quite plausible a priori that 'Bhogarāma' stood more specifically for a Kṛṣṇa temple. This seems to be endorsed by the Yadava inscription, which mentions Bhogarāma in the following stanza: 'And by seeing the illustrious Bhogarāma, whose image (body) is wonderful, the whole range of sins is destroyed in the refuge of the Enemy of Mura (i.e. Kṛṣṇa); and directly one shall taste all kinds of undiminishing enjoyments for a hundred world-periods, dwarfing the king of the gods.'[11] The Yadava inscription describes, apart from the Bhogarāma temple, another sanctuary dedicated to Kṛṣṇa-Gopāla, 'who is like the full moon (reflected) in the ocean of bliss of the *gopī* folk' (*gopījanānandasamudrapūrṇacandro*),[12] but this aspect of the Kṛṣṇa figure seems to have had little attraction for the ascetic Cakradhara, although 'patently this attitude did not survive him.'[13] The Mahānubhāvas have taken over a number of temples that could be linked with the stay of Cakradhara and thus they accommodated, for instance, the Gopāla Kṛṣṇa temple at Pujade.[14] The predilection of Cakradhara himself, however, seems to follow from his preferring the Bhogarāma temple above the temple dedicated to Gopāla.

With respect to the name Bhogarāma and the nature of the (original) deity to which it may refer different explanations seem possible. The Yadava inscription accounts for the name by a pun when it ascribes *bhoga* (enjoyment) to everyone who has darshan of the image, that is to say it connects the prefix *bhoga* with the root *bhuj* (class 7), 'to enjoy'. In the same line of thought one could think of terms like *bhoga-maṇḍapa* etc. signifying the hall where food (and other enjoyments) are offered to the deity. Bhogarāma could hence mean Rāma-Viṣṇu, who procures enjoyment, and in this way Dagens explains the name Śiva Bhogeśvara of three temples in Andhra Pradesh.[15] From the same root *bhuj* (7) derive the technical iconographic and architectural categories *bhoga*. The *bhoga* variety of images is described by Rao as follows: 'The *bhoga* form is the form best fitted to have the temple therefore constructed within towns and villages, as it is conceived to be the giver of all happiness to its worshippers and has therefore to be worshipped and prayed to by all sorts of men and women belonging to all conditions of life.'[16] The

Mānasāra (xix. 167) classifies a type of single-storeyed temple (building) as *bhoga*, viz. 'those that have similar wings'.[17]

None of these three possibilities provides an entirely satisfactory explanation for the name 'Bhogarāma'. The first etymological one gives the impression of being secondary, prompted by the desire to eulogize the temple. The iconographic designation of an image as *bhoga*-type could explain the name, but in that case we would expect to find many more Viṣṇu temples bearing the *bhoga* prefix. In fact, only one Viṣṇu temple with the word *bhoga* as part of its name is known to me, namely the Bhoganārāyaṇa temple in Paithan mentioned as a place of residence of Cakradhara in the *Līḷācaritra*.[18] The third archaeological term *bhoga* seems inapplicable on account of the fact that the temple does not have wings, unless the two parallel *garbhagṛhas* (about which more is said below) are to be considered as such.[19] Although a combination of the first two explanations seems to yield an adequate interpretation of the name, a close examination of the temple and its history will yield, as we shall try to demonstrate, yet another solution.

The *Sthānapothī* informs us that the temple was facing east and was enclosed by a wall. The main entrance gate was at the northern side, another opening was in the wall facing east. Through this opening Cakradhara went to defecate (for urinating he remained inside the enclosure). This description conforms more or less to the present situation (the opening in the eastern wall has recently been converted into the main entrance gate). This is also true for the surrounding temples and tanks mentioned in the *Sthānapothī*, the topography of which, as far as it is still extant and identifiable,[20] corresponds to the present situation. There can, therefore, be no doubt that the temple described as Bhogarāma is the same as the temple occupied today by the Manbhaus (Pl. 1). This temple is built with the red sandstone that is characteristic of the older temples of Ramtek. Graffiti in one of these temples, namely that of Narasiṃha,[21] and a Vakataka inscription in the same temple, seem to prove that this group of temples belongs to the period of the second quarter to the end of the fifth century AD when Ramtek was an important religious centre within the Vakataka realm. This is corroborated by stylistic architectural features such as, for instance, the dado of dwarflike figures on the wall of the Bhogarāma temple (Pl. 2), which corresponds to similar ornamentation on the remains of a Trivikrama temple on the hill and the above-mentioned Narasiṃha temple. Examining the latter two of these temples, but curiously enough ignoring entirely the splendid Bhogarāma temple, Joanna Williams arrived at the conclusion that these constructions possibly 'go back to the second quarter of the fifth century AD, when we know that nearby Nandivardhana was the capital', namely of the Vakatakas. 'Yet on the basis of stylistic correspondence with Nāchnā, and the mature phase at Ajantā, I would date the pieces just considered closer to the year 500 AD.'[22]

Plate 1. The Bhogarāma temple, Ramtek, seen through the eastern entrance

Plate 2. Dado of dwarflike figures on the north wall of the Bhogarāma temple

From the above it ensues that the Manbhaus took over a temple that, at the time, had a history of at least 800 years. A very peculiar feature of this temple is that, when we enter it through the pillared portico, we come across two parallel *garbhagṛhas*, separated by a narrow passage called *saṃdhi* in the *Sthānapothī*. The *oṭā* of Cakradhara is said to have been in between them.[23] This feature adds another enigma to the original character of the sanctuary. For which twin or pair of deities could a fifth-century temple have been erected? On account of the fact that all Vakataka remains on Ramtek are Vaiṣṇava, to wit a Trivikrama, a Varāha, and two Narasiṃha temples, and that the hill features as a religious centre dedicated to Viṣṇu in the inscriptions of Prabhāvatī Guptā,[24] it seems most likely that the Bhogarāma temple was also a Visnuite sanctuary from its inception, an inference that is consistent with the conclusion reached above of its probably Kṛṣṇaite character in the thirteenth century.

The first place to look for confirmation of this hypothesis is, of course, the sanctum and its images. However, the original idols are no longer there. They were probably replaced by the Manbhaus. One of these substitutes appears to be rather late and is therefore left out of account here (Pl. 3). The other in the southern *garbhagṛha* may date from the thirteenth or fourteenth century. On first sight it looks like a classical Viṣṇu image, one of the twenty-four *caturbhuja* types (Pl. 4). However, on closer inspection (Pl. 5) it appears that the image does not seem to wear a *vanamālā*. The right lower hand holds a

Plate 3. Images in the northern cella of the Bhogarāma temple

rudrākṣamālā instead of the *padma*. There are no other gods or flying celestials, nor are the two Viṣṇuite acolytes, Śrīdevī and Bhūdevī (or Sarasvatī), found at the bottom. The head-gear resembles the type of crown called *kirīṭa-makuṭa* found on images belonging to 'the Hoysala school of sculpture' that are depicted in Rao's *Hindu Iconography*.[25] Beside the lower hands are two blurred carvings which may represent lotus flowers. It is conceivable that we are concerned with a so-called syncretistic image, one that combines Śaiva and Vaiṣṇava elements, although the latter predominate. The image may therefore be typical for the Mahānubhāva sect, whose main deity, it is true, is Kṛṣṇa, but not Kṛṣṇa 'as an aspect of Viṣṇu. This Kṛṣṇa is independent, *sui generis* and at a pinch Kṛṣṇa the expounder of the *Gītā*.'[26] The subtle alterations in the iconography, made to distinguish the deity from his Hindu counterpart, conform to the Mahānubhāva theology, although one may doubt whether this had any real impact on the devotee in front of the idol, a question to which we return below. This analysis, however, does not provide us with an answer to the question regarding the original deities, yet the iconological considerations further underpin the hypothesized replacement of a Hindu Kṛṣṇa by a Manbhaus' Kṛṣṇa.

If, then, one of the original pair of deities must have been Kṛṣṇa, the other may have been his brother Balarāma. And although, admittedly, no fifth-century temples dedicated to Kṛṣṇa together with Balarāma are known,

Plate 4. Images in the southern cella of the Bhogarāma temple

those of Vāsudeva and Saṃkarṣaṇa, their two theological prototypes, are. A well-known inscription from Ghosundi (Nagari) in south-western Rajasthan, probably dating from the first century BC, records the erection of a wall around a place of worship for Vāsudeva and Saṃkarṣaṇa which is called Nārāyaṇa-Vāṭaka.[27] Images of Saṃkarṣaṇa-Balarāma, who is conceived of as a Nāga deity from the beginning, are known from the Sunga period onwards.[28] In the Vidarbha region, which is well known for its Nāga cult and where Nāga shrines can still be found everywhere, at a place 45 km. south-east of Nagpur, brick temples pertaining to the Vakataka period were excavated[29] along with twelve remarkable red sandstone images and several fragments.[30] Among these images is one that is identified by Professor A. M. Shastri as Balarāma on account of the serpent coil at the back and the (probable) backside of an ass seized by the left hand (Pl. 6),[31] which would make it a free-standing Dhenukāsuravadha image.[32]

The existence of a fifth-century Vāsudeva–Saṃkarṣaṇa/Kṛṣṇa–Balarāma temple on Ramtek Hill thus seems to have a certain plausibility in itself. Let us now turn to the texts of this period to see how this Balarāma is described. *Mahābhārata*: 'The head of him, who is strong-armed and Master of all Worlds, will be encompassed by the large hoods of noble serpents (*nāgair mahābhogaiḥ*)',[33] or *Harivaṃśa*: 'attached to a plough and sheltered by serpent coils (or hoods) (*bhujagābhogavartinā*) . . .',[34] or: 'he saw the Lord of

Plate 5. Central image in the southern cella of the Bhogarāma temple

Plate 6. Front and back of an image of Balarāma killing the demon Dhenuka found at Mandhal; kept in the Museum of the Department of Ancient Indian History, Culture, and Archaeology of the University of Nagpur. (Courtesy of Dr A. M. Shastri)

the Serpents (*bhogināṃ nātham*) . . . comfortably seated on a beautiful seat made up of serpent coils (*bhogodarāsane*) that formed part of his own body.'[35] This identity of Saṃkarṣaṇa-Balarāma with Ananta or Śeṣa and the iconographic description of him as possessed of a serpent body, i.e. of coils and/or hoods (Skt. *bhoga*), leads us to conjecture that the first part of the name of Bhogarāma should be connected with the root *bhuj* (class 6) meaning 'to bend' and that Bhogarāma thus stands for Balarāma. This would also account for the second part of the name *rāma*, which in the first millennium can hardly stand for Viṣṇu in general, but may only refer to a deity actually having *rāma* as part of his name. When in the second millennium the original meaning of *bhoga* was forgotten it became natural to interpret *rāma* as signifying Viṣṇu or Rāmacandra. If this interpretation is correct it could also provide an explanation of the name of the temple in Paithan, Bhoganārā-yaṇa, which may signify Nārāyaṇa resting on the coils of the serpent Śeṣa with a canopy of his hoods. This seems to be borne out by a beautiful Śeṣaśayanamūrti that is presently kept in a recently restored Narasiṃha temple in Paithan (Pl. 7). It is believed to have originally belonged to the Bhoganārāyaṇa temple, which is still in the possession of the Manbhaus sect.[36]

The Bhogarāma temple with its two cellae may hence originally have been dedicated to the divine couple of Vāsudeva–Saṃkarṣaṇa, alias Kṛṣṇa–Balarāma. The latter deity, who initially might have been the foremost of the pair, gradually had to give way to his increasingly celebrated brother Kṛṣṇa

Plate 7. Śeṣaśayanamūrti kept in the Narasiṃha temple in Paithan, thought originally to belong to the Bhoganārāyaṇa temple in Paithan

until, eventually, only the name of the temple served as a reminder of his former importance.

The thirteenth-century Yadava inscription in the Lakṣmaṇa temple provides a parallel for this punning concoction of temple names. As I have argued elsewhere this Lakṣmaṇa temple is referred to in the inscription by the name of Śaṅkharāma, not meaning Rāma or Viṣṇu who holds the conch (*śaṅkha*), but Rāma-Viṣṇu who is the Serpent (Śaṅkha), that is to say Lakṣmaṇa. The ninety-sixth verse of this inscription runs: 'Here, in the proximity of the spouse of Janaka's daughter, resides Lakṣmaṇa, who fulfils whatever desire is cherished by any of his devotees, who is the powerful Serpent (Śaṅkha), although he had not a serpent nature (*aśaṅkhātmakaḥ*), who is the companion of Hari during his descent as the illustrious Rāma, and who carries on his heads this world as if it were a garland made of flowers.'[37]

We can now attempt to reconstruct the events that took place in the second half of the thirteenth century. Like many others, the ascetic Cakradhara wended his way towards Ramtek, attracted by the fame of this holy place in the Yadava kingdom. Having a fancy for Kṛṣṇa, but not for the fanciful Kṛṣṇa-Gopāla 'joy of the *gopīs*', he stayed in the Bhogarāma temple. Not long after he left, however, when his followers started to organize themselves, the temple was purchased by the sect, despite Cakradhara's unequivocal depreciation of religious cults: 'holy places, gods, and men, these three you should avoid' runs *Sūtrapāṭha* xii. 39.[38] In conformity with the theology that was developed in the sect the original idol(s) (if they were still there) was (were) replaced by a Kṛṣṇa image that, for the initiated, was essentially distinct from its Hindu prototype, although for the lay followers who came to the temple this distinction might have been beyond their perception and experience.

These developments run to a great extent parallel with other religious currents of the thirteenth and fourteenth centuries. I am thinking in particular of the movement of the Sants. Like Cakradhara, many of these Sants moved from a Nāthyogī background to a more Vaiṣṇava type of bhakti religion, condemning, however, temple worship and idolatry. Instead they stressed the remembrance of God and the utterance of his Name, in case of Cakradhara called Parameśvara, in many other cases called Rāma. Thus *Sūtrapāṭha* xiii. 46: 'Recollect [Parameśvara's] Names (*nāmasmaraṇa*). [Parameśvara] identifies with [his] Names.' 'Recollection of the Name is Recollection of the absolute, and it is recollection of the Name' (xiii. 186). 'Recollection, repeated recollection, and once [a day] recollection. Keep Parameśvara in mind while you are lying down, sitting, and eating' (xii. 29–30), etc. And compare Kabīr's *sākhī*: 'Pilgrimages and ritual are a poisonous Creeper which has spread all over the world: Kabīr has pulled it up by the roots lest someone eat the poison'[39] with Cakradhara's laconic injunction: 'Do not go on pilgrimages or to holy places.'[40]

Elsewhere[41] I have argued that despite the transmitted utterances of some of the Sants, for the great majority of devotees 'Rāma' meant simply the Vaiṣṇava god Rāma, son of Daśaratha, and, notwithstanding sceptical remarks of the Sant holy men about idol worship etc., their followers went to the temple.[42] The story of Bhogarāma seems to confirm this picture. And, on top of this, the conduct of Cakradhara himself, as known from his biographies and the material remains of the world to which these refer, seems to have been continuously at odds with at least some of his own theological beliefs and precepts.

NOTES

1. *Līḷācaritra* 1978, *Pū*. 44.
2. See Feldhaus 1984, ch. 115 n. (p. 178).
3. Feldhaus 1984, pp. 60, 118.
4. Bakker 1989*a*, pp. 469 ff.
5. See Bakker, 1990, pp. 70 f.
6. *Līḷācaritra* 1978, *Pū*. 44.
7. *Sthānapothī* 1976, *Ek*. p. 4: *saṃdī pasīme bonebāiyāṃcī guṃphā/ javaḷīci bhairavāṃcīdeuḷī/ paṭisāḷa/ jagatīcā dāravaṭhā/ uttarābhimūkha/ jagatī āṃtu maḍhāmāge bonebāiyāṃcī guphā/ purvābhimūkha.*
8. Ramtek stone inscription of the time of Ramachandra, v. 94 (see Bakker 1989*a*, pp. 486, 494).

9. *Sūtrapāṭha* xi a 32–3. Cf. Feldhaus 1980, pp. 103 f.
10. Raeside 1976, p. 591.
11. Ramtek stone inscription of the time of Ramachandra, v. 100 (see Bakker 1989*a*, p. 487).
12. Ibid., v. 88 (see Bakker 1989*a*, pp. 485, 493).
13. Raeside 1976, p. 598.
14. Raeside 1976, p. 596.
15. Cf. Dagens 1984, vol. i, p. 609 with respect to Śiva Bhogeśvara. See also n. 19 below.
16. Rao 1971, vol. i, p. 20.
17. *Mānasāra*, quoted in Acharya 1978, p. 345. The text itself (*Mānasāra* xix. 91), however, seems to describe something else: *śīrṣaṃ ca śikhāgrīvaṃ vṛttaṃ syād vaijayantikam/ tad eva karṇakūṭaṃ ced vā bhogam iti kīrtitam*, which is translated by the same Acharya as follows: 'The [single-storeyed] building with circular head (*śīrṣa*), finial (*śikhā*) and neck (*grīva*) is called the Vaijayantika. The same with attic pavilion (*karṇakūṭa*) is known as the Bhoga.' In a note (p. 226) an 'attic pavilion' is defined as 'a little pavilion on the corner'. The Bhogarāma temple in its present state of conservation has neither pinnacle nor pavilions.
18. *Līḷācaritra* 1978, *Pū*. 105 (*Sthānapothī* 1976, p. 13).
19. If that were the case, the occurrence of the term might possibly have a parallel in the Bhoganandīśvara temple in Nandi (Kolar District, Karnataka). This ninth-century sanctuary is 'a double temple consisting of two separate shrines standing in a line with two Nandi-mantapas in front and having a small intervening shrine. The north shrine is dedicated to Bhoganandīśvara and the south shrine to Aruṇācaleśvara. Each consists of a *garbhagṛha* . . .' (*Mysore Gaz*. 1930, p. 345; cf. Harle 1986, pp. 183 f.). However, this explanation runs up against new difficulties. The Bhoganandīśvara temple has more storeys and only the name of one of the two shrines is prefixed with the word *bhoga*. The same applies to the Śiva Bhogeśvara temple in Damagatla (Andhra Pradesh) (see Dagens 1984, vol. i, pp. 449 f.). Dagens describes three Śiva Bhogeśvara temples, the names of which he explains as 'expriment le fruit attendu de la dévotion portée au Liṅga' (p. 609).
20. The shrines of Guptarāma and Guptabhairava are no longer known with certainty. A little cave-temple and a cave-reclusory, which both may belong to the Vakataka period and of which the first is identified by some with Guptarāma, are situated to the south-east of Bhogarāma instead of to the north-east as said in the *Sthānapothī* (cf. Bakker 1989*b*, pp. 92 f.).
21. These graffiti along with the inscriptions have been published in Bakker 1989*a*.
22. Williams 1983, p. 226. In Bakker 1989*b*, p. 81, it is argued that the Vakataka inscription in the Narasiṃha temple, published by Jamkhedkar 1987*b*, is not to be ascribed to Prabhāvatī Guptā herself, but to her children, in particular to her daughter, which places the Narasiṃha temple in the second quarter of the 5th century. In view of its advanced structure, the Bhogarāma temple should be dated in the second half of the fifth century.
23. The temple has been described by Jamkhedkar 1988, pp. 69 f. Cf. Bakker 1989*b*, pp. 89 f.
24. *CII* 1963, 7. 35.
25. Vol. i, pt. 1, pp. 229–31, 243.
26. Raeside 1976, p. 591.

27. Sircar 1965, pp. 90 f; cf. pp. 192 ff.; Agrawala 1987, pp. 328 ff. Cf. also the Mora Well inscription (near Mathura), which records the establishment of the five Pañcavīra, that is, of Vāsudeva, Saṃkarṣaṇa, Pradyumna, Aniruddha, and Sāmba, of whom the first two retain their status as major divine figures.
28. Joshi 1979, pp. 24 ff. Cf. Filliozat 1973.
29. *IAR* 1979, p. 36; *IAR* 1980, p. 39; Shastri 1977–8; Jamkhedkar 1987*a*, p. 337.
30. Three of these images are presently kept in the Central Nagpur Museum, the others are in the Museum of the Department of Ancient Indian History, Culture, and Archaeology of the University of Nagpur, which conducted the excavations in Mandhal. I am much obliged to Prof. A. M. Shastri and Dr Chandrashekhar Gupta for allowing me to study and photograph these findings.
31. Shastri 1977–8, p. 147.
32. Another Vakataka sculpture of Balarāma killing the ass-demon Dhenuka is found among the panels of Paunar (*c.* 55 km. SW of Nagpur). See Deo and Dhavalikar 1968; Williams 1983, p. 229 and Pl. 19; Jamkhedkar 1985, pp. 83 f. Cf. Bhandarkar 1909.
33. *Mbh.* (Bombay) 1979, 13. 147. 56.
34. *Harivaṃśa* 1969–71, 2. 83. 26.
35. *Harivaṃśa* 1969–71, 2. 70. 19–22.
36. Cf. Morwanchikar 1985, pp. 148 f. This Manbhaus temple no longer contains its original idols. The temple has been completely reconstructed, preserving, however, parts of the structure of the original *maṇḍapa.*
37. Ramtek stone inscription of the time of Ramachandra, v. 96 (Bakker 1989*a*, pp. 486, 494). That Lakṣmaṇa is conceived of as an incarnation of Śeṣa appears clearly from the fact that he is said to carry the world on his heads. The denial of a serpent nature to Lakṣmaṇa corresponds to the absence of snake-hoods and other Nāga characteristics in his iconography (cf. Mirashi 1964, p. 143).
38. Translations of the *Sūtrapāṭha* are from Feldhaus 1983.
39. *Sākhī* 26. 5a, trans. Vaudeville 1974.
40. *Sūtrapāṭha* xiii. 19.
41. Bakker 1987.
42. Cf. the great mental effort made by Rāmānanda to restrain himself from going to the temple: 'One day I did have an inclination to go, I ground sandal, took aloes paste and many perfumes. And I was proceeding to worship God in a temple, when my Guru showed me that God is in my heart . . .' (Pada ascribed to Rāmānanda in the *Guru Granth (Basant* I), quoted in Vaudeville 1974, p. 112).

REFERENCES

Acharya, Prasanna Kumar (1978), *An Encyclopaedia of Hindu Architecture*, Bhopal, repr.

Agrawala, R. C. (1987), 'Early Vaiṣṇava Icons from Rajasthan', in R. Parimoo, ed., *Vaiṣṇavism in Indian Arts and Culture*, Delhi, pp. 328–34.

Bakker, H. (1987), 'Reflections on the Evolution of Rāma Devotion in the Light of Textual and Archaeological Evidence', *WZKSA* 31, pp. 9–42.

——(1989*a*), 'The Ramtek Inscriptions', *BSOAS*, 52, pt. 3, pp. 467–96.

——(1989*b*), 'The Antiquities of Ramtek Hill, Maharashtra', *Journal of South Asian Studies*, 5, pp. 79–102.

——(1990), 'Ramtek: An Ancient Centre of Viṣṇu Devotion in Maharashtra', in Hans Bakker, ed., *The History of Sacred Places in India as Reflected in Traditional Literature. Papers on Pilgrimage in South Asia*, Panels of the VIIth World Sanskrit Conference, vol. iii, Leiden, pp. 62–85.

Bhandarkar, D. R. (1909), 'Two Sculptures at Mandor', *Archaeological Survey of India. Annual Report (1905–6)*, pp. 135–40.

CII (1963), *Corpus Inscriptionum Indicarum*, vol. v, Ootacamund.

Dagens, B. (1984), *Entre Alampur en Śrīśailam: Recherches archéologiques en Andhra Pradesh*, Institut Français d'Indologie no. 67, 2 vols., Pondicherry.

Deo, S. B. and Dhavalikar, M. K. (1968), *Paunar Excavation (1967)*, Nagpur.

Feldhaus, A. (1980), 'The *Devatācakra* of the Mahānubhāvas', *BSOAS*, 43, pt. 1, pp. 101–9.

——(1983), *The Religious System of the Mahānubhāva Sect: The Mahānubhāva* Sūtrapāṭha, ed. and trans. with introduction by A. Feldhaus, Manohar.

——(1984), *The Deeds of God in Ṛddhipur*, trans. from the Marathi and annotated by A. Feldhaus, with introductory essays by A. Feldhaus and E. Zelliot, New York and Oxford.

Filliozat, J. (1973), 'Représentations de Vāsudeva et Saṃkarṣaṇa au IIe siècle avant J.C.', *AA* 26, pp. 113–23.

Harivaṃśa (1969–71), *The Harivaṃśa being the* khila *or supplement to the Mahābhārata*, for the first time critically edited by Parashuram Lakshman Vaidya, 2 vols., Poona.

Harle, J. C. (1986), *The Art and Architecture of the Indian Subcontinent*, The Pelican History of Art, Harmondsworth.

IAR (1979), *Indian Archaeology 1975–6: A Review*, ed. B. K. Thapar, New Delhi.

——(1980), *Indian Archaeology 1976–7: A Review*, ed. B. K. Thapar, New Delhi.

Jamkhedkar, J. P. (1985), 'Narrative Sculptures from Paunar: A Reappraisal', *Indian Epigraphy*, pp. 83–6.

——(1987*a*), 'Vaiṣṇavism in the Vakata times', in R. Parimoo, ed., *Vaiṣṇavism in Indian Arts and Culture*, New Delhi, pp. 335–41.

——(1987*b*), 'A Newly Discovered Vakataka Temple at Ramtek, Dist. Nagpur', *Kusumāñjali*, pp. 217–33.

——(1988), 'Beginnings of North Indian Style: Early Vidarbha Style, *c.* A.D. 350–500: Vākāṭakas (Main Branch)', in *Encyclopaedia of Indian Temple Architecture*, vol. ii: *I: Foundations of North Indian Style* c. *250 B.C.–A.D. 1100*, ed. M. W. Meister, M. A. Dhaky, K. Deva, Delhi, pp. 59–72.

Joshi, N. P. (1979), *Iconography of Balarāma*, New Delhi.

Līḷācaritra (1978), *Śrīcakradhara Līḷā Caritra*, ed. V. B. Kolte, Bombay.

Mānasāra (1979–80), *Manasara on Architecture and Sculpture*, Sanskrit text, with critical notes and trans. from original Sanskrit by Prasanna Kumar Acharya, 2 vols., first pub. London 1934, repr. Mānasāra Series, Delhi, vols. iii, iv.

Mbh. (Bombay) (1979), *The Mahābhārata with the Bharata Bhawadeepa Commentary of Nilakantha*, ed. Ramchandra-Sastri Kinjawadekar, 6 vols., Delhi.

Mirashi, V. V. (1964), '*Ramagiri of Kalidasa, JIH* 42, pt. 1, pp. 131–43.

Morwanchikar, R. S. (1985), *The City of Saints: Paithan through the Ages*, Delhi.

Mysore Gaz. (1930), *Mysore Gazetteer. Compiled for Government*, vol. v: *Gazetteer*, ed. C. Hayavadana Rao, new ed., Bangalore.

Raeside, I. M. P. (1976), 'The Mahānubhāvas', *BSOAS* 39, pt. 3, pp. 585–600.

Rao, T. A. Gopinatha (1971), *Elements of Hindu Iconography*, Introduction and editorial notes by K. K. Das Gupta, 4 vols., Varanasi.

Shastri, Ajay Mitra (1977–8), 'Māṇḍhal Utkhanana', *Vidarbha Samshodhak Mandal Annual*, pp. 142–74.

Sircar, Dines Chandra (1965), *Select Inscriptions Bearing on Indian History and Civilization*, vol. i: *From the Sixth Century B.C. to the Sixth Century A.D.*, Delhi/Madras.

Sthānapothī (1976), *Sthāna Pothī: Prastāvanā, Mūḷa Pothī, Sthānasūcī, Kaṭhīṇa śabdāṃcā kośa ityadīsahita saṃpādilelā*, ed. Viṣṇu Bhikājī Kolte, Malkapur.

Vaudeville, C. (1974), *Kabīr*, vol. i, Oxford.

Williams, J. (1983), 'Vākāṭaka Art and the Gupta Mainstream', in *Essays on Gupta Culture*, ed. B. L. Smith, Delhi, pp. 215–33.

Formulation and transmission of religious attitudes

Singers' repertoires in western India

WINAND M. CALLEWAERT

Let us imagine we are travelling through north-west India in AD 1550, on sandy tracks or on bumpy roads after the rainy season. We spend the nights on the floor in temples and watch the audiences drawn by travelling singers singing songs of bhakti. These singers, like the purāṇic bards, received extended hospitality depending on the quality and depth of their performance. They may not have belonged to a particular *sampradāy* and they sang what appealed most to the local feelings. We are on the way to Rajasthan after a visit to Banaras, where, a few years before, Raidās had died, and where the oldest member in the singers' families had heard a person called Kabīr. These families of travelling musicians, a few generations before, may have been to Maharashtra, where they could have heard a poet called Nāmdev. Thus, their repertoire went on expanding and some started to feel the need to write down songs.

The singers sang the songs which were most in demand, such as those of Nāmdev and Kabīr, which they had learned from their fathers. They too were artists, and inspired by a particular environment they added new songs, sometimes their own, to the repertoire. This should not amaze us. Present-day musicologists in Rajasthan studying the Dev Nārāyaṇ or Pābūjī performance pay their performants by the hour. Some found the story never-ending, and on close analysis found gossip about contemporary politicians to have been interpolated in the story.

Memory was their only way of recording, but, as the repertoires grew bigger, some musicians started to keep little (or big) notebooks as an aid to their memory. The earliest manuscripts seem to have had these notebooks as their basis. The manuscripts of the seventeenth century that have been preserved are copies of these early notes now lost. Scholars of the twentieth century have to rely on seventeenth-century manuscripts which are copies of the scribbled notes of singers in order to reconstruct and edit what the singers were singing. I do not say: 'to reconstruct what Nāmdev or Kabīr or Raidās were singing'.

Indian musicians used to sing clusters of songs according to particular modes, called *rāg*. It appears that first the singer sang a particular *pada* in a particular *rāg*; they grouped together the *padas* which were to be sung in the same *rāg*. Consequently, a *rāg* is like an identity card for the earliest period of oral transmission. It was only later, when compilers took over, that *padas* were classified in *aṅgas*, according to the main theme.[1]

The same song could be sung to different *rāgas* and as a result we find songs classified under different *rāgas* in different manuscripts. This variation in classification is obviously not due to a scribe's intervention, but stems from the oral period itself, when the songs were in the hands of the singers. Subsequently, the songs were transmitted under different *rāgas* and appeared as such also in the manuscripts. Thus, looking at the *rāg* structure we are able to make a preliminary classification of the musical recensions.

When, for Nāmdev, Kabīr, and Raidās, we compare the *rāg* structure in the *Guru Granth* with that in the Rajasthani repertoires, we find considerable differences. The Panjabi singers handled a text which was not only morphologically but also musically very different from what their colleagues in Rajasthan had. We are tempted to propose that the *padas* which have the same *rāg* in the *Guru Granth* and in the Rajasthani manuscripts are likely to have belonged to a very early common source. In fact, what we find in the seventeenth-century Rajasthani manuscripts is a variant musical version which may well be as old as the musical version from which the Panjabi singers drew their inspiration, if not older. At what muddy or sandy crossroads did singing families go their own ways, and at what point in history?

Probably not more than fifty years were needed for the songs of Raidās to become the exclusive property of travelling singers. And when around AD 1600 they started to be written down in fancy and voluminous manuscripts, these songs had undergone numerous minor and quite a few important changes. Amazingly, scribes added very few variants, as appears from our study of eleven manuscripts of the seventeenth century which give the songs of Raidās.[2] Nearly all variant readings can be traced to the period of oral transmission, when singers took the songs to villages all over north-west India.[3]

Travelling singers knew no borders. They easily walked from the kingdoms in and around Banaras through the Mughal territories to the princely states in Rajasthan, or from the Maratha country to the Panjab. With an amazing ease also they moved from one regional language to another, using a supraregional medium, while at the same time picking up local idioms and words in an effort to adjust to local audiences. This effort is responsible for the linguistic and stemmatic chaos we find in the manuscripts.

The interaction between regional dialects, and between singers and audiences, is an exciting phenomenon which we can study only when looking carefully at manuscripts. Without doubt, most literature of fifteenth- and sixteenth-century north India has to be studied through manuscripts in which that literature is preserved. A special discipline, however, is required to study the songs which have been in the hands of singers for a long while before being written down. The textual critic cannot reconstruct a scribal archetype. There never was one. Corrupt readings need not be listed as text-critical clues, leading back towards an original, later emended, text. At best we can try to reconstruct oral archetypes (in the plural) and to reach beyond the period of creative changing by professional and other singers. We have several 'archetypes'.[4] Text-critical clues based on the variants of oral origin can only point to the possibility of originality in most cases and to relative certainty in some cases. We consider the songs as independent units and do away with the traditional, text-critical approach which treats a corpus of songs as a homogeneous, literary piece. The songs have to be treated and studied separately, because songs underwent creative changes by singers not only throughout each repertoire, but also independently. Consequently, we do not have a repertoire which gives the 'best' reading throughout.

Let us go back to the *rāgas* and the *Guru Granth.* Of the 61 songs of Nāmdev in the *Guru Granth,* only 25 are found in the Rajasthani manuscripts. When we look at the (only) 11 songs of Nāmdev which are classified under the same *rāg* in the *Guru Granth* and in the Rajasthani manuscripts, we notice that these songs are found in *all* the Rajasthani recensions (with only one exception), and we see that these songs have exactly the same *rāg* in all these recensions. On the other hand, when we look at those songs which do *not* have the same *rāg* in all Rajasthani manuscripts, they are also the songs which are not given in all the manuscripts, often occurring only in a few.

In the *Guru Granth* we find 40 (or 37)[5] songs attributed to Raidās; of these only 22 are found in the Rajasthani manuscripts. Here again the difference in *rāg* points to the rather independent position of the *Guru Granth* repertoire, which must have separated from other repertoires at a very early stage during or after Raidās's lifetime: only 8 songs are found with the same *rāg* as in the Rajasthani manuscripts.

For his critical edition of the *pada bhāg* of Kabīr, P. N. Tivārī finally selected 200 *padas*. Of these, 121 are found in the *Guru Granth* also, but only 55 are classified under the same *rāg* as in the Rajasthani tradition.

Singers' variants

The singers not only changed the *rāg* at times; they also brought an inversion of *antarās* (stanzas), of lines or half lines, and they added 'fillers'. Since the musical tradition in the Panjab was different from that in Rajasthan, these variants are most obvious when we compare these two traditions.[6] One of the most common singers' variants is the (dis)order of the *antarās*. As an example we quote in Hindi eight manuscripts giving song 91 of Nāmdev. If one treats this song (and many others) as one which underwent scribal tampering, the result is a hopeless and useless mess in the critical apparatus. A careful study of this sample shows that certain repertoires can be paired off; small units of lines are moved about by singers. Interestingly, this 'stemma' created on the basis of the study of this song may be totally contradicted if one studies the pairing off in another song in the Nāmdev repertoire.

९१

c;१ कोटि जौ तीरथ करै । तन जो हिवालै गलै । ।
j;१ कोटि जौ तीरथ करै । तन जो हिवालें गलें । ।
a;१ कोटि जौ तीरथ करै । तन जौ हिवालै गलै । रांम रांम रांम सरि तऊ न तूलै ।
m;१ कोटि जौ तीरथ करै । तंन जौ हिंवालै गलै । रांम रांम रांम रांम संमिं तउ न तुलै ।
p;१ कोटि जौ तीरथ करै । तन जौं हिवालै गलै ।
p;१ प्रिथी जे सकल परदक्षत दीजै करवत कासी मैं लीजै ।
p;१ सिव कौं जो सीस दीजै । रांम रांम - सरि तऊ न तुलै ।
g;१ कोटि जौ तीर्थ करै । तन जौ हिवालै गलै ।
g;१ प्रिथी सकल प्रदछन दीजै करवत कासी मैं लीजै ।
g;१ स्यौं कूं जे सीस दीजै । रांम रांम रांम सरि तऊ न तुलै ।
v;१ कोटि जौ तीरथ फिरै । तंन जौ हिवालै गलै । रांम रांम रांम सरि तउ नं तुलै ।
d;१ कोटि जौ तीरथ करै । तंन जौ हिंवालै गलै । रांम रांम रांम समि तउ न तुलै ।

c;२ । गया जो कुरषेति न्हइये । गोमती संगम गउ सहश्र दीजे ।
j;२ । गया जो कुरषेत न्हइयें । गोमती संगम गौ सहस्र दीजे ।
a;२ मांनसरोवरि - - जाइये । गया जौ कुरषेत न्हाइये । गोमती अष्नांनगऊ कोटि दीजै ।
m;२ मांन जौ सरोवर जईये । गया जौ कुरषेत न्हईये । गोमती सनांन गउ सहंश्र दीजै ।
p;२ । मांन जौ सरोवर जईये । गया जौ कुरषेत न्हइयै । गोमती सनांन गऊ कोटि दीजै ।
g;२ । मांन जौ सरोवर जइये । गया जौ कुरषेत्र न्हइये । गोमती अस्नांन गऊ कोटि दीजै ।
v;२ मांन - सरोवर जाइए । गया जौ कुरषेत्र न्हाइए । गोमती अश्नांन गऊ कोटि दीजै ।
d;२ मांन जौ सरोवर जईये । गया जौ कुरषेती न्हईऐ । गोमती अस्नांन गउ कोटि दीजै ।

c;३ । स्यंघ जो गोदावरी जइये । रांम रांम रांम समि तउ न तुलै ।
j;३ । सिघ जो गोदावरी जइये । रांम रांम रांम समि तौ न तुलै ।
a;३ कुंभ जौ केदारि जइये । स्यंघहस्त गोदावरी न्हइये । रांम रांम रांम समि तऊ न तुलै रे ।
m;३ कुंभ जौ केदारि जइये । सिंघहस्त गोदावरी न्हइये । रांम रांम रांम रांम संमिं तउ न तुलै ।
p;३ । कुंभ जौ केदार जइयै । सिंगहसत गोदावरी न्हइयै । रांम रांम रांम सरि तऊ न तुलै ।
v;३ कुंभ जौ केदार जाइए । स्यंघहस्त गोदावरी न्हइए । रांम रांम रंम सरि तउ नं तुलै ।
d;३ कूंभ जौ केदारि जईये । सिंघसत गोदावरि न्हईये । रांम रांम रांम सरि तउ न तुलै ।
g;३ । कुंभ जौ केदार जइए । स्यंघहस्त गोदावरी न्हइये । रांम रांम रांम सरि तऊ न तुलै ।

c;४ रांम नांम निज सार । जन भजि पावै पार । भनंत नांमदेव - अंमृत पीजे ।
j;४ रांम नांम निज सार । जन नजि पावे पार । भनत नांमदेव - अमृंत पीजे ।

Again let us compare the 'critical' text of song 91 with the version we find in the *Guru Granth*:

१ कोटि जौ तीरथ करै तन जौ हिवालै गलै ॥
रांम रांम रांम सरि तऊ न तुलै ॥
२ बानारसी तप करै पलटि तीरथ मरै ॥
काया जे अगनि मुषि कलेस कीजै ॥
हिरणग्रभ दांन दीजै अस्वमेद जगि कीजै ॥
रांम रांम रांम सरि तऊ न तुलै ॥
३ मांन जौ सरोवर जइये गया जौ कुरषेत न्हइये ॥
गोमती अस्नांन गऊ कोटि दीजै कुंभ जौ केदार जइये ॥
स्यंघहस्त गोदावरी न्हइये रांम रांम रांम सरि तऊ न तुलै ॥
४ अस्वदांन गजदांन भोमिदांन कन्यांदांन ग्रिहदांन सिज्यादांन दांन दीजै ॥
तन तुला तोलि दीजै मन जौ न्रिमल कीजै । रांम रांम रांम सरि तऊ न तुलै ॥

• बानारसी तपु करै उलटि तीरथ मरै अगनि दहै काइआ कलपु कीजै ॥
असुमेध जगु कीजै सोना गरभ दानु दीजै ॥
राम नाम सरि तऊ न पूजै छोडि छोडि रे पाखंडी मन कपटु न कीजै ॥
हरि का नामु नित नितहि लीजै ॥ रहाउ ॥
१ गंगा जउ गोदावरी जाईऐ कुंभि जउ केदार
नहाईऐ गोमती सहस गऊ दानु कीजै ॥
कोटि जउ तीरथ करै तनु जउ हिवाले गारै राम नाम सरि तऊ न पूजै ॥
२ असुदान गजदान सिहजा नारी भूमि दान ऐसो दानु नित नितहि कीजै ॥
आतम जउ निरमाइलु कीजै आप बराबरि कंचनु दीजै ॥
राम नाम सरि तऊ न पूजै ॥
३ मनहि न कीजै रोसु जमहि न दीजै दोसु । निरमल निरबाण पदु चीन्हि लीजै ॥
जसरथ राइ नंदु राजा मेरा रामचंदु प्रणवै नामा ततु रसु अंमृतु पीजै ॥

५ जमहि न दीजै दोस मनहि न कीजैय ॥
रोस निरषि न्रिबांणपद रांम नांम लीजै ॥
आतमां अंगि लगाइ सेइ लै सहज भाइ ॥
भणत नांमइयौ छीपौ अंम्रित पीजै ॥

This example illustrates that each *antarā* in a Sant song could have a life of its own. Within the song it could be moved about, dropped or added as an independent unit.

But the *antarā* was not the smallest unit that could be moved about. Even half *antarās*, consisting of two lines (or even one line), could be dropped or replaced by an entirely different reading. It appears that such units correspond to the minimum length of an *āvarta*, or the complete movement from one *sam* (beat) to another. Musicians *can* move it from place to place, if they feel that this does not really change the song, its sentiment, or message.[7]

Finally, let us compare the variation in *rāg* (brought about by singers, not scribes) and the singers' variants discussed above. I looked at the first 150 songs in our critical edition of the songs of Nāmdev from the viewpoint of variation in *rāg* and inversion of *antarās*. I was surprised *not* to find a consistent correlation. Of the 10 songs in this set common to the *Guru Granth* and the Rajasthani manuscripts, and with the same *rāg*, six or 60 per cent have an inversion of *antarās*. Similarly, however, of the remaining 10 common songs, with a *different rāg*, again six or 60 per cent have an inversion of *antarās*. In these first 150 songs, 130 are found *only* in the Rajasthani manuscripts. Of these, 106 have the same *rāg* in all the manuscripts: 27 or 25 per cent have an inversion of *antarās*. Of the 24 songs having a different *rāg* in one manuscript or more, six or again 25 per cent have an inversion of *antarās*. I conclude that both the changes in the *rāg* and the inversion of *antarās* are brought about by singers, not scribes, but in the songs of Nāmdev there is no relevant correlation between these two kinds of variant. A different *rāg* in some manuscripts does not necessarily bring about more inversions.

When we construct a tentative stemma on the basis of the similarity in the order in which the songs are classified under the heading of a *rāg*, then our effort will continually be contradicted by the dissimilarity of the order of *antarās* or of lines. The result is a totally blurred and confused pattern, if any pattern appears at all. As was displayed in my paper at the Leiden Conference (forthcoming), there is no consistent relation between manuscripts at all. Similar conclusions are the basis for the critical edition of the songs of Raidās.

In contrast with these conclusions I quote a translated passage from the introduction to P. N. Tivārī's *Kabīr-granthāvalī*, which is still the most authoritative edition of the songs of Kabīr.[8] His goal was to reconstruct the original text, but he failed to distinguish the *Pañcavāṇīs* as independent repertoires (as I did for the Nāmdev and the Raidās editions); he also does not seem to treat the variants as results of oral creativity and interaction.

> No single recension is absolutely authentic or original, as none is devoid of corrupt meanings and interpolations. They may, however, be regarded as different branches and offshoots of a single root. We shall reach the original root only if we follow these branches. The root is out of sight but, clinging merely to a single branch, if we presume to have reached the original branch, it would be a folly. Long, long ago, a place was built which was later divided between its occupants, who made many alterations in the portions they occupied according to their own taste. Some of them went to the extent of rebuilding their portion after having demolished it completely. Today the original design of the house is changed and distorted, but the bricks which built it are still there. We have to collect them and, after watching their original

cuttings carefully, to replace them in their original position as far as possible. In this way, we have to reconstruct the house, if we can, because we are now anxious to have it rebuilt.

NOTES

1. For the *Sarvāṅgī* compiled by Dādū's disciple Rajab (*c.* AD 1620), see my study *The Sarvāṅgī of the Dādūpanthī Rajab*, Leuven, 1978. For the Gopāldās *Sarvāṅgī*, compiled in AD 1627, see 'A 17th Century Anthology of Hindi Poetry', *OLP* 5, 1974, pp. 187–96. In the colophon at the end of the work it is stated that Gopāldās completed this immense work at the age of 37. An edition of the complete *Sarvāṅgī* is forthcoming.
2. *Life and Works of Raidās*, critical edn. and English trans., in collaboration with P. Friedlander, forthcoming.
3. For the *geyavikāras* or variants brought about by singers, see W. M. Callewaert and Mukund Lath, *The Hindī Padāvalī of Nāmdev*, Leuven, 1988, pp. 63 ff., 391 f.
4. For the 'archetypes' of the *Pañcavāṇī* see Callewaert and Lath, op. cit. pp. 99 f.
5. See *The Hindī Songs of Raīdās*, ch. 2.5; also chs. 1.2, 3.
6. For more details, see Callewaert and Lath, op. cit.
7. For a discussion at length of the importance of other singers' variants, see ibid., pp. 70 ff.
8. 1961, p. 54, Ph.D. thesis, Allahabad, 1956. The translation is from C. Vaudeville, *Kabīr*, vol. i, Oxford, 1974, p. 71.

An oral theology: Dādūpanthī homilies

MONIKA THIEL-HORSTMANN

In this paper I wish to give an introductory account of Dādūpanthī homilies, addressing in detail only two aspects, both of which have been issues in recent scholarly discussion. The first of these is the function of *sākhīs* in Sant tradition; the second is the issue of the identity of the Sant *satguru*.

In a comprehensive paper on 'The *Dohā* as a Vehicle of Sant Teachings', Karine Schomer suggests with regard to the *dohā* (referred to here by the alternative term *sākhī*, which includes didactic verses in other metres as well as in the *dohā* proper), that

> the status of the *sākhī* as a religious utterance is different from that of other Sant genres in that its statement of Sant teachings and themes is accepted as particularly authoritative. Indeed, the function of Sant *sākhīs* in popular religious culture may best be understood by analogy to the *sūtras* of the classical philosophical texts. . . . they are on a different level from that of ordinary proverbial sayings. While general proverbial lore transmits practical wisdom for daily life, *sākhīs* express . . . the spiritual vision and high moral ideals preached by the Sants.[1]

Schomer does not, however, point out in precisely what way the *dohās* are used for the transmission of religious teaching. My paper will therefore, I hope, supplement what she said by providing more information on the religious usage of *sākhīs* in a Sant sect.

The Dādūpanth (DP) is a Sant community with its centre in Rajasthan that emerged at the turn of the seventeenth century. It played a pivotal role in giving *sākhī* collections a characteristic shape, for it was the Dādūpanthīs (DPī) who first arranged *sākhī* corpuses thematically by grouping them in chapters (*aṅga*), each devoted to a particular topic. This originally DPī usage has been widely followed ever since, not only for its general convenience but also for the purpose of maintaining a large number of stock chapters which are of great importance for their subject-matter to the religious life of the Sant groups concerned.[2]

Sākhīs in liturgical and homiletic use

A common use of *sākhīs* which is fully in accordance with Schomer's view is that in the context of *bhajans*. Here *sākhīs* are used to introduce and to highlight thematically the repertoire of a given singer or to point out the message of subsequent *bhajans* in a repertoire.[3] They also abound in discursive contexts and are quoted in order to give argument conviction. In both these contexts, in *bhajan* singing and in speech, the use of *sākhīs* is random and depends on the personal choice of the singer or speaker.

In homilies *sākhīs* can have that random function, too. However, it is also in homilies – used in the sense of all discursive texts produced by preachers – and especially in sermons delivered at the most important festivals of the DP, that *sākhīs* cease to be used randomly and show their essential characteristic of being *śabda*, the word revealed that is proof in itself. Because the *sākhīs* have the quality of *śabda* they can be used as support for a speaker's statement as well as in less formal discursive contexts. After a brief description of the various types of homily and their place in the religious life of the DP, I will discuss the *śabda* character of *sākhīs*.

Homilies are mainly delivered on the occasion of one of the great festivals of the DP, which are held at the five main DPī *tīrthas* in turn and are concluded by the six-day celebration of Dādū's birthday[4] at the headquarters of the DP in Naraina. The day of Dādū's death[5] is also an occasion for preaching. Homilies are, finally, expected to be given by DPī monks during the *caumāsā*. The ceremonially most important sermons given during the main festival are delivered at the main shrines of the *tīrthas* and advertised long before the celebrations.

Those who preach are the most distinguished DPī scholars, several of them professors of philosophy or otherwise theologically accomplished dignitaries of the DP. As would be expected, the most distinguished preacher is the Abbot-in-Chief of the Panth, who also holds a *Śāstrī* degree in philosophy. His authority, notwithstanding his personal accomplishments, rests intrinsically on his ritual status, which is especially and obviously imposing when he preaches on the occasion of the main festival of the sect. For before the final stage of that observance he disappears ritually and is then brought back in a procession from the outskirts of Naraina and, along with his *gaddī*, is taken back to his residence in the temple there. In this ritual he becomes the avatār of the unmanifest God. When he preaches he is thus an avatār in the successional line of Dādū, who has himself been considered an avatār since the beginning of the DP. The fact that the Abbot's *gaddī* is transported in the procession in a palanquin of its own gives expression to that continuity.

The great ceremonial sermons are mostly called *pravacans*, but the term *kathā* may also be used. Less formal *kathās* are given at minor shrines within the precincts of the DPī headquarters during the six festival days as well as on different occasions.[6] Both the great ceremonial and the less formal sermons last about an hour and are usually given swiftly, which points to intensive training and practice on the part of the preachers. Written drafts are, to the best of my knowledge, never used, but the first part of the *Dādūvāṇī*, namely the *sākhī* portion, is kept in front of the preacher and is also used in the case of an exegetical sermon.

Sākhī *as* śabda

While in the less ceremonial sermons the use of the *sākhīs* is random even if the speaker concentrates on a topic provided by a particular *sākhī* chapter, the ceremonial sermons present a totally different picture. Here *sākhīs* may occur as illustrative devices as often as *bhajans*; but this usage is clearly subordinate. In the great sermons *sākhī* is *śabda*, as I indicated above: *śabda* in the sense of the word as revelation and supreme *pramāṇa*, proof. Here *sākhīs* are not comparable to *sūtras*, as hinted by Schomer,[7] but are equivalent to Vedic revelation. The whole corpus of the *sākhīs*, and for that matter also of the *bhajans*, which follow the *sākhī* section but which are not made the object of exegetical sermons, is taken as a continuous text of revelation where no arbitrary selection of a saying is possible. For the purpose of exegesis a portion of the *sākhī* corpus is selected as a pericope to become the object of *vyākhyā*, or *pravacan*, which is the usual term in the DP. It is in these exegetical commentary-like sermons on the words of revelation that the great theological issues are raised and explicated. The preachers have an audience fully competent to follow their sermons since reading of the *sākhīs* forms part of the *nityapāṭh* of lay DPīs. The *sākhī* section of the *Dādūvāṇī* comprises some 2,500 distiches, grouped in thirty-seven chapters. Only three of these, and among these three one chapter prescribed only partially, come under the *nityapāṭh*. These are *sākhīs* 1–19 of the first chapter (*Gurudeva kau aṅga*), the fourth chapter (*Paricaya kau aṅga*) and the thirty-fourth chapter (*Vinatī kau aṅga*). Thus the *nityapāṭh*, as far as the *sākhīs* are concerned, concentrates on the fundamental elements which are, according to the Sants, indispensable for access to bhakti: the guru without whom no bhakti can be performed; *paricaya*, the experience of God identical with the soul, which is the goal of the devotee's spiritual quest; *vinatī*, supplication, which is the way towards this goal. In all *aṅga* editions of *sākhīs*, in the DP and outside it, the chapter on the guru stands first, and chapters on *paricaya* and *vinatī* are present, naturally in positions varying according to the individual *œuvre* of a Sant poet. From the material that I have at hand it seems that the preachers prefer to base their sermons on portions of the *nityapāṭh*.

Sample sermon

In this section I will try to give evidence of the quasi-Vedic character of the *sākhīs* and to point to some key issues raised in sermons. I am basing my discussion on a single sermon, which I have selected for the following reasons: the preacher was the Abbot-in-Chief of the DP, hence the most authoritative interpreter of his faith; the occasion on which the sermon was given was Dādū's birthday, the main DPī festival; the Abbot-in-Chief told me before the sermon that he would for the sake of my analysis start with an outline of the presuppositions of DPī doctrine although I had not made any request to this effect. This is, I think, important to know in order to evaluate sectarian doctrinal emphasis correctly. It was thus perhaps not merely accidental that key issues also discussed by non-sectarian scholars figure prominently in his sermon.

The sermon was based on the following pericope:[8]

। श्री स्वामी दादूदयाल जी की अनभै वाणी ।।

The Words of Intuitive Knowledge by Sv. Dādū Dayāl

[title-line of the **Dādūvāṇī**];

गुरुदेव कौ अंग

Chapter on the Divine Guru [first chapter of the *sākhī* section of the *Dādūvāṇī*].

[*Maṅgala* Verses:]

दादू न्मो, न्मो निरंजनं, नमसकार गुरुदेवतह ।
वंदनं श्रव साधवा, प्रणांमं पारंगतह ।।१।।

Worship be paid to Nirañjana, homage to the Divine Guru,
Obeisance to all saints, obeisance to those who have attained.

परब्रह्म परापरं, सो नम देव निरंजनं ।
निराकारं निर्मलं, तस्य दादू वंदनं ।।२।।

The Supreme Being, Immanent and Transcendent, he is my God, Nirañjana,
Formless, Unsullied: to him Dādū does reverence.

[Beginning of the main part of the *Dādūvāṇī*:]

दादू गैब मांहि मिल्या, पाया हम परसाद ।
मसतकि मेरे कर धर्या, दष्या अग्म अगाध ।।३।।

Miraculously the Divine Guru met with me: I received the token of his favour;
He placed his hand on my head and made me see that which is Unapproachable and Unfathomable.

दादू सद्गुरु सहज मैं, कीया बहु उपगार ।
नृधन धनवंत करि लिया, गुर मिलिया दातार ।।४।।

Many are the blessings the Satguru has freely bestowed.
The poor he has enriched: a bounteous Guru I have found.

दादू सतगुर सौं सहजैं मिल्या, लीया कंठि लगाइ ।
दया भई दयाल की, तब दीपक दीया जगाइ ।।५।।

Without effort I found the Satguru: he clasped me to his breast;
The Compassionate had pity on me: he awoke me and gave me a lamp.

दादू देषु दयाल की, गुरु दिषाई बाट ।
ताला कूंची लाइ करि, षोले सबै कपाट ।।६।।

Lo, the Guru has shown the way to the Merciful One;
Key in hand, he has opened every door.

दादू सतगुर अंजन बाहि करि, नैंन पटल सब षोले ।
वहिर कानौं सुणणे लागे, गुंगे मुष सौं बोले ।।७।।

Applying his unguent, the Satguru opened the closed eyelids;
The ears of the deaf hear, the dumb begin to speak.

सतगुरु दाता जीव का, श्रवन सीस कर नैंन ।
तन मन सौंज संवारि सब, मुष रसनां अरु बैंन ।।८।।

The Satguru gives to the soul head and hands, eyes and ears;
The material of mind and body he arranges properly, he bestows mouth, tongue, and speech.

Like any religious act in the DP, the sample sermon, too, starts with the DPī *maṅgalācaraṇa*. This is, first of all, the first two stanzas, which in DPī editions of the *Dādūvāṇī* stand at the beginning. In early manuscripts only the first of these verses is to be found while the second stands in a different position. The programmatic similarity of the DPī *maṅgala* verses to *maṅgala* verses of popular advaitic texts, such as the *Vedāntasāra*, is obvious. In the case of a sermon, these two canonical *maṅgala* verses are followed by more verses which comprise the rest or a selection of the rest of a collection of stanzas forming the extended *maṅgalācaraṇa*.[9] These stanzas are all in praise of the Guru, in praise of Nirañjan, and in praise of the Divine Name. Some of them are in Sanskrit. To these often more stanzas are added, mostly taken from the *Guru stotra* which is universally used and forms also part of the orthodox *saṃdhyā* ritual and extols the identity of the Guru with the Supreme Self.[10]

After these *maṅgala* verses there often follows as an exposition, even in sermons that do not focus on the greatness of the Guru, a brief statement explaining the purpose of Guru Dādū's existence on earth.[11] In our sample sermon this section is integral to the actual sermon on the pericope selected, and I will return to this. Suffice it to say here that without exception the purpose of Dādū's earthly existence is described as 'work for the benefit of the creatures of *saṃsār*', consisting in teaching a *vāṇī* that is as authoritative as the Veda but, in order to benefit the common man, is in simple language.

After the *maṅgala* verses, the present preacher starts expounding the meaning of the title-line, concentrating on the term *anabhai vāṇī (anubhava-vāṇī)*, 'words coming from immediate intuition'. This title-line is in evidence from the time of the earliest manuscripts, sometimes with minor variations. This shows that it is considered to be an integral part of the *vāṇī* which is followed by the *sākhī* and the *pada* sections. As I said, the whole text of the *vāṇī* is considered to be immediate revelation. This naturally raises the question of how this text can claim such an extraordinary status. The present preacher, as much as authors of other homilies that I have studied for comparison,[12] explains that the *anubhava-vāṇī* is founded on *sākṣātkār*, immediate witness. That is, it is not mediated by other *pramāṇas*, valid proofs. The very act of according this rank to the text implies that it is now no longer at anybody's random disposal but that it is a *śruti* text of which every syllable is permeated by the eternal truth and which is thus eternal truth itself.

I see in this procedure of interpretation three implicit noteworthy aspects, the third of which I have reported as it was spelt out by the preacher.

1. As *anubhava* the words of the founder of the DP gain the status of indubitable truth, which is of crucial importance for the spiritual reassurance of his followers.

2. The term *anubhava* relates directly – and is also intended by the speaker to relate directly – to the philosophy of Advaita Vedānta by summing up the classical concept of *anubhava*. It is the supreme *pramāṇa*, proof, which makes all further proofs, of which six are considered valid in Vedānta, unnecessary. *Anubhava* is pure consciousness, self-knowledge in the sense of *brahman*-knowledge. In the advaitic setting this means that it is knowledge as such without an object of knowledge.[13] As the *vāṇī* has that quality it is not only equivalent to the Veda but it renders the Veda superfluous, for the Veda is only necessary as long as supreme knowledge does not yet prevail. The Veda is the way to the goal, not the goal itself.[14] As a consequence of the introduction of the *anubhava* concept, the objectless intuitive knowledge or pure consciousness, the words of Dādū are *brahman* themselves, that is the Veda itself and, for the reason just adduced, also the transcendence of the Veda.

In other words, by this concept the notoriously strained relationship between *nirguṇ* bhakti and orthodox Hinduism with regard to the acceptance or rejection of the authority of the Veda is somewhat eased, for the Veda is at the same time accepted and transcended by a classical advaitic strategy as old as Śaṅkara's commentary on the *Brahmasūtras*.[15] This strategy is by no means a *tour de force* superimposed upon the *vāṇī* and made up in order to plaster over conflicts. For instance, Dādū himself, who certainly does often flatly denounce Vedic authority, also emphasizes that his *anubhava* discloses the hidden meaning of the Veda, and for that matter also of the Qur'ān.[16]

3. The *anubhava*, which is *brahman* itself, can only be a single entity in all human beings endowed with it. Hence the Sant tradition transcends time, place, caste, and creed. All the *vāṇīs* of all Sants are identical to the Veda, all Sants are the embodiment of *brahman* (*brahmarūpī* is the word used here). As an example, the speaker, a little further on in his sermon, refers to Raidās, the Camār, and to Sadhnā, the butcher. Like all sermons of the DP that I have

heard, this sermon is not only unconcerned with problems of *vyāvahārika* truth but, in fact, avoids them. Its only concern is with theological reflection on the *paramatattva*. Applied to the mentioning of Raidās and Sadhnā, this means that the preacher can take a position fully consonant with the teachings of Dādū himself and that he can ignore socio-religious restrictions within his Panth, which consists of *dvijas* alone. For a DPī preacher, especially when he acts *ex officio* on a great ceremonial occasion, this is the only way to safeguard a theological continuity conformable to the teachings of Dādū. By commenting either positively or negatively on that socio-religious problem he would either demean the Muslim and low-caste DPīs who contributed to the sect during the first century of its existence, or he would antagonize the orthodoxy among his own followers. In brief, a restriction of subject to ontological issues, while passing over in silence all practical religious matters, seems to be a common characteristic of DPī sermons.

The *anubhava* section being finished, the speaker now gives a long summary of the pericope amounting to sixteen pages of the transcription of the tape.

The detailed exegesis then starts with the *maṅgalācaraṇa*, which contains the author's obeisance to his *iṣṭadeva* and his Guru. The *maṅgala* verses are important because they set the tone of the work and have to be corroborated by the main text if the author is to succeed in his purpose. The DPī exemplars emphasize the unity of the unqualified God, the Guru, and the Sants and sādhus,[17] as do innumerable like stanzas of other *nirguṇ* bhakti texts.

The actual beginning of the *vāṇī* is with the third *sākhī*. It is probably the *sākhī* quoted most often in homiletic texts. No sketch of the life of Dādū can do without it or some new adaptation of it. It is the distich taken to be Dādū's own testimony of his *anubhava*, his experience. This is the reason why this distich stands first. It sheds the light of authenticity on the whole *vāṇī*. It is the hinge of all reverence of the guru in the DP and the paradigm of all guru–disciple relationship, because on it the rite of initiation into the Panth is modelled. It is, finally, the *sākhī* that is illustrated pictorially most often, and it is this picture that will be found invariably at any DPī shrine, generally immediately behind the *vāṇī*, which is revered almost like an icon. In the homily concerned, exegesis of the preceding *anubhava* finds its conclusive continuation, for it is here that the way by which knowledge of *brahman* can be obtained is indicated: this way being the guru himself. The preacher, after a long discussion of the various ways in which ordinary men proceed in order to find a guru, without whom there is no salvation, embarks upon the crucial question of what Dādū's relation to a guru could have been like. For the rest of this paper I will dwell on this point, for distiches 4 to 8 of the pericope unfold the theme of the guru but no longer pose basic conceptual problems.

The preacher says that Dādū, unlike ordinary people, who strive for a guru over a long series of reincarnations, found the *gurudev*, the Divine Guru, *gaiba māṁhi*, 'secretly, mysteriously' or, as he also paraphrases the expression, 'unexpectedly'. Dādū obtained a guru, and Dādū was an avatār in the full sense of the word. Here the preacher refers implicitly to the earliest hagiography by Jangopāl, which is followed by all important sectarian treatises in making Dādū an avatār.[18] So, he continues, how could it be that Dādū had a guru? Here is his exegesis: Dādū had no need to search for a guru, for he was an avatār. But God himself transformed himself into a guru and appeared to Dādū, not to instruct him but so that mankind would learn, through this incident and Dādū's testimony of it, how essential it is to have a guru.

The conceptual problem that seems to arise here, namely of the corporeal duality of the Supreme Self as Bhagavān and as Dādū, the avatār, is best explained in light of the one Supreme Self that can take on multiple form.

In mainstream Indological writing on Sant bhakti the hitherto basically uncontested opinion, mainly put forth by P. R. Caturvedī, C. Vaudeville, and W. H. McLeod with regard to Kabīr and Guru Nānak,[19] has been that the *satguru* of these Sants is inner revelation or, ultimately, God. As far as Dādū is concerned, earlier literature, against Dādū's own testimony, took great pains to establish a human guru for him.[20] This procedure was abetted by the fact that tradition has handed down a name for Dādū's guru, namely Bābā Būṛhā or Vṛddhānand and that that guru was also represented pictorially on the icons mentioned earlier. I return to this below. Here it may be sufficient to remark that such a way of answering the question of the nature of the guru is strained and invalid as far as DPī sectarian theology is concerned.

Recently R. M. Steinmann and D. Gold raised the question of the Sants' *satguru* anew.[21] Steinmann doubts that the identification of the *satguru* with inner experience is correct. He says:

> If the institution of guru in the case of the Sants were purely spiritual, the Sants' popularity, which triggered one of the greatest popular religious movements in India, could hardly be accounted for. Moreover, the Sant institution lacks the epistemological presuppositions that would allow us to infer a merely autodidactic and purely interior experience of salvation.[22]

Gold, expressing doubt, too, and pointing to the so-called Western tradition of Kabīr (that is the DPī and *Gurū Granth* tradition) and the very human image of the guru that he feels emerges from it, and also retroactively applying socio-religiously relevant findings that form the heart of the book, says:

> So if Kabīr had no guru, he was either one of the very few exceptions that yogic traditions allows, or he adapted the *nāth* vocabulary in such an idiosyncratic way that it does not refer to yogic experience at all.[23]

And, after expressing his conviction that there is indeed a yogic basis for Sant experience, he concludes:

We are, then, led to suspect that Kabīr, like most *sants* and yogis, probably had some sort of living guru – though just who he was will probably never be known.[24]

This kind of reasoning catches us (with Morgenstern's Palmström) in a vicious circle: 'For, he reasons trenchantly, "That which must not, cannot be."' The reason why this is so seems to be a conceptual error, which I will analyse at least for the case of Dādū. My contention is that Dādū's concept of the *satguru* is phenomenologically different from the concept of the *satguru* as the true spiritual preceptor who interacts as a living person with his disciples.

First of all, what has DPī theology to contribute to the argument? The preacher, when flatly denying that Dādū had a human guru, is in agreement with the authoritative texts of his sect. In evidence of this I will quote three authors, namely Jangopāl, the hagiographer (*c*.1636); Sundardās, the poet-philosopher and main author of the DPī liturgy (mid-seventeenth century AD); and Caturdās (AD 1800), the commentator on Raghodās' *Bhaktmāl*. All of them, in an open or, in the case of Sundardās, in an ingeniously concealed fashion, state that Dādū's guru was God. Jangopāl describes the two mystical experiences of Dādū in the following way in the first chapter of his work:

7. When he was 11 years old, one day at dusk while playing with other children,
Bābū Būḍhā appeared to him.
8. 'The Supreme Lord is sporting,
He grants liberation, the Indweller.
He crosses and guides one over the ocean of rebirth.
Wealth, perfection and liberation are always found in his court'.
9. The old man came and begged for money, testing the discernment of every child.
Svāmījī gave without delay and the old man, giver of all happiness, was pleased.
10. If a child shows such intelligence, what love will he be capable of later?
The old man was happy, he called the boy close to him and touched him.
11. He put a sweet *pāṇ* roll in his mouth, giving him everlasting knowledge of Rām.
He gave him everything, putting his hand on the child's forehead.
The child did not grasp what was happening.
12. Dādū did different works for seven years and then Hari appeared to him.
He started to travel on the true path and his mind turned away from external things to the internal.

A variant in certain manuscripts (of the years 1654, 1700, and 1739) reads 'Hari in the form of an old man appeared to him.'[25] Even if we are content with the first, earliest reading, the text makes it clear that the Bābā is the Supreme Lord (1. 8) and 'the giver of all happiness' (1. 9), the latter an unmistakable epithet of God. At any rate, the 'old man' was no preceptor.

Sundardās talks of Dādū's guru in his allegorical treatise *Guru-sampradāya*, perhaps directed against the Rāmānandīs.[26] There he says that the guru granted a view of himself to Dādū suddenly and that nobody saw that guru, that his name was Vṛddhānand, who has no place of residence, who roams over the earth *sahaj rūp*, 'in an unconditioned way' or 'easily', who can go anywhere at his will, and whose ways are unknowable. It should be clear (and this is also how the commentator interprets it) that Vṛddhānand is God (sts. 8bc–9).[27] Caturdās, finally, speaks of Dādū's guru as of 'Hari who had put on the form of an old man.'[28]

From the intrasectarian theological discussion as reproduced here we have to conclude that the guru of Dādū is the personification of an interior revelatory experience. A strikingly similar case – striking, too, in its iconographical similarity – is that of the encounter of Jakob Böhme (1575–1624) with a 'stranger'. As in the case of Dādū, an unsought-after encounter in adolescence, a bargain with a stranger, the election to revelation by tactile contact with him, and the announcement of the future religious career by the stranger are prominent motives here.[29]

In light of DPī descriptions of Dādū's encounter with his *satguru* and of comparative evidence, I feel that the question whether Dādū had a human guru or not is of secondary importance, for an existent human guru would belong to a different phenomenological category from that of revelatory experience personified. To pursue the discussion on the *satguru* of the early Sants in the way that Gold does (see the first passage quoted from his book above) therefore also seems unpromising. Their indebtedness to Nāth tradition helps the Sants to express their own experience of revelation in Nāth terms. Organisationally, however, we cannot claim that the early Sants' indebtedness to Nāth tradition necessarily implies that the guru institution was part of their inheritance because Santism, in its formative phase, was not essentially an organised movement to which yogic initiation, relying on the institution of guruship, would have been necessary.

NOTES

The author wishes to thank the Abbot-in-Chief of the Dādūpanth, Svāmī Harirāmjī Mahārāj, for his hospitality, ongoing interest, and co-operation, and for much more that has to remain unexpressed here. My research in India was made possible by a grant from the Deutsche Forschungsgemeinschaft, for which I also express my gratitude.

1. Schomer 1987, p. 84.

2. Schomer 1987, pp. 75–7.
3. This is also attested by a relatively early MS of the *Dādūvāṇī* of vs 1765 (MS 35b, Dādūmahāvidyālay, Jaipur) in which *bhajans* are occasionally supplemented by *sākhīs*.
4. Phālguna *śuklā* 8, vs 1601.
5. Jyaiṣṭha *badī* 9, vs 1660.
6. These discourses are directed to a different audience from that of the ceremonial sermons, for while the latter are compulsory and are attended without regard for their entertainment value, the former are given in the leisure hours of lay people – mostly women who help with the preparation of the *paṅktis* and in other ways. Such sermons are often full of stories drawn from general Hindu mythology and narrative matter illustrated by examples (*dṛṣṭāntas*), although they, too, never lose sight of their central topic, always addressing one or several issues of Sant theology proper. Narrative matter, however, is almost completely absent from the great ceremonial sermons, which are pieces of exegesis.
7. (1987, p. 84.)
8. The sermon was given on 25 Feb. 1985. The text is as used in the sermon and identical with that in traditional editions of the *Dādūvāṇī*, such as that of C. P. Tripāṭhī (Dādū vs 1964). The translation follows Orr 1947, p. 84, but includes a few corrections. Above I have chosen the term 'pericope' but hasten to modify it as far as its usage in the DPī context is concerned. Unlike Christian pericopes, the portion of the scripture to be commented on is not read out in total at the beginning, although it may be summed up initially. The procedure is rather that a stanza is read out and then discussed.
9. See e.g. Svāmī vs 2030, pp. 151–2.
10. For the text, trans., and further comments see Steinmann 1986, pp. 248–51.
11. I am referring to a sermon in which the preacher bases this part of his discourse on Niścaldās' *Vicār-sāgar* (Niścaldās n.d.), Maṅgal Kavitta 6, p. 295.
12. See esp. Svāmī n.d., p. 23.
13. Potter 1981, pp. 52, 98.
14. This is how it is put in the sermon and is in accordance with orthodox tradition.
15. Deussen 1883, p. 95 n. 54.
16. In a different, printed homiletic text, the author when addressing the *anubhava* issue does, in fact, quote distiches by Dādū that testify to this. See Svāmī n.d., p. 23; the *sākhīs* quoted in evidence are four (*Paricaya kau aṅga*): '*dādū anabhai vāṇī agama kūṁ, lai gaī saṅgi lagāi| agaha gahai akaha kahai, abheda bheda lahāi*' (188); '*je kachu veda kurāṁṇa thaiṁ, agama agocara bāta| so anabhai sācā kahai, yahu dādū akaha kahāta*' (189) (Caturvedī 1972; in 188a Kanīrām Svāmī reads *brahma kī* instead of *agama kūṁ*).
17. 'Sants' are defined as those who have shaken off *māyā* and are about to attain the supreme truth; as 'sādhus' are described as those who have already obtained the supreme truth.
18. Jangopāl's hagiography of Dādū has been edited critically and translated by W. M. Callewaert (1988).
19. Caturvedī 1972, pp. 159–61; Vaudeville 1974, p. 116; McLeod 1968, p. 197.
20. Orr 1947, pp. 52–6.
21. Steinmann 1986; Gold 1987.
22. Steinmann 1986, pp. 141, n. 51; my translation.

23. Gold 1987, pp. 108–9.
24. Gold 1987, p. 109.
25. Callewaert 1988, pp. 35, 91 (Hindi text).
26. Sundardās 1978, pp. 268–80.
27. Sundardās 1978, pp. 270–1.
28. Manhar 549 on Raghodās' *Bhaktamāl* (Rāghavdās 1965).
29. Böhme's contemporary biographer Abraham von Franckenberg relates what Böhme told him about this encounter: 'Denn wie mir der selige Mann selber erzählet, hat sich einstmals bei seinen Lehrjahren zugetragen, daß ein fremder, zwar schlecht bekleideter, doch feiner und ehrbarer Mann vor den Laden kommen, welcher ein Paar Schuh für sich zum Kauf begehret. . . . Und als er ihm die Schuh (der Meinung, Käufern abzuschrecken) ziemlich hoch und über rechte Billigkeit geboten, hat ihn der Mann dasselbe Geld alsobald und ohne Widerrede dafür gegeben, die Schuh genommen, fortgegangen, und als er ein wenig von dem Laden abgekommen, stille gestanden und mit lauter und ernster Stimme gerufen: Jacob, komme heraus! Worüber er sich selbst erschrocken, daß ihn dieser unbekannte Mann mit eigenem Taufnamen genennet . . . Da ihn der Mann eines ernstfreundlichen Ansehens mit lichtfunkelnden Augen bei der rechten Hand gefasset, ihm strack und stark in die Augen gesehen und gesprochen: Jacob, du bist klein, aber du wirst groß und gar ein anderer Mensch und Mann werden, daß sich die Welt über dir verwundern wird' (Franckenberg in Böhme 1961, p. 9).

REFERENCES

Böhme, J. (1961), *Sämtliche Schriften*, facsimile of the 1730 edn. in 11 vols., begun by A. Faust, rev. W. E. Peukert, vol. x: *De Vita et scriptis Jacobi Böhmii oder Historischer Bericht von dem Leben und Schriften Jakob Böhmes: Das Leben Jakob Böhmes*, ed. W. E. Peukert, 2nd rev. edn., Stuttgart: Fr. Fromann Verlag.

Callewaert, W. M. (1988), *The Hindī Biography of Dādū Dayāl*, Delhi: Motilal Banarsidass.

Caturvedī, Paraśurām (1972), *Uttarī bhārat kī sant paramparā*, 3rd edn., Allahabad: Bhāratī Bhaṇḍār.

Dādū (vs 1964), *Śrīdādūbāṇī, aṅgabandhū saṭīk*, ed. and comm. Candrikāprasād Tripaṭhī, Ajmer, repr. Varanasi: Sant Sāhitya Akādamī, 1985.

——(vs 2023), *Dādudayāl (granthāvalī)*, ed. Paraśurām Caturvedī, Varanasi: Nāgarīpracāriṇī Sabhā.

Deussen, P. (1883), *Das System des Vedānta nach den* Brahma-sūtra's *des Bādarāyaṇa und dem Commentare des Çaṅkara über dieselben . . .*, Leipzig: F. A. Brockhaus.

Gold, D. (1987), *The Lord as Guru: Hindi Sants in the North Indian Tradition*, New York and Oxford: Oxford University Press.

McLeod, W. H. (1968), *Gurū Nānak and the Sikh Religion*, Oxford: Oxford University Press.

Niścaldās (n.d.), *Śrī vicār-sāgar, saṭīk*, Mathura: Shiam Kashi Press.

Orr, W. G. (1947), *A Sixteenth-Century Indian Mystic: Dadu and his Followers*, London and Redhill: Lutterworth Press.

Potter, K. H., ed. (1981), *Encyclopaedia of Indian Philosophies: Advaita Vedānta up to Śaṅkara and his Pupils*, Delhi: Motilal Banarsidass.

Rāghavdās (1965), *Bhaktamāl (Caturdās kṛt ṭīkā sahit)*, ed. Agarcand Nāhṭā (Rājasthān Purātan Granthmālā, 75), Jodhpur: Rājasthān Prācyavidyā Pratiṣṭhān.

Schomer, K. (1987), 'The *Dohā* as a Vehicle of Sant Teaching', in K. Schomer and W. H. McLeod, eds., *The Sants: Studies in a Devotional Tradition of India*, Berkeley, Calif., Berkeley Religious Studies Series, and Delhi: Motilal Banarsidass, pp. 61–90.

Steinmann, R. M. (1986), *Guru-Śiṣya-Sambandha: Das Meister-Schüler-Verhältnis im traditionellen und modernen Hinduismus* (Beiträge zur Südasienforschung, 109), Heidelberg: Südasien-Institut.

Sundardās (1978), *Śrīsundar-granthāvalī*, ed. Dvarikādās Śāstrī, pt. 2 (Śrīdādūdayālu-Śodh-Granthmālā, 2), 2nd edn., Varanasi: Śrīdādūdayālu-Śodh-Saṃsthān Trust.

Svāmī Kanīrām (n.d.), 'Sant śrī Dādūdayāl va unkī *Anbhaivāṇī*', *Jñānāñjalī* (Journal of the Dādū Ācārya Saṃskṛt Mahāvidyālay, Jaipur), 1983–4, pp. 21–4.

—— ed. (vs 2030), *Svādhyāy-saṃgrah*, Baṛāgāṁv: S. O. Bhānīrām.

Vaudeville, C. (1974), *Kabīr*, vol. i, Oxford: Clarendon Press.

Some aspects of the development of bhakti traditions, with especial reference to the Hindi poems attributed to Rāmānand

ENZO TURBIANI

When we speak of bhakti in late medieval India, we are immediately confronted with many complex problems involving philosophy, history, and even language. Bhakti is like a rising tide that carries everything with it, then when it recedes leaves its traces behind it. It cannot be considered a spiritual movement limited uniquely to Hinduism, since non-dogmatic and mystical Islamic thought has permeated it. From bhakti, Sikhism rises, after Kabīr has given poetic expression to his feelings of profound devotion towards the Supreme Being. Bhakti paves the way for the Sants' literature, in which typical Indian monotheism is represented without iconoclastic tendencies; and it is in the very bosom of bhakti that Dādū Dayāl's and Rajjab's poetry blooms, and even Rabīndranāth Ṭhākur gets his most genuine inspiration.

It may appear strange that I mention together the names of two Sants of the *nirguṇ* current and that of the most famous poet in modern Bengal. In point of fact, Ṭhākur's thought and literary production would not be conceivable without the *nirguṇ* devotional trends that reached their climax between the fifteenth and eighteenth centuries of the Christian era. In particular, Kabīr's bhakti and the Sants' message have deeply influenced Ṭhākur's mystical poetry; Śyāmsundardās rightly asserts that Rabīndranāth Ṭhākur 'found the seed of his own mysticism in Kabīr' (*apne rahasyavād kā bīj unhoṁne Kabīr hī meṁ pāyā*):[1] although the Bengali writer expressed his religious insight through formal structures and poetical patterns of a kind which could reconcile the traditions of his country with European ones.

It is the concept of *bīj*, the seed that Kabīr saw as the origin of all things,[2] that leads Ṭhākur to what we might call 'an extraordinary perspective of immortality' in his poem *Tājmahal*:

from your soul a squall of wind
once, all of a sudden,
blew a seed, after it was
freed from the garland of being.
You went far off;
that seed, having become an immortal gem,
rose up towards heaven
and cried in a deep tone:

– As far as I look into the depth of space
that wanderer does not appear, he does not appear.
His beloved has not stopped him,
his kingdom has let him go,
neither the sea nor the mountains have halted him.
Now his chariot
has left at the call of night,
while the stars are singing,
for the morning door.
For this reason
I am overwhelmed by the burden of my memories;
having cast away all burdens, he is not here.[3]

The phenomenological display of the Supreme Being in the two dimensions of time and space is potentially concentrated in the 'seed'. Having freed itself from cosmic illusion, the 'seed' shatters the material limits that have so far concealed its real nature as Śāhjahān's chariot moves towards 'the morning door', where the dawn and the sunset of the world come together.

I have quoted a translated passage from Ṭhākur's poetry since the author of *Gītāñjali* has thrown a bridge between our conception of the world and bhakti in its multifarious expression. Without a landmark which can be equally recognized by Westerners and Indians, it becomes extremely arduous, and a task for specialists, to grasp the development and salient features of the main bhakti trends: but the poems and philosophical essays of Rabīndranāth Ṭhākur are a reminder of the significance of bhakti attitudes in the modern world of mixed cultures.

In this paper I have started from the idea of the 'seed' of bhakti, which Ṭhākur imagines as intuited by the Emperor Śāhjahān. Śāhjahān realized the *vanitas vantitatum* while still on the throne of India, which is made a symbol here of the vastness of space and of limitless power; in the dichotomy between matter and spirit it is only an infinitesimal part of the emperor's being that is to reach freedom and become an 'immortal germ'.

Striving for liberation of the soul from the bonds of the world of contingency is the fundamental end to which bhakti tends. All-pervading love for the godhead becomes the only salvific medium for those who surrender themselves to him, casting off the illusory consciousness of *aham*, the individual self. As to the broad religious viewpoint of the bhaktas, we find a surprising identity with Sufism, but also with neo-Platonism and Christian mysticism, which can be ascertained by perusing the writings of Meister Eckhart, Suso, and Saint John of the Cross.

The Hindi poems attributed to Rāmānand

It has been suggested that the bhakti movement arose and developed within Hindu society as a means of self-assertion and confirmation of religious principles after India had almost entirely fallen into the hands of the Muslim invaders; also that Christianity was most probably the starting-point from which bhakti began spreading all over the Indian subcontinent. But an identity crisis and the mere search for one's spiritual roots can hardly have given rise to one of the most impressive religious movements in man's history; and Christianity has always played a secondary role in the development of philosophical schools and creeds in India, its early diffusion having been limited to a narrow environment in the south. By contrast it is much more likely that bhakti originated in south India under the stimulus of the devotional religion that characterized the *ā̤lvārs'* Viṣṇuism. The credit for spreading bhakti in the rest of the country has sometimes, especially earlier in this century, been granted to Rāmānuja, who asserted the prominence of devotional tendencies in the domain of religious practice.

About one of Rāmānuja's direct followers, Rāmānand, little is known with certainty. Some historical sources maintain that Rāmānand was born in the south of India and had left his *maṭh* (monastery) there owing to doctrinal dissensions with a guru, Śrī Rāghavānand, to settle in the northern part of the country, where Hindi is spoken at present. But the Rāmānandīs claim that their spiritual master's birthplace is Prayāg (Allahabad), where Eastern Hindi is the local language. According to this tradition Rāmānanda belonged to the brāhmaṇ subcaste Kānyakubja: his father's name was Śrī Puṇyasadan and his mother's Śrīmatī Suśīlā Devī. In the Rāmānandīs' opinion their guru moved to the sacred town of Banaras and became the disciple of Svāmī Rāghavānand, a descendant of Rāmānuja who had brought and spread the devotional worship of Viṣṇu and his principal avatārs, Kṛṣṇa and Rām.

A linguistic analysis of *Gyān-līlā* and *Yog-cintāmaṇi*, both of them mystical treatises in Old Hindi attributed to Rāmānand, would suggest that the guru's birthplace is to be looked for somewhere in the Hindi-speaking territory. The type of speech used by their author in *Yog-cintāmaṇi* (Rāmānand is also credited with authorship of two works in Sanskrit, *Vaiṣṇava-matābja-bhāskara* and *Rāmārcana-paddhati*) shows evident traces of what might be called Khaṛī bolī influence, since most nominal and verbal terminations are characterized by the morpheme *-ā* and not by the *-o*/*-au* distinctive of Brajbhāṣā and Kanaujī. The language of these compositions is akin to that employed by Kabīr and by the majority of Sants leaning towards *nirguṇ* bhakti in their doctrine. Moreover, a hymn by Rāmānand is included in the *Damdamī Bīṛ* (i.e. the authorized edition of the *Ādi Granth*).[4] This reminds us that the original compiler of the *Ādi Granth*, the fifth Sikh gurū Śrī Arjan, will have realized a close similarity between the metaphysical theories underlying Sikh doctrines and those professed by the supposed founder of the *Rāmāvat sampradāy*.[5] The same hymn is to be found also in a handwritten *Sarbāṅgī*, dating back to VS 1660 and preserved in the library of the Nāgarī-pracāriṇī Sabhā at Banaras.[6] This manuscript is thus contemporary with the compilation of the *Ādi Granth* under the supervision of the fifth Sikh gurū.

Little research has hitherto been carried out on the Hindi compositions attributed to Rāmānand.[7] The metaphysical principles expounded in the works in question represent a milestone in the development of bhakti in northern India. First of all Rāmānand purports to say that ascetics who devote themselves to excessive austerities and grievous penances waste their own existence if they do not realize Hari (Viṣṇu) in their inner self.[8] He adds also that such fasts as the Ekādaśī observed by the Hindus, or the abstinence from drink and food that the Muslims practise on the occasion of Ramadān, are ineffectual if one forgets the Supreme Being.[9] Rāmānand asserts that even the Vedas and the Qur'ān are no use if one does not purify oneself by reading them.[10] In this way, the founder of the *Rāmāvat sampradāy* appears as making a revolutionary stand for what will be called the 'Religion of Man' by Rabīndranāth Ṭhākur, and objects to brahmanical orthodoxy; his original position as here represented is more radically resumed by Kabīr and by the Sikh gurūs.

The teaching attributed to Rāmānand has undoubtedly opened new perspectives on doctrinal and philosophical thought in the northern part of the Indian subcontinent. It is not surprising that by making an active participation in the divine mysteries accessible also to the humblest classes, and to outcastes, it has also had the effect of checking the proselytism carried forward by Ṣūfī brotherhoods. As to Rāmānand's reformism, it is probable that he may have taken over some notions to be found in esoteric Islam, adapting them, or, more exactly, remoulding them, to Hinduism, which was able to preserve its position only by changing its formal and conceptual 'reality'.

Purity of heart, unceasing physical and mental effort, and constant recollection (*sumiran*) of the Supreme Being represent the pivots which the door of eternal bliss hinges upon. It is the seventh avatār of Viṣṇu, Rām, that for Rāmānand symbolizes the godhead. The following verses from *Yog-cintāmaṇi* seem to me particularly noteworthy for our understanding of the Rām cult:

अब उलटा चढ़ना दूर, जहाँ नगर बसता है पूर,
तन कर फिकिर कर भाई, जिसमें राम रोसनाई ।[11]

Now instead one must clamber a long way, where there rises a peerless town:
with all your force practise meditation, wherein Rām's light appears.

It is interesting to notice how the Rāmaite saint makes use of Arabic and Persian terms such as *phikira* (Arabic *fikr*), 'thought, reflection, meditation' and *rosanāī* (cf. Persian *roshnī*, 'light, illumination'). Clearly he lived in an epoch when the two classical languages of Islam had already permeated the vocabulary of the Indo-Aryan languages.

The style of Rāmānand's poems and the intrusion of Arabic and Persian words in modified form, which involves an acculturation process, inclines me towards Farquhar's hypothesis about the year when Rāmānand was born (AD 1400) rather than towards the traditional date (AD 1299). By the fifteenth century Arabic, Turkish, and Persian words had become so integrated into Hindi that it was difficult to distinguish them structurally from their Indo-Aryan counterparts; furthermore, the type of language employed by Rāmānand is itself an evolved one, with clear-cut morphemic and syntagmatic relationships, which are not found in *Pṛthvirāj-rāso*,[12] or in other near-contemporary literary compositions and epic poems.

In Rāmānand's opinion *sumiran* or *simaran* is one of the fundamental elements which raise the soul to *paramānand*, supreme bliss. In *Gyān-līlā* and in *Yog-cintāmaṇi* Rāmānand gives particular emphasis to the theory of *simaran*, recalling the sacred name of the Absolute:

रामानँद यूं कहै समुझाई: हरि सिमर्यौ जम लोक न जाई ।[13]

Rāmānand speaks thus by way of explanation: if one recalls Hari, he does not descend to hell.

Again, using allegorical terms such as are met with in poetic compositions by Muslim writers like Mullā Vajhī in his *Sab ras*, Rāmānand states:

सुरत नगर का कर सयल, जिसमें आत्मा का महल ।[14]

Go the round of the town of Remembrance, where there is the abode of the Soul.

Here Rāmānand employs the lexeme *surat*, whose meaning exactly corresponds to the one implied in the word *sumiran*. The 'abode of the Soul' (*ātmā kā mahal*) should be looked for in the 'town of Remembrance', a well-defined image of the metaphysical space one has to run through in order to reach the Final Goal.

Use of *rāg* Gujrī in the *Ādi Granth*

Another point at issue is represented by the employment of *rāg* Gujrī in many a mystical composition contained in the *Ādi Granth*. In the Holy Book of the Sikhs we meet with two *padas* composed by Nāmdev and adapted to *rāg* Gujrī. It is relevant that the poet is presumed to have lived in the fourteenth century, when Sufism had already set firm roots in the Deccan, especially in Maharashtra. In Nāmdev's *padas* and *abhaṅgas* is it easy to recognize a strong influence of *nirguṇ* bhakti, a few currents of which were most probably influenced by mystical Islam. We cannot exclude that Nāmdev, too, may have been well acquainted with the religion developed in Maharashtra and adjoining areas by the Ṣūfīs, with their monotheistic creed. Nāmdev asserts, in his first *pada* adapted to *rāg* Gujrī, that it is impossible to worship the godhead having made idols of stone;[15] in the second, employing highly figurative images, he says that God is not a visible Being.[16]

The language of the first *pada* by Nāmdev is akin to Old Hindi, whereas the second shows a clear influence of Marathi: as, for instance, in the genitive postposition *ce* in *nāme ce svāmī*,[17] 'possessor of the Name'. In reading the first *pada*, however, we find the contrasting usage *bahuri na hoi terā āvana jānu*,[18] 'you will not be subject to transmigration any longer', where *terā* and *āvana jānu* show specifically Hindi linguistic patterns.

As to *rāg* Gujrī itself, the famous Sikh scholar and theologian Tāran Siṅgh writes that it is the *rāg* of the *Gujarī jāti gavāri*,[19] 'the wandering Gūjar tribes', and is sung in the morning watch. Although originally a *rāg* proper to the cult of Kṛṣṇa, the Sikh gurūs and bhagats came to it also for themes connected with the blossoming of the inner self. Thus gurū Nānak in his 'Gujrī' compositions says that it is impossible to see any limits in the Supreme Being (*antu na jāī lakhṇā*) and that there is no difference between the gurū and God.[20] The third gurū, Amardās, in his hymns assigned to *rāg* Gujrī emphasizes the uniqueness of God: *Hari kī tuma sevā karahu, dūjī sevā karahu na koī jī*,[21] 'serve the Lord, do not serve anybody else'; further *guraprasādi rāmu mani vasai tā phalu pāvai koi*,[22] 'if Rām dwells in the soul through the guru's grace, some fruit is certainly obtained'. Finally, the fifth gurū, Arjan, in his poems assigned to *rāg* Gujrī, asserts that by means of the Name *apajasu miṭai hovai jagi kīrati daragaha baisaṇu pāīai*,[23] 'ill fame is destroyed, one gets renown in the world and is admitted into the court of Viṣṇu'.

Guru Rāmdās says, further, in one of his compositions in *rāg* Gujrī: *Hari binu jīarā rahi na sakai jiu bālaku khīra adhāri*,[24] 'the Being inside cannot remain without Hari, just as a child cannot do without milk'; for him, God is the very foundation on which the world rests and the only nourishment on which man's soul feeds.

The *Ādi Granth* compositions in *rāg* Gujrī deserve critical study as a group, since the above-mentioned *rāg*, used previously to sing and to extol Lord Kṛṣṇa, acquires quite a different 'value' in the language of the gurūs and of the bhagats. In fact, it becomes the *rāg* devoted *par excellence* to the only God, seen as an Absolute, who does not admit of any comparison. It is also the *rāg* which lays special emphasis on the worship of the inner self, to be identified as the microcosmic unit in the macrocosmic ocean where the *paramātmā*, the Supreme Being, abides. In *rāg* Gujrī we see all the main characteristics of Sikhism exemplified: firm monotheism, which abhors idols and figurative representations of the godhead; repetition of the Name, which brings one nearer the Supreme Being; belief in the transmigration of the soul, which will be overcome by remembering the Divine Being; God as an invisible, unlimited entity; the gurū who is identified with God; the 'fruit of salvation', which one can obtain through the grace bestowed by the gurū; and the impossibility for the individual *ātmā* to remain far from the Supreme Spirit.

NOTES

1. Śyāmsundardās, ed., *Kabīr granthāvalī*, new edn., Varanasi: Nāgarī Pracāriṇī Sabhā, 1965.
2. '*Baṭaka bīja mahi ravi rahyo jāko tīni loka nistāra*' (ibid., p. 236).
3. Trans. from *Balākā*, new edn., Calcutta: Vishvabhāratī Granthanvibhāg, 1970, pp. 30–1.
4. p. 1195.
5. E. Turbiani, 'Il sikhismo: la religione dei divini maestri', in E. Turbiani, *Classe di Scienze Morali: Memorie*, vol. xxix, series 8, Rome: Accademia Nazionale dei Lincei, 1987, p. 349.
6. Hajārīprasād Dvivedī *et al.*, eds., *Rāmānand kī hindī racanāeṁ*, Varanasi: Nāgarīpracāriṇī Sabhā, 1955, introduction, p. 1.
7. As Rāmānand's reputation is that of a major innovator of religious traditions in late medieval Hindustan, it appears highly advisable for some scholar to prepare a critical edition, with philosophical commentary, of the *padas* and mystical treatises in Old Hindi attributed to this disciple of Svāmī Rāghavānand. I would like to take up this research, but my present position as administrative principal of an Italian high school prevents me from collecting the handwritten and printed materials necessary to take the study further. I should be grateful for help in this regard.
8. Ibid., *pada* 42, p. 15.
9. Ibid., *pada* 49, p. 16.
10. Ibid., *pada* 51, p. 16.
11. Ibid., p. 9.
12. I suppose *Pṛthvirāj-rāso* to have been composed (in part at least) in the second half of the 14th century: cf. Rāmkumār Varmā, *Hindī sāhitya kā ālocanātmak itihās*, Allahabad: Rāmnārāyaṇlāl Benīmādhav, 1971, p. 166.
13. *Rāmānand kī hindī racanāeṁ, pada* 13, p. 7.
14. Ibid., *pada* 9, p. 9.
15. *Ādi Granth*, p. 525.
16. Ibid.
17. Ibid., 3/2.
18. Ibid., 1/1.
19. *Srī Gurū Granth sāhib dā sāhitak itihās*, Amritsar: Fakīr Siṅgh & Sons, n.d., p. 75.
20. Ibid., p. 260.
21. Ibid., p. 329.
22. Ibid., p. 329.
23. Ibid., p. 396.
24. Ibid., p. 367.

The Hindu model of social organization and the bhakti movement: the example of Vallabha's *sampradāya*

MAYA BURGER

The period that gave rise to devotional literature in vernacular language broadly corresponds to the bhakti revival and the spread of sectarian traditions. Bhakti, though an old spiritual practice of the Hindus, found new ways of expression during the medieval period, flourishing in a great variety of spiritual communities. This revival of the bhakti movement not only brought about deep changes in the prevailing orthodox and brahmanical vision of God and the world, it also carried new models of behaviour, social and ethical values that express historical compulsions and new aspirations through songs, myths, poems, or philosophical explanations. The general sensibility of this movement was such as to open up religion against a proprietary attitude to religion on the part of the twice-born castes, to all the people who wanted to voice and live it, regardless of their social origin, sex, or colour. The communication a devotee could establish with a personal God (*Īśvara*) of love and grace was recognized as unfitting to exclusiveness. Though most of the bhakti movement remained indebted in one way or another to the old tradition, and few would try to do away with it, there was none the less a need, among poet-saints especially, and even more among those of deprived origins, to claim religion as belonging to all. This egalitarian thrust became fully part of bhakti literature and oral tradition and was usually praised as one of its important features. In spite of many attempts, it would be wrong to view this aspiration as other than religious. I will show in this paper, however, that the bhakti movement reveals quite clearly that the Hindu social organization, with its stratified groups, can be viewed independently of religious beliefs.

The spreading of sects with their social and religious aspirations raises the important question of the status of religion in the Indian context. Besides the eternal, omnipresent, and permanent law, the sanātana dharma of the elitist brāhmaṇs, many religious beliefs, practices, and attitudes of mind exist among the sectarian groups. A sect, in the Indian context, defines a religious tradition that allows for a particular approach to God, and for specific ways and techniques to know and realize him. Based on the teaching of a master, these various traditions from a common root are the usual way of religion to grow and be lived. Devotional attitudes were to be shared among other followers of the same faith. This sharing resulted in the proliferation of sectarian communities that would create, maintain, and spread devotional messages. These spiritual communities with their recognized master became so important that it would be very difficult to find someone today who does not belong to one or the other spiritual community in one or another of the main streams (Viṣṇuism, Śaivism, Śāktism, etc.) or in one of the smaller communities. This adherence provides a Hindu with a religious identity embedded in a set of beliefs and ritual practices. Each sect emphasizes the worship of a deity and relies on a corpus of accepted (or refuted) scriptures. Besides, each family clan has its master and deity (*kuldevatā*), though this does not have to be exclusive. As K. N. Sharma puts it:

> these sects are of a non-church type or in other words there is no religious bureaucracy controlling the behaviour of the followers of the sect . . . One can observe the shivaites worshipping Vishnu and Mother Goddess in some form or the other, Vaishnavas worshipping deities of the other two sects and so on. . . . On an individual level also deviation occurs, because the non-church type of religion may emphasize individual religious responsibility; among the Hindus it is so. The result is that even in the same family one member may become a complete Vaishnava, leaving non-vegetarian food all together, while others may continue to be shaktists.[1]

This individual right (which can vary depending on the social background) to choose a personal worship in spite of the fact that one belongs to a jāti that normally upholds a religious tradition existing over generations provides a clue to our argument. It points to the fact that religious feelings can also belong to the personal sphere of the inner world of a human being and are not totally dependent on family and jāti tradition. Bhakti sect adherence allows one to live out religious feelings in a way independent of one's jāti, without, however, changing the status one belongs to by birth, hence the social model of the Hindus.

Let us now consider the jāti, the corner-stone of Hindu society, and view it in relation to bhakti religion and sectarian communities. The primal identity a Hindu gets is by birth, by belonging to a jāti. This group provides the pattern for the cultural, social, and economic life of its members. There are innumerable jātis, closed towards each other by strict endogamic rules, skilled in a specialized or specific function, and stratified by more or less changing hierarchical criteria, of which the pure/impure criterion seems to be the most important. Brāhmaṇs explained the jātis by a cosmo-ideology that frames them in an abstract, perfectly explainable, all-pervading hierarchical order that does not correspond to actual reality. Throughout history up to the present day, we have to admit a moving character to this pluralistic social order (change of status, jāti fusion and fission) provided each jāti, old or new, can be localized and retains defined group criteria.

Observing the bhakti movement and sectarian divisions from a more social point of view may help to bring out a different understanding of the jāti system which appears in brahmanical literature, by showing, for instance, that jāti organization and religion are of a different nature. On an ideological level the bhakti movement clearly destroys the brahmanical assumption of the fusional nature of religion and caste, wanting worship to be free of social bounds and love of God open to all. On the level of social reality, however, jāti organization seems to be independent also of this new religious discourse. It appears, rather, that the jāti and its regime structure sectarian movements.

There were quite a few members of the Dādū-panth living in the villages where I did field-work (Rajasthan). They were totally anti-brāhmaṇ, and opposed to Vedic orthodoxy in their verbal expressions and religious beliefs. In the social context, however, they considered themselves equal to brāhmaṇs, lived endogamically in the jātis, and established social relations on hierarchical criteria. In this respect the example of the Jains in Rājasthān is very relevant. Members of the Jain religion belong to precise jātis, very much like those of the Hindus. Religious sects among Jains (*gacchas*) are formed along jāti lines, or a Jaina jāti may adhere to an existing sect.[2]

Jāti is fundamental to Hindu society: religious content may change, rituals be modified, views altered, many religious systems may coexist, yet the basic structure of endogamous groups remains. Neither religion nor even occupation seem to be permanent criteria for caste identity, but both can produce various effects on the status of jāti.

To illustrate, I shall briefly analyse the social history and implementation of the *sampradāya* of Vallabhācārya and its establishment in the city of Nāthadwārā.[3] After introductory remarks on the history of the *sampradāya* and an analysis of the philosophy of Vallabha, I shall focus my attention on the social aspects of the formation and evolution of the sect.[4]

Vallabha (1479–1531) founded a *sampradāya* that has its centre in the worship and service (*sevā*) of the Lord Nāthajī – Śrī Kṛṣṇa as a child – in the homeland of Braj. Vallabha taught a non-ascetic religion where the world and existence are viewed as real and as destined to enjoy and serve the omnipresent Lord. Through a loving relation to God, the devotee is able to leave the ordinary plane of reality for a purified mode of existence, where everything rejoices in the manifestation and presence of the Lord. God comes closest to man in the child Kṛṣṇa, who brings out in his devotees the most tender and caring attention. He invites them to experience in a joyful, playful, and innocent way how to relate and serve him. Besides *vātsalya* and other *bhāvas*, Vallabha, in his commentary on the *Bhāgavata Purāṇa*, emphasizes also the passionate (*mādhurya*) ideal of devotion as realized in the total love, devoid of any social or ethical constraints, of the gopīs.[5] This living presence of the Lord among his bhaktas made the *sampradāya* evolve around its worship and service. The *sevā* of the Lord became a model of worldly existence and temple rituals created social organization. Many crafts and arts were cultivated to please the Lord, offering him the finest of this world, and favouring the ecstatic union of the bhakta with the Lord.

This path to God was basically open to all, and Vallabha created a spiritual community including members of low castes. The rite (*saṁskāra*), called *brahma-sambandha* could be performed by any person irrespective of caste or creed. As we shall see, this spiritual initiation into the sect did not change the social origin of a sect member. Besides belonging to the spiritual community of brotherhood, one belonged to one's jāti, an identity one would carry into the *sampradāya* and that would put one, as a devotee, in a specific position in the *sevā* of Śrī Nāthajī.

During his lifetime, Vallabha instituted the crucial role of the guru, or master. Initiation into the *sampradāya* was to be directly bestowed to the candidate by the guru himself. The process made the devotee a possession of the Lord and purified an ordinary, but by nature impure, state of manhood. With the immediate followers of Vallabha, his sons, guruship became a right of birth and not of spiritual qualification. The second son, Viṭṭhalnāthajī (1516–86), played a crucial role in the growing and shaping of the sect. He also travelled over the country, spreading the new creed, collecting funds and new adherents, negotiating with local and Mughal authorities: in brief, establishing the importance of the sect. After his death the sect was divided among his seven sons, who each established a new sectarian line, symbolized by the possession of one of the idols of Kṛṣṇa from the original temple of Braj. At the same time that these brothers spread the sect over the country, they institutionalized spiritual lineages through the installation of the *svarūpas* of Kṛṣṇa in different parts of the country, and the seven main centres of the *Puṣṭimārg* of Vallabha came into existence.[6]

Through Mughal pressure, the main idol was brought by Bade Daujī (1655–67) to Sinhad village near Udaipur, which was to become the pan-Indian pilgrimage city of Nāthadwārā. The power of the heads (Tilakāyat/Mahārājas) of the *sampradāya* became even more important when they not only represented the spiritual force, but were endowed with worldly powers. In the case of Nāthadwārā, the Tilakāyat's spiritual and worldly power was sanctioned by the rulers of Udaipur themselves, making Nāthadwārā a state within the state.[7] A guru was next to God, if not God himself, and history, up until now, relates many cases of abuse of authority and of debauchery on the part of the leaders of Nāthadwārā. Let us now consider the relation between caste and *sampradāya* that occurs in the case of Nāthadwārā.

Vallabha was a Telenga brāhmaṇ of the Panchdravidian group; he promulgated the real identity of the statue of Kṛṣṇa found on Govardhan Hill and created the *sampradāya*. His caste came to represent the leading group of the sect along with other Panchdravidians that joined Nāthadwārā (Sanchihar, Girnara, Nagar, Audichya jātis). Other jātis had a link with the statue of Govardhan Hill in Braj, and they were to form the party that would bring the idol to Nāthadwārā. They came to be known in Nāthadwārā as the people from Braj (*Brajvāsī*). Due to their direct association with Lord Kṛṣṇa, they occupy until today a privileged position among the local followers of similar jātis. Besides keeping their specific caste, they also formed a group having the distinct features of the Braj background: they kept their original language, food, and clothing habits and were little influenced by local customs. They would normally not mix with local jātis of similar status and had to split up, over the years, in numerous exogamical gotras to allow marriage. These Braj jātis are ranked according to their relation to the service of the Lord in the temple, as follows:

1. Sanāḍhya brāhmaṇs: they have a special position among the local brāhmaṇs of Nāthadwārā, because a member of this jāti discovered the mūrti of Govardhan Hill, and since then they have been associated with the worship of the idol.
2. Gūjars: this cowherd caste is a part of the story of Kṛṣṇa in his village life in Braj; they are needed for cattle-rearing and dairy supply to the temple.
3. Gorva (Rājpūts) and jāṭs (mixed caste) are responsible for the protection of the statue and the important members of the *sampradāya.*
4. Serving jātis are composed of barbers (*nāī*) in charge of minor ritual works in the temple and the Loda, a jāti in charge of manual work. Besides the jātis and outside the group come those in charge of the polluting occupations.

These Braj communities form a group inside the *sampradāya* that can join together to defend economic interests and privileged positions.

The original inhabitants of Nāthadwārā also became directly or indirectly involved in the temple service. Many of them were initiated in the *sampradāya*. Only one brāhmaṇ jāti (Pālīwāl) became directly associated with the service rendered in the sacred parts of the temple; the other jātis remained in charge of the services outside the sacred parts of the temple.[8]

It is interesting to mention here the status of the artist castes. For the *pichhvāīs* and the fabrication of small icons painters were needed. Though we do not know exactly when they reached Nāthadwārā, they were divided among two jātis, the Jangid and Adi Gaud, who still live in different areas near the Havelī. Due to their close association with the Lord they rose in status, and are considered not as serving castes, but as two brāhmaṇ subcastes. They are ordered hierarchically, the Adi Gaud being superior, and they do not intermarry. Members of the similar jātis elsewhere in the country do not enjoy such a high status,[9] which shows the adaptive character of the jāti regime when necessary.

The temple in Nāthadwārā is in fact called a Havelī, a mansion inhabited by the Lord, which underlines the worldly character of the *sampradāya*. The Havelī is ruled, as we have shown, by a strict internal hierarchy. The innermost centre of the Havelī, where the Lord leads his daily existence, is an extremely sacred place, under strict rules of purity. It is the domain of the high-caste Panchdravidian group. The further we move from the centre, the less strict the degree of purity. Yet everything pertaining to the service inside the temple remains in the hands of upper castes or people from the Braj group, and a highly complex assignment system is made according to one's position in the temple service. This position can be modified or allocated by the Tilakāyat, which leads to caste frictions and competition in order to get into the more privileged positions. Jātis from the Braj group and members of the Panchdravidian jātis have a hereditary right to serve the Lord and enjoy a privileged situation. Even if they only occasionally serve in the temple, they receive through a so-called 'siddha' system their share of the temple income.[10]

Other jātis will seek initiation into the *sampradāya*, which is given by the direct male descendant of Vallabha's lineage. This initiation process has become very selective over the years. Low jātis and impure ones are not admitted to the *sampradāya*, which became mainly composed of elite jātis and merchants from Rajasthan, Gujarat, and Bombay. After Independence, the Nāthadwārā Temple Act put the temple activities under Government control. However, as shown by Verdia, the temple board employs high-caste Hindus and its secular character is even more undermined by the fact that the chairman of the board is the Tilakāyat himself.

The worship of Śrī Nāthajī in the Nāthadwārā temple has produced an original local hierarchy and given rise to a special jāti regime. The temple itself physically bears the mark of caste, as well as the city, this being divided into jāti and ethnic (Braj-derived) clusters. Local jātis that are associated with the temple service gain in prestige and importance over the other local jātis of similar background. The jātis of Braj origin had to adjust to their expatriate situation that demanded a frequent splitting into exogamic gotras to allow survival of endogamic jātis. Verdia[11] counted two gotra lineages among Gūjars when they reached Nāthadwārā, as against seven today.

The important elements provided by the example of Vallabha's *sampradāya* for our purpose can be summed up as follows: Nāthadwārā is a city ruled by the temple and its activities. The people of the temple belong, on the one hand, to a spiritual community that preaches a religion of horizontal brotherhood and direct sacred participation. On the other hand, they belong to their birth group. This latter identity dictates the place one occupies in the temple service, one's economic position, as well as the physical closeness or distance to the main living place of Śrī Nāthajī. The members of the *sampradāya*, especially those of the temple, define themselves by a double identity.

The people who were the original inhabitants of the region are considered of lower status than those of the same jāti but associated with the temple service. Among the local people only one brāhmaṇ caste was allowed to partake of the inner life of the temple. Entry into the *sampradāya* is reserved to upper castes. Lower castes, foreigners, tribals, etc. are not allowed to enter the sacred shrines.

Strictly from the point of view of the jāti system, the case of Nāthadwārā and the local implementation of the sect is extremely interesting. Our example shows the flexible character of jāti ranking. A local situation and specific cases can produce a caste situation of a unique character and feature. In our case it shows how people of the region had to integrate a new religious belief into the caste system that was able to modify their local way of defining social relations without changing the system's basic feature. A striking example of this is the adjustment of the status of the painters and the difference of status advocated between usually equal jātis on religious grounds. R. Burghart shows in his field-work and historical study of caste that there is traditionally no unique model of hierarchy in the Indian context. In his case-study, he speaks of three models of hierarchy, against the hierarchical model of the brāhmaṇ spokesman.[12]

Nāthadwārā reveals that a sect, besides incorporating caste, can produce a new type of caste system locally and define new social relations, without ever being able to change the jāti regime. A similar phenomenon, among many others that would confirm our point of view, is the sanskritized Śukla varṇa founded at Galtājī (near Jaipur) by the four Vaiṣṇava sects.[13] They view themselves, through religious adherence, as superior to the traditional four varṇas and their jātis, by forming a fifth varṇa. Their social relations (food-sharing, marriage, etc.) follow their pretensions to be of a superior varṇa. We do not know, however, how much these claims are taken into consideration by the existing castes.

In spite of Vallabha's claim to establish a religion that would take into its fold whoever wanted it, his followers made the sect into a caste-dominated institution. One could even say that it became the opposite of its founder's intention, creating new barriers among the people by means of sectarian identity that could give the right to claim a superior status and bring about a better position in the caste ranking. On the social level, sectarian identity could have an impact on local stratification of the society.[14] On the level of the *sampradāya*, among the members of the sect, there remains an inconsistency between participation in shared rituals (kīrtan-singing, darśan, etc.) and the fact that one's identity is based on jāti ranking.

Sect identity is different from social-caste identity. Sect identity pertains to a religious level, guiding one's relation to God and to other members, whereas social identity is ascribed by birth and remains unmodified (except in rare cases) by adherence to the sect, or can exclude it. Yet the relation between religion and social order appears through our sectarian example as highly complex: for on the one hand the sect dominates the caste regime not by doing away with it, but by adjusting it when needed; while on the other hand, jāti dominates the sect by the very fact that caste structures the sect.

Jāti identity controls one's situation in the *sampradāya*, especially when this is as worldly as the sect of Vallabha. The living presence of the Lord in the Havelī and the sacred city established a hierarchical model of life very close to the worldly pattern of court existence. In many ways the Havelī life and the political and landowning character of the Tilakāyat reminds us of what is known of court life in Rajasthan.[15]

The specific case of the *sampradāya* of Vallabha may help (though one has to be very careful with generalizations) to clarify the intricate relation between bhakti and sectarian movements and Hindu social organizations. It may clarify the position of religion in this context, and the nature of the jāti regime.

The early bhakti movement, in the realm of religion or, even, on a social level by virtue of its more antinomian tendencies as found among the Sant traditions, produced a possibility of sharing religious beliefs and practices by grouping around a special worship or master. This characteristic is still of enormous importance today. It allows one, besides daily or individual rituals, to enjoy on certain occasions (pilgrimage, moments of darśan, kīrtan-singing) very strong and intense devotional feelings which are shared among group members.

These religious groups were to be formed without regard to social considerations, but had to incorporate the jāti regime, as is shown by the example of Nāthadwārā. The very fact that religious identity remained embedded in the primal identity group, but could also build up a new type of caste ranking inside the general frame of jāti organization may yield more general information on the social system. Jāti is not a religious phenomenon, though one has to underline the fact that religion is present in the entire life of the Hindus, and that, in the case of India, one has to be careful in applying dichotomous categories, such as 'secular/religious'. The Indian regime appears more as a solution to a given economic, social, and political situation, sustained by corresponding religious attitudes. Even if these go against caste divisions, the jāti remains and survives, appearing as the only way of living in an organized way in the political context of Indian society. In a recent book,[16] Jean Baechler, in search of the origin of the system, which he views as a morphological solution in a given Indian context, talks of jāti as the storehouse of Hindu civilization. This seems a very adequate way to name the jāti, able as the latter is to absorb into its system many explanations and speculations which, because of the lack of chronological and historical data on its origin and expansion, will always escape final and definitive explanation.

Religion did not invent the social system of jātis, even though the highly refined explanations it produced give a secure feeling to man, who searches to understand the reason for his existence. It is through the existence of the diversified jāti regime that religious feelings could grow and change outside a church administration and inside varied religious traditions. A multitude of personal ways to relate and communicate with God corresponds to a strong social control.

If we leave aside the institutional character of the sect, we notice in Nāthadwārā that all jātis worship the image of Lord Kṛṣṇa. Even in the most remote parts of the city, and among non-Hindus also, one can find a shrine to Śrī Nāthajī. I would emphasize, finally, that personal worship and very deep devotional love is independent of any institution and can be found everywhere among true bhaktas.

NOTES

1. K. N. Sharma, 'Hindu Sects and Food Patterns in North India', *Journal of Social Research*, Ranchi, 4, 1–2, Mar.–Sept. 1961, pp. 45–58, p. 48.
2. N. K. Singhi, ed., *Ideal, Ideology and Practice*, Studies in Jainism, Jaipur: Printwell Publishers, 1987: see esp. Singhi, 'Study of Jains in a Rajasthan Town', pp. 149–79, and M. J. Banks, 'Caste, Sect and Property: Relations of the Jain Community of Jamnagar, Gujarat', pp. 180–96.
3. I am grateful to members of the Tilakāyat's family for the information they gave me, which has helped me to understand the life of the Nāthadwārā Havelī.
4. H. S. Verdia, *Religion and Social Structure in a Sacred Town: Nāthadwārā*, Delhi: Research Publications, 1982. I am indebted to Verdia's recent research on Nāthadwārā, which provided me with much of the required information. Verdia's study shows national integration at a grass-roots level, where religion is viewed in a perspective of integration and disintegration.
5. Śrī Pt. Jagannātha Caturvedī, Hindi commentary on *Rāsapañcādhyāyī Śrī Subodhinī* (a commentary on the five rāsa chapters of Śrīmad Bhāgavata, by Mahāprabhu Śrī Vallabhācārya), Varanasi: Chowkhamba, Sanskrit Series Office, 1971.
6. A. Ambalal, *Kṛṣṇa as Śrī Nāthajī*, Ahmadabad: Mapin, 1987, p. 46.
7. J. Tod, *Annals and Antiquities of Rajasthan*, new edn., New Delhi: M. N. Publishers, 1978, vol. 1, pp. 415–24.
8. Verdia, op. cit.
9. Ambalal, op. cit., p. 93.
10. See Verdia, op. cit. on the 'siddha' system.
11. Ibid.
12. These three models of hierarchy are brāhmaṇ, king, and ascetic. R. Burghart, 'Hierarchical Models of the Hindu Social System', *Man*, 13, 1978, pp. 519–36.
13. Ibid., p. 526.
14. To measure this impact, one would have to consider carefully the historical fact that, from the time when the Muslims were first present in India (from the 8th century onwards), the jāti was reinforced and justified by religious beliefs, alongside the more egalitarian movements.
15. If we were to take the models of hierarchy proposed by Burghart, Nāthadwārā would appear as a mixed case of brahmanical model and kingly administration (op. cit., p. 523).
16. J. Baechler, *La Solution indienne*, essay on the origins of the hierarchy of the castes, Paris: PUF, 1988. This book appears to me among the most relevant analyses of the origin and development of the jāti–varṇa system in India.

Interaction between Islamic and Indian religious attitudes

Ṣūfī influence in the *Ekanāthī-bhāgavat*: some observations on the text and its historical context

H. VAN SKYHAWK

I

As early as 1958 V. S. Bendre presented the Marathi reading public with strong hagiographical evidence of Śrī Sant Ekanāth's links to the Qādirī Ṣūfīs via a mysterious *malaṅg* known as Dattātreya, Cānd Bodhale, or Sayed Cāndasāheb Kādirī.[1] In 1966 and 1967 R. C. Ḍhere presented additional hagiographical and historical materials as a supplement to Bendre's argument and advised the Marathi reading public to 'accept the truth, even if it is unpleasant.'[2] In 1979 S. G. Tulpule confirmed Bendre's and Ḍhere's findings and offered the following appraisal of Janārdana's and Ekanāth's spiritual milieu:

> The blend of Hinduism and Islam inherent in the cult of Dattātreya is reflected by Janārdana, the guru of Ekanātha, who, according to recent researches, belonged to the Ṣūfī tradition. Refuting the hitherto popular notion that Janārdana was initiated directly by god Dattātreya, Bendre has, on the evidence of the *Yogasaṅgrāma* of Sheikh Muhammad, convincingly shown that he was a disciple of Cānda Bodhale, who belonged to the Ṣūfīs and whose appearing before Ekanātha in the form of a Muslim mendicant (*malaṅga*) is a clear twist of the historical truth about the guru of Ekanātha being the disciple of a Ṣūfī in the line of Sijrā-i-kādirī. Ekanātha himself concealed this fact in order not to invite the displeasure of the orthodoxy and traced his spiritual lineage to god Dattātreya through his guru Janārdana. Modern research has, however, laid bare this connecting link between the tradition of later Marāṭhī poet-saints and the Ṣūfīs.[3]

Whilst a number of important scholars of the literature of the Maharashtrian Sant poets have accepted that the Ṣūfīs significantly influenced religious and social customs in the medieval Deccan,[4] up to now it has been generally believed that Ṣūfī influence was not reflected in the medieval Sant literature.[5]

Unfortunately, only some few *abhaṅgs* of Janārdana-svāmī and his spiritual master Cānd Bodhale, alias Sayed Cāndasāheb Kādirī, have come down to us.[6] In the writings of Janārdana's *śiṣya*, Ekanāth, however, we have a voluminous corpus of literature in which not only spiritual teachings, but also fascinating details of everyday life in sixteenth-century Mahārāṣṭra, have been preserved. It is evident from the *bhārūḍ 'Hindū-Turk-saṃvād'* that

Ekanāth had a good knowledge of the basic tenets of Islam and of the habits of contemporary fakirs.[7] However, the *Hindū-Turk-saṃvād* does not prove that Ekanāth was influenced by the Ṣūfīs in his teachings as the dialogue of the opponents in this bucolic religious debate does not necessarily represent Ekanāth's point of view. The Hindu and the Turk serve as stereotypical figures and alternate in being the object of Ekanāth's humour.

In contrast to the language of the *abhaṅgs* – which must be close to the spoken Marathi of Ekanāth's times – the language of the *Śrī-Ekanāthī-bhāgavat (EBh)* has very few words of Arabic, Persian, or Hindustani origin. Thus, at first reading, it gives the impression of being a work from a much earlier, pre-Muslim period of Indian history, and not of the sixteenth-century Deccan. Though Ekanāth uses metaphors taken from all aspects of daily life, his language contains grammatical forms that were considered archaic even in Jñāneśvar's times.[8] But, by consciously avoiding words of Muslim origin in the final redaction of the *EBh*, Ekanāth imposed an important restriction upon himself: should any phenomenon peculiar to the Ṣūfīs be described in the commentary, it would have to be translated into or paraphrased in Sanskrit terminology. When placed next to the polished concision of the *composita* used in philosophical Sanskrit, such an improvised *compositum* immediately reveals its makeshift character.[9] Such is the case when one juxtaposes *pratyagātman* (*EBh* 2. 643), the technical term used in *advaita* Vedānta for the *ātman* experienced by the empirical individual, the 'personal *ātman*' as it were, with *svarūpa-phuṃju-vismṛti* (*EBh* 1. 49 and 2. 436), which I translate as 'the loss of memory that occurs as a result of the swelling that takes place when the bhakta experiences the *svarūpa*'. The first occurrence of *svarūpa-phuṃju-vismṛti* in the *EBh* is at 1. 49, in a *naman*, or homage, to the unnamed Sants who ordered Ekanāth to compose the *EBh*. Here we are told that the Sants

> . . . don't show off their learnedness, nor do they make a display of their madness (*pisepaṇa*). They swallow their *svarūpa-phuṃju-vismṛti* and abide in their own true nature. (*EBh* 1. 49)

> They absorb their *prema* in their very bodies and forget the astonishment that was caused by it. *prapañca* and *paramārtha* become one for them, but even from this they are detached. (*EBh* 1. 50)

From this brief excerpt we learn that the Sants do not regard public exhibitions of 'madness' as being the highest spiritual state. While Ekanāth's description of the Sants in 1. 49–1. 50 might not harmonise with the description of the ideal bhakta in the *Bhāgavata Purāṇa* (*BhP*), such as in 11. 2. 40 ('and when he hears the names of Hari that are dear to him, he becomes passionate. Loudly he laughs, cries, shouts, and sings. And like a madman, who has been cast out of society, he dances'), it suits the popular notions of the ideal conduct of a yogi or *advaitin* well enough that there is no real need to explain the *compositum* further here. And, when *svarūpa-phuṃju-vismṛti* is mentioned again, some 500 *ovīs* later, in the second *adhyāya* of the *EBh*, the reader or listener would not necessarily recall the brief reference to it in the first *adhyāya*. But, for an understanding of the various components of Ekanāth's bhakti the extensive description of *svarūpa-phuṃju-vismṛti* in the second *adhyāya* of the *EBh* is very useful. The passage begins with a metaphor that is well known in *advaita* Vedānta, the wave in the ocean:

A wave in the ocean says: 'It is really because of me that the clouds cool down and enliven the earth and quench the thirst of the *cātaka*-bird.' (*EBh* 2. 395)

Because of me the grain ripens. Because of me the rivers rise in spate. In me they flow together and regain their ocean-ness. (*EBh* 2. 396)

In the same way [the bhakta] feels conceit (*abhimāna*) when he regains the perfection of his source. Note well the characteristics of his worship! (*EBh* 2. 397)

He says: I am the creator of all the worlds. Although I do deeds, I remain a non-doer. Though I am the enjoyer of all enjoyments, I remain the only eternal non-enjoyer.' (*EBh* 2. 398)

In all the worlds there exists only my power. I am the tamer in all and of all. Through my all-ness (*sakaḷatveṃ*) I am the illuminator and the punisher (*śāstā*) of all. (*EBh* 2. 399)

I am the first among the gods. The divinity in God is really my *bhāva*. I am the unborn imperishable one. The immortal characteristics in the unchanging one arise through my body. (*EBh* 2. 401)

Whatever power *Īśvara* has, is in reality my power. Know ye that the lordliness in the Lord really [derives] from me. (*EBh* 2. 402)

Through me the unborn one is born without birth. Though I am a non-doer, I nevertheless make deeds come to pass without action. Through me Puruṣottama gets his glory as the Highest Being. (*EBh* 2. 405)

Through me Sūrya gets the power of vision in his eye. In me is the space in which the ether of consciousness exists. In my body dwells *Jagannivāsu* in comfort (*sāvakāśa*). (*EBh* 2. 407)

Hari, Hara, and Brahmā – these too are certainly partial incarnations that have arisen from my parts. I am the *avatāra* who has incarnated himself in ten *avatāras*. Even I do not fully comprehend my own greatness! (*EBh* 2. 413)

Up to this point the swelling of the bhakta's *abhimān* bears a striking resemblance to the *stotras* of Śaṅkara's *Nirvāṇamañjarī*.[10] But then Ekanāth interrupts the ecstasy of the imaginary bhakta and, unlike Śaṅkara, subordinates this spiritual experience to bhakti by making the expansion of the I-principle first a sacrifice to the *brahman* and, ultimately, to Śrī Kṛṣṇa. In a striking departure from the 'normative ideology'[11] Ekanāth boldly states:

'Brahmāhamasmi' – that is only a saying. Such egotism the bhaktas call *bhagavadbhajan*. Then the bhakta takes on the form [of the *brahman*] and worships the *brahman* by sacrificing his *abhimāna* to the *brahman*. (*EBh* 2. 416)

The *citta*, the object of thought, and thought itself – when these three have been pacified [through spontaneous sacrifice to the *brahman*] the pacification itself naturally becomes a sacrifice to Kṛṣṇa in every respect. (*EBh* 2. 422)

When the identification with the material body has vanished, the swelling [caused by the experience] of the *svarūpa* does not afflict [the bhakta]. Nor does ignorance with regard to that which one should do and that which one should not do, afflict him. (*EBh* 2. 436)

In the foregoing passage we have seen that even the experience of 'being the *brahman*' is offered as a sacrifice to the *brahman* and, ultimately, to Śrī Kṛṣṇa. For, even if the wave is not different from the ocean, it is nevertheless not the ocean in its entirety. Just as the wave cannot be the ocean, so the bhakta cannot become Śrī Kṛṣṇa. Though he may experience the *svarūpa*, this experience is not his ultimate goal. Therefore, even this sublime experience is considered to be an offering to Śrī Kṛṣṇa.

Loss of memory, or *vismṛti*, caused by the experience of one's divine nature is not a typical phenomenon in yoga or *advaita* Vedānta. Moreover, loss of memory, or *smṛti-vibhrama*, is used in the *Bhagavadgītā* to describe the very opposite condition to the experience of the divine *jñāna*.[12] The term Ekanāth uses to describe the experience of divine swelling has an unmistakable negative connotation. Such a negative evaluation of the expansion of the individual into the all-encompassing divine is well known in the literature of the Ṣūfīs. Together with its opposite, contradiction, or *qabḍ*, the condition of *basṭ*, or expansion, represents an advanced but dangerous step on the path of the Ṣūfī. With regard to *basṭ*, R. C. Zaehner has drawn attention to Abu'l Qāsim Qushayrī's description of the danger of this phenomenon:

'... the expanded man experiences an expansion great enough to contain (all) creation; and there is practically nothing that will cause him fear. He is so "expanded" that nothing will affect him in what ever state he may be ... expansion comes suddenly and strikes the subject unexpectedly so that he can find no reason for it. It makes him quiver with joy, yet scares him. The way to deal with it is to keep quiet and to observe conventional good manners. There is the greatest danger in this mood, and those who are open to it should keep on their guard against an insidious deception ... Both conditions, that of expansion, as well as that of contraction, have been considered by those who have investigated the truth of these matters to be things in the face of which one should take refuge in God, for both must be considered to be a poor thing and a harmful one if compared with the [spiritual states] which are above them, such as the annihilation of the servant [of God] and his gradual upward progress in the truth.' In this remarkable passage Qushayrī obviously has his rival Abū Sa'id in mind, for the latter seems to have regarded 'expansion' almost as an end in itself, for in that state he felt that he was God, and since God was all, he too was all. This is obviously what Qushayrī is referring to when he speaks of 'an expansion great enough to contain [all] creation.' Such ideas are, he says, 'an insidious deception' and extremely dangerous. Qushayrī, however, was a voice crying in the wilderness: Abū Yazīd had injected into the body of Ṣūfīsm a dose of the Indians' Vedānta that was soon to transform the whole movement. It was now within the power of every Ṣūfī to realise himself as God, and this entitled him to live in total disregard of the Muslim religious law.[13]

It is not my intention here to enter into the discussion concerning the possible Indian origins of the monastic teachings of Ṣūfīs such as Abū Yazīd al-Bistamī, Ḥusayn ibn Mansūr al-Ḥallāj, or Abū Sa'īd ibn Abī'l-Khayr. My argument is far more limited in scope. Specifically: Did Ekanāth learn of the spiritual phenomenon of the swelling of the individual identity into the divine directly from the brahmanical tradition? Or was he initiated into a Ṣūfī variant of this phenomenon? Does not the *ovī* 2. 413 ('Even I do not know [the extent] of my own greatness!') bear a striking resemblance to Abū Yazīd's ecstatic outburst '*subhānī, mā a'ẓama sha'nī!*' (Glory be to me! How great is my glory!)?[14]

In the homage to the Sants in the first *adhyāya* of the *EBh*, immediately following *ovī* 49, in which we are told that the Sants 'swallow' the *svarūpa-phuṃju-vismṛti*, we also learn that they 'absorb their *prema* in their very bodies and forget the astonishment that was caused by it . . . *prapañca* and *paramārtha* become one for them. But even from this they are detached' (*EBh* 1. 50). In a remarkable passage in the ninth *adhyāya* of the *EBh* we are given an example of what absorbing *prema* into one's body meant for Ekanāth. In a digression from his commentary on *BhP* 11. 9. 31 Ekanāth tells of his guru Janārdana's *guruparamparā*, and of an encounter with Janārdana's guru Dattātreya:[15]

The *paramparā* of the disciples of Dattātreya [is as follows]: Sahasrārjuna [was the first], Yadu, the second. Verily, Janārdana was the third disciple that he accepted in the *kaliyuga*. (*EBh* 9. 430)

The longing for a *sadguru* in Janārdana's mind was so strong that because of thinking constantly about a *sadguru*, he forgot the three conditions [of human mental activity, i.e. *jāgṛta, svapna, suṣupti*]. (*EBh* 9. 431)

But God enjoys *bhāva*. He recognised this firm condition [in Janārdana]. [By means of Janārdana's *bhāva*] he became Śrī Datta, who laid his hand on Janārdana's head. (*EBh* 9. 432)

As soon as he had laid his hand [on Janārdana's head], Janārdana understood the complete spiritual instruction. By means of the pure teachings on the nature of the *ātman*, he recognised that *prapañca* is completely illusory. (*EBh* 9. 433)

When Janārdana perceived this in his *mana*, his *mana* dissolved in its own essence. When this condition (*avasthā*) became clear, Janārdana fell down in a swoon. (*EBh* 9. 436)

Then [Dattātreya] brought him back to consciousness immediately and said: 'You should swallow even the *prema* in this *sattvāvasthā*. Always conduct yourself according to the *nija-bodha* [spiritual teachings]. (*EBh* 9. 437)

As Janārdana laid his head on Dattātreya's feet, Dattātreya vanished by means of his *yoga-māyā* [supernatural yogic powers]. (*EBh* 9. 438)

Apart from the conspicuous brevity of the *guruparamparā* given above, V. S. Bendre has called attention to the fact that the Dattātreya mentioned in the foregoing passage should not be taken to be the god Dattātreya, as it would have been improper for Janārdana-svāmī to take *upadeś* from a divine guru. For that, a human guru is required.[16] And this human guru was none other than Cānd Bodhle alias Cāndra Bhaṭ alias Dattadigambar alias Sayed Cāndasāheb Kādirī.

Ekanāth's description of Janārdana's swoon upon experiencing a *sattvāvasthā* and Dattātreya's immediate intervention to bring him back to consciousness may be an example of the suppression of a *ḥāl*, which is the technical term for an ecstatic condition in Sufism. Falling into a trance as a result of comprehending the inner, or mystic, meaning of a spiritual teaching is a well-known phenomenon in Sufism. The following description of *ḥāl*, which was written by a contemporary Biyābānī-Qādirī shaykh of the Deccan, bears a striking similarity with the foregoing description of Janārdana's *sattvāvasthā*:

The best example of a fully God-realised person in Islam is the holy Prophet himself who was one with Unity and dwelt in duality, leading a well-balanced life. His submission unto God was of the highest degree. The self was humbled down to the status of a slave of God, gradually dissolving into nonentity leaving God and God alone. And in spite of this it is simply wonderful and marvelous to see him leading a balanced life on the material stage. This is indirectly explained in the Quran by a parable that 'Had the Quran descended on a mountain, the mountain would have been humbled and rent asunder'. Well, what sort of descent is this? We keep the Quran in a cupboard, but the cupboard remains intact. Therefore, this descent is through the revelation of words and sentences with their actual meaning and actual experience, i.e. we call it Haal. Sometimes a single mystic sentence from the Holy Quran uttered by a realized person, may send an ardent devotee into trance and forgetfulness of his personal existence. It was only through the Grace of God that the Holy Prophet [May peace be upon Him!] possessed a heart that could stand the full reception of the Holy Quran with experience, without damaging his mental equilibrium . . .[17]

As a rule, Qādirīs and Chistīs favoured the suppression and mastery of the *aḥwāl*, or ecstatic conditions, and the attainment of *saḥw*, or sobriety. According to Dārā Shikūḥ, the famous Qādirī shaykh Mīyān Mīr always maintained his self-control in public.[18] And the famous Chistī *pīr* of Gulbarga, Sayyid Muḥammad al-Ḥusaynī-i-Gīsūdirāz, considered it praiseworthy if the devotee does not lose himself in a *ḥāl*:

Reflecting over the incident when a young companion, under the orders of Junayd, died in trying to control himself in *samā*, Gīsūdirāz exclaims, 'Bravo! to the preceptor that Junayd was, for he knew the states and [rightly] prohibited the young man from displaying his state (*ḥāl*). Bravo! to that young disciple who controlled himself to the extent that he died.' Elsewhere Gīsūdirāz says that the display of a state is not an 'aid' (*musā'adat*) but it is hypocrisy (*riyā*).[19]

As the Sants are said to 'swallow their *prema* and abide within themselves' (*EBh* 1. 50), Janārdana is exhorted by Dattātreya in *ovī* 9. 437 of the *EBh* to 'swallow his *prema* and always conduct himself according to the *nijabodha*', which in this case means maintaining self-control. Clearly, for the Sants, as for Dattātreya, madness or unconsciousness is a lesser state than abiding serenely in the unity of the self. Ekanāth's notion of the ideal conduct of a spiritual master is very similar to Gīsūdirāz's description of the Ṣūfīs who have achieved the permanent unity of their spiritual state. Gīsūdirāz calls these realised persons the 'abiding lords', or *arbāb-i-tamkīn*. He further observes that unconsciousness means that the individual has not yet achieved the unity of his spiritual state. According to Gīsūdirāz:

The state of a resider is that his heart is delighted with God . . . The words *talwīn* and *tamkīn* are two technical terms. *Talwīn* literally means 'colouring'. In Ṣūfīsm it is an unbalanced condition of a mystic on whom one state descends and disappears, while another appears and disappears. *Tamkīn* literally means 'establishing'. It is the 'established' state of a mystic in whom no change occurs. Such a person is called *mutamakkin*, a 'resider'. This state is peculiar to the adepts or *ahl-i-ḥaqā'iq*. Gīsūdirāz calls them 'residing lords' or *arbāb-i-tamkīn*. This state is achieved after one passes through the states of *talwīn*. A resider is one who has reached the stage of union, or *ittiṣāl*.[20]

II

Janārdana-svāmī Deśpaṇḍe was born in Caḷisgāv on *phālgūn vadya* 6 in *śaka* 1426, corresponding to February–March AD 1504.[21] Around *śaka* 1462 or AD 1540, when Ekanāth, who was then a young boy,[22] entered his service, Janārdana-svāmī was the *killedār* of Fort Daulatabad. The atmosphere at the Nizām-Shāhīn court at that time was liberal and cosmopolitan. Owing largely to the efforts of Shāh Tāhīr, Burhān Nizām Shāh's Iranian peshwa, Aḥmadnagar had become a centre of Shī'a learning in the Deccan. Scores of sayyids and mullahs from Iran, Sistan, and Khurasan had taken up residence at Burhān Nizām Shāh's court.[23] In assessing the character of Burhān Nizām Shāh and the atmosphere at his court Radhey Shyam writes:

His faith in religion was unshakeable; and his regard for justice unimpeachable. He was kind and generous towards masses and classes alike. His indefatigable energy, his uncommon physical strength, his keen and penetrating intellect, his pleasing manners, his love for scholarship made him the idol of his people. Even the contemporary

Portuguese chroniclers speak highly of him, saying that Burhān Nizām Shāh 'was endowed with great natural and political sagacity, his court being the hospitable resort of the best men of his time.'[24]

Owing to a lack of historical material we are not in a position to describe Janārdana-svāmī's relations to Burhān Nizām Shāh in detail. However, there can be little doubt that he held a position of high esteem at the Nizām Shāhī court, as the Fort of Daulatabad was as a rule entrusted to a Muslim *killedār*.[25] As a trusted high official of the Nizām Shāhī government, Janārdana-svāmī Deśpaṇḍe must have had frequent contacts with the Shī'a scholars at Burhān Nizām Shāh's court. On the other hand, the proximity of Daulatabad to Khuldabad, a famous centre for Ṣūfīs since the fourteenth century, would have made it inevitable that Janārdana and Ekanāth have frequent contacts with Ṣūfīs. These conjectures are borne out by the evidence contained in Janārdana's true *guru-paramparā*, or should we say *shajrā*, the *Sijrā-jadi-Kādirī*, in which we find, in addition to the usual Qādirī shaykhs, the names of the twelve imāms of the Shī'i, and a remarkable description of Abdu'l Qādir Jīlānī as being the descendant of Imām Ḥusain, the martyr and 'Sant' of Karbala.[26] The synthesis of bhakti, Sufism, and Shi'ism could hardly be expressed more succinctly. In this *shajrā* Janārdana's own shaykh, Sayed Cāndasāheb Kādirī, is the twenty-fourth in succession from the Holy Prophet. The contents of the *sijrā-jadi-Kādirī* remind one of the peculiar mixture of Sufism and Shi'ism in the *shajrās* of Ahmad Shāh Walī, the ninth Bāhmanī sultan (1420–35), who was a disciple of Nūr ud-Dīn Muḥammad Ni'matullāh bin 'Abdallāh of Kirmān (1330–1431), the first shaykh of the *Nī'matullāhī-silsila*. On the ceiling of Aḥmad Shāh Walī's *dargā* at Bidar are inscribed a Qādirī *shajrā*, a Junaydī *shajrā*, the names of the twelve imāms, and the names of the *pañjatanpāk*, Muḥammad, 'Alī, Fāṭima, Ḥasan, and Ḥusain. In addition, a *jaṅgam* of the Liṅgāyats is always in attendance at the *dargā*, as the Liṅgāyats regard Aḥmad Shāh Walī as '*Allama Prabhū*'.[27]

Ekanāth spent his childhood and adolescence in a similar milieu of religious syncretism. When one considers his intense devotion to and identification with his guru, Janārdana-svāmī, there can be little doubt that he was influenced by the same religious syncretism as his guru. Was the influence of Sufism evident in the first five *adhyāyas* of the *EBh*, which were written at Pratiṣṭhan? Was Ekanāth summoned to Varanasi by the Maharashtrian paṇḍits to explain the improprieties of his Marathi commentary on the *Bhāgavata Purāṇa* for this reason?[28] This would account for the absence of Persian words in the *EBh*, and for such a makeshift *compositum* as *svarūpa-phuṃju-vismṛti*. Though it would have been relatively easy for the Marathi-speaking paṇḍits at Kāśī to purge the *EBh* of Persian words, it would have proved far more difficult for them to purge the Ṣūfī ideas – especially when expressed in a Marathi almost as pure as Jñāneśvar's.

Up to now, two theories have been advanced to explain, or better, explain away Ekanāth's falsification of his *guru-paramparā*: (1) that he was afraid of being persecuted by the orthodox brāhmaṇs (Tulpule);[29] (2) that he hoped to encourage the resistance of the Hindus against Muslim rule by concealing his own links to the Ṣūfīs (Ḍhere).[30]

In this connection I find it significant that in the 18,810 *ovīs* of the *EBh*, not one clear-cut example of criticism against Muslims can be found, while scathing attacks on orthodox paṇḍits and *yājñikas* are numerous.[31] Moreover, in Janārdana-svāmī's *caritra*, it is said that Janārdana was so 'just and compassionate, that everyone held him in awe'. And that 'Hindus and Muslims alike felt equal reverence for him'.[32] Considering the importance Ekanāth placed on assiduously following his guru's example, it is difficult to imagine that he would have departed from a principle of conduct that was said to be characteristic of his guru.

The assimilation of Ṣūfī teachings in the *EBh* does not mean that Ekanāth was a crypto-Ṣūfī. For there is certainly nothing in the *EBh* that is irreconcilable with the Vaiṣṇava bhakti of the *BhP* or the Vārkarī *saṃpradāya*. What Ṣūfī influence in this context means is that Ekanāth incorporated a number of Ṣūfī teachings and practices in the *EBh* that were similar in form and content to elements of devotional Hinduism. A good example of such an assimilation is the absorption of Ekanāth's individual personality into the personality of his guru, Janārdana-svāmī – a process that was so complete that Ekanāth even merged his own name with that of his guru, thus becoming Ekājanārdana. This process as it is described in the *EBh* is very similar to the spiritual discipline known as *fanā-fi-sh-Shaykh* among Ṣūfīs: the personality of the *murīd* is absorbed into the personality of the *shaykh*. Certainly, Arjuna's absorption into Śrī Kṛṣṇa in the *Bhagavadgītā* would have provided Ekanāth with an authoritative precedent for seeing in *fanā-fi-sh-Shaykh* a Ṣūfī variation on a theme that had its origin in his own religious tradition. And, on the level of folk deities, Śiva as Mallāri (*Malla ari*, the enemy of the demon Malla) was also known to absorb rather than destroy the demons he conquered. In the *Mallāri-māhātmya* (17. 36) the defeated demon Malla, who has become a *Śiva-bhakta*, obtains from Śiva the boon of fusing his name with that of Śiva, i.e. Mallāri, the enemy of the demon Malla.[33] It would be wrong, however, to see in Ekanāth's absorption into the personality of his guru just another example of the fusion of the bhakta with the divine, or even with the divine guru (Kṛṣṇa). For Ekanāth, Janārdana is both the divine guru and the very human man who fell into a trance at the feet of his guru (see above). Absorption into his personality means both internal spiritual fusion as well as external behavioural fusion. What behavioural fusion means has been described in a popular pamphlet of the Chistī Ṣūfīs:

> In the first stage the disciple is expected to love and look to his Shaikh as his all in all. He acts, talks and prays like the Shaikh; he eats, drinks and walks like the Shaikh and constantly meditates upon him. Having been, by this process, spiritually transformed into the Shaikh, the student (*murid*) [*sic*] is spiritually introduced to the Prophet.[34]

Ekanāth usually described the fusion of the personality of the *śiṣya* with that of the guru in the most self-effacing terms. The ideal *guru-bhakta* negates his own personality and merges himself with the guru through continuous service to the guru, for example, he becomes the water for washing the guru's feet (*EBh* 12. 527), the particles of dust of the guru's feet (*EBh* 12. 528), the seat on which the guru sits (*EBh* 12. 528), the living cuspidor that catches the guru's spittle in mid-air (*EBh* 12. 551), the fly-whisk (*cavarī*) that chases away the flies from the mouth of the guru's cuspidor (*EBh* 12. 552), and so on (*EBh* 12. 519–12. 581). But Ekanāth also emphasises that the ideal *śiṣya* assumes both the internal and external form (*sābahya*) of the guru (*EBh* 12. 518). In this connection the hagiographer Mahīpati relates the following incident in Ekanāth's life:

108. Now it happened one day, when it was about the fourth *ghatika* [the word *ghatika* indicates a period of twenty-four minutes. We can infer from the next verse that it was probably 5. 36 in the morning, as the fourth *ghatika* would begin at 5. 36 if one considers 4 a.m., the traditional time for beginning the day, as the first *ghatika*] that a great invading army suddenly arrived to capture Devagiri. 109. Spies announced that a certain enemy of the king was approaching with an army. The king fell into a great fright. 110. The mace-bearers hurried to the house of Janārdan, to tell him that a great invading army had arrived, and that he should come at once. 111. Now Janārdan had just completed his ablutions and devotions, and was sitting in meditation. To convey to him the news at such a time would be overstepping the grounds of propriety. 112. Eknāth, an *avatār* able for miraculous deeds, now performed a miracle. He assumed the form of Janārdan, but no one, other than himself, was aware of the fact. 113. He hurriedly put on the garments of his *Svāmi* [*sic*], and changed his own form to that of his. He took his dagger in hand and sat in his palanquin. 114. In his talk and carriage he differed not in the least from his *guru* . . .[35]

As an isolated example, Ekanāth's absorption into the personality of his guru would only represent an interesting coincidence. Taken together with several other similar examples, a pattern begins to emerge that points to the type of influence I have described above. By further research into the historical context in which Ekanāth lived and wrote, we may gain additional insights into the nature of Hindu–Muslim religious syncretism in the medieval Deccan.

NOTES

1. Vāsudeva Sītārāma Bendre, *Tukārāmāṃce-saṃta-saṃgatī*, Bombay, 1958, p. 71.
2. Rāmacandra Cintāmana Ḍhere, *Vividhā*, Poona, 1966, pp. 110–58, esp. p. 136. Also see Ḍhere's *Musalamāna-marāṭhī-saṃtakavi*, Poona, śaka 1889 (AD 1967), pp. 84–118.

3. Shankar Gopal Tulpule, *Classical Marāṭhī Literature: From the Beginning to 1818*, Wiesbaden, 1979, p. 453.
4. Shankar Gopal Tulpule, *Mysticism in Medieval India*, Wiesbaden, 1984, p. 1.
5. Setu Mādhavarāva Pagaḍī, *Sūfī-saṃpradāya*, Bombay, 1953, p. 106.
6. Tulpule, *Classical Marāṭhī Literature*, p. 453.
7. E. Zelliot, 'A Medieval Encounter between Hindu and Muslim: Ekanāth's Drama-Poem *Hindū-Turk-saṃvād*', in F. W. Clothey, ed., *Images of Man: Religion and Historical Process in South Asia*, Madras, 1982, pp. 171–95.
8. Shankar Gopal Tulpule, *An Old Marāṭhī Reader*, Poona, 1960, p. 55.
9. H. Berger, 'Hochsprache und Volkssprache in Indien', in *Jahrbuch des Südasien-Instituts, 1966*, Wiesbaden, 1967, p. 30.
10. e.g. Heinrich Zimmer's translation of Śaṅkara's morning *stotras* in *Philosophie und Religion Indiens*, Zurich, 1961, repr. Baden-Baden, 1973, pp. 412 ff.
11. F. Hardy, *Viraha Bhakti: The Early History of Kṛṣṇa Devotion in South India*, Delhi, 1983, pp. 534–41.
12. See *Bhagavadgītā*, 2. 63.
13. R. C. Zaehner, *Hindu and Muslim Mysticism*, London, 1960, repr. New York, 1969 and 1972, pp. 118 f.
14. Ibid., p. 117.
15. For a discussion of Janārdana's *guru-paramparā* see Bendre, *Tukārāmāṃce-saṃta-saṃgatī*, pp. 77 ff., Ḍhere, *Vividhā*, pp. 136 ff., and *Musalamāna-marāṭhī-saṃta-kavi*, pp. 86 ff., and my dissertation, *Bhakti und Bhakta: Religionsgeschichtliche Untersuchungen zum Heilsbegriff und zur religiösen Umwelt des Śrī Santa Ekanāth*, Stuttgart, 1990, 310–25 and *passim*.
16. Bendre, p. 80.
17. Śekh Abdul Rajhākśāh Biyābānī, *God, Realization and Religion*, Poona, 1980, pp. 6 f.
18. Sayyid Athar Abbas Rizvi, *A History of Sufism in India*, vol. i, New Delhi, 1978, pp. 107 f.
19. Sayyid Shah Khusro Hussaini, *Sayyid Muḥammad al-Ḥusaynī-i-Gīsūdirāz: On Sufism*, Delhi, 1983, pp. 134 f.
20. Ibid., pp. 170 ff. and n. 253.
21. Lakṣmaṇa Rāmacandra Paṃgārakara, *Śrī-Ekanātha-Mahārā-jāṃceṃ-saṃkṣipta-caritra*, Poona, śaka 1832 (AD 1911), p. 33.
22. The generally accepted date of Ekanāth's birth is 1533 (see Tulpule, *Classical Marāṭhī Literature*, p. 354). As Burhān Nizām Shāh reigned in Aḥmadnagar for nearly half a century (1505–53), we can be relatively sure that it was during his reign that Ekanāth, who was then perhaps 7 or 8 years old, entered Janārdanasvāmī Deśpaṇḍe's service.
23. Postscript, July, 1991: Until the publication of Farhad Daftary's *The Ismā'īlīs: their history and doctrines* Cambridge (Cambridge University Press), 1990, it was generally believed that Shāh Tāhir was a twelve *Shī'ī (Ithnā'ashariyya)* who succeeded in converting Burhān Nizām Shāh, his entire court, and numerous Hindus to twelver Shī'ism (see Shyam, Radhey, *The Kingdom of Ahmadnagar*, Delhi, 1966, pp. 81, 83, 85). Daftary has shown, however, that Shāh Tāhir was none other than Shāh Ṭāhir bin Raḍī al-Dīn II al-Ḥusaynī al-Dakkanī, the thirty-first *imām* of the Muḥammad-Shāhī Nizārī Ismā'īlīs, who had come to Aḥmadnagar in 1522 via Bijāpūr after narrowly escaping execution at the hands of Shāh

Ismā'īl, the Ṣafawīd Shāh of Persia. Shāh Tāhir then pursued his *da'wa* (mission) in the guise of twelver Shi'ism and Sufism. At the invitation of Burhān Nizām Shāh he began giving weekly lectures on various religious subjects inside the fort at Aḥmadnagar. The sessions, which were attended by numerous scholars and Burhān Nizām Shāh himself, soon made Shāh Tāhir famous throughout the Deccan. About the form in which Shāh Tāhir conveyed his spiritual teachings, Daftary writes: 'Shāh Tāhir apparently expressed his Nizārī ideas also in the guise of Ṣūfism, though specific details are lacking on the matter. In this connection, it may be recalled that the authorship of the already-cited Ismā'īlī commentary on the *Gulshan-i-nāz* is sometimes attributed to Shāh Tāhir. At any rate, these associations are well reflected in the *Lama'āt al'ṭāhirīn*, a versified Muḥammad-Shāhī treatise composed in the Deccan around 1110/1698 by Ghulām 'Alī b. Muḥammad. In the *Lama'āt*, the only Muḥammad-Shāhī work preserved in India, the author clearly camouflages his scattered Nizārī ideas under Ithnā'asharī and Ṣūfi expressions. He often eulogizes the twelve imāms of the Ithnā'asharīs whilst also alluding to the imāms of the Muḥammad-Shāhī line ... Shāh Tāhir was the author of numerous works on theology and jurisprudence, which do not seem to be extant; but many of his poems have been preserved.' (Daftary, op. cit., pp. 488 ff.). Daftary's findings have far-reaching implications for the religious and cultural milieu in which Janārdana-svāmī and Ekanāth lived. For, it was the Nizārī Ismā'īlīs who adopted the *Vaiṣṇava avatāra*-doctrine as the allegorical medium for conveying their concept of the successive *imāms* (who were held to be identical in status and authority with 'Alī b. Abī Ṭālib) to Hindu converts (most striking in the *ginān 'Dasa-avatāra'*; see Daftary, op. cit., pp. 484 ff.). Similarly, for the Hindu convert to Nizārī Ismā'īlism the term '*sadguru*', which occurs so frequently in the *EBh*, was a familiar epithet for the Nizārī *imām* of the times.

24. See Radhey Shyam, *The Kingdom of Ahmadnagar*, Delhi, 1966, p. 93.
25. Ibid., p. 376.
26. Vāsudeva Sītārāma Bendre, *Kavitā-saṃgraha*, Bombay, 1961, p. 124.
27. Gulam Yazdani, *Bidar: Its History and Monuments*, London, 1947, pp. 114 ff.
28. See the *Bhakta-līlāmṛta* of Mahīpati, 21. 37–22. 34.
29. *Classical Marāṭhī Literature*, p. 353.
30. *Vividhā*, p. 136.
31. See e.g. *EBh* 11. 510–11. 556 and *BhP* 21. 37–21. 202, 22. 1–22. 44. Ekanāth's extensive criticism of the *mīmāṃsakas, karmavādins, karmaṭhas*, and *paṇḍitas* raises a number of questions. On the one hand, such criticism is not exactly new; Ekanāth does not introduce the theme of criticism of orthodox brāhmaṇs, rather, he expatiates upon the theme of the *śloka* as it is given in the *BhP* (on the criticism of orthodox brāhmaṇs in the *BhP* see J. A. B. van Buitenen, 'On the Archaism of the *Bhāgavata Purāṇa*', in M. Singer, ed., *Krishna: Myths, Rites and Attitudes*, Chicago, 1966, repr. 1968, pp. 23–40). On the other hand, his criticism of the *yajñikas* and *paṇḍitas* is far more caustic than the magisterial tone of condemnation in the *BhP* (e.g. 11. 10. 21 and 11. 11. 18; for a discussion of Ekanāth's satirical treatment of orthodox brahmins see my article 'Satire in the Writings of Śrī Sant Ekanāth', in Giovanni Bandini, ed., *South Asian Digest of Regional Writing*, vol. ix, Stuttgart, 1988, pp. 42–64). Moreover, his satirical targets also include the *advaitins*, who 'in the scholarship of *advaita* have obtained something very difficult to obtain. But they sell it in order to get *viṣayas*. Such learned men

are surely fools' (*EBh* 11. 544). We do not know who read Ekanāth's Marathi commentary during his stay at the *pañca-mūdra-pīṭhā aśram* (*EBh* 31. 527 f.) in Varanasi (*c*. 1574). Perhaps Ekanāth's vehement criticism was acceptable to the orthodox brahmins at Kāśī owing to the precedent given in the *ślokas* of the *BhP*. Perhaps the more caustic passages were added to the *EBh* later, after Ekanāth had returned to Pratiṣṭhān. Be that as it may, the text of the *EBh* as it now stands contains (1) very few words of Muslim origin, but (2) no clear-cut criticisms of Muslims; however, (3) extensive passages of invective against all types of *'paṇḍitas', 'yājñikas'*, and *'karmaṭhas'*. In view of Mahīpati's narrative of the persecution of Ekanāth by an important brāhmaṇ *mahant* of Vārāṇasī (*BhP* 21. 37–22. 34) and Ekanāth's own remarks concerning his residence in Kāśī during the composition of the *EBh*, we can be relatively sure that the *EBh* was subjected to the scrutiny of the Marathi-speaking paṇḍits at Kāśī. Unfortunately, we are not in a position to say with certainty why the passages containing invective against orthodox brāhmaṇs would not have also been expurgated along with the words of Muslim origin.

32. Paṃgārakara, op. cit., p. 34.
33. G. D. Sontheimer, *Birobā, Mhaskobā und Khaṇḍobā: Ursprung, Geschichte und Umwelt von pastoralen Gottheiten in Mahārāṣṭra*, Wiesbaden, 1976, p. 92.
34. Quoted by J. Spencer Trimingham in *The Sufi Orders in Islam*, Oxford, 1971, p. 164.
35. *Bhaktalīlāmṛta*, 13. 108–13. 114, trans. J. A. Abbott, under the title *Eknath* [*sic*], Poona, 1927, p. 12.

How a Muslim looks at Hindu bhakti

PETER GAEFFKE

When Muhammad Gaur laid the foundation for the Muslim conquest of India, he may have had little idea of how large the enterprise he undertook would be and how mixed the eventual results. Although the Muslim population of the South Asian subcontinent is by far the largest in any geographic region, the phenotypes of this religion have grown so confusingly diversified that not only in popular beliefs but also in scholarly literature a bewildering multitude of 'Islamic' practices and concepts are entertained which give the term 'Indian Islam' nearly a polytheistic meaning.

In more recent times, this meeting of the oceans has prompted a number of Hindu scholars and scholars of Hinduism to assume that a golden age existed when Muslims and Hindus created a common culture because some Muslim rulers patronized Sanskrit and translations from Sanskrit into Persian, while there were poets with Muslim names who wrote about Kṛṣṇa and Rādhā, yoga techniques and *nāthapantha* ideology. Modern Indian Hindus, confronted with the large Muslim minority in their country and adopting the inclusivistic approach, see in these writers the forerunners of an accommodation on which the future of India as a secular multireligious state rests. As a prominent example I quote here from Jagadish Narayan Sarkar and Jadunath Sarkar, who, after discussing Muslim *pañcālīs* in their *Hindu–Muslim Relations in Bengal: Medieval Period*,[1] introduce Muslim poets with Vaiṣṇava sentiments, such as Nawāziš, 'Alī Raẓā, Lālan Faqīr, Sayyid Murtaẓā, and Hachhan Raja Chaudhary, and say: 'remaining within the fold of Islam, but crossing the narrow limit of communalism, and casting off all hesitations, these Muslims composed books on Hindu religion, wrote songs in honor of Kali' (p. 106).

According to these two authors, this beginning of a harmonious fusion of both religions was, however, thwarted 'by orthodox reformers of the 18th and 19th centuries' who called the syncretistic practices and ideas polytheism (*širk*), and 'vices of heresy, association of God, abuses or innovations in religion and a mode of performing religious duty and worship, which must be shunned by every true Mohammedan' (p. 109).

When we try to separate the facts of this argument from its intra-Indian political relevance, we can compare them to the discussions every fully developed religion has to face sooner or later: political circumstances or social changes create forces working for inclusion of their own interests within the main dogma. Very recently we observe attempts to accommodate a female aspect in the Christian Trinity or to extend Christian monogamous ethics beyond their heterosexual limits. In both cases, on one side of the fence one speaks about the necessary adaptation of a traditional religion to changed circumstances, and on the other we can see how carefully and slowly the established religious authorities react. Their reluctance to clamp down on dissenters is not only in accordance with our times but also shows the general difficulty of dealing with innovations. However, as early as 1517, the learned Cardinal Cajetanus, in a preparatory note for his talks with the rebellious Luther, criticized Luther's statement that the sacraments would bring damnation even to the contrite person if he should not believe that he was being absolved: 'hoc enim est novam Ecclesiam construere'.[2]

The position which Cajetanus took is similar to that of Muslim theologians when looking at the Indian innovations. For both, there existed a fully developed dogma which was the result of centuries of theological debates. For Cajetanus this dogma had found its ultimate expression in the *Summa* of Thomas Aquinas and Muslim scholars could rely on a comprehensive *tafsīr* and *ḥadīth* literature which stated in all details what is Islam and what are its deviant sects. All this was available already before the establishment of the Delhi Sulṭānat and did not leave any room for innovations which might have been necessary due to the conquest of India. In his remarkably clear representation of Islamic theology W. Montgomery Watts writes:

Während der zu besprechenden Jahrhunderte [i.e. 1250–1850] nahm das theologische Denken wahrscheinlich quantitativ zu, aber man ist gewöhnlich der Auffassung, daß seine Qualität – insbesondere im Bereiche des *kalām* . . . abnahm. Eines der Anzeichen dieses Verfalls ist der Mangel an Originalität. Statt neuer Werke scheinen die Theologen hauptsächlich bestrebt gewesen zu sein, Kommentare, Superkommentare und Glossen zu früheren Werken zu verfassen.

He characterizes this period as 'theologische Starrheit oder Rigidität' and as 'Mangel an Originalität'.[3]

Built into this orthodox framework was a basic Islamic attitude against non-believers which is already available in qur'ānic statements. Due to historic circumstances the Qur'ān and other early Muslim writing were more concerned with the conversion of Jews and Christians, who as 'People of the Book' (*ahlu 'l-kitāb*) belonged to the same religion of Abraham but did not obey the messages of their prophets. But the Qur'ān enjoined again and again on its followers:

أُدْعُ اِلىٰ سَبِيْلِ رَبِّكَ بِالْحِكْمَةِ
وَالْمَوعِظَةِ الْحَسَنَةِ
وَجَادِلْهُمْ بِالَّتِىْ هِىَ اَحْسَنُ (xvi. 125)

Summon thou to the way of thy Lord with wisdom and with kind warning: dispute with them in the kindest manner.

And even the *ḥadīth* literature, which is primarily concerned with non-believers in the chapters on *jiḥād*, has passages such as: 'May God remove far from His mercy anyone who goes from us to them. But God will make an escape and a way out for anyone who comes to us from them.'[4]

The Arabic polytheists, however, get short shrift in the Qur'ān and nobody finds it a loss that Lāt, Manāt, 'Uzzā and all the other pre-Islamic idols were destroyed because along with them existed barbaric customs which were uprooted by the harbingers of a new, more human culture.

So while the Islamic writings of before the twelfth century contain numerous references to Christians and Jews and reflect debates with Jewish and Christian theologians and with Greek philosophers, the Muslims generally overlooked Hinduism. The only exception is Abū Raiḥān al-Bīrūnī (eleventh century), who had travelled to India and in his *Kitābu 'l-Hind* has given us a remarkable account of Hindu philosophy, religion, and literature by which he placed himself squarely among the best of the early Orientalists. However, in the Islamic world his book remained unnoticed for centuries, and its author was known only as an astronomer. The religious ideas of the Hindus did not become a topic of the transmitted debates of the Muslims and when it happened that in India a leading Muslim took a serious interest in Hindu philosophy and religion in order to bring together the two communities, virulent 'orthodox' reaction was the consequence. Such a reaction caused both the demise of Akbar's Dīn-e ilāhī and the death of Dārā Šikoh, the translator of the Upaniṣads. Neither fitted into the conception of the true Muslim as described above.

The general attitude of the Muslims is clearly expressed in 'Umar Miḥrābī's *Ḥujjatu 'l-Hind* ('The Case of India', *c.* 1645), which equates the gods of the Hindu pantheon to the *dīvs* of Persian folklore and makes them responsible for the many schisms and the caste system of the Hindus. It calls phallic worship obscene, and it demonstrates licentiousness and impotence on the part of the Hindu gods with examples from purāṇic stories. It states that no prophets were born in India and, therefore, the country remained in the grip of paganism which could only produce devilish scriptures. It rejects the concept of reincarnation and disapproves of the custom of *satī* as of a pagan rite.[5] Under these conditions there could be no bridge built from Islamic theology to all those so-called 'Muslims' who venerated Kṛṣṇa or identified Allāh with *nirañjana* or gave Śiva a place in their writings. For they were indeed 'establishing a new church'. For this insight one does not have to wait for the 'orthodox' reformers of the eighteenth and nineteenth centuries. As early as the twelfth century anybody versed in Islamic theology could state that Hindus were polytheists (*ahlu'šširk*) and that all religious ideas passing from Hindu sources into Muslim belief are such as amount to an assault on the *tauḥīd*, the basic tenet of Islam.

In this paper we shall deal with Muslims who take this position, and we can be assured that such Muslims were around from the beginning of Islamic teaching in India. That their view did not always prevail (and the writers quoted above prove this abundantly) is not a literary but a political question: Islam was never able to dominate India completely, and partial domination and peaceful persuasion did not break the backbone of Hinduism, though in certain regions of the subcontinent it came close to it or it actually happened.

Generally speaking, it was from the *ḥaram* that Hindu rituals and stories entered orthodox Muslim homes. Not only female servants but also the wives of many Muslim nobles and common men came from Hindu families. In Nuṣratī's *Gulšan-i 'Išq*[6] we come across a passage where a wet-nurse is comforting a young man in pain. Although this story is set in an indistinct pre-Islamic world, many of the described customs and patterns of behaviour are those of the seventeenth-century Deccan. The wet-nurse says:

چلاون منتر کهم پو کر هم مین آ   اتارون اب اتا اندر کی اچهرا
کر افسون پتهاون تو دهرتی منجهار   نکالون سو پاتال تی سیس بهار

(1674 f.)

> If, in the right mood, I send a magic formula to the sky,
> I shall bring down many apsaras of Indra.
>
> When I place a spell on the earth,
> I shall bring Śeṣa from the nether world.

In this way Hindu mythology was taught a young Muslim, so to say, with his wet-nurse's milk. However, this did not prevent most young men from becoming good Muslims when they grew up.

Looking into the Muslim literature in Indian languages of the fifteenth and sixteenth centuries, we find that very little or, rather, nothing can be learned about Muslim attitudes toward bhakti. The only religion which comes across loud and clear is that of the Aghora and Gorakhanātha yogis. Their magic tricks are feared and readers are warned not to fall into their trap, otherwise it can happen (as happened to king Padamrā'o in Niẕāmī's *mat͟hnawī Padamrā'o o Kadamrā'o*) that your soul is cast out into the body of a bird while the Aghora's soul takes residence in your body and enjoys your possessions and your wife. This crude image of Hinduism may have been part of the phenotype of Hinduism which Muslims of the age of the Salṯanat encountered in their dealings with the lower classes of the Indian populace, and this image of Hinduism lingered on in sixteenth-century literature, where Hindu ascetics and Hindu gods are introduced mostly for their magic abilities, which are nothing other than the eight *siddhis* of the yogins. Islam from its very beginnings took magic powers very seriously because in a very prominent passage of the Qur'ān Muhammad prayed for protection from the ones 'who spit on knots':

قُلْ اَعُوْذُ بِرَبِ الْفَلَقِ

مِنْ شَـرِّ النَفّٰثٰـتِ فِى الْعُقَدِ

(cxiii. 1 and 4)

Say: 'I seek refuge with the Lord of the Dawn . . . from the mischief of those [fem.] who spit on knots' [i.e. who practise secret acts].

But magic is not a theological question in Islam and in the Hindu context the magic of the Nāthayogīs was superseded by unascetic bhakti cults. It would be, of course, completely futile to expect a true Muslim to have sympathy with devotion to an idol, even if this idol is not of stone or wood but just in the imagination of a poet or a devotee, but the glorification of love in Hindu devotion could create a common ground on which a bridge could be built. However, its foundations on the Islamic side are of a peculiar type. There is no doubt that the Qur'ān has no sympathy for sexual love except in the framework of the heterosexual marriage. However, the limitation of multiple love in this framework is left to the husband, who not only may marry up to four women but also may have any number of female slaves 'to his left hand'. The rules for these relationships are legalistic and made to serve certain purposes not only for the Muslim community in early times but also for mankind in general, as Muslims believe. Love outside these parameters was madness at best and a grave sin at worst. There was no general concept of love to be praised or venerated. This changed when Islam familiarized itself with Platonic writings, especially with neo-Platonic concepts prevalent in the Eastern Mediterranean world since pre-Christian times. While the official theology struggled with Aristotelian concepts which led to a similar result (as, at a later age, the encounter with Aristotle in the medieval West), the impact of Plato and his successors was much more subtle in the Islamic world. Of course, by as early as the seventh century of the Christian era, Platonism and Aristotelianism had already merged in many minds, especially in the schools of neo-Platonic thinking. This development provided Islam with a particularly cheerful type of Platonism, which grew stronger and stronger in the Persian area, especially after the beginning of our millennium. While the earliest Ṣūfīs still adhered to a pessimistic view of the world, quite in tune with Plato's myth of the cave, the confidence of Plotinus and his followers that the absolute soul in all her beauty participates in the forms of this world and leads the seeker to higher and higher levels of accomplishments has become the trademark of the most developed Sufism. Here in our world, which is the lowest level of its cosmological manifestation, the Divine Soul appears as beauty in its various forms. By a congenial sympathy, the human soul is drawn to the beautiful form of the beloved, as the first experience of the Divine for a mortal. From there it will rise to the experience of beauty free from sexuality, i.e. beautiful virtues and exemplary lives, etc. The way of the soul will thus be a constant progress from the lower levels of existence to the higher, and the propelling force which pushes it upwards is Love. This is what Dante is talking about in the last line of his *Commedia*:

> l'amor che muove il sole e l'altre stelle.

The creative energy of God which acts without the creator's involvement is described in Plotinus' works in different metaphors, for example when he speaks of God as a geometer who 'sees' the lines of his calculation on the land, or when he compares God and his creation with an original and its copy. The basic Platonic metaphor for the presence of the divine on all levels of the cosmos is, however, the sun and its light. So just as the sun illuminates the world without itself being involved in it, God is present in the beautiful forms of the world without being there. In the seventeenth century Nuṣratī writes:

جتی جیو روشن هین پا تجتی نور   او تابع دسین جنکی بالضرور

> They whose life has been illuminated by Your light,
> will necessarily appear to be followers of beauty.

The concept that the beauty of this world is the work of a great artist was stressed repeatedly by Plotinus in passages such as:

καὶ ἡ μὲν ὅλη καὶ ὅλου τῷ αὐτῆς μέρει τῷ πρὸς τό σῶμα τὸ ὅλον κοσμεῖ ὑπερέχουσα ἀπόνως, ὅτι μηδὲ ἐκ λογισμοῦ, ὡς ἡμεῖς, ἀλλὰ νῷ (ὡς ἡ τέχνη οὐ βουλεύεται).

Περὶ τῆς εἰς τὰ σώματα καθόδου τῆς ψυχῆς, iv. 8. 8. 13

And the soul which is a whole and is the soul of the whole by its part which is directed to the body, maintains the beauty and order of the whole in effortless transcendence because it does not do so by calculating and considering, as we do, but by intellect, as art does not deliberate.

So it does not come as a surprise that Nuṣratī compares God with an artist and the world as his painting:

نظارا کرین نقش جن بیمثال   لجاوین او تج نقشبند پر خیال
(31)

> Those who inspect these incomparable paintings,
> will think about Your art of painting.

But the most striking parallel is to be found in his light metaphors, and who would not recognize Goethe's famous lines:

> Wär nicht das Auge sonnenhaft,
> Die Sonne könnt es nie erblicken;

(*Zahme Xenien*, i. 7)[7]

while Nuṣratī's words are:

تون ایسا دیا ذره پتلے کون نور   سماتی هین جس جوت مین چاند سور
(57)

> You gave the little pupil such a light;
> in its shine sun and moon are contained.

Both the Dakkini poet of the seventeenth century and the German poet of the nineteenth drank from the same source:

> Οὐ γὰρ ἄν πώποτε εἶδεν ὀφθαλμὸς ἥλιον ἡλιοειδὴς μὴ γενόμενος.
> Περὶ τοῦ καλοῦ, i. 6. 9. 31)

> No eye could ever see the sun, if it was not sunlike.

In another passage of the same context on the power of Love we come across the first mention of a Hindu bhakta:

کری تونچ بتخانه دلکی نین   نپاتا هی عابد کون تون برهمن
(697)

> You make the eyes of the heart into the shrine of an idol,
> you turn its worshipper into a brāhmaṇ.

It may seem as if the attraction of human beauty is enough to allow comparison of the lover with the temple priest. The comparison has, however, much deeper roots. The great Persian masters especially, such as Rūmī and Aḥmad Ghazzālī, who all lived before the establishment of the Delhi Salṭanat, and also Ibn ʿArabī, who for other reasons is anathema for many Muslims, provided the ideas on which Sunni Sufism thrived in India. Of course it was out of the question for Rūmī's love for Šamsu 'l-Tabrīz to receive popular display in stories in Indian languages, but the divine nature of heterosexual love appealed very much to Indian Ṣūfīs and offered an excellent explanation for understanding the great Persian *mat͟hnawīs* with their sometimes very open erotic descriptions and all their hidden innuendoes. Moreoever, in this manner it also became possible to treat 'pre-Islamic' love between Indian princes and princesses as a manifestation of the Divine. So the door was opened for stories not connected with the Muslim traditions.[8]

Of course, we would be mistaken to look for a deification of the beloved in such stories as a sign of sympathy with the main bhakti sects. This is not the case. The revelation comes, however, at a completely different place. There is no doubt that the culmination point of a whole *mat͟hnawī* is the meeting between lover and beloved. This is the goal for which all the toils and sufferings are undertaken and which attracts the lover with a force which lets him think about his own life as being nothing. It is this passage where Nuṣratī introduced a remarkable image:

لی بیٹھی اسی جب چترسال مین   دسیا یون او عاشقکون تس حال مین
کہ جون صبح صادق نی دامن تہ بہار   نکالیا ہی خورشید ادک تابدار
یو عاشق نی پا روشنی نین کی   سٹیا دلتی دھو تیرہ کی رین کی
دیکھیا سوچ خورشید کون برھمن   لگیا یک توجہ سون سیوا کرن
او سورج مکھی جون درس خوش دکھای   ادک ھونی برس برھمن پو آی
اپس مہربانی کی کر نین باز   او زریکون کرنی بدل سر فراز
محبت سون لی کھینچ آپس منی   ڈبای اپس چھبکی رنگ رس منی
ھوی یک او جون برھمن ھور صنم[9]   چلی وانتی او صبح سی راست دم

(3015–22)

When she sat in the picture gallery,
she appeared to her lover in this condition:

As if out of its skirt the faithful morning
had brought forth a very dazzling sun.

Her lover took the light of her eyes
and washed off the darkness of the night from his heart

As if a brāhmaṇ looks at the dazzling sun
when he begins to worship it with humility.

This sun-faced one showed her beautiful appearance
and came to shower profusely upon that brāhmaṇ.

She did not withhold her kindness
in order to turn him into proud gold.

Full of love she drew him into herself
and immersed him in the passion of her beauty.

It was as if the brāhmaṇ and his idol had become one,
and he went from there exactly like the early morning.

In these verses the well-known *sāndhya pūjā* of the Hindus is turned into a bhakti act. This makes it possible to compare a brāhmaṇ with an *ʿāšiq* and at least show some understanding of a religion which from a Muslim point of view is on a level with the pre-Islamic idol-worshippers. The basis of this understanding is neo-Platonic, and this is a key to the inclusion of pre-Islamic Indian characters of the Ṣūfī stories in the stations on the Ṣūfī's path in search of God. Moreover, if the brāhmaṇ who worships the sun is an example of the Platonic doctrine of the mysterious relationship of the human soul with the beautiful form, then he in his love for beauty has reached the same goal to which the Ṣūfī also aspires.

NOTES

1. Delhi, 1985.
2. G. Henning, *Cajetan und Luther*, Stuttgart, 1966, p. 56.
3. W. Montgomery Watts, A. T. Welch, M. Marmura, *Der Islam*, 2 vols., Stuttgart, 1980 and 1985, vol. ii, p. 463 f.
4. *Miškatu 'l-Masabhih*, book XVII (*jiḥād*), ch. 10.1).
5. Quoted from Aziz Ahmad, *Studies in Islamic Culture in the Indian Environment*, Oxford, 1964, p. 85.
6. The quotations from Nuṣratī's *Gulšan-i 'Išq* (1667) follow the text and the spellings of Aḥmad Nādkār's MS (Hyderabad, 1743–4), which is now in the possession of the Art Museum of Philadelphia. The only existing lithographic print, edited by Sayyid Muḥammaḍ (Hyderabad) is uncritical and unreliable.
7. The poem continues: 'Läg' nicht in uns des Gottes eigene Kraft / Wie könnt' uns Göttliches entzücken?' (*Goethes Werke*, complete edn. in 40 vols., ed. Karl Alt *et al.*, vol. i, Berlin, n.d.). For a history of prints of the poem and literature on it see *Goethes Werke*, Hamburg Edition, n.d., vol. i, p. 681.
8. For a very different approach to the same issue see A. Wali, 'Hinduism according to Muslim Sufis', *JASB* 11, 1923, pp. 237–52.
9. In the MS the last words of this quotation are '*rāst dam*', which makes no sense.

Muslim devotional literature in Gujarati: Islam and bhakti

FRANÇOISE MALLISON

In Gujarat, Islam originated a rich literature in the vernacular, but the texts remain quite unknown as they concern groups who often wish to retain their secret character, or groups who are not very numerous or in some cases belong to less favoured social strata. However, as early as at the end of the nineteenth century, some of the texts of these groups attracted the attention of non-Islamic philologists who had become aware not only of their interest but also of their aesthetic qualities.[1] This paper intends to review three groups of texts:[2]

The *gināns* by the Ismāʻīlī Pīrs belonging to the Nizārī (Khojā) branch dating back to the thirteenth century and composed between then and the nineteenth century;

the *bhajans* written by the disciples of the Ṣūfī Pīr Kāyamadīn Bāvā Sāheb of Māṃgaroḷa (Mangrol, Surat) of the eighteenth century;

the poems of Rāje Bhagat, a Molesalām Muslim (Rajput Garāsīā) from the Broach area, who lived before 1720.

The *gināns*

The word is derived from the Sanskrit *jñāna* (i.e. knowledge acquired through meditation) and denotes various compositions by the Ismāʻīlī Nizārī missionaries (*dāʻī*) in the vernaculars of their converts, in order to provide them with a sacred literature. The Nizārī form one of the main branches of Ismailism,[3] as an outcome of the 1094 schism in the Egypt of Fāṭimid decline where the followers of Nizār, the elder son of Imām Al Mustanṣir, were opposed to those of his younger brother Mustaʻlī. Both groups were to have a long history, but were finally reunited in India.[4] The present-day Nizārī, mainly at Bombay, in Gujarat, in Kutch, and in Sind, are known as Satpanthī or Khojā.[5] The Nizārī Ismāʻīlī are the only Shīʻite sect to acknowledge a living and physically present imām who is regarded as the perfect incarnation of God, being the 'imām of the time'. Persecution, conquest, and schism were the lot of the successive imāms in Iran until 1840 when the imām who had just received the title of Āgā Khān had to fly to Sind and then on to Bombay. There, his privileges in respect of the Khojā community converted by the missionaries who had been sent by his predecessors, but who at that time were more or less cut off from the Iranian Imāmat, were officially recognized. From this period onwards, scholarly research was stimulated among the Ismā'īlī themselves as well as among Western scholars. The manuscripts of the *ginâns* surfaced, and were copied and published openly, not any longer in the secret Khojkī alphabet, as there was no more threat of persecution by orthodox Islam.[6]

The history of the conversions in Gujarat is difficult to assess as the *ginâns*, the only source, are of an apologetic nature by definition.[7] The first Nizārī missionary of Pīr to have reached Gujarat is the legendary Satgur Nūr, said to have converted the king Siddharāja Jayasiṃha (1094–1143). His mausoleum can be seen at Navasari, south Gujarat. Among the following envoys (dā'ī), three are traditionally associated with the corpus of the *ginâns*: (1) Pīr Shams, who is said to have reached India during the fourteenth century and to have been active in Kutch and in Multan, where he was buried; (2) Pīr Ṣadruddīn (*c.* 1400), who founded the *Jamā'atkhāna* (places of prayer and worship) and gave the name of Khwājā (Lord) to his converts belonging to the Lohāṇā caste in Kutch; (3) Pīr Ḥasan Kabīr al-Dīn, son of Pīr Ṣadruddīn, at whose death (at the end of the fifteenth century) the community was unable to agree on a successor.[8] The followers of his eighteenth and youngest son, Imām Shāh, declared themselves independent and founded with Nūr Muḥammad Shāh, son of Imām Shāh, the new sect of the Imām-Shāhī, the seat of which is in the vicinity of Ahmadabad at Pirana. The corpus of the *ginâns* of the Imāmshāhī is closely similar to that of the Nizārī: thus, if a *ginân* is found in both the traditions, it may be assumed that it is anterior to the sixteenth century, a precious indication. The Imāmshāhī remained exclusively Gujarati, whereas the Nizārī persuasion extended to other parts of India (the Panjab), to Pakistan (Sind, and the remote Hunza valleys), and to Iran. Syncretist tendencies are more prevalent among the Imāmshāhī, in spite of different reform attempts during the subsequent centuries, than among the Nizārī Āgā-Khānī, who from the nineteenth century onwards tended to redefine themselves in terms of the Islam of the Near East. In any case, the Imāmshāhī schism stopped any further proselytizing of the Nizārī from Iran in India.

The core of the teaching of the Pīrs depends essentially on the doctrine of the Imāmat as defined by the successive imāms of Alamut. The believer undertakes a spiritual quest which is to lead him into mystical union; its hidden meaning can only be revealed with the help of a guide, the Pīr, who provides an instrument of meditation: the *dhik* or *bol*; exterior customs and rites are to be discarded for the benefit of the interior practice of religion. The preaching methods of the Pīrs, as revealed in the *ginâns*, very clearly draw on a Hindu–Islamic synthesis. The Pīrs seem to have borrowed from Hinduism on more than one level:[9] on one side there is the group of unavoidable concessions made in order to be understood by the crowds of the faithful belonging to predominantly illiterate low castes. The most popular Hindu customs and beliefs, such as the *garabā* dances to honour the Devī and the belief in reincarnation, are taken up. The very mission of the *dā'ī* implied that they had to be aware of the customs and the language of the country where they were preaching. But apart from these more or less sociological concessions, the Pīrs even elaborated a complete Ismā'īlī system on the basis of the doctrine of the avatārs of Viṣṇu, so that Kalki, the saviour announced by the Vaiṣṇavas for our present era (*Kali yuga*) was said to have been incarnate in Ḥaẓrat 'Alī, the son-in-law and successor of the Prophet, as well as in the imām of the time. In this system, the Hindu identities become Islamic, thus 'Alī is equated with Viṣṇu, the Prophet Muḥammad with Brahmā, his daughter Fāṭima is either Śakti or Sarasvatī, whereas Ḥasan is Śiva, etc. The Imāmshāhī of Gujarat attach more importance to the *dasa-avatāra* doctrine than the remaining Khojās of the subcontinent. But the notion of a saviour is of little importance to Hindus, and Kalki is much less important when compared to Rāma and Kṛṣṇa, who became the only forms of godhead absolute (among the ten avatārs of Viṣṇu). Thus, however conclusive might appear the transposition of the *dasa-avatāra* myth into the Ismā'īlī cosmogony, it remains artificial. Yet the Hindu religious atmosphere as conveyed by the *ginān* lyrics is a different matter.[10]

Composed between the thirteenth century and the beginning of the twentieth century, they number about 800, of varied lengths. Many of their features – their origin, mode of transmission, literary form, and actual use – are reminiscent of those of the *padas* and *bhajans* of the medieval Vaiṣṇava bhakti of north India.[11] The *gināns* were first transmitted orally, which implies a lack of stability of the texts. The earliest manuscript is dated AD 1736 but manuscripts are dated as existing as early as the sixteenth century.[12] The *gināns* were actually written in several languages: Multani, Panjabi, Sindhi, Kacchi, Hindi, but mainly in Gujarati, not to speak of the jargon of the sādhus, the *Sādhukaḍa bolī*.[13]

The *gināns* are in verse, adopting the *caupāī* and *dohā* forms.[14] Their length varies much; the shortest *gināns* count four to five stanzas. The lengthier usually have an abridged version (*nāno* or *niḍho*) and some *gināns* – so it seems – were provided with a longer version (*moṭo* or *vaḍo*). Each *ginān* contains the signature of its author (or *bhaṇitā*); they are supposed to be sung or recited; each having its *rāga*, and transmitted orally from generation to generation. The use of the musical element is essential to the transmission of the sacred message, as in Hindu devotional poetry.[15] According to A. Nanji,[16] the decision was taken in the sixteenth century to put the texts into writing and to attribute each *ginān* to one of the great Pīrs (Pīr Shams, Pīr Ṣadruddīn, Pīr Ḥasan Kabīr al-Dīn), and the printed texts group the *gināns* according to their presumed authors.

The themes of the *gināns* are manifold (missionary, mythological, ethical, ritual), but the most interesting of the corpus are the *gināns* dealing with the mysticism of the Indian Ismā'īlī. They describe the ultimate experience of a spiritual unity of the interior reality of the believer on the one hand, and the interior reality of the imām on the other, i.e. they struggle to describe union with God. They are popular because of their emotional character. On the other hand, the *gināns* also faithfully reflect preoccupations of the Vaiṣṇava Sants of north India,[17] such as the cult of the divine name (*sata-śabda*) as being the only means of crossing the ocean of existence, the abandon of the stress laid on the exterior aspects of religious practice, and the exaltation of devotion extended to the interior guru (*sat-guru*). They use the *virahiṇī* symbol[18] and advocate the cult of absolute godhead: both impersonal under the names of Nīrīṃjan, Sāmī (for Svāmī), Nāthajī, Pūrṇa Paribrahman, etc., as well as personal in its Vaiṣṇava forms of Tribhovan Śām, Harajī, Jadurāy. The authors of the *gināns*, like the Sants, take up the symbolism and the tantric practices of the Nāthayogīs. Thus the repetition of the *bol* (or *dhikr*), being a kind of *mantra* offered to the neophyte on his way towards illumination (*didara*), may be *ajapa* (mental); and the elixir of immortality (*amī, amṛta*) may accompany the experience of the union with God. In their practice as well as in their texts, the Khojā Ismā'īlī echo the popular forms of Hindu mysticism of the fourteenth, fifteenth, and sixteenth centuries, and their poetry is related beyond doubt to the poetry of the medieval bhakti of the *nirguṇī* Sants.[19]

The *bhajans* of the disciples of Pīr Kāyamadīn Bāvā

Pīr Kāyamadīn Bāvā is considered to be the founder of the Chistī Ṣūfī gādī of Mangrol, a tālukā in the district of Surat. But the annual fair at Mangrol is observed in honour of a successor of Kāyamadīn, namely Pīr Moṭā Mīyāṃ, who was an enlightened religious leader at the beginning of the twentieth century with a Western type education and ecumenical views. He handed over in the early years of this century to Haragovindadās Dvārakādās Kāṃṭāvāḷā the Gujarati *bhajan* and *kalām* texts composed by the disciples of Kāyamadīn. Kāṃṭāvāḷā drew attention to them as being good samples of medieval Gujarati literature in his address to the Sixth Gujarati Sāhitya Pariṣad. They were later printed in his monthly *Sāhitya* (January–December 1922), before being collected in book form under the title of *Bhakti-sāgar*.[20]

The tomb of Pīr Kāyamadīn Bāvā is situated, however, not at Mangrol but at Ekalbara, in the Padara tālukā of Baroda district, and there is an annual fair at Ekalbara in honour of Pīr Kāyamadīn. The fairs of both Mangrol and Ekalbara gather the faithful of all Islamic communities (especially of the Ismā'īlī Bohrā) as well as the Hindus of the neighbourhood. An essential item on their programme is the singing of the Gujarati *bhajans* composed by the disciples and successors of Kāyamadīn.

The Ṣūfī community of Mangrol does not seem to have attracted the attention of the specialists in Islam in Gujarat, who do not mention it apart from in the Gazetteers,[21] and the lives and the works of its authors remain little known. According to Kāṃṭāvāḷā, who collected parts of their tradition, Pīr Kāyamadīn belonged to the lineage of Bābā Farīd of Pāk Paṭṭan through his father Badruddīn Mastāna, and was of imperial descent.[22] Nothing is known precisely about how he came to Gujarat; some of the *kalāms* printed in the *Bhakti-sāgar* by Haragovanadās Harakīśanadās as a supplement to the collection of Kāṃṭāvāḷā (pp. 255–66) are written in Urdu, as is his *Nūra-rośana*, dated 1703. He is supposed to have died in 1722. In the hagiographic texts concerning him stress is put on his religious syncretism, and specially on his strict vegetarianism.[23] His disciples, the composers of the *padas* to be mentioned now, are Gujaratis of humble origin.

Ratanabāī

The most prolific writer among these disciples is a woman: Ratanabāī. Although she figures in the last line of the title page of the *Bhakti-sāgar*, the editor begins his collection with her poems. She is said to be the cousin of Jīvaṇa Mastāna, another disciple, but one knows little more about her than that she lived at the end of the eighteenth century and that she had little schooling.[24] The wide range of the topics touched upon by her in her *bhajans* and *kalāms*, ranging from philosophy to bhakti, *nīti*, and mysticism, is said to be due to a competence acquired exclusively through the teaching of her guru. Her poems are pleasant, with a personal touch unusual for the period.[25] It is a pity we cannot know to which community she belonged. She has been compared to Mīrābāī,[26] not without reason as she complains about the persecutions she endured from her family, who disliked her mystical preoccupations and her attachment to the teaching of Pīr Kāyama.

Ratana used the *garabī* form and her models are the *padas* of Kṛṣṇa bhakti as written by the Bhagats of the eighteenth century.[27] She reminds us also of the Nāgar lady authors Kṛṣṇabāī or Dīvāḷībāī, as well as of the Svāmīnārāy-aṇī authors. When she invokes the divinity, she sometimes makes use of the name of Hari[28] or Harikṛṣṇa,[29] more often of Kiratāra[30] (the Creator), but essentially Kāyamadīn[31] is her favourite.

Abharām Bāvā

Pīr Kāyamadīn was succeeded by Abharām Bāvā (or Amarām, or Ibha-rāhīma Bhagat) from Pariyeja, a village in Broach district. Like Ratana, he is said to have had no education and to have owed whatever he knew to Pīr Kāyama.[32] In some of his *padas*, he assumes the female part of the lover, *sakhī*, as, for instance, in his *garabī* where he cries for his Lord (*Nāth*).[33] His

Gujarati is mixed with Urdu, and he has also written entire *padas* in Urdu. He emphasizes his lineage:[34]

Among the four sufi *panth*
  my house is *Cīstī*,
I hold Khvājā Moinudīn
  in high esteem . . .
Śāha Kāyamadīn is my *pīr*
  and my true master.

Puṃjā Bāvā

Puṃjā Bāvā was a Khāravā, a sailor, from Cambay but is said to have lived at Broach. He also owed his education to Pīr Kāyamadīn and he has many followers nowadays among the Khāravā of Gujarat.[35] His poetry has a *nirguṇī* touch with plenty of tantric symbolism.

Heaven rings high with the word of Sahaja,
  Trikama beats the time;
    So'ham So'ham, this is the word . . .[36]

Nabī Mīyāṃ

The editor of the *Bhakti-sāgar* does not tell anything about the life of Nabī Mīyāṃ.[37] A *pada* published in the journal *Sāhitya* puts side by side the names of the gurus of Nabī and those of Kṛṣṇa in an astonishing manner: Pharīād, Abharām, Śāha Kāyam, and Morārī, Śyām, Viśarām, etc.[38] It is also very interesting to note that several *bhajans* of Nabī Mīyāṃ bear at the beginning the phrase *Dhīrā bhagata no rāha* (according to the way of Dhīro Bhagat). Dhīro was a Hindu Bhagat (1753–1824) whose *padas* are powerful warnings against *māyā* and the world's illusion. Nabī could identify himself with Dhīro, so it seems.

The Gujarati Bhagats are a group of poet-saints who, in the eighteenth century, were in favour of an austere creed imbued with the Kabīrian thought quite in fashion there at that time. The Bhagats were the heirs of the north Indian Sants of the fifteenth and sixteenth centuries. They preached against the darkness of their time and the excessive number of false sādhus and religious men of all sorts. If they invoked Kṛṣṇa or Viṣṇu, it was merely by way of a name given to the unqualified Brahman. They were all independent one of the other; they did not found any school; they were of humble origin and lived a family life. They are sometimes called *jñān-mārgī-kavi* on account of their strong monistic Vedantism. Their link with Islam has not been sufficiently noticed. One of them, for instance, Nirānt (1747–1824), a Rājpūt or a Patidar, was converted to *nirguṇī* worship by a Muslim.[39] It is obvious that there was a mutual influence between the Hindu Bhagats and their contemporaries, the disciples of Pīr Kāyama. Some followers of the Pīr bear the surname Bhagat, as Sulemān Bhagat, for instance.

The *ginān*s had portrayed the *nirguṇī* bhakti of before the fifteenth century, and we cannot know for sure whether this was the outcome of a premeditated move on the part of the Ismā'īlī Pīrs to identify their preaching with a predominant trend at the time or whether it was the result of an unconscious and irresistible assimilation. But as far as the disciples of Pīr Kāyama are concerned, their poetry was not meant for proselytising, and their integration into the Bhagat movement of the time seems quite natural.

The poems of Rāje Bhagat

Rāje, who is known for an exclusively *saguṇa* Kṛṣṇaite poetry, precedes in time the followers of Kāyama, and in fact he holds a special place. His poetry does not reveal him as a Muslim, unlike Kāyamadīn's followers, who acknowledge their lineage. Little is known about him except that he was a Molesalām. The Molesalāms are Rājpūts converted at the time of Sultān Maḥmūd Begaḍā (1459–1513), but who remained somewhat unconcerned by Islam as they stuck to their social system and Hindu cultural patterns.[40] They live in the districts of Broach, Baroda, Banaskantha, and Kaira. They belong to several Rājpūt clans. Rāje's was the Garāsīā,[41] the most numerous among the Molesalām. The Garāsīā Molesalām are poor and backward, usually uneducated. They use the services of Hindu priests and, only when they are well off, of the Muslim clergy.

Rāje was a Garāsīā from Keravada village in the Amoda tālukā of Broach district. We have no information concerning his family; we do not know when he died nor where his tomb lies. From a single manuscript mention one may conclude that he was alive in 1720.[42] The name Raṇachoḍ appears after his name in his *Jñān cusarā*, and that is why, according to the tradition, his father's name was Raṇachoḍ. But the double meaning which can be given to this surname of Kṛṣṇa each time it appears in the *cusarā* makes one doubt the validity of this conclusion.[43] In any case, the language of Rāje's poetry definitely belongs to the Broach area and seems contemporary with that of the great *ākhyānakār* Premānand (mid-seventeenth to eighteenth century). The inevitable legends in his hagiography are, meanwhile, the proof of his popularity. His first miracle is to have secured an abundant harvest of *jovana* for his father in spite of the fact that he had neglected to watch the fields properly. According to another story, he changed meat into sugar.[44]

His written output is manifold.[45] Like other poets of Braj bhakti he wrote about *Rās-līlā, mān*, and *dāṇ-līlā*, and composed *Hiṇḍoḷā-nā-pada, bāramāsī kāvya, garabī, vrehegītā, Vasantanāṃ pada*, and *bāla-līlā*. Some of his *padas* come, however, under the headings of *vairāgya* and *nīti*. His *thāḷas* (poems describing food offerings to Kṛṣṇa) recall the Vallabhan *sevā*.[46] In his *sākhīo*, Rāje fancies himself a *gopī* or Rādhā, for such are *Brija bāsī kī rīta* (the ways of Braj people).[47] His *Rās-paṃcādhyāyī* describes the *mahārās* in conventional language in 18 *kaḍavās*.[48] His style is elegant, rich with assonances. More vivid is the inspiration of his description of the secret marriage of Rādhā.[49] All this remains puzzling, however, if one considers the poet's origins. One wonders why Rāje was not known as a major author of the Gujarati Kṛṣṇa bhakti. His work announces the poetry of Dayārāma (1777–1853),[50] and the very time of its composition (the early eighteenth century) shows it to be one of the links between the Vallabhan missionaries of the sixteenth century and Dayā. Why was he ignored by the historians of literature until the edition of Rāvaḷ in 1931? Was it because he was a Muslim? It is hardly possible to speak of a synthesis between the two religions in the case of Rāje, as he was entirely immersed in Hinduism.[51] But Rāje was not a Hindu convert, and the Molesalām still acknowledge him with pride. Kṛṣṇaism, in the extreme form of *Premalakṣaṇā* bhakti in Gujarat, was chosen to be the unique medium for Rāje's religious experience. Is it possible to go further from Islam towards bhakti?

NOTES

1. See e.g. the first edition of *padas* of Rāje by I. S. Desai in his *Bṛhat kāvyadohan*, Bombay, Gujarati Printing Press, vol. i, 1890, 7th edn., 1925, pp. 822–7, and vol. vii, 1911, pp. 771–83, and the discovery by H. D. Kāṃṭāvāḷā of the poems of the disciples of Pīr Kāyamadīn made known at the 6th Gujarati Sāhitya Pariṣad and published in the monthly *Sāhitya* of the year 1922.
2. For the texts not covered, see K. M. Jhaveri, 'Musalamān jevā parasaṃskār ane gujarātī sāhitya' in K. M. Munshi, ed., *Gujarātī sāhitya*, Bombay, 1929, pp. 189–98. See A. Schimmel, *Islam in the Indian Subcontinent*, Leiden: E. J. Brill, 1980, p. 67, on the popular devotional poetry called *jikrī* (from *dhikr*) and the mystical works of Shāh ʿAlī Muḥammad Jīv Jān; p. 70 on the *Khūb tarang* composed by Khūb Muḥammad Chishtī (d. 1614) in a mixture of Gujarati and Urdu. Not only devotional poetry was composed, but a variety of didactic and theological literature, including a translation into Gujarati of the Qur'ān. On the works of Pīr Mashā'ikh II (b. 1650), the reformer of the Pīrāṇā panth, see S. C. Misra, *Muslim Communities in Gujarat*, London: Asia Publishing House, 1964, pp. 62–5.
3. Ismailism branched off Shīʿa Islam in AD 765 when there was disagreement concerning the authority of the 7th imām, the successor of Jaʿfar al-Ṣādiq, because Jaʿfar's son and successor Ismāʿīl had died before him. At that time, Ismāʿīl's followers acknowledged his son Muḥammad as the 7th and last imām, thus founding Ismailism, whereas the main Shīʿa branch, which was to acknowledge 12 imāms, chose as successor Ismāʿīl's brother, Mūsā'al-Kāẓim.
4. On the history of Ismailism and of its Nizārī branch in the Indian subcontinent, see Y. Marquet, *Poésie ésotérique ismaïlienne*, Paris: Maisonneuve et Larose, 1985, introduction: 'L'Ismaïlisme', pp. 7–25; Schimmel, op. cit.; Misra, op. cit.;

K. M. Master, *Mahāgujarātanā musalamāno*, Baroda: M. S. University, 1969; W. Ivanow, 'Satpanth', in *Collectanea*, vol. i, Leiden: E. J. Brill, 1948, pp. 1–54, and 'The Sect of Imam Shah in Gujrat', *JBRAS*, NS 12, 1936, pp. 19–70; A. Nanji, *The Nizārī Ismā'īlī Tradition in the Indo-Pakistan Subcontinent*, New York, Caravan Books, 1978; A. Asani, *The Ismā'īlī Ginān Literature, its Structure and Love Symbolism*, Harvard University B.A. thesis, forthcoming.

5. From the branch of the Musta'lī resulted the Ṭayyibīya in Yemen, who in 1539 emigrated to Gujarat, where they became the Dā'ūdī Bohrā. See F. Mallison, 'Hinduism as Seen by the Nizārī Ismā'īlī Missionaries of Western India: The Evidence of the Ginān', in G. D. Sontheimer and H. Kulke, eds., *Hinduism Reconsidered*, Heidelberg University Studies, no. 24, New Delhi: South Asia Institute, 1989, p. 93. Although both communities are settled in Gujarat, the Bohrā use Arabic and Urdu (in addition to Gujarati), whereas the Khojā prefer Persian and Gujarati.
6. Several alphabets are in use, with a preference for the Gujarati script, as the headquarters of the community are located in Bombay with the majority of the Gujarati faithful not far away. On Khojkī see A. S. Asani, 'The Khojkī Script: A Legacy of Ismaili Islam to the Indo-Pakistan Subcontinent', *JAOS*, 107, 3, pp. 439–49.
7. See Nanji, op. cit., p. 7, and Ivanow, 'The Sect of Imam Shah in Gujrat', pp. 21 f.
8. The following collections of their *ginān*s were made available to me: (1) *Mahān īsamāīlī sant Pīr Śams racit gīnānono saṃgrah* (106 *ginān*s, out of which 28 *garabī*); neither the place and date of the publication nor the name of the editor are indicated; (2) *Mahān īsamāīlī sant Pīra Sadaradīn racit gīnānono saṃgrah*, 1 (217 *ginān*s), Bombay, 1969; (3) *Mahāna īsamāīlī sant Pīr Hasan Kabīradīn ane bījā sattādhārī pīro racit gīnānono saṃgrah* (78 and 23 *ginān*s), without any indication of place, date, or the name of the editor.
9. See F. Mallison, 'La Secte ismaélienne des Nizārī ou Satpanthī en Inde: Hétérodoxie hindoue ou musulmane?', sect. 2: 'Hindouisme des Satpanthī' in S. Bouez, ed., *Le Renoncement en Asie du Sud: Formes populaires et savantes*, forthcoming. On the Islamic identity of the Khojā see A. S. Asani, 'The Khojahs of Indo-Pakistan: The Quest for an Islamic Identity', *Journal of the Institute of Muslim Minority Affairs*, 8, 1, pp. 31–41.
10. Mallison, 'Hinduism as Seen by the Nizārī Ismā'īlī Missionaries of Western India', pp. 96–8.
11. See Nanji, op. cit., p. 14, and Schimmel, op. cit., p. 73.
12. See Nanji, op. cit., pp. 10–13.
13. Ibid., p. 9, and Ivanow, 'The Sect of Imam Shah in Gujrat', p. 29.
14. These are the most common metres used to express the medieval devotional poetry of the Sants of north India (see K. Schomer, 'The *Dohā* as a Vehicle of Sant Teachings', in K. Schomer and W. H. McLeod, eds., *The Sants: Studies in a Devotional Tradition of India*, Delhi: Motilal Banarsidass, 1987, pp. 90 ff.). The *dohā* is a verse of two lines, each of 24 instants. Each line is divided into two *caraṇa* and six feet: 6 + 4 + 3, 6 + 4 + 1; the *caupāī* is a verse of four lines of 16 instants each: 6 + 4 + 4 + 2.
15. On the importance of the actual performance for the appreciation of this medieval devotional poetry, see J. Bloch, 'Les Mystiques de l'Inde médiévale: Kabir', in *Recueil d'articles de Jules Bloch, 1906–1955*, texts collected by C.

Caillat, Paris: Collège de France and Institut de Civilisation Indienne, 1985, pp. 230 f.

16. See op. cit., pp. 12 ff.
17. See Mallison, 'Hinduism as Seen by the Nizārī Ismā'īlī Missionaries of Western India', pp. 96–8, and 'La Secte ismaélienne des Nizārī ou Satpanthī en Inde: Hétérodoxie hindoue ou musulmane?'
18. The soul symbolized by the bride awaiting the nuptials expresses its desire of union with God in a special type of *ginān* called *venti* (request), such as the *venti* of Ḥasan Kabīruddīn (*Gīnānono saṃgrah*, pp. 14 f.) commented upon by Asani in *The Ismā'īlī Ginān Literature*, pp. 30–40 and app.
19. On the reciprocal influences of the Sants and the medieval Muslim saints, see Y. Husain, *L'Inde mystique au Moyen Age: Hindous et Musulmans*, Paris: Adrien Maisonneuve, 1929. For a documented survey of identical themes in Ṣūfī and Sant texts, see B. B. Lawrence, 'The Sant Movement and North Indian Sufis' in Schomer and McLeod, op. cit., pp. 336 ff.
20. *Bhakti-sāgar, jemāṃ pīr kāyamadīn bāvā sāheb, abharām bāvā, umar bāvā, puṃjābāvā, jīvaṇ mastāna, ratanabāī, baḍā sāheb, nathubāvā vigerenāṃ bhajano che*, Surat: Haragovanadās Harakīśanadās 1925. The address of H. D. Kāṃṭāvāḷā to the 6th Gujarati Sāhitya Pariṣad is given in the introduction, pp. 1–6. The publisher adds that much more material exists which has not yet become available to him.
21. *Gazetteer of India, Gujarat State, Surat District*, rev. edn., Ahmadabad, 1962, p. 939, and *Vadodara District*, Ahmadabad, 1979, p. 804. *Census of India, 1961*, vol. v: *Gujarat*, pt. 7B: 'Fairs and Festivals', ed. R. K. Trivedi, Delhi, 1965, pt. 2, pp. 145 and 168.
22. See *Bhakti-sāgar*, introduction.
23. According to A. Schimmel (*Mystical Dimensions of Islam*, Chapel Hill: North Carolina University Press, 1975, p. 358), strict vegetarianism on the part of Ṣūfīs in India is not necessarily borrowed from Indian ascetic practice or Hindu customs.
24. See *Bhakti-sāgar*, introduction, p. 6.
25. Ibid., *kalām*, p. 10, and Munshi, op. cit., p. 198, *ṭek*: 'He has come and has taken me by his hand, Our Pīr Kāyamadīn. He has come and has taken me by his hand. Drowned I was in household worries, Yet I obtained the company of Pīr Kāyamadīn'; or *garabī*, p. 15, and Munshi, op. cit., p. 198, v. 2: 'Within me I was cleansed, Within my mind detachment arose. The world's deceit has disappeared, Why did I have such luck?'
26. The Rajput princess Mīrābāī, a Hindu Vaiṣṇava Sant, happens to be mentioned in some of the lists of the five Hindu–Muslim saints, the *Paṃca pīriyā*, whose cult is very popular among low Hindu or Muslim castes of north India (see Husain, op. cit., p. 31).
27. However, as happens frequently in the case of the *Bhagats*, she may reveal a highly *nirguṇī* type of bhakti poetry with reminiscences of the Nāth form of tantrism. See poems attributed to a Ratanabāi in the collection *Santavāṇī (Lokapriya bhajano), ātmajñānanāṃ bhajano*, vol. iii, ed. H. M. Patel, Ahmadabad: *Sastuṃ sāhitya vardhaka kāryālaya*, 1972, pp. 67f.: *Sahejanuṃ jñāna ne sahaja samādhi, suratā samāve brahmākāramāṃ* (*pada* 55, v. 3); *Śūrā nara koṇa batāve śabde laḍe samsaramāṃ* (*pada* 56, v. 1).
28. See *Bhakti-sāgar*, *kalām*, p. 25, v. 6: *Bāī Ratane Harī rasa pīdho.*

29. See *Santavāṇī, padas* 55 and 56, pp. 67 f.: *Jñāna Ratana guru Harikṛṣṇa maḷiyā* and *Jñāna Ratana guru Harikṛṣṇa maḷatāṃ*.
30. Kiratāra is certainly more appropriate in an Islamic context. See Bloch, art. cit., p. 250.
31. See *Bhakti-sāgar, sākhī*, p. 8, v. 5: *Kāyamadīna japanā meṃ japuṃ*.
32. Ibid., p. 38.
33. See *Bhakti-sāgar* (*garabī* no. 7), pp. 45 f.
34. Ibid. (no. 9), p. 47, vv. 3–4.
35. *Bhakti-sāgar*, p. 66.
36. *Bhakti-sāgar* (*bhajan* no. 10), p. 75, *ṭek* and v. 1. The Khāravā are famous for their devotion to the Devī. See also the case of the musicians and servants (named *Kamaliyā*) of the temple of Bahucarājī (Mehsana district), who are at the same time Muslims and Devī-worshippers (see V. T. Padmaja, 'Three Śakti Pīthas of Gujarat', *JOIB*, 35, 1985, p. 245). Conversely, devotees of the Devī may make extensive use of Muslim words and expressions in their compositions in honour of their deity.
37. Seven *bhajans* of Nabī Mīyāṃ are found on pp. 112–17 of *Bhakti-sāgar*, and six more in the suppl., pp. 148–53.
38. Munshi, op. cit., p. 198.
39. See K. M. Jhaveri, *Milestones in Gujarati Literature*, Bombay: Gujarati Printing Press, 1914, pp. 175–7.
40. See Master, op. cit., pp. 335 ff. There have been continuing attempts to islamize this kind of superficial Muslim in Gujarat during the last 150 years, according to Schimmel, *Islam*, pp. 68 f. At present, an opposite movement of reconversion to Hinduism is being attempted.
41. Misra, op. cit., p. 70.
42. C. V. Rāvaḷa, ed., *Prācīn kāvya sudhā*, pt. 5: *Kavi Rāje Bhāī kṛt kavitā saṃgrah*, 1931, introduction, pp. 1–12.
43. Ibid. (*Jñān cusarā*), pp. 1–10. On the possible meanings of the name Raṇachoḍ, see F. Mallison, 'Development of Early Krishnaism in Gujarāt, Viṣṇu-Raṇachoḍ-Kṛṣṇa' in *BCR*, pp. 247 f. Speaking of Kṛṣṇa, Rāje uses the names of Śamaḷiyā, Viṭṭhal, or Trikam; all are typical of Gujarati bhakti, as is Raṇachoḍ.
44. Rāvaḷa, op. cit., introduction, pp. 13 f.
45. Rāvaḷa (ibid.) compiles a lengthy list of 4,951 *padas* collected in different MSS, pp. 15–53.
46. Ibid., pp. 140–6. *Thāḷa* compositions are in use among the Vallabhans but did not originate among them, as an author such as Narasiṃh Mahetā (15th cent.) is known to have composed a *thāḷa* (see F. Mallison, *Au Point du jour: Les Prabhātiyāṃ de Narasiṃha Mahetā*, Paris: École Française d'Extrême-Orient, 1986, p. 43).
47. Rāvaḷa, op. cit., *sākhīo*, p. 167.
48. Ibid. (*Rās paṃcādhyāyī*), pp. 11–20, and I. S. Desai, ed., *Bṛhat kāvyadohan*, vol. vii, Bombay: Gujarati Printing Press, 1911, pp. 772–6.
49. *Rādhakājī svapnāmāṃ paraṇyāṃ te viṣe*, in Rāvaḷa, op. cit., pp. 124–6, and Desai, op. cit., 7th edn., 1925, pp. 826 f.
50. Especially in his *garabī* compositions, for which he is better known (see the sample quoted in D. A. Patel and I. N. Trivedi, *Love Poems and Lyrics from Gujarati*, Ahmadabad: Gurjar Grantha Ratna Karyalaya, 1987, p. 90: *Gopīno kāgaḷ*).

51. That was apparently also the case (in the 17th cent.) with a famous Oriya devotee of Kṛṣṇa-Jagannāth of Puri who had been born a Muslim: Salabega. Some of his poems are translated in N. Mohanty, 'Salabega: Poet of Immaculate Devotion', *Indian Literature*, no. 118, New Delhi, 1987, pp. 19–32.

The Ismaili *gināns* as devotional literature

ALI S. ASANI

Almost twenty-five years ago, His Highness the Aga Khan, the imām (spiritual leader) of the Nizari Ismaili community, visited Karachi.[1] As is customary during such visits, the Aga Khan met with his followers at several gatherings, offering them advice on a variety of religious and secular issues. At one such gathering of his followers ('spiritual children' as he calls them) he said:

> Many times I have recommended to my spiritual children that they should remember *gināns*, that they should understand the meaning of these *gināns* and that they should carry these meanings in their hearts. It is most important that my spiritual children . . . hold to this tradition which is so special, so unique, and so important . . .[2]

Four years earlier, while addressing his community in East Pakistan, now Bangladesh, the Aga Khan had, in fact, designated the *gināns* a 'wonderful tradition'. The *gināns* were, according to him, a distinctive religious and literary heritage which the community should strive hard to preserve for future generations.[3]

The *gināns* the Aga Khan refers to are the over 800 hymnlike poems that his followers, popularly known in the subcontinent as 'Khojas' or 'Aga Khanis', recite almost daily during their prayer meetings. Composed in the various Indic languages and dialects of Gujarat, Sind, and Panjab, these *gināns* may vary in length from four to over 1,000 verses. On account of their linguistic and cultural background, they represent an important regional and ethnic element in a broader corpus of Ismaili devotional literature that includes works in Arabic, Persian, and even Burushaski, a language of the northern areas of Pakistan. The subcontinent's Nizari Ismailis employ the term *ginān*, meaning contemplative or meditative knowledge or simply knowledge,[4] to designate and distinguish a special type of poetic composition: specifically, a composition whose authorship is attributed to Ismaili *pīrs* or preacher-saints. These *pīrs*, the community's traditions assert, came to the Indian subcontinent from Iran as early as the thirteenth century. Unfortunately, as is the case with many of the poet-saints (Sants and Ṣūfīs) of medieval India, we possess remarkably little accurate historical information about these reputed authors of the *gināns* and their activities.[5] What we do have, however, are hagiographic and legendary accounts, some of which are incorporated in the *ginān*s themselves. According to these accounts, the *pīrs* were entrusted by the Ismaili imāms, then residing in Iran, with the responsibility of propagating and sustaining the Ismaili form of Islam within the subcontinent. Their target population, largely consisting of the lower and illiterate classes of rural Gujarat, Sind, and Panjab, seems to have been heavily influenced by the Vaiṣṇava Hindu tradition.[6]

In order to maximize their impact on this Hindu population, the Iranian Ismaili *pīrs*, like several of their Ṣūfī contemporaries, adopted an approach that stressed indigenization of Islam to the local Indic linguistic and cultural milieu.[7] As the Russian orientalist Wladimir Ivanow puts it, they avoided conservatism of forms by separating 'the meaning and spirit of Islam from its hard Arabic shell'.[8] In other words, they presented Islam, in its Nizari Ismaili form, in languages, terms, and concepts that were familiar to their Indic audience. For example, in an environment that was filled with cults and sects, several *pīrs* used an indigenous Sanskritic term *panth* – path, doctrine, sect – to refer to the religion they were preaching. In fact, their preferred term for Ismaili Islam was *satpanth*, the true or correct path, a term that echoes the quranic concept of *ṣirāṭ al-mustaqīm*, the right or straight path. More significantly, in their concern to facilitate a smooth transition and a continuum from one religion to another, the *pīrs* portrayed Nizari Ismaili Islam as the completion or culmination of the Hindu tradition.[9] Typically, in *ginān*s, such as the 'classic' *Dasa avatāra*, the *pīrs*, many of whom even took on local Indian names, represented themselves as guides who knew the whereabouts of the awaited tenth Kalki avatāra of Viṣṇu. Through a process of mythopoesis, they created an ostensible correspondence between this Vaiṣṇava Hindu concept and the Ismaili concept of the imām. The tenth avatār of Viṣṇu, renamed in the tradition as Nakalaṅkī 'the stainless one', was identified with ʿAlī, the first Shii imām. Other basic Hindu deities were redirected to Islamic personalities: Brahmā, for example, was identified with the Prophet Muḥammad, while the Prophet's daughter, Fāṭima was identified with Śakti and Sarasvatī.[10]

What is particularly striking about the *pīrs*' manner of acculturating Islam to the Hindu tradition is that it fostered amongst their converts a complex religious identity, an identity that allowed them to regard themselves simultaneously as 'true Hindus' and 'true Muslims'.[11] On the other hand, the society that surrounded them, as it became entangled with issues of religious identity, perceived these Ismaili converts as inhabiting a kind of a half-way house between Islam and Hinduism. Naturally, in the community's later history, these differing perceptions gave rise to intriguing issues concerning the definition of religious identity, issues that we have considered elsewhere.[12] Here we simply note that it is precisely during their proselytizing activities that the *pīrs* are believed to have first composed the several hundred poems known as *ginān*s. In keeping with the emphasis on indigenization, the *ginān*s not only employed indigenous Indic languages – tradition claims, rather exaggeratedly, the use of thirty-six languages – and indigenous poetic forms and metres, but also indigenous musical modes, for like most medieval Indian vernacular poetry the *ginān*s were meant to be recited or sung. Not surprisingly, in their literary forms, symbols, and manner of recitation, the *ginān*s are reminiscent, on the one hand, of the *padas* and *bhajans* of the north Indian bhakti tradition and, on the other, of Ṣūfī poetry in the Indic vernaculars. Through the poetic medium of the *ginān*s, the *pīrs* provided guidance on a variety of doctrinal, ethical, and mystical themes for the edification of those embarking on the *satpanth*.[13]

The *ginān*s and their role in Ismaili religious life

The *ginān*s are the focus of intense veneration within the community. For those who revere them, they are the embodiment of the faith; the substantiation of the truth that the *pīrs* conveyed. The intention here, therefore, is to focus on the 'relational, contextual, or functional quality' of ginānic literature.[14] By this we mean the role the *ginān*s have played within the context of the community's religious life and in individual piety, that is, the interaction between these texts and the people who memorize them, recite them, and listen to them.

Though initially associated with the process of conversion, today, several centuries later, the *ginān*s dominate the community's religious life not only in the subcontinent but also in other parts of the world to which Ismailis of Indo-Pakistani origin have immigrated, such as East Africa, Europe, North America, and Australia. According to a 1980 Canadian Ismaili monograph entitled 'Observations and Comments on our Modern Ginanic Literature', through the *ginān*s, members of the community have been able to inspire their lives by learning about key concepts of their faith. The *ginān*s have provided the community with an understanding of the 'true meaning' of the Qur'ān as well as the true meaning of religion.[15] During a recent lecture, an *al-wā'iẓ̈* (preacher), prominent in the Ismaili community of Pakistan, observed that the *ginān* literature forms 'an unbounded and immeasurable sea of knowledge, a unique storehouse of wisdom and guidelines for everyday life'.[16] Another publication, espousing a view that not all Ismailis would subscribe to, goes so far as to declare the *ginān* literature 'a divine literary corpus in its own right, with all the honors and dignity that pertains to any divine literature'.[17]

These comments suggest that the *ginān*s have attained a scriptural status within the community – a position, as we shall presently see, that has provoked questions, both within and outside the community, about their relationship *vis-à-vis* the Qur'ān, the primary scripture of Islam. Ivanow, the Russian orientalist, noting 'the strange fascination, the majestic pathos and beauty' of the *ginān*s as they are recited, observes that their 'mystical appeal [for the Nizari Ismailis] equals, if not exceeds that exercised by the Coran on Arabic speaking peoples'.[18] Indeed, the care and reverence with which members of the community physically handle books containing *ginān* texts resembles the care and reverence shown by all Muslims, Ismailis included, towards physical copies of the Qur'ān. It is common to see older members of the community, in particular, lightly kiss a *ginān* book or touch it to their forehead out of respect before and after they recite from it. Great care is taken to avoid mutilating pages containing *ginān* texts, be they in manuscript or print form. In conservative circles, placing a *ginān* book on the ground is considered highly disrespectful.

The reverence shown to the *ginān* as written word should not, however, mislead us. Though they have been embodied in a written textual form, the *gināns* are primarily an oral scripture.[19] Their greatest impact is through the ear. They are intended to be chanted and recited aloud according to prescribed *rāgas* and folk tunes. Singing *gināns*, alongside the performance of ritual prayers, is one of the mainstays of the worship service in the mornings and evenings when the community congregates in the *jamā'at khānah* for prayers. Memorization of at least a few *gināns* and their tunes constitutes an essential part of the religious education of Khoja Ismaili children. In fact, like much Indian devotional poetry, the *gināns*, through much of their history, were transmitted orally and only committed to writing rather late.[20] As I have shown elsewhere, even after being recorded in Khojkī, the community's special script, oral knowledge of *ginān* texts was still necessary to ensure correct reading of an ambiguous alphabet.[21] Nowadays, the oral and memorized text continues to be functionally more important than the written text which appears to be more of an *aide-mémoire* for the man or woman who leads the congregation in recitation. The members in the congregation usually accompany the lead singer by recalling from memory the text of individual stanzas as they are being sung. Those who are unfamiliar with the text of a particular composition can usually participate in the singing of the refrain, a common structural element in most *gināns*. Illustrative of the significance and effect of the oral/aural dimension of *ginān* recitation are the following comments by the Pakistani writer and poet G. Allana, as he reminisces about a childhood experience:

> my mother Sharfibai start[s] singing a ginan. Her voice was unmatched. Everybody listened to her bewitching voice singing a ginan. No other person, as is normally customary, dare join his or her voice with hers to sing in chorus, whether she sang a stanza of a ginan or the refrain of the ginan. The fragrance of that spiritual atmosphere still lingers in my mind. One seemed to live and be so near to the presence of the Omnipotent and the Omniscient One. The weight of life's burdens dissolved.[22]

The singing in unison of the entire congregation, which on Fridays and special religious holidays may number, in some areas, up to one thousand or more, can also be very powerful in its emotional and sensual impact. Even those who may not fully understand the meanings and significance of the words they sing may experience an emotion difficult to describe but which sometimes physically manifests itself through moist eyes or tears. An oft-repeated story within the community concerns the penitence and redemption of Ismail Ganji, a not exactly pious Ismaili of Junagadh, induced one evening while he was sitting in the *jamā'at khānah* listening to the recitation of a *ginān* stanza.

He heard the stanza very attentively and tears poured through his eyes. Immediately on conclusion of the Ginan recitation, this faithful [one] got up, went to the honorable Mukhi [a religious official], Rai Rahmatullahbhai, and sought forgiveness of all his sins. This was the moment signifying the day he started his life anew.[23]

Subsequently, he became the chief minister to the nawab of Junagadh. According to one community publication, Ismail Ganji even had the unique honour, at his death, of receiving the title of *pīr* from the imām on account of his high spiritual development.[24] The *ginān* texts themselves reflect an awareness of their transformative effect on the individual. A verse from a commonly recited Gujarati *ginān* attributed to the Pir Ṣadr ad-Dīn (*c.* 1350–1400) instructs the faithful: *ginān bolore nīt nure bhareā; evo haiḍe tamāre harakh na māejī* (recite *gināns* which are filled with light; boundless will be the happiness in your heart).[25] The use of the symbol of light appropriately points to the role of the *gināns* in bringing about an inner transformation through enlightenment and the banishing of the darkness of ignorance.

While the recitation of one or more *gināns* constitutes an important ritual in itself, individual *ginān* verses or sometimes entire *gināns* are also an integral part of other rituals of worship. Consequently, manuscripts, lithographs, or books containing *gināns* frequently classify and arrange them according to ritual usage. We may cite a few noteworthy examples. Verses concerning the importance of prayer and the auspiciousness of the sunset as a time for prayer are recited in almost every *jamā'at khānah* before the evening ritual prayer.[26] Similarly, before the early morning meditation, a selection of verses on aspects of the mystical experience are recited in order to evoke the appropriate mental and spiritual disposition within the mediators. Verses from *gināns* belonging to the supplicatory genre of the *veñtī* are often sung at the beginning of the *giriyāzārī tasbīḥ*, a special prayer in which the congregation seeks the bestowal of spiritual and material blessings. An entire set of *gināns* has been identified as a genre to be sung during the ritual called the *ghaṭpāṭ*.[27] Another genre – the *prabhātiyā* – is intended specifically for the early morning ceremonies. Some *gināns* are heard only on certain religious festivals and holidays: the *ginān sāt swargnā kāīṃ khuliyā ćhe dwār* (the doors of the seven heavens have swung open) on the birthday of Prophet Muḥammad; *dhan dhan ājno dahaḍo* (happy and blessed is this day) on the birthday of the imām; and *navaroznā din sohāmaṇā* (on this auspicious day of Navrūz) at the beginning of the Persian New Year. Finally, on a night of special spiritual significance such as *Layltul-Qadr* on which the Qur'ān was first revealed, appropriate *ginān* verses alternate with the names of God and other religious formulas in an entrancing meditative chant called the *zikr* (Arabic *dhikr*).

Beyond their role in worship, the *gināns* permeate in many ways communal and individual life. At a communal level, the commencement of any function or meeting, be it religious or secular, is marked by a short Qur'ān recitation followed by one from the *gināns*. The intent of such recitations is to bestow auspiciousness on the occasion. During sermons, religious discussions, and in religious education materials *ginān* verses are often cited as proof-texts. Recently, some members of the community have even interpreted certain *gināns* as predicting modern scientific developments such as synthetic foods, robots, atomic bombs, cardiac resuscitation, or as documenting scientific facts related to the human body and the world of nature.[28] Occasionally, for both entertainment and religious edification, a special concert or *ginān mehfil/mushā'iro* takes place during which professional and amateur singers sing *gināns* with musical accompaniment. In deference to the reluctance among many Muslims to permit the use of musical instruments in explicitly religious contexts, such concerts are not usually held within the premises of *jamā'at khānahs*. Again, outside the context of formal worship or liturgy, community institutions responsible for religious education may sponsor *ginān* competitions in which participants are judged on their ability to sing and properly enunciate *ginān* texts. Such competitions are a popular method among religious educators to encourage the learning of *gināns* among young students and adults. At a personal and family level, too, *gināns* are used in many different contexts: individual verses can be quoted as proverbs; verses can be recited in homes to bring *barakah*, spiritual and material blessing; housewives, in a usage that stresses the links between the *gināns* and the folk tradition, often recite them while working or as lullabies; audio cassettes with *gināns* sung by 'star' singers or recordings of *ginān mehfils* can be found in many an Ismaili home and even car!

The scriptural status of the *gināns*

That the *gināns*, a literary corpus originating within a folk tradition, should have attained a scriptural role is by no means unprecedented in the history of north Indian vernacular literatures. We can discern, in medieval Indian literature, similar developments in poetry attributed to sages or holy persons. Two prominent examples come to mind: the *Ādi Granth*, the scripture of the Sikhs, is an anthology of religious poetry of devotional saints and preceptors (Nāmdev, Kabīr, Ravidās, and the Sikh Gurus); and the *Dādū-bānī*, the scripture that the Dādūpanthīs revere as the collection of their founder's sacred poetic utterances.[29] What is unusual about the *gināns'* scriptural status is the implication this has for the status of the Qur'ān within the Khoja

Ismaili community. As the principal scripture of Islam, the Qur'ān is an important hallmark of Islamic identity – a fact that the *gināns* themselves acknowledge by recognizing it as the scripture (*veda*) of the present age. Nevertheless, in their function and importance within the community, the *gināns* seem to eclipse the Qur'ān. Naturally, to many non-Ismaili Muslims and scholars on the religious life of the Khoja Ismailis the community's attitude to the Qur'ān remains unclear, provoking questions concerning the extent to which the Khoja Ismailis could be called Muslims. For example, one scholar, Syed Mujtaba Ali, writes:

The present writer has not been able to grasp the attitude taken by the Khojahs towards the Koran and Hadith (Shii and Sunni). It seems that they consider them to be holy scriptures but do not regard studying them as necessary. By the more up to date sectarians the Koran, at least, is held in some respect as can be seen from the articles regularly published in the Ismaili journals which use the Koran for supporting their contentions.[30]

The need to clarify the ambiguous relationship between the Qur'ān and the *gināns* became urgent in the late nineteenth century. From this time onwards, on account of a complex interaction of political and historical factors, questions of religious identity became crucial for Ismaili and other Muslim communities in the subcontinent who practised forms of Islam which were unusual by the standards of Islamic orthodoxy and orthopraxy. Furthermore, in an atmosphere in which lines between Hindu and Islamic groups were being firmly delineated, literatures in indigenous Indic languages, particularly those that displayed characteristics considered to be syncretistic, stood in danger of being regarded with suspicion and branded as non-Islamic.[31] These developments have impacted and will continue to impact the *ginān* literature.

The response of the Nizari Ismaili community to the issue of the relation between the *ginān* literature and the Qur'ān is a complex one. It can be summarized as follows: first, the literature is perceived within the community as a kind of commentary on the Qur'ān. This was the clarification given by Aga Khan III, the community's forty-eighth imām, in his pronouncements (*farmāns*) giving guidance on this issue:

In the *gināns* which Pir Sadardin has composed for you, he has conveyed and explained the gist of the Qur'ān in the language of Hindustan.[32]

The *gināns* composed and presented before you by Pir Sadardin are from commentaries of the Qur'ān.[33]

If there were amongst you individuals who had read the Qur'ān and were well-acquainted with the *gināns*, I would be able to point out to you each verse of the *gināns* from the Qur'ān.[34]

According to this interpretation, the *gināns* serve as secondary texts generated in the vernacular for the transmission of the teachings of a primary scripture – the Qur'ān – to non-Arabic speaking peoples. In the process, these secondary texts have acquired scriptural qualities. Not surprisingly, contemporary religious education material in the community often matches Qur'ān verses with *ginān* ones to demonstrate that the *pīrs* have successfully delivered the message and gist of the Qur'ān in the language and idiom of the *gināns*.[35] A recent monograph on this issue states:

We [Nizari Ismailis] should be proud to possess such a literary divine corpus [the *gināns*] and proclaim that we are the true followers of the Holy Quran and all the parables, stories, metaphors, allegories which appear in our Holy Ginans are nothing but the true message of the religion of Islam.[36]

The same monograph, reflecting the traditional preoccupation with the esoteric (*bāṭin*) in Ismaili thought, also explains:

the *ginans* serve to penetrate to the inner (*batin*) signification of the Quran rather than the external (*zahir*) aspects.[37]

In this manner, while affirming the primacy of the Qur'ān in its theology, the community has been able to preserve a significant role for the *gināns*. Viewed within the context of Islamic religious literature, the community's perception of the *gināns* as playing a mediating role is not without its parallels. In parts of the Islamic world influenced by Persian culture, Mawlānā Jalāl ad-Dīn Rūmī's *Mathnawī*, popularly called the 'Qur'ān in Persian', is regarded as a vast esoteric commentary on the Qur'ān, many of its verses being interpreted as translations of Qur'ān verses into Persian poetry. Similar interpretations exist about the poetic masterpiece so influential among Sindhi-speakers – Shāh 'Abdu'l Laṭīf's *Risālo*, the 'sacred book for Sindhis, admired and memorized by Muslims and Hindus equally'.[38]

In a second development, terms and idioms within the *gināns* that could be perceived as 'Hinduistic', and hence likely to provoke questions regarding their identity as an Islamic literature,[39] have been replaced by Perso-Arabic ones considered to be more in consonance with the greater Islamic tradition. In recent editions of *ginān* texts published by community institutions, for example, the word 'Harī' is replaced by 'Alī' and so on. Such changes, while generally accepted within the community, have also generated much debate on the appropriateness of interfering with sacred texts which presumably have been handed down intact through the centuries. *Ginās* in which the *pīrs* elucidate Ismaili concepts through reformulations of Hindu mythology are sung less frequently. The *Dasa-avatāra*, which used to be so central in the tradition, is hardly ever recited in the *jamā'at khānah* today.[40] In fact the younger generations are, generally, not even aware of the existence of this work. The definition of what constitutes a Hindu element as opposed to an Islamic one has been another focus of controversy, especially when terms from Indic languages with no specific theological connection to the Hindu tradition have been replaced by Perso-Arabic ones. 'Do we think', says one angry tract on this controversial subject, 'that Islam can be preached and understood only through the medium of Arabic and Persian languages and the same teaching presented in any other [Indic] language should be regarded as a Hindu element?'[41]

Such questioning and debate, symptomatic of tensions between localized, ethnic, or vernacular expressions of Islam and pan-Islamic forces, reveals the strength of the Nizari Ismaili community's attachment to the *ginãns*. While their functions may change and evolve over time, they will nevertheless remain a part of the communal religious life. They provide us with a particularly vivid and powerful reminder of the significant, and unfortunately underestimated, role played by Indic vernacular literatures in the development of Indo-Muslim civilization.

NOTES

1. As Shii (*shīʿī*) Muslims, the Nizari Ismailis believe that, after the death of the Prophet of Islam, the leadership and guidance of the Muslim *ummah* (community) is the prerogative of his direct descendants. They regard Shāh Karīm Al-Ḥusaynī, currently Aga Khan IV, to be the 49th in an unbroken chain of imāms or leaders directly descended from the Prophet's daughter Fāṭima and son-in-law ʿAlī, b. Abī Ṭālib. The hereditary title Aga Khan was first bestowed in 1817 by the Qajar Shah of Iran on the 46th Ismaili imām, Ḥasan ʿAlī Shāh (d. 1881).
2. Speech made at Karachi, 16 Dec. 1964, in *Farman Mubarak Pakistan Visit 1964*, pt. 1, repr. edn., Mombasa, n.d., p. 40.
3. Speech made at Dacca on 17 Oct. 1960. As quoted in *Wonderful Tradition Transliteration of Holy* Ginans, pts. 1 and 2, comp. Al-waiz Sultanali Mohamed, Kisumu, Kenya, 1966, p. [1].
4. The term is generally held to be from the Sanskrit *jñāna*. An alternative, though highly unlikely, derivation from the Arabic *ǵanna* (to sing) is mentioned by G. Khakee, 'The Dasa Avatāra of the Satpanthi Ismailis and the Imam Shahis of Indo-Pakistan', Ph.D. thesis, Harvard University, 1972, p. 3.
5. For a discussion of the 'historicity' of these *pīrs* and the use of *ginãns* as sources of information concerning the arrival and establishment of Nizari Ismailism in the subcontinent, see A. Nanji, *The Nizārī Ismāʿīlī Tradition in the Indo-Pakistan Subcontinent*, Delmar, NY, 1978, pp. 33–96.
6. There is also evidence, some of it from the *ginān* literature, suggesting the strong presence, in this region, of a cult devoted to the Hindu goddess Śakti. See R. E. Enthoven, *Tribes and Castes of Bombay*, Bombay, 1922, vol. ii, p. 227, and W. Ivanow, 'Satpanth', in *Collectanea*, vol. i, Leiden, 1948, pp. 36–9.
7. For brief summary descriptions of the indigenization of Sufism to the Indian cultural environment, see A. S. Asani, 'Sufi Poetry in the Folk Tradition of Indo-Pakistan', *Religion and Literature*, 20, pp. 81–94; A. Schimmel, 'Reflections on Popular Muslim Poetry', *Contributions to Asian Studies*, 17, pp. 17–26; and R.

Eaton, 'Sufi Folk Literature and the Expansion of Islam', *History of Religions*, 14, 2, pp. 115–27.

8. Ivanow, op. cit., p. 21.
9. The *pīrs*' manner of representing the relationship between Islam and the Hindu tradition echoes the traditional Muslim conception of Islam as the culmination of the Judaeo-Christian religion. The Ismaili *pīrs* were by no means unique in expressing such a formulation. For parallel developments in Bengali Islam, see A. Roy, *The Islamic Syncretistic Tradition in Bengal*, Princeton, NJ, 1984, pp. 87–110.
10. Nanji, op. cit., pp. 110–20, discusses the mythopoeic character of the *ginān* literature and the reformulation, within a Hindu framework, of Ismaili concepts such as that of the imamate. His definition of mythopoesis – a re-creation that reflects 'a critique of the existing social norms and points to a futuristic order' – is based on that by Harry Slochower, *Mythopoesis*, Detroit, 1970.
11. Azim Nanji suggests that this ambiguous identity may, in fact, have been a form of *taqīya*, the pious dissimulation practised by Shii groups to avoid persecution. See his article '*Sharī'at* and *Ḥaqīqat*: Continuity and Synthesis in the Nizārī Ismā'īlī Muslim Tradition', in K. P. Ewing, ed., *Sharī'at and Ambiguity in South Asian Islam*, Berkeley and Los Angeles, 1988, p. 69.
12. A. S. Asani, 'The Khojahs of Indo-Pakistan: The Quest for an Islamic Identity', *Journal of the Institute of Muslim Minority Affairs*, 8, 1, pp. 31–41.
13. For a summary of the main themes in *ginān* literature, see my article '*Ginān*' in M. Eliade, ed., *Encyclopaedia of Religion*, New York, 1987.
14. I borrow this term from William A. Graham's study of sacred texts *Beyond the Written Word: Oral Aspects of Scripture in the History of Religion*, Cambridge and New York, 1987.
15. His Highness the Aga Khan Shia Imami Ismailia Association for Canada, 'Observations and Comments on our Modern Ginanic Literature', Paper presented at the Ismailia Association International Review meeting, Nairobi, 1980, p. 26.
16. 'Ismaili Tariqah Board: Two Special Evenings', *Ismaili Mirror*, Aug. 1987, p. 33.
17. His Highness the Aga Khan Shia Imami Ismailia Association for Canada, 'A Suggestive Guide to the "Islamic" Interpretation and Refutation of the "Hindu" Elements in our Holy *Ginans*', Paper presented at the Ismailia Associations International Conference, Nairobi, 1979, p. 11.
18. W. Ivanow, 'The Sect of Imam Shah in Gujarat', *JBRAS* 12, 1936, p. 68.
19. The *ginān*s provide a particularly strong case for scriptural texts functioning as oral phenomena. The significance of the oral–aural dimensions of written scripture for the history of religions has been most ably explored by William Graham in his book *Beyond the Written Word* and his article 'Scripture', in Eliade, ed., *Encyclopaedia of Religion*.
20. The earliest extant *ginān* MS dates to 1736, though there is considerable evidence that the tradition of writing down *ginān* texts goes back much earlier. See Nanji, *The Nizārī Ismā'īlī Tradition*, pp. 9–11, and Z. Noorally, 'Catalogue of Khojki Manuscripts in the Collection of the Ismailia Association for Pakistan', MS, Karachi, 1971, MS 25.
21. A. S. Asani, 'The Khojkī Script: A Legacy of Ismaili Islam in the Indo-Pakistan Subcontinent', *JAOS* 107, 3, pp. 439–49.

22. G. Allana, *Ginans of Ismaili Pirs*, Karachi, 1984, vol. i, p. 2.
23. *The Great Ismaili Heroes*, Karachi, 1973, pp. 98–9. The verse that was effective in bringing about Ismail Ganji's 'conversion' is reputed to be one from the Gujarati *ginān*, attributed to Pir Ṣadr ad-dīn (*c*. 1350–1400): *sheṭh kahe tame sāṁbhaḍo vāṇotar*.
24. Ibid., p. 99. Whether Ismail Ganji was in actual fact given this title seems to be a matter of controversy; several Ismailis vigorously assert that Ismail Ganji did not receive this title, which is usually reserved for members of the imām's immediate family.
25. *Collection of Ginūns Composed by the Great Ismaili Saint Pir Sadruddin* (*mahān īsmāīlī sant pīr sadaradīn raćit gīnānono saṃgrah*), Bombay, 1969, p. 61 (my translation).
26. Especially popular for this purpose are several verses from a long *ginān* entitled *Anant Akhāḍo*. Attributed to the late 15th-century *pīr* Ḥasan Kabīr ad-Dīn, this *ginān* has been described as a sort of 'Pilgrim's Progress' in a Ṣūfī vein (Nanji, *The Nizārī Ismā'īlī Tradition*, p. 143).
27. For a description and analysis of the *ghaṭpāṭ* ritual, see Nanji, *The Nizārī Ismā'īlī Tradition*, p. 175 n. 2, and '*Sharī'at* and *Ḥaqīqat*', pp. 65–7.
28. To cite one example of this trend: a lecture at a communal function in Toronto on 29 Jan. 1982 was entitled '*Ginans*: Prophesies and Science in *Ginans*'. The use of scriptures as 'scientific proof-texts' is a common phenomenon in the history of religion.
29. Another poetic anthology revered among the Dādūpanthīs is the *Pañc-bānī*, which contains the utterances of five poet-saints especially honoured in the Dādūpanth: Dādū, Kabīr, Nāmdev, Raidās, and Haridās. See W. G. Orr, *A Sixteenth Century Indian Mystic*, London, 1947, p. 69.
30. Syed Mujtaba Ali, *The Origin of the Khojahs and their Religious Life Today*, Bonn, 1936, p. 59.
31. For a discussion of the attacks of 19th-century reformist–revivalist movements on the 'syncretistic' *pūthi* literature of rural Bengali Muslims, see Rafiuddin Ahmed, *The Bengal Muslims 1871–1906: A Quest for Identity*, Delhi, 1981, pp. 39–105, and a paper by the same author, 'Conflict and Contradictions in Bengali Islam: Problems of Change and Adjustment', in Ewing, ed., *Sharī'at and Ambiguity*, pp. 121–34.
32. Quoted in *Ginãne Śarīf: Īsmāīlī pīroe āpel pāk dīnnī rośnī*, Karachi, 1966, p. [2] (original in Gujarati; my translation).
33. *Bahare rahemat yāne rahematno darīyo*, comp. Hāsham Boghā Māsṭar, Bombay, 1911, p. 17 (Khojki text in Gujarati; my translation).
34. Ibid., p. 13.
35. Illustrative of this comparative tendency is a paper, 'Our Holy *Ginans* (Devotional Literature) and the Holy Quran', *Holy Quran and the Ismaili Faith*, Nairobi, n.d., pp. 31–8. This paper compares *ginān* verses with Qur'ān ones on a variety of religious concepts: *tawḥīd* (unity of God), remembrance of God, repentance, etc.
36. 'A Suggestive Guide to the "Islamic" Interpretation', p. 32.
37. Ibid., p. 10.
38. A. Schimmel, *Sindhi Literature*, ed. J. Gonda, A History of Indian Literature, vol. viii, pt. 2, Wiesbaden, 1974, p. 14.

39. Aziz Ahmad, for example, judges the 'literary personality' of the *gināns* to be 'un-Islamic' (*An Intellectual History of Islam in India*, Edinburgh, 1969, p. 126).
40. Writing in the early years of this century, Menant observes: 'Le *Desavatar* est le livre le plus sacré de la littérature religieuse des Khodjas: on en récite des passages au lit de mort des fidèles; au *Jamat Khana* quand on commence la lecture du dixième chapitre la congrégation se lève et reste debout en s'inclinant chaque fois que le nom d'Ali est prononcé,' 'Les Khodjas du Guzarate', *Revue du Monde Musulman*, 12, 10, p. 224.
41. 'Observations and Comments on our Modern Ginanic Literature', p. 30.

Literary and religious traditions in Maharashtra

A grammar of bhakti: *Pañcavārtika*

V. D. KULKARNI

Preamble

The study is based on ten manuscripts of *Pañcavārtika (PV)* by Paṇḍit Bhīṣmācārya I (AD 1338) and the commentary on it. The oldest available dated manuscript of *PV* is of *śaka* 1506 (AD 1584).[1] The oldest manuscript of the commentary is some decades earlier than that date, i.e. *śaka* 1452 (AD 1530). *PV* is supposed to be the first grammar of the Marathi language.[2] I am of the opinion that it is not a grammar of the Marathi language as such, but rather a semantic analysis, composed in a spirit of devotion (bhakti) with the aim of understanding the true and real meanings of the *sūtras* uttered by Śrī Sarvajña Cakradhara, the Supreme God of the Mahānubhāva sect. *PV* and its commentary are set up on Mīmāṃsā lines and according to the principles of Indian semantics. I have not used the word 'grammar' here in its ordinary sense. *PV* is not a structural study of language, but a study of the structural aspect of words and an exposition of meaning aimed at proper understanding of the utterances on which the entire philosophy of the Mahānubhāva cult is based. It represents an effort to provide correct guide-lines for the interpretation of Mahānubhāva thought.

Introductory

The Supreme God, Śrī Sarvajña Cakradhara, spoke these *sūtras* from time to time to his disciples and followers. They are doctrinal utterances and are regarded as *śruti*: the very Veda of the sect.[3] Cakradhara himself explained how to derive the proper and real meaning of these *sūtras* in Marathi in order to understand his philosophical thought. He narrated the *sūtras* to Mahīṃbhaṭa, who disclosed them to Paṇḍit Ānerājabāsa. Ānerājabāsa rendered illustrative examples into Sanskrit in *Lakṣaṇaratnākara* (*LR*). The Mahānubhāvas believe that the utterances from the mouth of their Supreme God, Śrī Sarvajña Cakradhara, are *śruti*, revelation; as is illustrated in Nāgadevācārya's statement that the analytical meaning of *śruti* is only to be grasped from *śruti* itself.[4]

Paṇḍit Kesobāsa (AD 1288) compiled and classified the *sūtras* and parables of Śrī Sarvajña Cakradhara.[5] After the completion of the writings of *Ratnamāla-stotra* in Sanskrit, Nāgadevācārya described this work as 'the worship of God with verbal flowers'.[6] Ānerājabāsa, who was a contemporary of Kesobāsa, analysed and explained thirty-two semantic categories in *LR*.[7] Rāmeśvarabāsa, Nāganāthabāsa, Siddhānte Haribāsa, Gurjara Śivabāsa, Taḷegāoṅkar Dattobāsa, Bhīṣmācārya, Sāraṅgdhara Pujadekara and Viśvanātha Bīdakara are the foremost commentators in the Mahānubhāva sect. *Ācārabhāṣya, Vicārabhāṣya, Lakṣaṇabhāṣya, Dṛṣṭāntasthaḷa, Hetusthaḷa, Lāpikā, Lāpanikā, Prakaraṇavaśa*, etc. are commentaries based on the *Sūtrapāṭha* and on the *Dṛṣṭāntapāṭha*, the compilation of *sūtras* and parables attributed to Śrī Cakradhara. There are a few other commentators who discussed *caupadīs* of Dāmodar Paṇḍit (AD 1287). I have discussed these at length in my earlier work.[8] In the same way, *PV* is also a commentary on the *sūtras* and not a grammar of Marathi. Ostensibly a grammatical study of the *sūtras*, it is in fact an interpretative study of their meaning composed for the use of scholars of the sect.

Pañcavārtika

PV is a composition of five expository chapters (*vārtika*), namely:

1. characteristic features of the *sūtras* (*sūtra-lakṣaṇa*);
2. essential nature of the *sūtras* (*sūtra-prakṛti*);
3. case in the *sūtras* (*sūtra-kāraka*);
4. features of exposition of the *sūtras* (*sūtra-vyākhyāna*);
5. essential form of the *sūtras* (*sūtra-svarūpa-lakṣaṇa*).

The first chapter deals with number, sentence, context, and composite utterance (*mahāvākya*). It discusses gender, noun, pronoun, assimilation (*sandhi*), suffixes and prefixes, verbs, compounds, etc. The different types of sentence are classified. For all this material the examples provided are from the *sūtras* only. The second chapter defining the essential nature of the *sūtras* distinguishes ten categories. The third chapter elaborately discusses case (*kāraka*) and the relationship of a noun or pronoun with the verb or other words in its sentence, emphasising the dependence of true or real meaning on these. Along with the importance of case it stresses a threefold system of analysis of meaning, namely, (1) lexicological (*śabdārthākhya*); (2) traditional or sectarian (*sampradāyārthākhya*); (3) metaphysical (*rahasyārthākhya*). If one attains the true meaning of the *sūtras* with the help of this threefold system and with the knowledge of grammar, the Supreme God as revealed in disguise in the *sūtras* will never be distressed. The fourth chapter of *PV* presents six features, namely, analyses of: (1) word division (*praccheda*); (2) sense of words (*padārthokti*); (3) compound sentences, to determine their meaning (*vigraha*); (4) syntax (*vākya-yojanā*); (5) hidden meaning (*ākṣepa*); (6) inner content (*samādhāna*). This classification agrees with that found in

LR. The fifth chapter gives an account of all thirty-two categories of meaning as laid down by Paṇḍit Ānerājabāsa in *LR*. Paṇḍit Bhīṣmācārya concludes the work by observing that with the help of *PV* in this way the complete teachings of Śrī Sarvajña Cakradhara can be understood in proper perspective; that this is a religious treatise in grammatical garb; that if it is not studied as such God will be grieved; and that *PV* is to be studied under oral instruction of a spiritual guide. Then only it will be perfect (*sampūrṇatva hoe*).[9]

The commentary

The commentator of *PV* stresses need for the study of *PV*, stating that the complete teachings of Śrī Cakradhara on Parameśvara will thereby be made clear:

heṁ paṃcavārtika abhyāsije tari sakaḷahī parameśvaraśāstra prakāśe.[10]

He asserts the same at the beginning and end of his commentary on each chapter.

1. It is stated that the Supreme God Śrī Sarvajña Cakradhara gave this religious teaching (*brahmavidyā*) in twelve chapters to Bhaṭobāsa, i.e. Nāgadevācārya, his first disciple.[11] The characteristics of these *sūtras* were elaborated by Kavīśvara Mahānubhāva (perhaps Bhāskara-bhaṭṭa Borīkara, AD 1288) in *Ācārasthaḷa*, 'Commentary on Practice'. But that was very obscure to the followers. So at the very beginning of the commentary the characteristic features of the *sūtras* are explained; for even though one realises the outward sense of the *sūtras* one cannot grasp their essence.[12]

2. Similarly, without the knowledge of case (*kāraka*) no one attains to the decisive and true meaning of the *sūtras*. So Paṇḍit Ānerājabāsa in his *LR* refers along with the thirty-two categories of meaning to the principle of judgement (*nirṇaya*) in determining meaning. This is analysed (as in *PV*) as threefold, namely, (1) lexicological; (2) traditional or sectarian; (3) metaphysical.

'Lexicological' judgement applies in the sciences of grammar, prosody, music, etc. 'Sectarian' judgement is based upon audition, meditation, contemplation, and 'metaphysical' judgement comes via the mouth of a spiritual guide. Without the knowledge of case the true meaning of the *sūtras* cannot be attained, only a deceptive meaning; and Bhaṭobāsa says to Keśavadeya that to explain *PV* (in effect, the Supreme Being) otherwise would deprave the text and cause hurt to God. But with the help of grammar and through a knowledge of case, the true meaning can be determined. Otherwise the result will be as in the story of 'Wākam and Digam'.[13]

3. Similarly proceeding again via the consideration of characteristic features of the *sūtras* and of case, the commentator comes to the features of

exposition of the *sūtras*. This is now illustrated with reference to each chapter of *PV* to bring out the full sense hidden in the *sūtras*.[14]

Illustrative text from *PV*

At the very outset Paṇḍit Bhīṣmācārya describes the term *sūtra*:

अल्पाक्षरमसंदिग्धं सारवद्विश्वतोमुखं
अस्तोभमनवद्यं च सूत्रं सूत्रविदो विदुः ।[15]

Those who know *sūtras* know a *sūtra* to be short, clear, pithy, universal in scope, of free application and without fault or reproach.

Chapter I: Characteristic features of sūtras (sūtralakṣaṇa)

1. One-word *sūtra*:
   kṛpāḷu 'merciful' (*AM* 6);[16] *nirālambī* 'independent' (*AS* 3).
2. Two-word *sūtra*:
   ānanda to 'he is joy' (*N* 2); *brahma to* 'He is brahma' (*N* 3); *ātmajñāneṁ mokṣa* 'liberation is brought about by knowledge of self' (*V* 132).
3. Three-word *sūtra*:
   ānandaśabdeṁ īśvaru bolije 'the word "joy" refers to Īśvara' (*N* 1).

Likewise number, gender, assimilation, classification of verbs, suffixes, and prefixes are discussed with examples from the *Sūtrapāṭha* only.

4. Compound words (*samāsa*):
   (*a*) Copulative compound (*dvandva samāsa*):
   saccidānanda in *jīvaprapaṃcavyatirikta saccidānanda svarūpa parameśvara eku āti*
   'there is a single Parameśvara, distinct from the jīva and the world and composed of being, consciousness and joy. He possesses all power' (*M* 1).
   (*b*) Adjective compound (*bahuvrīhi samāsa*):
   anantaśakti parameśvaru sakaḷāsīhi viṣaya vyavasthā karīti 'Parameśvara, who is endowed with infinite powers, orders all things' (*V* 223).
   (*c*) Determinative compound (*tatpuruṣa samāsa*):
   (i) Case-determinative (*vibhakti tatpuruṣa*):
   jīvaprapaṃcavyatirikta . . . (as above).
   (ii) oppositional compound (*karmadhāraya samāsa*):
   nityabaddha devatā : *baddhamukta jīva* : *nityamukta parameśvaru* 'deities are eternally bound : *jīvas* are both bound and released : *Parameśvara* is eternally free' (*V* 45).
   (iii) numeral adjective (*dvigu samāsa*):
   tribhuvana.

(*d*) Adverbial compound (*avyayībhāva samāsa*):
yathocita, yathāśakti, etc.

5. Syntax:
The sentence is classified into fifteen categories, e.g.
   (*a*) four-word sentence:
   kṛtayugīṁ ātmopāsti hā dharmu 'in the Kṛta age, meditation on the self is prescribed' (*Y* 2).
   (*b*) seven-word sentence:
   nityatva : *vyāpakatva* : *sarvātmakatva*: *sarvakartṛtva* : *sarvasākṣitva* : *evamādika ananta dharma bolijeti* 'the infinite properties are eternalness, pervasiveness, being the self of all, being beyond all, being the doer of all, and so on' (*M* 9).
   (*c*) fourteen-word sentence:
   sacchabdeṁ brahma bolije : *citchabdeṁ māyā bolije* : *ānanda śabdeṁ īśvaru bolije - brahma* : *māyā* : *īśvaru* : *aisa tryaṃśu parameśvaru eku āti* 'the word "being" refers to brahma: the word "consciousness" refers to Māyā: the word "joy" refers to Īśvara: brahma : māyā : Īśvara : thus the single Parameśvara is tripartite' (*M* 5).
6. Simple sentence (*kevala vākya*):
jīvaprapaṃcavyatirikta . . . āti (as above) (*M* 1).
7. Compound sentence (*saṃbhukta vākya*):
tuṣṭalā jana tari vikho sampādila : *rusalā tari prāṇā ghataila* : *bhaṇauni ubhayatā jana saṃbandhu tyājye* 'if you please people, they will give you a sense of pleasure; if you displease them, they will threaten your life; so renounce both kinds of attachment to people'.

When three or more *sūtras* are interlinked they form a context (*prakaraṇa*) and three or more contexts combined form a composite utterance (*mahāvākya*). A complete spiritual teaching is referred to as *peṃḍhī* 'a sheaf of corn', and a grouping of these 'sheaves of corn' is termed *dhārā*. The *bhāvās* again form contexts, and ten types of context again comprise a composite utterance; these are classifiable into supra-ordinate units.

Chapter II: Essential nature of the sūtras

These *sūtras* are of varying types both in structure and in meaning, but are assembled in one chapter. Their subjects are classified into ten categories. Before giving the examples for each category, the author states the rule for it, e.g. where the explanatory part of *atideśa* is missing, the figure is called *pratiṣedha*. Bhīṣmācārya lists the categories in the following verse:

संज्ञा च परिभाषा च विधिर्नियमेव च
अतिदेशोऽपवादश्च विभाषा च निपातनं
प्रतिषेधोऽधिकारश्च सूत्रं तद्दशधां विदुः ।[17]

1. Terminology (*saṃjñā*):
   parā : *paśyanti* : *madhyamā* : *vaikhari* (*V* 15).
2. Definition (*paribhāṣā*):
   battīs lakṣa yuga : *kṛtayugīṁ lakṣabhari āyuṣye* 'the Kṛta age is 3,200,000 (years long): in the Kṛta age, (human) life span is a full 100,000 years' (*Y* 1 and 24).
3. Sacred precept (*vidhi*):
   nāmasmaraṇa kije 'recollect (*parameśvara*'s) names' (*AM* 46); *prāptārthācā tyāgu karāvā* 'give up sense pleasure which has been yours' (*AM* 108); *tumhā sayanāsanīṁ bhojanīṁ parameśvaru hoāvā kīṁ gā* 'keep Parameśvara in mind while you are lying down, sitting and eating' (*A* 30); *kaupinu dhāraṇa karāve* 'wear a loin-cloth' (*AM* 160).
4. Law (*niyama*) with four divisions:
   (*a*) Law (*niyama*):
   apamṛtyu eku āti 'some die suddenly' (*VM* 120).
   (*b*) As to nature (*vastusvarūpa niyama*):
   striyāṁcāṃ svarūpīṃ agraho eku āti 'there is an element of obstinacy in the nature of women' (*V* 20).
   (*c*) As to cause (*vastukāraṇa niyama*):
   anantaśakti parameśvara sakaḷāsihi viṣaya vyavasthā karīti 'Parameśvara, who is endowed with infinite powers, orders all things' (*V* 223).
   (*d*) As to function (*vastukārya niyama*):
   ayogyāsi yogya karīti; *yogyāsi parameśvaru jñāna deti* 'he makes the unworthy worthy; to the worthy, Parameśvara gives knowledge' (*V* 117).
5. Transferred application (*atideśa*):
   jaisā tumhā śvāna sukarācā vikho : *taisā indrādika tumacā* 'your object of sense pleasure seems to Indra and his company what that of a dog or pig seems to you' (*VM* 91).
6. Special case or exception (*apavāda*):
   jñānāpasi prema uttama 'love is much better than knowledge' (*VM* 32).
7. Specification (*vibhāṣā*):
   jīveśvara svāmī-bhṛtya saṃbandhu hā anādīcā 'the master–servant relationship between jīva and Īśvara is beginningless' (*V* 124).
8. Irregularity (*nipāta*):
   taḷicila hānitaleyā varīla paḍe utaraṇḍī gaḍabaḍī 'when the bottom is struck, the one above it falls; the stack of pots comes clattering down' (*U* 56).
9. Negation (*pratiṣedha*):
   kṣīrābdhīcā śeṣaśāyā devatā hoe pari parameśvara navhe 'Śeṣaśāyā of the sea of milk is a deity, but he is not Parameśvara' (*AV* 6).

10. Authority (*adhikāra*):
    nitya vyāpaka parameśvaru 'Parameśvara is the eternal pervader' (*VM* 2).

Chapter III

The third chapter deals with the cases, their varied suffixes, and concord (*prayoga*), and with illustrations in detail.

1. Nominative (*prathamā*):
   māyā jīvātem̐ vikhare '*māyā* changes the jīvas' (*SS* 4).
2. Accusative (*dvitīyā*):
   maga jīva prapaṃcātem̐ racitī 'then the jīva constructs a world' (*SS* 16).
3. Instrumental (*tṛtīyā*):
   ātmajñānem̐ mokṣa 'liberation is brought about by knowledge of the self' (*V* 132).
4. Dative (*caturthī*):
   jñāniyāsi mokṣa deti 'he gives the knower liberation' (*U* 63).
5. Ablative (*paṃcamī*):
   parameśvarapāsauni vidyā hoe kā vidyāvantā pāsauni hoe 'enlightenment comes from Īśvara, or it comes from one who is enlightened' (*V* 261).
6. Genitive (*ṣaṣṭhī*):
   kavāḍācām̐ deuḷī na baisāve '(they) should not sit in a temple with doors' (*A* 270).
7. Locative (*saptamī*):
   īśvarīm̐ sampūrṇā śakti : jīvīm̐ aṃśatā śakti 'in Īśvara there is complete śakti : in the jīva there is partial śakti' (*U* 11).

Chapter IV: features of exposition of the sūtras

The fourth chapter of *PV* deals with principles of exposition, mainly as bearing on analysis of sentence structure to extract correct meanings. It is stated that there are six principles:

पदच्छेदः पदार्थोक्तिर्विग्रहो वाक्ययोजना
आक्षेपश्च समाधानं व्याख्यानं षड्विधं मतम् ।[18]

1. Division of words (*padacchedaḥ*):
   maga jīva prapaṃcātem̐ racitī 'then the jīva constructs a world' (*SS* 16).

In this sentence nouns with nominative and accusative cases, verbs and adverbs are pointed out with their internal relations.

2. Purport of words (*padārthokti*):
   māyā kārya jīvu : jīva kārye prapaṃcu 'the jīvas are the product of māyā; the world is the product of the jīvas' (*SS* 9).

3. Derivation (*vigraha*):
   vasudevācā putra to vāsudeva 'the son of Vasudeva is Vāsudeva'.
4. Syntax (*vākyayojanā*):
   aisiyā māyāpurāteṁ svīkārauni karmabhūmisthitāṁ manuṣyadehayuktāṁ jīvā jñānaparyanta āpulā saṃbandha deti 'having taken on such a *māyā*-body he (Parameśvara) gives union with himself, until (they attain to) knowledge, to the jīvas having human bodies who are in karmabhūmi' (*U* 12).

The author expounds the syntax of a given sentence by question and answer in commentarial style in order to clarify the meaning. In the present *sūtra*, the subject is 'Parameśvara': who unites? Parameśvara; whose union? his own; with whom? with the jīvas; in which form? in the form of human bodies; where? in *karmabhūmi*; how long? until they attain to knowledge; how? by taking on an illusory body.

5. Hidden meaning or implication (*ākṣepa*):
   yāpari parameśvara śrī cakradhara sakaḷa jīvāteṁ uddharitī 'in this way Parameśvara Śrī Cakradhara uplifts the jīvas' (*U* 66).

What is the purpose of referring both to Parameśvara and to Śrī Cakradhara? This kind of question is implicitly raised here.

6. Inner context (*samādhāna*):
   In the same *sūtra*: Śrī Cakradhara is manifested as a human being whereas Parameśvara is not manifest. How then will Parameśvara uplift the jīvas? What is the point, or justification, of the word 'Parameśvara' here? Is it Cakradhara only who uplifts the jīvas? If, as is the case, Cakradhara is himself the incarnation of Parameśvara then both the expressions 'Parameśvara' and 'Śrī Cakradhara' are meaningful. This is the inner meaning.

All these examples make it clear that *PV* is a study of semantics and syntax undertaken to extract the correct, true, and real meaning of *sūtras* uttered by Śrī Sarvajña Cakradhara, the Supreme God of the sect. In this sense *PV* is a grammar of bhakti, not a grammar of the Marathi language or a philosophical study of Marathi, as has been thought by scholars in Marathi, but a work of implicit devotion.

Bhīṣmācārya: the author and the commentator

There is a great controversy over the period of Bhīṣmācārya. Moreover, scholars do not agree about the authorship of *PV*, its tradition, its author's acquaintance with other works, the guru of Bhīṣmācārya, or the identity or otherwise of author and commentator. V. L. Bhāve in his history of Marathi literature writes that there are five Bhīṣmācāryas, and that the *PV* of

Bhīṣmācārya is an essay on Marathi philology.[19] In introducing old Marathi prose he again indicates that *PV* is a grammatical work by Paṇḍit Bhīṣmācārya with commentator of perhaps the sixteenth century.[20] The first edition of *PV* was published by Moreśvar Sakhārām Mone in 1927; in the preface to this work Mahant Dattarāj Mahānubhāva describes *PV* as the first Marathi grammar.[21] Y. K. Deśpāṇḍe is uncertain about the authorship of *PV* and its period, and lists three Bhīṣmācāryas of different times.[22] H. N. Nene in his edition of *LR* gives some evidence bearing on the date of *PV* and its author, Bhīṣmācārya.[23] Dr I. M. P. Raeside refers to four Bhīṣmācāryas and describes *PV* as a short grammatical work of five sections in prose, based in part on *LR*.[24] Dr Bhīmrāo Kulkarnī notes eight Bhīṣmācāryas and is uncertain about the authenticity of *PV* and Bhīṣmācārya.[25] In a supplement to *Mahārāṣṭra Sārasvat* Dr S. G. Tulpule places Paṇḍit Bhīṣmācārya (the author of *PV*) in the thirteenth rather than the fourteenth century.[26] He sees *PV* as a paraphrase of *LR* and as the first grammar of Marathi.[27] Later Tulpule considered it possible that Bhīṣmācārya could be of the fifteenth century;[28] but with the new research material at his disposal he writes: 'The *Pañcavārtika* of Bhīṣmācārya I is in a way a commentary on the aforesaid Sanskrit work (*Lakṣaṇaratnākara*) but it also happens to be the first grammar of Marathi prepared with sūtras as its central idea.'[29]

In view of recent developments in the availability of dated manuscripts both of the text of *PV* and of commentaries on it, I have again addressed this subject. In earlier papers I have pointed out clearly that *PV* is neither a grammar nor a treatise on philology, but work on semantics prepared in the manner of *mīmāṃsakas* to illustrate examples from the *Sūtrapāṭha*. It was never the intention of Bhīṣmācārya to compose a grammar of Marathi. His work is on the interpretation of Cakradhara's sayings.[30] I have come to the conclusion that Paṇḍit Bhīṣmācārya I (*śaka* 1260, AD 1338) belongs to the Upādhāya tradition (*amnāya*) and is the disciple of Paṇḍit Bopadeva and the composer of *PV*, while another Paṇḍit Bhīṣmācārya (*śaka* 1310, AD 1388) of the Pāramāndilya *āmnāya*, a disciple of Nāganāthadāsa, is the commentator on *PV*. This Bhīṣmācārya belongs to the tradition of Ānerājabāsa, and is also the author of the *Battīsa lakṣaṇācī ṭīpa*, a commentary in Marathi on thirty-two categories of meaning laid down by Ānerājabāsa.[31]

Conclusion

In the commentary on *LR* Bhīṣmācārya refers to *PV* and stresses the need for its study in determining the real and true meanings of *sūtras* quoted in the commentary on *PV*.[32] He also remarks that *PV* should be studied through the teaching of a spiritual guide, otherwise dharma will perish and caste practice will be destroyed: yet why worry (he asks) when the Supreme Being, Parameśvara, is with us in the form of *sūtras*?[33]

PV and its commentary closely resemble the traditional type of commentary in Sanskrit on various Vedas (such as that by Sāyaṇācārya) which examine grammatical forms of a text to determine its exact meaning. It takes cognisance of the personality of Śrī Sarvajña Cakradhara as well as of the *sūtras* uttered by him which form the revealed (*śruti*) basis of Mahānubhāva doctrines. Both Bhīṣmācāryas, the author of *PV* and the commentator, worked with full devotion for the realisation of the Supreme Being in the form of Cakradhara's *Sūtrapāṭha*. *PV* is, then, a semantic and syntactical study of *śruti*, and thus a grammar of devotion.

NOTES

1. Mahant Kṛṣṇadāsjī Mahānubhāv, Director, Shri Gita Ashram, Hyderabad has been kind enough to hand over this MS to me for editing. Apart from the MSS mentioned above, two printed texts of *PV* and its commentary were also consulted in the course of preparation of this paper.
2. Dr V. B. Kolte, an erudite scholar and authority on Mahānubhāva literature, has kindly handed over a copy made by himself of an MS of the commentary on *PV*. This copy, Dr Kolte thinks, is of the MS dated *śaka* 1452.
3. V. B. Kolte, 'Siddhānte haribāsa va dhākute soṅgobāsa kṛt *Anvayasthaḷa*', *MSP*, vol. 106, 1953.
4. V. V. Pārkhe, ed., *Smṛtisthala*, Bombay, 1970, no. 236, 61.
5. Ibid., nos. 16 and 17, p. 6.
6. Ibid., no. 14, p. 5.
7. H. N. Nene, ed., '*Anvayasthaḷa* and *Vṛddhācāra*', in *Saṃśodhan lekh saṅgrah*, Nagpur, 1957, vol. i, p. 144; *Mahānubhāva* (special issue of *Anvusthal*), July–Aug. 1964.
8. V. D. Kulkarni, 'A Semantic Study of "Vachāharan" by Dāmodar Paṇḍit, a Mahānubhāva Poet of the 13c.', Ph.D. thesis, Osmania University, Hyderabad, 1979, pp. 207–33; 'Arthanirṇaya-śāstra āṇi mahānubhāvīya bhāṣyapaddhati', in B. L. Bhole, ed., *Saṃśodhanācī kṣitije* (Dr. V. B. Kolte commemoration volume), Nagpur, 1985, pp. 53–69.
9. MS of AD 1584.
10. MS of AD 1530.
11. Nene, op. cit., p. 144.
12. MS of AD 1530 (*sūtra-prakṛti lakṣaṇa*).
13. A story about an illiterate servant and his master's horse, which ran away leaving only the bridle and the reins in his hand. MS of AD 1530.
14. Ibid. (*sūtra-vyākhyāna lakṣaṇa*).
15. MS of AD 1584.
16. The English version of the *sūtras* is from the edition of the Mahānubhāva *Sūtrapāṭha* by Dr A. Feldhaus, *The Religious System of the Mahānubhāva Sect*, New Delhi (for South Asia Institute, Heidelberg), 1983. The abbreviated references are to the following materials: *A Ācāra*; *AM Ācāramālikā*; *AS Asatipari*; *AV Anyavyāvṛti*; *LR Lakṣaṇaratnākara*; *M Mahāvākya*; *N Nirvacana*; *PV Pañ-*

cavārtika; *S Saṃhāra*; *SS Saṃsaraṇa*; *U Uddharaṇa*; *V Vicāra*; *VD Vidyāmārga*; *VM Vicāramālikā*; *Y Yugadharma*.

17. MS of AD 1584.
18. Ibid.
19. V. L. Bhāve, *Mahānubhāva mahārāṣṭra granthāvalī kavi-kāvya sūcī*, Thane, *śaka* 1846, pp. 19–20; and in *Mahārāṣṭra Sārasvat*, 5th edn., Bombay, 1963, pp. 181–3.
20. Ibid., p. 595.
21. M. S. Mone, *Marāṭhī bhāṣāce vyākaraṇkār va vyākāraṇ-prabhandhkār*, Poona, 1927, p. 87; *PV*, pp. 84–118.
22. Y. K. Deśpāṇḍe, *Mahānubhāvīya marāṭhī vāṅmay*, Yeotmāl, 1925, pp. 42 and 57–8.
23. H. N. Nene, *Lakṣaṇaratnākara*, Nagpur, 1937, p. 37.
24. I. M. P. Raeside, *A Bibliographical Index of Mahānubhāva Works in Marāthi*, *BSOAS* 33, 3, 1960, pp. 506, 491.
25. B. Kulkarnī, 'Mahānubhāvīya vāṅmay', in S. G. Māḷaśe, ed., *Marāṭhī vāṅmayācā itihās*, Poona, 1982, vol. ii, pt. 1, pp. 509–11.
26. ed. V. L. Bhāve, pp. 747–9.
27. Māḷaśe, op. cit., vol. i, p. 311; and *Mahānubhāva panth va tyāce vāṅmay*, Poona: Venus, 1976, pp. 247–52.
28. Māḷaśe, op. cit., vol. i, pp. 753–4.
29. *Classical Marāthi Literature*, ed. J. Gonda, A History of Indian Literature, vol. ix, pt. 4, 1979, pp. 349–50.
30. V. D. Kulkarnī, 'Pañcavārtika', *Marathi Research Journal*, Osmania University, Hyderabad, 14, 1988, pp. 1 ff.
31. Nene, op. cit., pp. 1–167.
32. Ibid. (*Battīsa laksaṇācī ṭīpa*).
33. MS of AD 1530.

Authorship and redactorship of the Jñāndev *Gāthā*

CATHARINA KIEHNLE

The question whether there are one or two or even more Jñāndevs dates back to the end of the last century, when scholars started to view the Vārkarī tradition with a critical eye. The debate initiated by S. A. Bhārḍe (alias Bharadvāj) and S. R. Bhiṅgarkar (1898–1900) was continued by Patwardhan (1917), J. F. Edwards (1941), C. Vaudeville (1969), and many others on the two-or-more-Jñāndevs-side, and R. D. Ranade (1933), K. V. Gajendragaḍkar, and S. G. Tulpule (1970), etc. on the one-Jñāndev-side. The reason why the discussion has not yet come to an end lies of course partly in the emotions involved in matters concerning the great saint of Maharashtra. It also lies partly in the source material, which is not only limited and often legendary, but also, in the case of most of the literary sources, poorly edited and thus unreliable. I would not go into the whole problem were it not for new material that I have found in some of the archives in Maharashtra. The material consists in manuscripts (and some early prints) containing songs with the *mudrikā* of the famous poet-saint. Therefore I will concentrate in the following on the *abhaṅga* literature attributed to Jñāndev (the so-called Jñāndev *Gāthā*), on what it has to offer for the solution of the authorship problem, and on indications of redaction.[1]

My search in the Samartha Vāgdevatā Mandir, the Rājvāḍe Saṃśodhan Maṇḍal (both in Dhuḷe), the Bhārat Itihās Saṃśodhak Maṇḍal, and the University library (both in Poona), brought to light 1,656 Jñāndev songs altogether, plus 160 songs printed in rare and old editions.[2] Some songs appear more than once, so that the number of individual songs is 784, 150 of them unpublished. Thus the total of Jñāndev songs available so far is about 1,250, as against 1,100 of the latest print by P. N. Joshi.[3] It is on this material, and the editions of the Jñāndev *Gāthā* since 1891, that my studies are based.

As is well known, there are several *mudrikās* considered by the Vārkarīs and their partisans to be Jñāndev's, namely 'Jñānadeva', 'Jñāneśvara', 'Bāparakhumādevīvara Viṭṭhala', 'Nivṛttidāsa', and some rarer ones.[4] 'Jñānadeva' occurs in about 600 cases, 'Bāparakhumādevīvara Viṭṭhala' in about 500, 'Jñāneśvara' in about 100, 'Jñāneśvara rājayogī', 'Jñāneśvara satyayogī, 'Jñāneśvara pūrṇayogī', 'Jñāneśvara jñānī', 'Jñāneśvara tattvajñānī' in seven, 'Nivṛttidāsa' in about thirty, 'Jñānarāja' twice, and 'Jñānobā' and several others once.[5] There are also a few songs in which 'Jñānadeva' and 'Bāparakhumādevīvara' occur together. Although Gajendragaḍkar has only an ironical smile for those who might try to suspect a different author behind each of those *mudrikās*, I at least admitted that possibility. There are indeed some differences between the groups, and some arguments why or why not a certain *mudrikā* might be the 'signature' of the *Jñāneśvarī* author.[6]

'Jñānadeva' and 'Nivṛttidāsa' are the names of the author of *Jñāneśvarī, Anubhavāmṛt*, and *Cāṅgdevpāsaṣṭī* uses for himself, so that nothing stands against the assumption (at least from the point of view of *mudrikā*) that he might have 'signed' songs in the same way. Yet one has to be careful, because there are also some Nāmdev compositions that contain 'Jñānadeva mhaṇe'. Therefore one cannot exclude the possibility that a song may have been formerly meant as a quotation, and ended up as an 'original'.[7] More 'Jñānadeva' songs that are wrongly attributed to the *Jñāneśvarī* author will be dealt with presently. Most probably the songs containing 'Jñāneśvara' also belong to the latter category. 'Jñāneśvara' is frequently used in songs about Jñāndev by other authors, for example in Muktābāī's *Tāṭīce abhaṅga*, and sometimes with Nāmdev and Janābāī.[8] 'Jñāneśvara rājayogī' etc. does not fit into the picture of the humble author of the *Jñāneśvarī* who attributes all he knows to the grace of his teacher, and who likens himself to a young bird compared to the eagles of spiritual knowledge.[9] 'Jñānobā is not supported by the variants in the manuscripts, and 'Jñānarāja', like 'Jñāneśvara', might also be a designation given by the devotees.[10].

Especially when it comes to 'Bāparakhumādevīvara Viṭṭhala' one has to take into account that the *mudrikās* were not so limited in their usage as the present-day scholar might wish. They could be dedicated to a person or a god out of friendliness or devotion, or in memory of someone.[11] The latter was the case with the names of the (human) couple Viṭho and Rukmiṇī, who appeared in songs composed by their children (according to the *Līḷācaritra*), or with 'Viṭṭhala' alone in the case of 'one brāhmaṇ' who put that name into the last line of the song (according to the *Smṛtisthaḷa*).[12] All that makes one suspect that the 'Bāparakhumādevīvara Viṭṭhala' songs may be the products of various authors who for some reason or other felt a special affinity to the divine couple of Paṇḍharpūr, or to human beings of that name. Among those authors may have also been the *abhaṅga* composer Jñāndev, because there are occasionally songs of one type, which are 'signed' in one case with the *mudrikā* 'Jñānadeva', and in the other with 'Bāparakhumādevīvara'.[13]

Yet one notes also some differences between the 'Jñānadeva', and the 'Bāparakhumādevīvara Viṭṭhala' camps.[14] 'Guru Nivṛtti' is mentioned in one-third of the 'Jñānadeva' songs, but only in one-seventh of the 'Bāparakhumādevīvara Viṭṭhala' ones. Bhakti and personal experiences are more often the subject of 'Bāparakhumādevīvara' songs than of 'Jñānadeva' ones, whereas yoga and instructions are more frequent in 'Jñānadeva' compositions. The greatest difference pertains to the metres. Most of the 'Jñānadeva' songs are *moṭhā abhaṅgas*, and only one-sixth of them are composed in other metres.[15] Only half of the 'Bāparakhumādevīvara Viṭṭhala' songs are *moṭhā abhaṅgas*, a quarter are *lahān abhaṅgas*, and a quarter are in other metres. The reason for those divergences need not necessarily or exclusively be a difference of authors. 'Bāparakhumādevīvara Viṭṭhala', for example, matches the *lahān abhaṅga* form better than the *moṭhā abhaṅga* because of its great number of syllables. When further research has been done, the features just mentioned may become more meaningful. Still, it is even now interesting to see that the (almost) amorphous mass of *abhaṅgas* can be structured in the way suggested here.

More detailed research could be done so far on only 200 *abhaṅgas* which I am preparing for an edition. The 200 songs were not selected at random but for special reasons. When one counts the frequency with which individual songs occur in the manuscripts and editions, it becomes apparent that some are more popular than others. The most popular group is of course the *Haripāṭh*, the 'creed' of the Vārkarīs, which has been edited by Charlotte Vaudeville.[16] Its songs appear, as a group or separately, 21–12 times. Next in favour (19–21 times) are eight songs that turned out to be a group as well, but a forgotten one. They are about yoga and seem to be something like the 'creed' of the yogis who considered themselves as followers of (a) Jñāndev from the Nāth *sampradāya*. That group of eight songs is called *Lākhoṭā*, 'sealed letter', and the first group I will deal with here. The second group consists of about 140 songs that are available in one to six manuscripts. They resemble the *Lākhoṭā*, and have been very aptly called by their first editors *Yogapar abhaṅgamālā*, 'garland of songs about yoga' (*Mālā* from now onward). The third group consists of two subdivisions. Firstly, of twenty-seven Vaiṣṇava songs which I call *Anuṣṭhānapāṭh*, 'litany of observances'. Secondly, of twenty-three songs which in several respects are similar to the *Anuṣṭhānapāṭh*. The *Anuṣṭhānapāṭh* is available only in the journal *Mumukṣu* of 1927, and the latest Jñāndev *Gāthā* edition by P. N. Joshi, who took it from *Mumukṣu*.[17] The remaining twenty-three songs appear only in the editions, so that nothing can be said about their degree of popularity.[18] Except for a few songs in this last subgroup, all of the *abhaṅgas* under discussion have the name 'Jñāndeva' in the *mudrikā*.

One can examine the three groups from various angles. In the case of the *Lākhoṭā* with its numerous manuscripts, the methods of philology are applicable with good results. It is similar with the *Mālā*, where also the manuscript situation is quite acceptable, and where the metre proved a great help for the establishment of the text. In the case of the *Anuṣṭhānapāṭh* and the related songs, criteria could be applied that in various respects resemble those used by R. K. Ramanujan.[19] The following is the outcome of my research as far as it concerns questions of authorship and redactorship.

Lākhoṭā

When one takes into consideration the fact that at least from the time after Cakradhar's death onward (he died in 1272 or 1274), and in the Nāmdev circle (fourteenth century) there was a tradition of writing down events and songs, one cannot deny the possibility that *abhaṅgas* and groups of *abhaṅgas* may have been transmitted in that way also from the time of the Jñāndev of the *Jñāneśvarī* onward, that is, from the end of the thirteenth century.[20] The manuscripts available at present, though, are not older than 200 or 300 years on an average. Nevertheless, the versions of the *Lākhoṭā* preserved in them show some of the stages the songs have undergone in the course of transmission, and allow for conclusions about what a comparatively old version may have looked like. This oldest version which one can reconstruct, is of course not necessarily the 'Urfassung'.

There are basically two versions of the *Lākhoṭā*.[21] Their main difference is that one of them contains an extra stanza (see below) in the last song that the other does not. Other differences concern details. Contrary to what one would expect, the version without the extra stanza shows in many respects more modern traits. For example, instead of *dāvī*, a form that nowadays is used only in the Marathi of the peasants, it has *dākhavī*; instead of the *tadbhava* form *pālīṃ/pāyīṃ* it has Sanskrit *padīṃ* (sanskritization being a sign of recent standard Marathi). It often contains the easier readings; for example, instead of the ancient *pātaleṃ*, which has been preserved only in poetry, the inoffensive *āle*. Or, in one case when the word *muktā* leads to misunderstandings, it substitutes the unambiguous *motī*. In other cases, syntactical constructions are simplified. The changes go so far that they even spoil the metre in some instances. The two versions developed into subversions, that is, there are variants restricted to the one or the other group. In a few manuscripts the transmission is contaminated.

The *Lākhoṭā* songs as they are available in the editions and a few separate publications belong to the version with the extra stanza. Otherwise they are characterized by further standardization – although not only in the direction of modern Marathi.[22] On the one hand, the correct Sanskrit form *aṅguṣṭha* is substituted for the form *aṅguṣṭa* that occurs in the majority of manuscripts. Furthermore, standard Marāṭhī *mūsa, otalī, otīva, ekasarā* are introduced instead of *musa, votilī, votīva*, and *yekasarā*. On the other hand, the difficult *Nivṛttikṛpe[m]* (a questionable instrumental preferred by most of the scribes) is exchanged not for a modern form, but for the correct Old Marathi *-kṛpā*. Similarly, Old Marāṭhī *navā[ṃ]ciyā* stands for *navāṃce, -cya, -ciye*, of which the first one is still present in Marathi, but considered substandard. All that might be corrections by language-conscious editors, such as G. N. Dātār.[23] There are also cases of simplification; for example, when we find *pāhe pāṃ*, a frequent exclamation in *abhaṅgas*, instead of the more unusual *jāṇa pāṃ*. Or we find 2nd sg. imperative *pāhī* instead of *pāhatāṃ*, in a sentence where the present participle is supported by the manuscripts but difficult to translate. *Bharūni ṭhelā* of the editions, although not impossible at the time of the *Jñāneśvarī*, sounds more colloquial than *bharuni ase* of the manuscripts. *Śūnyā[ṃ]varatī* (instead of *śunyāṃvari*) is wrong because the context does not demand a feminine adjective but a designation of place. In one case a whole sentence was misunderstood, perhaps due to wrong hearing: *avyaktem̥ te kelī vasti tethem̥*, 'the unmanifest made [its] abode there', became *avyakta dekhilī vastū tethem̥*, 'the unmanifest reality was seen there'.

Of course, the identification of strands of transmission does not throw any light on the author. So much, however, shows clearly that the songs were committed to periodical changes according to the respective trends of language and the understanding of the scribes. That the *Lākhoṭā* was not only changed by chance but underwent actual redactorship is shown by the suspicious extra stanza.[24] The first way to account for its absence or presence is to assume that the 'Urfassung' did not contain it, and that it was added by a redactor. The new version would have been transmitted by a separate tradition, which only in some rare cases came into contact with the transmitters of the old version. The old version, in turn, would have been modernized at a later stage, which would explain the fact that it contains the more modern forms. I think, however, that there is a better solution.

The stanza runs:

अपार अधिष्ठान सप्त या अभङ्गीं
सत्य या
सातव्या
जाणोनियां वेगीं जीवीं धरा

The difficulties lie in *caraṇ b*. First, one has to decide whether or not the word *abhaṅga* has here its literal meaning 'without break', or the specialized meaning 'devotional song in the *abhaṅga* metre'. In the Jñāndev *Gāthā* in general, the word is used several times literally, but in the *Mālā*, it occurs in the sense of 'devotional song'. The respective passages of the *Mālā* conclude something: in the case of song no. 17 the *abhaṅga*, and in the case of song no. 100 (where the word is found as many as three times) the whole collection of songs. Just as in the *Lākhoṭā*, the listener is made aware of the impending end, and told about the immense value of what he has been listening to. *Mālās* 17 and 100 stick out from the rest of the collection also in so far as they belong to a group of eight songs that are longer than the rest, and contain systematic descriptions of the theories dealt with separately or alluded to in the shorter songs. *Lākhoṭā* viii is quite similar. It is longer than the other seven *abhaṅgas*, and sums up what is contained in them. In the *Mālā* as well as the *Lākhoṭā* one can suspect that those songs were added by a redactor who felt the necessity to systematize the impact of the shorter songs, and to supplement them in some way or other.

That means in all probability the original number of songs in the *Lākhoṭā* was not eight but seven. That is supported by the fact that it is called in one manuscript and by its first editor *Saptapadī*, 'the collection consisting of seven songs'. It is also supported by the readings in viii. 6*b* quoted above, which show considerable disagreement. Disagreement is often a sign that something was no longer understood properly, and I think that is the case here. All the readings have something to do with seven, even *satya*, which looks very similar to *sapta* in the manuscripts. I suspect that the following development has taken place: in the beginning there was Old Marathi *sātai[ṃ]*, a virtual oblique of *sāta*, 'seven', which would make the whole sentence mean 'know quickly the boundless basis in all these seven *abhaṅgas*'.[25] Some scribes were no longer aware that song no. viii was the addition of a redactor, and started doubting the number seven. Some of them arranged the songs in such a way that the outcome was seven again, as some manuscripts show. Others substituted *satya* for *sātai[ṃ]*, which is similar not only in writing but also in pronunciation. The next generation of scribes felt again the necessity of a number in that context, and substituted Sanskrit *sapta*, because they did not know the archaic *sātai[ṃ]* any more, and perhaps because they liked Sanskrit better anyway. The ordinal number *sātavyā* is another outcome of the endeavours to emend the strange passage, although one wonders why the value of the song should only be in the seventh *abhaṅga*. A more resolute scribe realized the jungle of difficulties opening up with the stanza and therefore dropped it, at the same time modernizing the rest of the songs.

So (provided the above theory is correct) there were at least three people who had a hand in the two main versions: first, the author of the seven songs; second, the redactor who added the eighth song; third, the redactor who dropped the difficult stanza and modernized the little collection. As far as the authorship is concerned, that leaves us with seven songs to be compared with the *Jñāneśvarī*.[26] Except for some instrumental singulars in *-neṃ*, which, as in the *Haripāṭh*, may be later additions, there are no grammatical forms contradicting the theory that the songs date back to the time of Jñāndev's *Gītā* commentary. The vocabulary in general, too, is quite similar to that of the *Jñāneśvarī*. There is a fair amount of Sanskrit, some Kannaḍa, and some compounds composed of *deśī* or *tadbhava* words and Sanskrit. Arabic–Persian words are lacking as in the Jñāneśvarī; this, however, does not mean anything because it might be due to a special effort as in the case of Eknāth's *Bhāgavata* commentary.[27] There are also several terms and images that remind one of the *Jñāneśvarī*.

Still, the songs sound more simple than the *Jñāneśvarī*, and one also finds differences of vocabulary that need some explanation. As to the simplicity, a great amount of skill was undoubtedly necessary to employ the popular *ovī* song form for a highly technical subject like yoga. Moreover, the *Lākhoṭā* is surprisingly poetical. As to the vocabulary, most of the Sanskrit words or compounds that are lacking in the *Jñāneśvarī* (such as *abhāgya, dāmbhika, pīṭha, bhāsa, gaganasaritā, brahmāṇḍageha*) may have been known to the author, who would just have had no reason to use them. Much more astonishing is the fact that the terms Ādinātha, Pārvatī (and Umā in some manuscripts) for Śiva and Śakti do not occur in the *Jñāneśvarī*, and that one does not come across terms like *(nīla)bindu, masurapramāṇa, aṃguṣṭha-pramāṇa, mahākāraṇa*, and *auṭapīṭha*, which are of major importance for the theories about the *Lākhoṭā*.

The partisan of the two-or-more-Jñāndevs-theory will stop here and decide that the Jñāndev of the *Lākhoṭā* is different from that of the *Jñāneśvarī*. He has my sympathy because what I have to say in favour of a faint possibility that the *Jñāneśvarī* author also composed the *Lākhoṭā* is partly an argument *ex silentio*. One part, though, is quite obvious. In both works the teachings are considered to be products of the Nāth school of yoga, and in both works not only is the reconciliation of Vaiṣṇavism and Śaivism propagated, but also their identity is declared.[28] Both the *Jñāneśvarī* (especially in the sixth chapter), and the *Lākhoṭā* describe or presuppose the same kind of spiritual practice, namely Kuṇḍalinī yoga. They agree in the idea that the syllable AUM is identical with Kuṇḍalinī, and that it is perceived on the last part of Kuṇḍalinī's way up to the *brahmarandhra*, bringing about the return of creation to its origin in the human body. The *Lākhoṭā*, and especially the *Mālā*, depict that process in a more technical language than the *Jñāneśvarī*, and, perhaps for that reason, in terms that do not occur in the latter. Among them are the designations for the subtle bodies, for example the *kāraṇadeha*, which is said to be the size of a thumb (*aṅguṣṭhapramāṇa*), or the *mahākāraṇadeha* the size of a lentil (*masurapramāṇa*), which is also called the 'blue dot' (*nīlabindu*). The *auṭapīṭha* is one of the places in the body on which the yogi puts special attention. Another reason why such notions are lacking in the *Jñāneśvarī* may be that it was meant for a general public, and the yoga songs for specialists. Among the initiates the poet may have felt more inclined than among strangers to use Śiva's Nāth name Ādinātha. The absence of 'Pārvatī' in the *Jñāneśvarī* may be accidental.

The theory of the four bodies, in any case, belongs very probably to the oldest stock of Nāth teachings, since it is related to the theories of *kāyas* as one finds them in Vajrayāna.[29] The similarity between the Nāth and the Buddhist *siddhas* in the early days of the Nāth school is manifest in the stories of the eighty-four *siddhas* where both groups are treated as belonging together, and in their yoga, which differs more in terminology than in practice.[30] One cannot exclude that the teachings (which are still alive in present-day Maharashtra) were also known to the author of the *Jñāneśvarī*, well informed about the philosophies of his time as he was.[31] Still, these are only suggestions, and not yet full-fledged theories. Before anything can be taken for granted, much more investigation has to be done into the affiliation of the Nāths in general, and of Jñāndev in particular, to Mahāyāna Buddhism.

Mālā

The *Mālā* is a collection of 138 songs on yoga. The two main manuscripts and the editions have exactly 100 of them in common, a fact that leads to the assumption that this is the original number. Most probably later scribes no longer realized that the number 100 was intended by the first compiler, and felt free to add similar-sounding compositions here and there. In the manuscripts, the Jñāndev songs are, moreover, interspersed with songs by Nivṛttināth, Muktābāī, Sopāndev, and some other poets of the Jñāndev circle.

The *Mālā* as a group seems to be comparatively old, since the earliest editors, V. N. Jog and G. N. Dātār (1906 and 1907), mention that they took it from a tattered manuscript where the songs already formed a homogeneous collection.[32] The exact age, and the age of the individual songs, is difficult to ascertain. The language of the songs is like that of the *Lākhoṭā*, and also their import is in accordance with the little collection. Just as in the *Lākhoṭā*, one finds in the *Mālā* passages where Vaiṣṇavism and Śaivism are identified. Such tendencies were in vogue at the beginnings of the Maharashtrian bhakti movement, and at the time of the composition of the *Jñāneśvarī*. The stress on Śaiva–Śākta ideas in the *Mālā* may also be an indication of some antiquity. It is true that most of the Vārkarī saints, such as Nāmdev, Janābāī, Muktābāī, Cāṅgdev, Eknāth, Tukārām, and even Bahiṇābāī composed Nāth-influenced songs. The earlier the author, the greater is the number of such compositions. With none of the authors just mentioned, however, does one find as many yoga songs as in the *Mālā*.

Therefore, just as with the *Lākhoṭā*, one cannot altogether exclude the possibility that at least some of the songs might be by the author of the *Jñāneśvarī*. With some of them, though, there is reason to believe that they were added by a compiler or redactor. One such group of eight was mentioned already in connection with the extra stanza of the *Lākhoṭā*. Since the last song of the *Lākhoṭā*, and especially songs no. 17 and 100 of the *Mālā*, bear some similarity with each other, one and the same person may have had a hand in both collections.[33]

One interesting feature of the *Mālā*'s transmission is brought to light by the analysis of its metre. As one would expect, there are many irregularities.[34] Most of them can be corrected by means of the manuscript readings. Yet a small number of them (eighteen to be exact) remain even then. They are disturbing from the point of view of metre, and wrong or unnecessary from the point of view of meaning. Since they occur in all manuscripts and editions they most probably crept in at a time when there was only one text. Here is an example:

Mālā 94.1

तुर्येमध्यें माझा अखंड रहिवास ।
निवृत्ति म्हणे अविनाश तुर्या का रे ।।[35]

My constant abode is in *turīyā* [state of consciousness].
Cessation [of mental fluctuations], indeed, is the imperishable *turīyā*.

The form *mhaṇe* in the third *caraṇ* was inserted because of the frequent *mudrikā caraṇs* like 'Nivṛtti mhaṇe', or 'Jñānadeva mhaṇe'. Here, however, the word *nivṛtti* has to be taken literally, and *mhaṇe* is out of place.

So again some stages of redaction can be counted, namely the one in which there were no mistakes (a stage that is not preserved in the manuscripts), and one in which there were some (the eighteen mentioned above). One cannot say whether the compiler came in at the first or the second step. In any case, his *Mālā* in turn was transmitted by various scribes with the old and additional blunders.

Anuṣṭhānapāṭh

Anuṣṭhānapāṭh, 'litany of observances', is an artificial title I gave to the twenty-seven Vaiṣṇava songs because they consist mostly of rules for the behaviour of the pious Vaiṣṇava. Since the collection occurs only in the edition of P. N. Joshi, who took them from the *Mumukṣu* of 1927, the philological situation is not at all satisfactory. In spite of that, the *Anuṣṭhānapāṭh* proved to be useful for the investigation into the authorship of the Jñāndev *Gāthā*, although in a negative way, for it differs strongly from *Haripāṭh, Lākhoṭā, Mālā*, and most of the remaining *Gāthā* songs.

The *Anuṣṭhānapāṭh* represents the attitude of a conservative Vaiṣṇava with a brahmanical background.[36] The author propagates the religion of the name, that is, mainly *nāmajapa* and *kīrtana*, but also *dhyāna* of Hari, combined with the observance of traditional values such as obedience to elders and guru, and respect of, and generosity towards, the brāhmaṇs. He promises to his listeners heaven and hell in accordance with their behaviour, and on the whole seems to be more interested in outer appearances than in inner experiences. In comparison to the *Haripāṭh* his songs sound rather stiff, not only because of what he says, but also because of how he says it.[37] The language consists of a limited number of sentence patterns, and abounds in nominal clauses. It contains a lot of Sanskrit – Sanskrit being what the early bhaktas in Maharashtra tried to avoid as far as possible. Especially Jñāndev, in his *Bhagavadgītā* commentary, put great stress on the fact that Marathi was as beautiful as Sanskrit, constantly admiring the flow of language that poured out of him due to the grace of his teacher. The metre of the *Anuṣṭhānapāṭh*, too, underlines its affinity to 'structure' in the sense of Victor

Turner and A. K. Ramanujan, who connect that term with conservatism and tradition, in contrast to the 'anti-structure' spontaneity of new religious movements.[38] Instead of the lively *ovīs* of the *Jñāneśvarī*, or the popular *abhaṅga* form, the author uses a more monotonous metre that gained its greatest popularity at the time of Eknāth (sixteenth century). The *mudrikā* stanzas are all knitted together after a similar model, another indication that the songs are not the product of a poet like the Jñāndev of the *Jñāneśvarī*. Also the *Haripāṭh* sounds quite refreshing when compared to the *Anuṣṭhānapāṭh*.

Other than the *Haripāṭh*, which represents the ideas of a sort of counter-culture acting independently from (though never against) caste-oriented society, the *Anuṣṭhānapāṭh* shows that the original impetus of what Victor Turner calls a 'communitas' ended up partly in brahmanism. Moreover, it proves beyond doubt that anyone could put the name of the author of the *Jñāneśvarī* into the *mudrikā*, and that any such songs were added indiscriminately to the *Gāthā* collection. The criteria established by the analysis of the *Anuṣṭhānapāṭh* have helped in picking out some more songs (twenty-three in number) that might belong to the same category. The assumption that these are later products as well is supported by the fact that some of them contain remarks about the Jñāndev of the *Jñāneśvarī*, which can only with great difficulty be interpreted as communications by this Jñāndev himself. Thus the general outcome of my studies is that, hidden under layers of redactorship, there may be songs by the great Nāth yogi Jñāndev in the *Gāthā*, but that many of the *abhaṅgas* were composed by his real or would-be followers.

NOTES

For a discussion of the whole history of the authorship and redactorship of the Jñāndev *Gāthā*, see C. Vaudeville, *L'Invocation: Le Haripāṭh de Dnyāndev*, Paris, 1969, and C. Kiehnle, *Lākhoṭā: The Letter on Yoga, Texts and Teachings of the Mahārāṣṭrian Nāths*, forthcoming, introduction.

1. The arguments are dealt with in detail in my forthcoming publications: *Lākhoṭā* (see first note); *Yogapar Abhaṅgamālā: A Garland of Songs on Yoga*; *Anuṣṭhānapāṭh, 50 Anonymous Songs of the Jñāndev Gāthā.*
2. One MS was contributed by Dr R. C. Ḍhere.
3. P. N. Joshi, *Sārtha Śrī Jñāndev abhaṅga gāthā*, Poona, 1969.
4. The orthography 'Jñānadeva' reflects the pronunciation in prosody, and 'Jñāndev' that in modern Marathi.
5. I say 'about' because the songs so far unpublished have not yet been fully evaluated. Moreover, the MSS contain contradictions in some rare cases.
6. K. V. Gajendragaḍkar, *Śrījñāndevmahārājāṃce abhaṅga Śrījñāneśvardarśan*, 1st edn., Ahmadnagar, 1934, pp. 312–14.

7. e.g. Nāmdev *Gāthā* (in *Sakalasantagāthā*, ed. K. A. Joshi, 1923, repr. 1967), 914. 1, 905. 11, 974. 1. Nāmdev *Gāthā* 1349, with 'Jñānadeva mhaṇe' in the *mudrikā* line, might belong to the Jñāndev *Gāthā* as well.
8. S. K. Dāṇḍekar, *Vārkarī bhajan saṃgraha*, 2nd edn., Poona, 1980, pp. 130–2; Janābāī *Gāthā* (in *Sakalasantagāthā*, see n. 7), 119, 266. 3, 268. 1, 3; 269. 2, 270. 1, 272. 2, 286. 1; Nāmdev *Gāthā* 900. 5, 1100. 8, 1335. 1.
9. *Jñāneśvarī* 18. 1713 (Government ed., Bombay, 1977).
10. 'Jñānobā' occurs in song 89 of the *Mālā*, which will be dealt with presently. 'Jñānarāja' is found in MSS nos. 702 and 1559 of the Samartha Vāgdevatā Mandir.
11. For this and most of the following references see S. G. Tulpule, *Abhaṅgavāṇītīl* Pantharāj, Poona, 1970, pp. 6–8.
12. *Līḷācaritra* ii. 2. 411 is discussed by S. G. Tulpule in 'The Origin of Viṭṭhala', *ABORI* Diamond Jubilee Volume, 1977–8, pp. 1009–15.
13. See e.g., in P. N. Joshi's *Gāthā* edition, songs no. 265 and 266, which describe the experience of the colour blue.
14. *Lākhoṭā*, ch. 3 B.
15. For the *abhaṅga* forms, see N. G. Joshi, *Marāṭhī chandoracanā*, Bombay, 1955, pp. 134 ff., and C. Kiehnle, *Lākhoṭā*, ch. 3 C 1, 2.
16. See first note.
17. L. R. Pāṅgarkar, *Mumukṣu*, varṣa 20, mās 6, Poona, 1927, pp. 8–14; Joshi, op. cit. pp. 103–21.
18. For a history of the editions, see *Lākhoṭā*, ch. 2 C.
19. *Anuṣṭhānapāṭh*, introduction; R. K. Ramanujan, *Speaking of Śiva*, Harmondsworth, 1973, 1979, introduction.
20. For the age of Cakradhar see A. Feldhaus, *The Religious System of the Mahānubhāva Sect: The Mahānubhāva Sūtrapāṭh*, South Asian Studies, vol. xii, New Delhi, 1983, p. 5, and S. G. Tulpule, *Classical Marāṭhī Literature from the Beginning to A.D. 1818*, A History of Indian Literature, vol. ix, fac. 4, Wiesbaden, 1979, p. 317. The authors disagree by two years. For Nāmdev see J. F. Edwards, *Dnyāneshṿar, the Out-Caste Brāhmin*, The Poet-Saints of Mahārāṣṭra, vol. xii, Poona, 1941, pp. 103–4.
21. For this and the following see *Lākhoṭā*, ch. 5 B.
22. Ibid., ch. 5 C.
23. In the introduction to his *Gāthā* edition (*Śrī Jñāneśvar Mahārājācyā abhaṃgāṃcī gāthā*, Bombay and Baroda, 1906) some interest in language matters is visible.
24. *Lākhoṭā*, ch. 5 D.
25. A. Master, *A Grammar of Old Marāṭhī*, Oxford, 1964, p. 104, thinks that *sātaiṃ* is locative, because of the *Jñāneśvarī* passages *sātaiṃ sāgarīṃ milijo* and *sāteṃ satīṃ*. The form, however, would be extremely difficult to explain. It would be better to interpret it as *sāta-hī[ṃ]* 'all the seven' (suggestion by S. G. Tulpule). It seems to have been used as an indeclinable, or as a sort of oblique (like *tīhīṃ*), as the examples given by Master show (*Lākhoṭā*, chs. 4 C 3, 5 D).
26. See esp. ibid., ch. 4 D 2.
27. Ibid., ch. 6 D 1. I owe this information to Hugh van Skyhawk.
28. Ibid., chs. 6 E, 7 B, C.
29. S. Dasgupta, *An Introduction to Tantric Buddhism*, 2nd edn., Calcutta, University

of Calcutta, 1958, pp. 148 ff.; *Obscure Religious Cults*, Calcutta, 1946, p. 91; *Lākhoṭā*, ch. 6 A 3.

30. J. B. Robinson, *The Eighty-Four Siddhas*, University Microfilms International, Ann Arbor, Mich., 1984; Dasgupta, *Obscure Religious Cults*, pp. 238, 248; *Tantric Buddhism*, pp. 118, 119, 148–53, 164, 165, etc.
31. The yoga described by Muktānanda (Svāmī), *Chitshakti Vilas: The Play of Consciousness*, Ganeshpuri, 1972, is in many details identical with that of the *Lākhoṭā*.
32. V. N. Jog, *Jñāndevācī Gāthā*, Poona, 1907; for Dātār's edition, see note 23.
33. *Lākhoṭā*, ch. 3 D 2.
34. The limits within which an *abhaṅga* can be called 'correct' are discussed at length in ch. 3 C of *Lākhoṭā*.
35. d) *Kā re* S1, otherwise *karī*.
36. *Anuṣṭhānapāṭh*, ch. 4 A–D.
37. *Anuṣṭhānapāṭh*, ch. 4 E.
38. Introduction to A. K. Ramanujan's *Speaking of Śiva*; V. Turner, *The Ritual Process, Structure and Anti-structure*, Chicago, 1969; *Dramas, Fields, and Metaphors, Symbolic Action in Human Society*, Ithaca, NY, and London, 3rd impression, 1983, pp. 272–99.

Mātāpitṛbhakti: some aspects of the development of the Puṇḍalīka legend in Marathi literature

ERIK REENBERG SAND

In this paper I shall deal briefly with some Marathi versions of the legend of Puṇḍalīka, which, being the founding myth of the Pandharpur *kṣetra*, have played a major part in the legitimization of this sacred town in Maharashtra ever since the Vaiṣṇavization of this place.[1] The paper is thus a continuation of an earlier paper,[2] in which I dealt with the hitherto hardly noticed Sanskrit sources of the Puṇḍalīka legend[3] in an effort to demonstrate the futility of all the speculations about the historicity of Puṇḍarīka[4] found in much of the earlier research on Pandharpur and the cult of Viṭhobā. Thus, the Sanskrit sources suggest that we are dealing with an ordinary aetiological legend of purely purāṇic character, explaining how Kṛṣṇa came to stay in Pandharpur in the form of Pāṇḍuraṅga or Viṭhobā.

In several respects the traditions found in the two main Sanskrit māhātmyas are reflected in the Marathi literature dealing with Pandharpur. This is most obvious in the case of Śrīdhara's *Pāṇḍuraṅgamāhātmya*,[5] which in the long version is almost nothing but a translation of the *Pd.Pdm.* But the *Sk.Pdm.* has also influenced Marathi literature: for example, parts of it are reiterated in a long *abhaṅga* of Viṣṇudāsa Nāmā,[6] and the *Pāṇḍuraṅgamāhātmya* of Pralhāda Mahārāja[7] is also an adaptation of this text. Furthermore, in the case of the Puṇḍalīka legend, it seems quite clear that the Marathi versions fall into two groups, one which follows the simple version found in the *Sk.Pdm.*, and one which consists of more elaborate versions, probably inspired by the version found in the *Pd.Pdm.*

In 'The Legend of Puṇḍarīka' I suggested that one reason for the more elaborate version of the *Pd.Pdm.* may have been a feeling of inconsistency in the fact that the simple version of the legend makes the *mātāpitṛbhakti* of Puṇḍarīka, and not Kṛṣṇa-bhakti, the cause of the arrival of the god in Pandharpur. Thus, it would probably have been hard for a Vaiṣṇava bhakta to understand how the service of one's parents could lead to the vision of Kṛṣṇa.

In the present paper my main aim will be to show how several of the developments of the legend in Marathi literature may likewise be understood against the background of the inadequacy of this somewhat special kind of bhakti. Thus, some elements of the more complex Marathi versions may also be understood as different attempts to justify the relevance of *mātāpitṛbhakti* in the religious context of the legend.

Mātāpitṛbhakti in classical Indian literature

Let me begin, however, with a brief survey of the *mātāpitṛbhakti* motif in the classical Indian tradition. The first time we encounter it is probably in the story of the pious hunter, or Dharmavyādha, in the *Mahābhārata*.[8] Here the motif seems to be used as a somewhat anti-brahmanical alternative to contemporary ascetic traditions, represented in the story of the brāhmaṇ Kauśika, who was first instructed by an anonymous *pativratā* woman and afterwards by a pious hunter who regards his two old parents as his highest deity.[9]

The motif is also found in the *Rāmāyaṇa*, in the story of the young boy Śravaṇa, who took care of his old and blind parents, but by mistake was killed by King Daśaratha.[10] Here, however, it is not the religious significance of the motif which is important, but rather its narrative function, which is to explain why Daśaratha has to see his son Rāma exiled in the forest.[11]

The motif of *mātāpitṛbhakti* also plays a part in the Bhūmikhaṇḍa of the *Padmapurāṇa*, most prominently in the story of Sukarmā, called Pitṛtīrthamāhātmya, in which Sukarmā spends all his time in the service of his parents.[12] Whereas *mātāpitṛbhakti* in the Dharmavyādha story represents an alternative to asceticism, it seems here to represent an alternative to the popular practice of going on pilgrimage (*tīrthayātrā*), along with devotion to one's guru and husband.

In 'The Legend of Puṇḍarīka' I tried to indicate that the Bhūmikhaṇḍa of the *Padmapurāṇa* and the legend of Sukarmā might have been the inspiration for the introduction of the *mātāpitṛbhakti* motif in the 'original' Sanskrit version of the Puṇḍalīka legend. In what follows we shall see how several of the above-mentioned classical examples of the *mātāpitṛbhakti* motif are likewise reflected in the various, more elaborate Marathi versions of the legend of Puṇḍalīka.

The simple versions

The *Sk.Pdm.* version of the Puṇḍalīka legend is very simple. It describes how, after he had built an āśrama on the banks of a pond, Puṇḍarīka served his parents with devotion (bhakti), and how, as a result of this, Kṛṣṇa came from Govardhana in order to offer him a boon which finally resulted in the constant presence of the god in Pandharpur.

Apart from a few of the *abhaṅgas* of Ekanātha which seem to reflect traditions of the *Pd.Pdm.*,[13] the many references to Puṇḍalīka and his legend in the *abhaṅga* literature seem to presuppose this simple version of the *Sk.Pdm.* Only exceptionally, however, do the *abhaṅgas* present us with the legend in detail,[14] most probably because it must have been too well known to the authors and their audience. Generally, the authors of the *abhaṅgas* are satisfied with praising Puṇḍalīka as the instrument of Pāṇḍuraṅga's or Viṭṭhala's presence in Pandharpur, most often without any specific attributes, but sometimes with various epithets such as the king of bhaktas (*bhaktarāyā*)[15] or brother or relative (*bandhu*) of the bhaktas,[16] or gem or chief of the bhaktas (*bhakta śiromaṇī*).[17]

Although the *Yogasaṃgrāma* of Śekh Mahaṃmadbābā[18] shows acquaintance with the later and more elaborate version of the *Pd.Pdm.*,[19] Śekh Mahaṃmad seems on the whole to have chosen the *Sk.Pdm.* version of the legend, perhaps because he felt it to be the older and more authoritative one.

Apart from the *abhaṅgas* and the *Yogasaṃgrāma*, two more versions of our legend basically follow the version of the *Sk.Pdm.*, namely the *Pāṇḍuraṅgamāhātmya* of Pralhāda Mahārāja and the *Bhaktalīlāmṛta* of Mahīpati.[20] In both these versions, as well as in most of the more elaborate ones,[21] we find, however, an additional feature: whereas in the earlier versions it is the *mātāpitṛbhakti* of Puṇḍalīka which alone causes Kṛṣṇa to come to Pandharpur in order to give him a boon, in these versions the *ṛṣi* Nārada is introduced as an intermediary between Puṇḍalīka and Kṛṣṇa. Thus, the *Pāṇḍuraṅgamāhātmya* of Pralhāda Mahārāja describes how one day, on his wanderings around the world, Nārada reached Pandharpur, where he observed Puṇḍalīka engaged in serving his parents. This marvel he reported to Kṛṣṇa, who then went to visit Puṇḍalīka, in this and some other versions[22] accompanied by Nārada. As I have pointed out elsewhere,[23] Nārada seems to have been connected with the area around the present Viṣṇupada temple south of Pandharpur at a very early date, since, in several passages of the *Sk.Pdm.*,[24] he is said to be standing there in the form of a liṅga, which is still found to the north of the Viṣṇupada temple. And as the arrival of Nārada still, as is seen from the local legends found in various Marathi pilgrim guidebooks,[25] plays an important part in the local mythology of the area around the present Viṣṇupada, it is clear that this feature might have been inspired by local religious circumstances. However, in a narrative perspective, this introduction of Nārada as go-between between Puṇḍalīka and Kṛṣṇa, like some of the other elaborations upon the simple version of our legend, may be seen as a way of compensating for the dubious relationship between Puṇḍalīka's parental devotion and the arrival of Kṛṣṇa, by associating him with the famous Viṣṇu-bhakta, and by providing Nārada with an opportunity to praise Puṇḍalīka's *mātāpitṛbhakti*.

The complex versions

In the last part of this paper, I shall deal with the more elaborate versions of the Puṇḍalīka legend, starting with Śrīdhara's version of the *Pd.Pdm.*, which is probably the first example of changes in the conception of Puṇḍalīka. A common feature of these versions is that they are all more elaborate in their descriptions of Puṇḍalīka, investing him with a more or less personal prehistory. As I argued in 'The Legend of Puṇḍarīka' with regard to the *Pd.Pdm.* version, one reason for this might have been the desire to make his parental devotion more easily intelligible; and another, the wish to make him more human, to make him look more like an ordinary bhakta.

On the structural level, these versions show some common features in their descriptions of Puṇḍalīka's prehistory. First of all, they all make him undergo a change or conversion from something negative to something more positive: that is, he becomes a *mātāpitṛbhakti.* In most versions this change takes place in connection with a pilgrimage,[26] and is effected through the teaching of gods or saintly persons. Furthermore, in filling out this structure these versions very often return to one of the motifs found in the classical tradition referred to at the beginning of this paper.

In the version of Śrīdhara, Puṇḍalīka is described as a married man who originally lived a sinful life and ill-treated his old parents – here even given the names Jānudeva and Satyā – in such a way that they decided to go on a yātrā to Kāśī. He and his wife, both on horseback, joined them and on the way he was converted to *mātāpitṛbhakti* in the āśrama of the *ṛṣi* Kukkuṭa, who, due to his devotion to his parents, was so sacred that the three rivers Gaṅgā, Yamunā, and Sarasvatī came to his āśrama every night to purify themselves. After this he returned with his old parents to Pandharpur, here called Lohadaṇḍakṣetra, and spent his life in their service, after which the story continues more or less as in the *Sk.Pdm.* version.

In this version we see that a change is taking place in Puṇḍalīka's character, from a man who ill-treats his old parents to a *mātāpitṛbhakta.* This change takes place on a pilgrimage to Kāśī and is effected by the teaching of the river-goddesses, who point to the *mātāpitṛbhakta* Kukkuṭa as a moral and religious example. As I pointed out in 'The Legend of Puṇḍarīka' this is in fact a doubling of the *mātāpitṛbhakta* motif, which may have been inspired by one of the sources of the 'original' Puṇḍarīka legend, namely the story of Sukarmā in the Padmapurāṇa, already referred to earlier, and which could have been introduced in order to justify the *mātāpitṛbhakti* of Puṇḍalīka.

The version which is most reminiscent of Śrīdhara's and *Pd.Pdm.*'s is the one found in a text called *Lohadaṇḍa urph Paṇḍharapūra kṣetra kaiphiyat,* which was finished by an anonymous author in 1807.[27] However, this is shorter and here Puṇḍalīka's bad behaviour towards his old parents consists in leaving them and going with his wife on a pilgrimage to Kāśī.[28] Furthermore, the name of the *mātāpitṛbhakti* saint is not Kukkuṭa but Citrakūṭa.

The version of Bahiṇā Bāī, called *Puṇḍalīkamāhātmya*,[29] seems also to be influenced by the *Pd.Pdm.* version of the legend. With the only differences that she does not tell under what circumstances on the pilgrimage the conversion in Puṇḍalīka's character took place, and that, as in the māhātmya of Pralhāda Mahārāja, the role played by Nārada in bringing Kṛṣṇa to Pandharpur is here accentuated.

Finally, I shall deal briefly with two versions which seem to be more literary and less dependent upon the *Pd.Pdm.* version. The first of these, the *Puṇḍalīkacaritra* of Kānhā Trimaladāsa,[30] in order to explain the *mātāpitṛbhakti* of Puṇḍalīka combines two stories, namely a story about a demon named Hiraṇyākṣa who lived in Pandharpur, and a story about a childless brāhmaṇ couple named Kuṇḍalīka and Gaṅgā who performed *tapas* at a place called Sūryatīrtha. The *ṛṣi* Nārada visits the couple and tells them to go to Pandharpur. Thereafter he visits the demon, who asks him to tell the secret through which he may meet Parabrahma. In answer to this Nārada, strangely enough, tells him that if he serves his mother and father properly in this life he will meet the Supreme Being.[31] Unfortunately the demon has no parents, and Nārada therefore tells him to be born as the son of Kuṇḍalīka and Gaṅgā.[32] In this way the demon is born as the dutiful Puṇḍalīka and the rest of the story runs like the *Sk.Pdm.* version.

One notes that, instead of the motif of pilgrimage and conversion,[33] Trimaladāsa has in a very original manner used the theme of rebirth, making Puṇḍalīka an incarnation of the demon Hiraṇyākṣa. In this way the conversion of Puṇḍalīka is placed back into his earlier life. Structurally the two versions are, however, similar, since the change of a sinful man into a dutiful one instead becomes a transformation of a demon into a saint.[34] Furthermore, just as we saw a reintroduction of purāṇic motifs in order to legitimize the *mātāpitṛbhakti* of Puṇḍalīka in some of the other versions, it is clear from the name of Puṇḍalīka's father, Kuṇḍalīka, that Trimaladāsa was acquainted with and inspired by the legend of Sukarmā found in the Padmapurāṇa, since this is also the name of Sukarmā's father.

Lastly, I will deal with the version of the Puṇḍalīka legend found in the Ādiparvan of Kṛṣṇadāsa Dāmā,[35] which is the most complex of the versions known to me. Here Puṇḍalīka is a brāhmaṇ who left his parents and started doing *tapas* on the banks of the river Revā. Hearing here about the power (*siddhi*) of Dattātreya he went to meet him. On the way he fancied that he himself had acquired great power (*tapaḥsāmarthya*), since he assumed that he had killed with a mere glance a young brahmacārin who was evacuating his bowels on the middle of the road. As he arrived at the āśrama of Dattātreya he went to the door of Anasūyā to ask for food. Engaged in serving her husband, the *ṛṣi* Atri, she kept Puṇḍalīka waiting, and when she came out Puṇḍalīka was extremely angry. His anger and arrogance, however, disappeared as she told him that she was the brahmacārin whom he had met on the road. After that she told him about three kinds of bhakti, the bhakti of a son towards his elderly relations, the bhakti of a disciple towards his guru, and the bhakti of a servant towards his master.[36] She said that if he would serve his elderly relations at home, then Hṛṣīkeśa would come and give him a fortune.[37] Then Puṇḍalīka went to Varanasi, where he heard a Purāṇa praising Pandharpur.[38] Finally, he left Varanasi and reached Pandharpur, carrying his father in a yoke (*kāvaḍa*), after which the story is very similar to the *Sk.Pdm.* version.

In this version we again find the motif of conversion in connection with a yātrā. Instead of the *mātāpitṛbhakta* Kukkuṭa, Puṇḍalīka here meets the famous *pativratā* Anasūyā, and, as he does not originally belong to Pandharpur, he is inspired to go there by listening to a māhātmya of this place in Varanasi, where, just like in the *Pd.Pdm.* version, he had gone after his conversion. With regard to his former character, his sinfulness in this version mostly consists in his self-conceit. This seems to accord well with what is probably one of the main inspirations of this version, namely the story about Kauśika and Dharmavyādha in the *Mahābhārata*, referred to above, except that the author seems to have replaced the *pativratā* women of this story with Anasūyā, and, with the help of the motif of 'conversion', combined the characteristics of both Kauśika and Dharmavyādha in one person, namely Puṇḍalīka.

Conclusion

In this paper I have tried to show how some features in the development of the legend of Puṇḍalīka may be understood as attempts to solve a basic difficulty in its 'original' version, namely that the *mātāpitṛbhakti* motif lacks relevance in a bhakti context. Further, if we compare the position of the *mātāpitṛbhakti* motif in the simple version of the Puṇḍalīka legend with the epic and purāṇic legends referred to at the beginning of the paper, we note that the difference is mainly contextual. Thus, whereas in the classical legends the motif has a clear contextual function which is either narrative, as in the *Rāmāyaṇa*, or religious, as in the legends of Dharmavyādha and Sukarmā, it does not have this function in the 'original' version of the Puṇḍalīka legend. (In the legends of Dharmavyādha and Sukarmā, it is used to oppose either anti-brahmanical behaviour, like asceticism, or the excessive practice of pilgrimage, both of which may be understood as threats to the family structure.) On the contrary, it might here have been felt by the bhakti milieu to contrast with ordinary bhakti, which would have been a more logical method for Puṇḍalīka to have used in attracting Kṛṣṇa.

Furthermore, I have tried to show how, in compensating for this lack, the later versions have employed various narrative means which give opportunities of explaining the behaviour of Puṇḍalīka, first of all by letting Puṇḍalīka go through a conversion (either through some spiritual instruction on a pilgrimage, or through rebirth), and perhaps also by introducing Nārada as intermediary, and how in this endeavour they often seem to go back to the classical formulations of the *mātāpitṛbhakti* motif for inspiration.

NOTES

1. The theory that Śiva was originally the main god of Pandharpur goes back to Sir Ramkrishna Gopal Bhandarkar, *Vaiṣṇavism, Śaivism and Minor Religious Systems*, Strasbourg, 1913, p. 88.
2. The Legend of Puṇḍarīka: The Founder of Pandharpur', to be published in the proceedings of the 7th World Sanskrit Conference in Leiden, 1987.
3. There are two main Sanskrit māhātmyas of Pandharpur, namely the *Pāṇḍuraṅgamāhātmya* attributed to the *Skandapurāṇa* (*Sk.Pdm.*), of which I have prepared an *editio princeps* to be published soon, and the *Pāṇḍuraṅgamāhātmya* attributed to the *Vārāhasaṃhitā* of the *Padmapurāṇa* (*Pd.Pdm.*), which has been printed in a rather poor edition in Bombay, 1869. Of these the former is almost certainly the older.
4. 'Puṇḍalīka' is the Marathi form, while the Sanskrit texts use 'Puṇḍarīka'.
5. *Pāṇḍuraṅgamāhātmya*, ed. R. C. Dhere, Poona, 1981 (long version), and *Pāṇḍharīmāhātmya*, Bombay, 1980 (short version). Both probably date from the beginning of the 18th century.
6. *Sakalasantagāthā*, ed. R. C. Dhere, Poona, 1983, vol. ii, *abhaṅga* no. 973.
7. Pandharpur, 1929. Probably also from around the beginning of the 18th century.
8. *Mahābhārata*, Āraṇyakaparvan 196–206, ed. V. S. Sukthankar, Poona, 1942. Several MSS call this section of the *Mahābhārata* 'Pativratopākhyāna', but it is interesting to note that it has also been published separately with the title *Pativratamāhātmya tathā mātāpitṛsevāmāhātmya*, by Gaṅgāviṣṇu Śrīkṛṣṇadāsa in Bombay, 1898.
9. पिता माता च भगवन्नेतौ मे दैवतं परम् ।
   यद्दैवतेभ्यः कर्तव्यं तदेताभ्यां करोम्यहम् ।।
   (*Mahābhārata* 3. 204. 17).
10. *Rāmāyaṇa* 2. 63–4, ed. Shastri Shrinivasa Katti Mudholkara, Bombay, n.d.
11. As is commonly known, Śravaṇa Kumār nowadays is a well-known figure on posters and in popular literature. For example, in part one of the *Saṃskṛti-*

mālā of Śrīmatī Premā Sarīn (Gorakhpur, vs 2021) there is a Hindi version of the Śravaṇa story along with other stories from the *Mahābhārata* and the *Rāmāyaṇa*, such as the stories of Prahlāda, Dhruva, and Sāvitrī. Furthermore, I have at hand a poster illustrating the Śravaṇa story accompanied by the following verse:

मांकी पूजा से कोई भी अच्छा पूजनीय स्थान नही है ।
पिताकी आज्ञा से बढ कोई भी वेद मंत्र नही है ।।

The story of Śravaṇa Kumār is not found in the *Rāmacaritamānasa* of Tulasīdāsa, and I have not been able to trace this verse elsewhere. In this case it seems that the motif still holds some of the moral and edifying significance that it had in the Dharmavyādha story of the *Mahābhārata*.

12. *Padmapurāṇa*, ed. Ānandāśrama, Bhūmikhaṇḍa 63 ff.
13. e.g. the tradition that Kṛṣṇa came to Pandharpur in search of his wife Rukmiṇī or Rakhumāī, who had left him in anger because of his relationship with Rādhā, found in *Sakalasantagāthā*, vol. iii, no. 319.
14. Such an exception is the case in an *abhaṅga* by Nāmadeva, ibid., vol. ii, no. 974.
15. e.g. in an *abhaṅga* of Ekanātha, ibid., vol. iii, no. 330.
16. As in the famous *abhaṅga* of Ekanātha: *mājhe māhera Paṇḍharī*, ibid., no. 424.
17. Thus in an *abhaṅga* of Ekanātha, ibid., no. 436.
18. Ed. V. S. Bendre, Bombay, 1959. According to S. G. Tulpule, *Classical Marāṭhī Literature*, Wiesbaden, 1979, p. 378, this work was written in 1645.
19. Thus, Śekh Mahaṃmadbābā calls Pandharpur Lohadaṇḍakṣetra, and makes Kṛṣṇa arrive from Dvārakā instead of Govardhana. Later in the work he has a whole section about Kukkuṭa, here called Kurkoṭa, who, strangely enough, is not described as a *mātāpitṛbhakta*. I am indebted to Dr Michael Martinec of the South Asia Institute of Heidelberg for referring me to this work.
20. According to Tulpule, op. cit., p. 431, this work was written in 1774. I am indebted to Dr Tulpule for a xerox copy of the 6th adhyāya of this work.
21. The only exception is the version of the *Pd.Pdm.*, and the Marathi versions of Śrīdhara, in which Rukmiṇī or Rakhumāī is the cause of Kṛṣṇa's arrival in Pandharpur.
22. This element is only expressed in the versions of Pralhāda Mahārāja, Bahiṇā Bāī, and in the text called *Lohadaṇḍa urph Paṇḍharapūra kṣetra kaiphiyat*, whereas in the *Puṇḍalīkacaritra* of Kānhā Trimaladāsa, Kṛṣṇa goes to Puṇḍalīka in the form of Nārada (*nāradamūrti*) in order to test him. In the versions of Mahīpati and Kṛṣṇadāsa Dāmā, Nārada's accompanying Kṛṣṇa is not explicit. Furthermore, the version of Mahīpati is only a summary one.
23. In 'Gopālpur-Kālā: Some Aspects of the History of Rites and Sacred Places to the South of Pandharpur', read at the Third International Conference on Maharashtra, held in Heidelberg in June 1988, forthcoming.
24. e.g. *Sk.Pdm.* 2. 28cd–29ab:

    सिद्धानामीश्वरो देवि दक्षिणद्वारमाश्रितः ।।
    विष्णुना स्थापितः प्रीत्या नारदो लिङ्गमूर्तिमान् ।

25. G. V. B. Jośī, R. J. Karakambakar, and P. J. B. Gurujī, *Śrīkṣetra paṇḍharapūra darśana*, Poona, 1960, p. 55; S. C. Kulkarnī, *Śrīkṣetra paṇḍharapūra mahātmya*,

Belgaum, 1981, p. 22; S. S. Suṇṭhaṅkar, *Asā āhe Śrīviṭhṭhala*, Belgaum, 1980, p. 84; K. J. Bhiṅgārkar, *Śrī Viṭhṭhala mahātmya*, Poona, 1981, p. 38; and S. Cendavaṅkar, *Paṇḍharapūracā Viṭhobā*, Bombay, 1965, p. 77.

26. This motif might very well have been adopted under influence from the purāṇic legend of Puṇḍarīka, *Padmapurāṇa*, Uttarakhaṇḍa 81, and *Narasiṃhapurāṇa* 64, in which a *ṛṣi* named Puṇḍarīka, leaving his mother and father, family, and friends behind him, sets out on a pilgrimage which finally leads him to Śālagrāma, where he attains his vision of Viṣṇu.
27. Ed. K. Thjulajaram Kshirasagar, *Bulletin of the Government Oriental Manuscript Library*, Triplicane, Madras, 15, 1961, pp. 101–6, and 16, pp. 109–12.
28. A motif which reminds one of the legend about Puṇḍarīka found in *Padmapurāṇa* and the *Narasiṃhapurāṇa*, and referred to in n. 26.
29. Ed. and trans. J. E. Abbott, Poona, 1929, and written some time in the second half of the 17th century.
30. Ed. M. Dhanpalvar, Hyderabad, 1972. The date of Kānhā Trimaladāsa is not known, but according to M. Dhanpalvar a MS of his Pātālakhaṇḍa is dated AD 1701, and it seems probable that he flourished sometime in the 17th cent.
31. मुनी म्हणे तयासी । मी सांगेन परियैसी
    सेवा बरवी आचरसी । पितयाची ।।
    मातापितया सेवा । भवीं करावे तुवां
    तरि भेटेल स्वभावा । नादमूर्ती । ।७६-७ ।।

    (vv. 76–7)
32. मग नारद तयासी म्हणे । आणिक नाहीं उधरणें
    मातापितया कारणें । अवतारू घेई ।।
    इतुकिया अवस्वरीं । कुंडलीक अवधारी
    लोटांगणीं निर्धारीं । आला देवा ।।
    पुत्रकारणें दुखिया । लागे विष्णच्चिया पायां
    मग प्रसन्न जाला तया । देखा । ।७९-८० ।।

    (vv. 79–80)
33. This motif is only indirectly employed in the description of the old couple's travel from Sūryatīrtha to Pandharpur.
34. This is in fact a variation of the motif of the demon devotee so often found in bhakti literature, the most important examples of which are the stories of Prahlāda and Bali.
35. Ed. J. S. Despande and N. D. Patil, Bombay, 1979. According to R. C. Dhere, *Srīviṭhṭhala eka mahāsamanvaya*, Poona, 1984, p. 205, Kṛṣṇadāsa Dāmā was writing earlier than Ekanātha, i.e. probably some time in the first half of the 16th century.
36. अगा पुत्रें भक्ति करावी पित्रुव्यांसि । कां शिष्यें
    भक्ती करावी गुरुचि । कां सेवकें स्वामिचि । करावी भक्ती । ।६.३५ ।।

    (v. 6. 35)

    The term used here is *pitruvya*, which normally means a paternal uncle. However, to judge from the context, Dāmā is referring to Puṇḍalīka's parents.
37. तरी तुं आतां ऐसें करी । तुज पित्रुव्यें आहेत घरीं । तुं
    त्यांचि सेवा करीं । मनोभावें ।।
    मग तुझेया भक्ति आदरसि । चरीत्र पाहों येईल रुषिकेसि ।
    कांहीं वचन मागतां तुजसि । देवो सर्वस्व देईल आपुलें । ।६.३७-८

    (6. 37, 6. 38)

38. In between this and the rest of the Puṇḍalīka story follows an episode about a brāhmaṇ called Trimbaka who went to Pandharpur after listening to the same Purāṇa.

Tukārām: the making of a saint

S. G. TULPULE

The writings of all saints, whether Eastern or Western, are in a way autobiographical, because they write only about spiritual matters, and spirituality is their very life. But Indian saints as a whole have generally no autobiographies, in the literary sense of the term, to offer. The only exceptions, perhaps, are Nāmadev (1270–1350) and Bahiṇā (1623–1700), who have given us brief accounts of some of the important events in their lives. But their autobiographical writings cannot be compared with the masterly and exhaustive lives of Christian saints like St Augustine or St Teresa of Avila as narrated by themselves. When we speak, therefore, about the autobiographical poems of Tukārām we do so with certain reservations. Certainly he is not an autobiographer, and yet his devotional poems show us the making of the man as he developed into sainthood.

Tukārām (1598–1649) spent the whole of his life in Dehu, a village near Poona. His parents died when he was still young and the burden of maintaining the family fell upon him when he was not mature enough to shoulder it. He tried to carry on the hereditary profession of petty trader cum money-lender, but suffered heavy losses because of his over-generous and rather impractical ways. To add to this misery, his first wife and son died of starvation in one of the repeatedly occurring famines. The second wife he married, if not exactly a Xantippe, was a very practical and down-to-earth woman. Tukārām has called her *karkaśā*, a virago. All these things made him forlorn and he turned towards God in order to seek internal peace. If the incentive to spiritual life in the case of Jñānadev, the doyen of Indian saints, was intellectual, it was emotional in the case of Tukārām. In the words of Carlyle it was sorrow that remarried him to God. He has told us very plainly that he was afflicted by the miseries of *saṃsāra* and hence turned to God:

संसाराच्या तापे तापलो मी देवा ...
म्हणौनि तुझे अर्थविले पाया ।

(no. 33)

But it was not an easy way for Tukārām. His was a warring mind, warring against both himself and the outside world. 'Day and night I am fighting against odds,' he says. And the result is a long story of ups and downs, hopes and despairs, deserts and frustrations, ending in a blissful vision of, and union with, God. It is the story of his heart. It begins with his retiring to the hills surrounding Dehu for spiritual reading and contemplation, and ends in his becoming one of the greatest mystics of the world. Every day was a day of awakening for him, and he could have very well said with St Augustine that he died daily. But his daily dying was a further step on the pathway to God, the 'endless end' which he reached around the middle of his life when he was hardly 32 years old. He spent the remaining years of his life in awakening the people from the sleep of ignorance and directing them to the way of bhakti. From the time of his own enlightenment onwards Tukārām lived only to oblige others for their spiritual good. '*Uralõ upakārāpuratā*' ('I now live for others'), he says. He can be fitly compared with Kabīr, who reputedly said towards the end of his life:

> कहै कबीर मै कहि कहि हार्यो ।
> अब मुझे दोस न दइओ ।।
>
> I tried to teach the people again and again; and I have failed.
> So do not blame me any more [for their faults].

Both Tukārām and Kabīr lived for the uplifting of the world after they had reached the acme of spiritual life. In the case of Kabīr it was free play in *behad*, or the spaceless, while in the case of Tukārām it was a symbolic marriage with *mukti*, 'liberation'. These two are like twin stars on the horizon of bhakti vying with each other in their spiritual glory. Neither of them wrote any autobiography. But unlike Kabīr, who is peculiarly silent about his past, Tukārām gave us a few poems (*abhaṅgas*) in which he narrates some important events in his life, though a little reluctantly.

There were two occasions when the admirers of Tukārām approached him for enlightenment about his own spiritual life, and how he developed into a saint. At first Tukārām scorned the idea. He said to them (in the poem beginning *āikā vacana he santa*):

> Listen, oh saints, I am verily a sinner.
> I really wonder why you should honour me;
> for I know in my heart of hearts
> that I have not reached the goal of my life,
> have not been liberated.
> But people blindly follow one another
> and go on calling me a saint, which I am not.
> If you want,
> here is an account of my so-called sainthood.
> As regards my much talked-about renunciation,
> I may tell you that I spent what money I had
> for my family, and not in charity.
> That is my *tyāg* (for which you praise me!)

Regarding my taking to the woods, here is the truth:
I got wearied with my relatives, wife and children,
and I could not show my face to the world.
That is why I preferred to spend most of my time
in the solitude of the hills surrounding Dehu.
Believe me, there was no spiritual urge behind it.
It is true that I worship the Lord Viṭṭhal;
but then, this is only the continuation
of what my ancestors were doing.
But I lack their faith and devotion. (no. 36)

This poem of Tukārām is a masterpiece of self-effacement, of what the *Bhagavadgītā* calls *amānitva*.[1] Commenting on this last term Jñānadev says: 'The real saint hides his cleverness, denies his greatness, and shows himself as a madman to the world.'[2] This is exactly what Tukārām has done in the present poem. Elsewhere he calls himself 'mad' (*tukāveḍā*) and asks the Paṇḍits to spit him out: '*aho paṇḍita jana, tukā ṭākāvā thunkona*' (no. 551).

His devotees, however, knew that he was not to be taken seriously when he denied that there was anything holy about himself. So they insisted upon their demand for his life story, and finally Tukārām succumbed to their wishes. He promised them that he would at some time unfold for them his spiritual travail. And he kept his word. He composed for them a twenty-one line *abhaṅga* narrating the major events in his spiritual life. The line beginning with the words *naye bolo, pari pāḷilẽ vacana* is the refrain of this poem. It means: 'I should not really speak about myself; but I have given you my word and must keep it.' The very fact that this line enjoys the status of refrain is enough to show the extreme self-denial of Tukārām. In this rather long *abhaṅga* (no. 35) he tells us the following things:

1. He was born into a family of śūdras and belongs to a low caste. He followed a hereditary profession (as grocer and money-lender) and worshipped his family deity. (Elsewhere Tukārām thanks God for being born a śūdra; for this has saved him from hypocrisy.)
2. His parents died and he became extremely afflicted by *saṃsāra*, worldly life.
3. He lost all prestige and money in a famine when his wife (and son) died of starvation.
4. That put him to shame; in his profession, too, he suffered loss.
5. Then he thought of renewing a temple in the village which had become delapidated. (This reminds us of a similar act of St Francis of Assisi on receiving a divine message which said: 'Francis, go and repair my House, which is wholly falling into ruin.')
6. He started performing *kīrtana*, devotional singing, in that temple, on the Ekādaśī (eleventh day of each fortnight). He was, however, a total novice in that art, and a little insincere too.

7. So he learnt by heart some sayings of the poet-saints with faith and respect.
8. He began by repeating the refrain sung by the main singers, or playing second fiddle, and this he did while purifying his mind with *bhāva*, loving devotion.
9. Not feeling ashamed of it, he consumed the water used in washing the saints' feet.
10. He performed obligations to others as far as lay in his power, not minding any physical hardships.
11. He paid no heed to what people said about him, for he was wholly disgusted with life.
12. Not caring for the opinion of the majority, he relied on his mind to distinguish between the true and the false.
13. Believing in the instruction received from his guru in a dream he held firm faith in the Divine Name.
14. At this stage he was inspired to compose poetry, which he did with full faith in God (Viṭṭhal).
15. But there was a stroke of prohibition from certain quarters which upset his mind.
16. (Eventually) he immersed the scripts of his poems in the river (Indrāyaṇī) and sat fasting at the door of God, who finally solaced him.
17. If he goes on narrating the many incidents in this way, it will take him long.
18. He may, therefore, say in brief that he is content with the present. As regards the future, it is known only to God.
19. He has come to know this, that God is merciful, and will never neglect His devotees.
20. He is Tukā's whole and sole treasure, and it is He who has made him speak out.

Tukārām has enlarged elsewhere upon some of the events narrated in this *abhaṅga*. For example, there are a few poems on the incident of his manuscripts being saved by God from the waters (nos. 122–4). There are also some other events described elsewhere; e.g. his response to an invitation from King Śivājī (68–80), or his instructions to the brāhmaṇ sent to him by Jñānadev (129–53). But it is the above-mentioned twenty-one line *abhaṅga* which is the nucleus around which to construct the spiritual biography of Tukārām. It describes in a nutshell the history of the making of this great saint, who became the pinnacle of the cult of devotion, the Bhāgavata Dharma, the foundation of which was laid by his predecessor, Jñānadev. The events it mentions are few. But then we have to remember that great men have short biographies to tell. Plotinus, according to his biographer-disciple Porphyry, refused even to say anything about his personal life. So we are fortunate that Tukārām gave us at least an outline of his spiritual career. It tells us how, starting from the life of a low-born agriculturist-trader, Tukārām ultimately merged into the godhead. Tukārām's poems are the history of his soul: how he commenced his spiritual life, what difficulties he met with on the way, what heart-rending experiences he endured in his lone journey, how ultimately a gleam of light began to shine on him, until finally he realised God, and became one with him. As Ranade says, there is a sort of 'Hegelian dialectic' in Tukārām's soul.[3] In the first stage of his spiritual career, he seems to have resolved to withdraw himself from the life of the world with a determined effort to win spiritual knowledge. This is the stage of positive affirmation. Then comes the stage of negation, the dark night of Tukārām's soul, a stage where he is warring with his own self. Finally, there is the stage of a new affirmation, namely the transforming of the original determination and the following negation into a final vision of the godhead, a stage which supersedes them both.

Tukārām is thus unique among Indian saints in sharing with us the story of his spiritual development.

NOTES

The English word 'saint' denotes in this paper (wherever used in an Indian context) a Sant poet of west or north India. The Marathi verses cited have the same numbers in P. N. Jośī, ed., *Sārtha Tukārām gāthā*, 3 vols., Bombay, 1966, 1967, 1968.

1. *Bhagavadgītā*, 13. 7.
2. *Jñāneśvarī* (ed. S. V. Dandekar, 8th edn., Poona, 1986), 13. 191.
3. R. D. Ranade, *Mysticism in Maharashtra*, Poona, 1933, p. 281.

Sadguru and the Holy Spirit

CHRISTOPHER SHELKE, SJ

Sant Rāmdās (1608–81), a Maharashtrian mystic akin to the Vārkarī movement of Pandharpur, not only influenced Śivājī, the founder of the Maratha kingdom, but gave spiritual and moral vigour to the thousands of Marathas who helped Śivājī to establish Hindu self-rule (*svarājya*). Rāmdās has considerable influence even today on the social and political life of Maharashtra. In this paper I shall examine the concept of the Sadguru (divine guru) in his compositions, and I would like to point out how this concept is close to that of the Holy Spirit that dwells in the heart of men. Therefore I will make some references to the spiritual growth of Rāmdās, as well as to some Christian mystics.

Rāmdās' teaching about the Guru

In the *Dās-bodh* (in the fourth *samās* of the first *daśak*), Rāmdās praises the Sadguru. According to Rāmdās, the Sadguru pervades the universe; he is the highest *puruṣa*, the flag of heaven and brother of the poor. The Sadguru is greater than the touchstone (*parīs*), the wishing tree, or the wishing cow. Rāmdās bestows such great praises on the Guru because the latter imparts real knowledge to the disciple and teaches him the way of right behaviour.

Rāmdās accepts traditional doctrine about the guru. According to this the brāhmaṇ is guru to all castes because it was his duty to teach the Vedas and religion (*dharma*) to all others: 'The brāhmaṇ is a guru to all, even if he becomes actionless. One must always surrender oneself to him with complete submission.'[1]

This is an acceptance not merely of traditional Vedic doctrine on the part of Rāmdās but also of the ritualistic worship performed by a brāhmaṇ as a pujārī, and therefore Rāmdās says that words uttered by a brāhmaṇ can make even a casteless person a brāhmaṇ. The 'actionless' brāhmaṇ cannot give *brahmadnyān (brahmajñāna)*, true knowledge. For the attainment of this one requires the Sadguru; without the Sadguru there is no possibility of salvation:

> You may say that the God of gods gives grace through the brāhmaṇ: then why should one require a Sadguru? I answer, truly, that there is no attaining to the real treasure without a Sadguru. (5. 1. 19)

Therefore the one who desires salvation must have a Sadguru; without a Sadguru none has achieved salvation; this will not happen until the end of ages. (5. 1. 44)

Rāmdās had no guru

Although Rāmdās states the extraordinary importance of a sadguru in the spiritual life, he did not take anyone as his own guru. In childhood he continually urged his father to give him *anugraha* (initiation), but the father refused, considering Rāmdās' young age; then Rāmdās persistently besought his elder brother, but he too refused for the same reason. Then Rāmdās, still a child, took shelter in the temple of Hanumān and sat in meditation. Neither during his childhood nor during his quest for spiritual life in Takali, nor during his mendicant days, do we learn of anyone whom Rāmdās made his guru.[2]

Rāmdās' entire *sādhanā* thus takes place without a guru. However, in spite of his own experience of achieving *brahmajñāna* without a guru, he states that without a (sad)guru there is no *brahmajñāna*. Here there seems to be a contradiction between Rāmdās' life and his teaching.

Readiness of a disciple to serve

Initiation by a guru without the readiness of a disciple to serve is of no use, and if the disciple is ready, then the initiation becomes merely an empty sign, or a word, or mere ritual. The above-mentioned incidents in the childhood of Rāmdās show clearly that there is no absolute need of initiation or of a guru, but that what is required is the will, the readiness, on the part of the devotee. It is traditionally accepted that through initiation the disciple puts himself under his guru's protection. The latter then secretly transmits to him a mantra, which he must faithfully repeat, and sometimes the guru adds some rite that must be observed. The disciple is made to believe that he will make wonderful progress by the quasi-magical power of the sacrament, and will profit enormously, both spiritually and temporally, if he repeats the mantra and carries out the rite. But Rāmdās' life indicates that it is not a guru's mantra but the search made by the disciple that makes the mantra fruitful. Abhishiktananda, the modern Christian swami who lived for years completely in the Indian monastic way of life, writes of mantra and initiation that 'either the disciple is not ready, in which case the so-called initiation is no more than the empty word, or else the disciple is ready, when neither a word nor a sign is necessary. The initiation then happens spontaneously.'[3]

Functions of a sadguru

Rāmdās narrates various functions of a sadguru (earthly guru). The sadguru unites the devotee with God; he frees him from the troubles and pains of *saṃsāra* (life and the world); by giving knowledge he liberates the disciple from the bondage of wishes and offers him the knowledge of things and their nature; further he explains his teaching, and advises abstinence. Thus he destroys *avidyā*, ignorance, in the disciple. At the end of his explanation about the guru, Rāmdās reduces all these functions to one: the real guru proposes the knowledge of the self and of God. The one who has achieved *ātmajñāna* also achieves *brahmajñāna* (i.e. 'knowledge of the Highest'). Through the achievement of *ātmajñāna* one realises God and achieves unity with him: 'Listen to the characteristics of *jñāna*: *jñāna* means *ātmajñāna*, to see oneself by self, yes, this is the real knowledge. To realize the God of gods, to acknowledge the true nature, to ask about the eternal and passing; this is knowledge' (5. 6. 1–2).

Ātmajñāna

The realisation of *ātmajñāna* by a person is simultaneously the realisation of *brahman*. It is an experience of the assertion *aham brahmāsmi*. The devotee comes to the realisation that he is not different from the infinite *brahman*. However, this realisation comes at a moment when the devotee (*jīvātmā*) is still existing by itself. This is the ultimate existential experience of finiteness and infinitude, of the reality of both self and the infinite *brahman*. Some call this experience *māyā*, 'illusion', because here the experience of the finite and the infinite comes to the mind as something deceptive or illusory: this illusion can exist in the mind, but only in so far as the mind does not realise its true being. This state is referred to by Rāmdās as *turyā*.

In *turyā*, then, a certain dualism persists. *Turyā* is not *śuddhajñāna*, which is a single state of knowledge. The soul can achieve such knowledge because the Sadguru dwells in its heart, but not by study of the scriptures nor of any other book. This is possible only by recognising the self (5. 6. 19). *Śuddhajñāna* means realisation of the self by the self; it is a process of going into the self:

> I have not looked for Sanskrit books; I did not look for Marāṭhā books; the grace-bestowing person abides in my heart; he is the *sadguru-svāmī*. Now, there is no need for Sanskrit scriptures nor for Prakrit books, for my Lord with his grace dwells in my heart. (5. 6. 33–4)

Ātmajñāna and the Sadguru

Rāmdās has clearly stated that the only way of achieving self-knowledge, *ātmajñāna*, is to go into the depth of one's own heart. The one who dwells in the depth of the heart is the voice of a Guru, the Sadguru himself. Here in the depth of the heart we find three things: the voice of the Guru, the hearer of this voice, and the content of the hearing. These three are not separate entities in the heart, but amount to a single reality perceived in three different forms. The devotee hears a voice that makes certain demands on him; these demands spring from his own heart; the hearer of the word, the word heard, and the word spoken are one and the same reality, as are *sādhaka*, 'devotee', *guruvacana*, 'the Guru's voice', and Guru. Here is the reality of the devotee's self.

From another perspective we can say that these three principles are united in the same person. The first is the voice of the Guru, the second the Guru that speaks, and the third the inner voice, or that infinite one who enables the inner voice to come to expression in the devotee's heart. Are these three different principles? No, there exists only a single reality here: the mystery that is sensed in the heart, of God dwelling in the heart of man. Therefore we say that the Sadguru imparts to his disciple the very mystery of himself, that this mystery is his word, and knowledge of the *mahāvākya*, 'great utterance': *aham brahmāsmi*. In this process we find that the word of the Guru, the Guru, and the disciple or devotee are united.

Stages in spiritual life

In the development of spiritual life Rāmdās proposes four different stages. These are the *baddha avasthā*, the *mumukṣa avasthā*, the *sādhaka avasthā*, and *siddha avasthā*. In the first or *baddha avasthā*, an individual finds himself in the bondage of the world, of passions, of worries, and of other miseries of this *saṃsāra*. He is full of vices and his inclination is to the lower things. He takes delight in wealth and women. Day and night he is given to the satisfaction of the senses.

The second stage is the *mumukṣa avasthā*, one of being thirsty and hungry for a higher nature. The devotee realises the various bonds that keep him tied, he desires abstinence, he strives for the company of saints, he is hungry for heaven and hopes to achieve it. He desires to be the servant of good people.

In the third stage, *sādhaka avasthā*, the individual renounces vice, surrenders himself to the virtuous, and listens to the explanation of non-dualism. He breaks the bonds of dualism, holds firm to *ātmajñāna* and allows it to grow in his soul. During this stage, in spite of having a body, he behaves as if he has no body: *dehī asūni videhī jāhālā*. At this stage the soul at times experiences doubts and bondage and weakness of resolve.

By contrast the one who has achieved *siddha avasthā* has firm resolve, has no doubt in his mind, sees that all things are empty and vain, and has satisfaction only in his resolve, never forgetting that he is the *ātman*, the *brahman*. One cannot describe him because he is already beyond attributes and body. The *siddha puruṣa* knows his own nature (*svarūpa*) and his inner state becomes the *svarūpa* itself. The highest dharma, according to Rāmdās, is to be in the *svarūpa*. The *siddha*, or *sādhu, puruṣa* always abides here, performing his rightful *svadharma*.

Ātmajñāna and *svarūpa*

Although according to Rāmdās spiritual development takes place in a soul through these four stages, with awakening of spiritual life in the disciple in the *mumukṣa* stage and this life reaching completion in *siddha avasthā*, the devotee does not leave this life when in *siddha avasthā*; he is very much alive, but all his attention is centred on knowledge of the self and of the *brahman*. All things are equal to him. This is the stage of equanimity or dispassion.

Rāmdās has nowhere stated that in this stage the individual loses his individuality. He is one with the *brahman*, but not totally lost in (or completely united with) *brahman*. Here the individual neither ceases to be, nor does his being taken into the *brahman* make him lose his individuality. He remains his own individual, aware of his own self.

Svarūpa and the ideal of life

We may ask ourselves whether this state is merely notional, or existential. Considering its characteristics we have to say that it is not merely notional, but is one to be achieved by practice, abstinence, and meditation. It is a state to be experienced in his whole being by one who is *sādhu*: comprising not merely a knowledge of *svarūpa*, but the experience of *svarūpa* and of its identity with the self. We have noted that Rāmdās did not take anyone as his guru. In Jamgaon, as a child named Nārāyaṇ, he began the practice of worshipping in front of Hanumān; after coming to Panchwati he established an idol of Hanumān, and changed his name from Nārāyaṇ to Rāmdās.[4] After his mendicant days he established eleven images of Māruti (Hanumān) all over southern Maharashtra. Māruti was thus an ideal for Nārāyaṇ; and it was thus that he adopted the name Rāmdās, 'servant of Rām'. Hanumān is the ideal servant of Rām, always ready for the service of his master, he knows his master's mind and acts according to it, not waiting for his order. This devotion of service, *dāsyabhakti*, is the characteristic of the spiritual life of Rāmdās. The worship of Tulajābhavānī and of Rām, as the powerful ones, are only different expressions of this devotional service.

The Ideal and the Guru of Rāmdās

For Rāmdās Hanumān is not a guru but an ideal and an example. This ideal is not proposed to Rāmdās by anyone, nor prescribed nor given to him; it is the fruit of a gradually increasing devotion and of his long search for truth and meaningful life. It is an outcome of self-search, an expression of Rāmdās' very self.

Dāsyabhakti is an expression of the *svarūpa* or *svadharma* of Rāmdās, who has experienced in his life how religion (dharma) had been destroyed and morality ruined, and how supposed leaders and guardians of society had become selfish and given up to servitude. In this *svarūpa* of Rāmdās is included consciousness of the foreign rule of the Muslims, the oppressive rule of the Mughals, and that of Bijapur. This experience indicates to him the need for power, for vigour and the support of the Almighty. The *svarūpa* and *svadharma* of Maharashtra could only be rebuilt by a restoration of this vigour: the real 'śakti'. The *svadharma* of Rāmdās has become the realization of such a *sāmarthya* (capacity); he also realises that he must possess this *sāmarthya* if he is to approach others and impart it to them. Rām, Tulajābhavānī, and Hanumān are the beloved objects of Rāmdās' worship, by the brightness of which his spiritual life had developed. One characteristic common to all these three deities is that they are known as vigorous and powerful. Their worship can allow their devotees to challenge heroes. Rām, the glory of the kṣatriya family, is an example and an ideal for all kṣatriyas; Tulajābhavānī is the powerful mother who appeared for the destruction of evil ones in Parghat, while Māruti is the incarnation of Rudra, who had achieved many feats by his own strength. Rāmdās brought to his own life the aspect of each of these deities that they destroyed the unrighteous, and re-established Dharma; and he keeps their example constantly before him in his labour. For him, the spread of their worship in Maharashtra and Bhārat will encourage vigour and promote abstinence, and people will guard religion by building up its foundations of morality. To encourage devotion for these three deities Rāmdās started various new celebrations and feasts, built temples, and taught; and through his temples to Rām, Tulajābhavānī, and Hanumān he created a new, bright wave of vigour in Maharashtra.[5]

Ātmajñana and the inner voice

The spiritual progress of Rāmdās and his entire spiritual life shows us that the latter is merely a realisation of the self in historical context. In his heart Rāmdās sees the self and its obligations; seeing the self includes hearing the voice of the innermost being. Hearing this voice brings the responsibility to be faithful to it. This inner experience of Rāmdās has become the ideal, and also the measure, of his spiritual life. We can thus say that the *ātmajñāna* which he proposes to strive after is the voice that speaks in his innermost heart, revealing to him what he should do. It is not a revelation from outside himself of the method and aim of his spiritual life, nor a receiving from outside himself of new thoughts transmitted through the senses. It is an opening of the self, and going into the cave of one's heart where the inner voice is heard. The inner voice heard and the inner word spoken are one and the same. This amounts to the self being revealed and realised, as the inner voice reveals itself to the person. The mystery of the depth of the heart and that of the Guru are identical, and the experience of being face to face with 'oneself' in the most secret corner is that of being face to face with the Guru. (Cf. Abhishiktananda, quoted below.)

The inner voice in some other saints[6]

Now we turn to other saints of the Vārkarī tradition. Sant Tukārām speaks of his guru, saying that he appeared to him in a dream and gave him a mantra of Rāmkṛṣṇahari, whereupon he was overwhelmed with joy.[7] Nāmdev accepts Visobā Khechar as his guru: and what has Visobā done for Nāmdev? When Visobā was resting with his feet on the *piṇḍ* of Śiva, Nāmdev was scandalised at such conduct; whereupon having seen Nāmdev's reaction Visobā asked Nāmdev to put his foot on the place where God was not present. In that very moment, the truth of the omnipresence of God came vividly to Nāmdev's mind. Visobā gave Nāmdev neither a mantra, nor a lecture, nor revealed any mystery to him; it was Nāmdev himself who realised the mystery of the omnipresence of God. Eknāth also had no contact with a human guru. These examples show that it is not a master–disciple relationship, as with the ancient Greeks, which is important. The important thing is that the disciple, the one who is on the path of bhakti, seriously reflects on his own life and its various events and with the help of these goes into the depth of his own heart. There he experiences truth and enlightenment and finds strength and guiding force.

> The guru is most certainly not some master or professor, or preacher or spiritual guide, or director of souls who has learned from books or from other men what he, in his turn, is passing on to others. The guru is one who has himself first attained the Real and who knows from personal experience the way that leads there; he is capable of initiating the disciple and of making well up from within the heart of his disciple the immediate ineffable experience which is his own – the utterly transparent knowledge, so limpid and pure, that quite simply 'he is'.
>
> Is it not in fact true that the mystery of the guru is the mystery of the depth of the heart? Is not the experience of being face to face with the guru that of being face to face with oneself, in the most secret corner, with all pretence gone?[8]

The one who reveals and what is being revealed can, as far as they are being revealed, be considered as being outside the person, but, as far as they are being heard and comprehended by a person, are in the person himself. That one who is there is nothing other than the spirit of the creator that is within an individual. This is called in Christian theology the indwelling spirit and is the gift of God to every person at his creation.

In the Christian tradition

Now I proceed to the experiences of some mystics from the Christian tradition. The first is that of the renowned mystic St Teresa of Avila, the second that of St Bernard, and the third that of a Carmelite nun.

St Teresa:

> I felt that his presence was there. Ignorant people told me that he was there only through his grace; I could not accept it, for as I have said, it appeared to me that He

himself was present. Therefore I found myself in difficulty. One learned man from the order of the Dominicans freed me from my doubt; he said to me that God was present as he has communicated it to us. This was a great relief for me.[9]

An inner peace is there, and neither pleasure nor pain would be able to take away from this presence of the three persons, as long as it is there. This presence is of such a nature that it cannot be doubted: it is self-evident; one lives it; as St. John says, 'he comes into the soul to indwell there', and this is not only through grace alone, but in the very fact that he allows this presence to be felt. It brings so much good along with it.[10]

St Teresa of Avila has here experienced the presence of the three persons in her own self. She has no doubt about this presence. It was self-evident to her. This indwelling, as Teresa describes, was not only through grace but was there on account of the presence of God. Here Teresa experienced in her inmost self the presence of the Holy Trinity.

St Bernard:

I must say (I speak as if a fool) the Word has visited me and this has happened quite often. Although It has entered me many times, I did not feel its coming but only that It was present. I recollect that It was with me; sometimes I did manage to perceive its coming, but never felt It enter, nor that It was departing from me. It neither entered through the eyes, because It has no colour, nor through the ears, because It produces no sound, nor through the nose, because It is diffused not in the air, but in the spirit . . . Certainly It did not come from within my own self, because It is good, and I know that there is no goodness in me. I came out of myself completely, and behold, the word was still high above. I searched eagerly below and in spite of my search, I found it was still deeper. I looked out of myself, far away, and discovered that the Word was there too. I looked into myself and It was still further within me. In this way I learnt that what I read is true: we live in him, we move in him and we are in him.[11]

In this experience St Bernard perceives the Word as a reality which is in himself as well as outside himself. It is a reality that cannot be merely perceived by any sense, for it remains beyond sense-perception yet it is always felt and continuously experienced.

Mother Isabelle Dourelle (d. 1914), a Carmelite nun, writes in her diary:

during my prayers on the evening of the third day, I entered the interior of my soul, and seemed to descend into the giddy depths of an abyss where I had the impression of being surrounded by limitless space. Then I felt the presence of the Holy Trinity, realizing my own nothingness, which I understood better than ever before, and the knowledge was sweet. The divine immensity in which I was plunged and which filled me had the same sweetness.

Without seeing anything with the eyes either of the body or the soul, I realized that God was present, I felt His gaze bent on me full of gentleness and affection, and that he smiled kindly upon me, I seemed plunged in God. My imagination was submissive and did not act. I did not hear any noise that might be going on around me. My soul looked fixedly into the gaze invisibly bent on me, and my heart repeated untiringly, 'My God, I love Thee!'[12]

The experience of the Ground of our being

What has this Carmelite nun seen? In the depth of her being she realises her own nothingness. This is the spirit of the Father that groans in every heart. As St Paul says, 'likewise, the spirit also helps our infirmities, for we know not what we should pray for as we ought: but the spirit itself makes intercession for us with groaning which cannot be uttered. And he that searches the hearts knows what is the mind of the spirit, because he makes intercession for the saints according to the will of God' (Rom. 8: 26–8).

What is experienced by this Carmelite nun is nothing other than the groaning of the spirit of God in her heart. This is the presence of the Holy Trinity in herself. She feels that God is looking at her with love. The realisation of her own nothingness brings into her a realisation of God's infinitude. Such an experience is always of the infinite, which some experience as God, others as the Trinity, some as the infinite Word, and some again as *brahman*. Yet it is the same reality that is experienced: that of the Ground of our being.

The object of this ultimate experience is always one's own being, with its finite realities or concrete existence: oneself, as well as the limitless power that is given in the self. It includes one's helplessness and the power that is given to one, which is realised either as a supporting hand or as a mere hope allowing one to look into the future. The experience is one of weakness and strength, of unity and duality, of the self and the divine, of disappointment and hope. Some have verbalised this experience as one of nothingness, others as of God, of the Trinity, of *brahman*, or of *ātmānubhava*.

Ātmānubhava as communion with the infinite

After this experience the soul – the devotee – looks at every creature, at every event of his life, and at himself from a totally different perspective. For him nothing is important now. All seems without any value. The only value for him is in feeling the presence of his self or of this ultimate reality. He wishes to remain within the Ground of his being, with God himself.

Finally we come to some important questions: Who has taught the devotee this knowledge? Who has given him this realisation? Is it a gift bestowed on him by someone outside himself or one given to him from within his own existence? One thing is certain: that it is at once a realisation of one's own being, or self, being loved or cared for, and also the ultimate knowledge of the self and of one's own existence, that makes a person conscious of what he is and is not, and also what he should and should not do. It is the consciousness of what one is and what one should be. It is the experience of the self, an *ātmānubhava*. Rāmdās and other Indian mystics attribute this *anubhava* as *ātmajñāna* to a Guru, while the Christian mystics attribute it to the Holy Spirit that dwells in the hearts of men. One thing is common here: the idea of a gift given to man in his own self, at his creation and in his existence, of God's self-communication to each individual, of the Ground of being, and of communion between man and God.

NOTES

1. Translation of the *ślokas* of *Dās-bodh* is my own. All the quotations from *Dās-bodh* are from S. S. Dev, *Saṭīp Dās-bodh*, 10th edn., Bombay, 1978.
2. K. Śeḷake, *Don Sākṣātkārī*, Poona, 1981, p. 106.
3. Abhishiktananda, *Guru and Disciple*, trans. H. Sandeman, London, 1974, p. 25.
4. S. K. Altekar, *Śrī samartha caritra*, Karahad, *śaka* 1845 (1923), p. 22.
5. Śeḷake, op. cit., p. 202.
6. i.e. Sant poets. – Ed.
7. V. P. Paṇḍit, *Tukārāmbāvācyā abhaṅgāmcī gāthā*, vol. i, Bombay, vs 1869, *abhaṅga* 369.
8. Abhishiktananda, op. cit., p. 29.
9. Cf. A. Barrientos, *Obras Completas: Santa Teresa de Jesus*, Madrid, 1976, 2nd edn., p. 1135.
10. Ibid., p. 135.
11. Cf. *Sermo cantica canticorum*, 74. 5, *St. Bernardi opera*, Rome, 1958, pp. 242 f.
12. D. C. Butler, *Western Mysticism*, London, 1927, new edn., p. 16.

Special features of the Vārkarī cult as regards *sādhanā*

G. MORJE

This paper gives a brief description of the background and aspects of the ritual of the modern Vārkarī cult. The distinctive character of the cult is to be found in its particular combination of elements of *smārta* tradition and popular belief. It is probable that the Vārkarī cult came into existence during the period of the Yādavas of Devagiri (1187–). The cult is essentially that of bhakti or devotion in Maharashtra. It is also known as Vārkarī Panth, Vārkarī Sampradāy, or Bhāgvat Sampradāy, all of which expressions carry the same meaning; and as Mālkarī Panth, because its followers wear a rosary of tulasī beads around their necks. This symbolic rosary plays a very important role in the religious life of a Vārkarī. The cult is essentially Marathi-orientated. The history of Marathi literature begins with the literature of the Vārkarī Sant poets. It is chiefly due to these poets that Marathi literature took shape and developed. From the literature of Jñāndev and Nāmdev (thirteenth century AD), it can be inferred that the tradition of the Vārkarī cult was in existence before Jñāndev and Nāmdev. Both poets link together two names, Puṇḍalīka and Viṭhobā, many times in their *abhaṅga* poetry. The available data and research done in this field does not allow a date to be given for the emergence of the Vārkarī cult. But it is certain that although Jñāndev was not the founder of the cult, he was the first and the greatest of its exponents.

The cult is a spiritual movement, or, more exactly, a body of groups gathered around spiritual leaders, gurus. The only public manifestation of this cult is the pilgrimage to Pandharpur, made at least once in a year. For entry into the cult there is no ceremony or rite of initiation which the Vārkarī must undergo comparable to the *upanayan* or sacred-thread ceremony among some high-caste Hindus, or to baptism among Christians. For one who wishes to enter the cult there is only a very simple ceremony, akin to the taking of a monastic vow. The candidate presents himself together with Vārkarī friends before the head of one of the Vārkarī groups, and expresses his desire to join the cult. He must bring a rosary of tulasī beads. The guru tells him to place it on any religious book, such as *Jñaneśvarī, Eknāthī Bhāgvat*, or *Tukārām Gathā* (these three books are known together as *Prasthān-trayī*). Thereupon the guru places the *tulasīmālā* round the initiate's neck (every Vārkarī must wear this rosary) and then gives him spiritual advice, as follows:

1. to speak the truth throughout life;
2. to respect women other than one's wife, as one's mother or as Rukmiṇī (the wife of Viṣṇu);
3. to pray God and request him to keep him away from sin;
4. to be a strict vegetarian;
5. to visit Pandharpur as a pilgrimage at least once a year, on the eleventh day of the bright fortnight of the lunar months of either Āṣāḍh or Kārttik (if possible, to go to Alandi, the place of Jñāndeva);
6. to fast on Ekādaśī days;
7. to recite a six-letter mantra (Rāma-Kṛṣṇa-Hari), with the help of *tulasīmālā*, as a daily ritual;
8. to read some portion from *Jñāneśvarī* or any religious book approved by the cult, and to recite *Haripāṭh* (a collection of *abhaṅgas* of Jñāndev);
9. to carry out all the worldly duties of life honestly, keeping in mind God (Viṭhobā).[1]

A man wears the rosary of tulasī beads around his neck, and markings (*mudrā*) of *gopicandan* (a kind of white clay) and *bukkā* (black, scented powder) on the forehead and on the hollow of the face along the ears, and has a small flag (*patākā*) of red ochre-coloured cloth on his shoulder. These are the main signs distinguishing a Vārkarī from others, and they are of great importance to the Vārkarī in his devotion. In daily rites and rituals these emblems also play an important role. To understand why they are considered so important by the cult, and what are regarded as their special qualities, it is necessary to study the ethnological background of the cult: where it came into existence and flourished. It is first necessary to note its geographical background.

To a Vārkarī, Pandharpur is the holy city of Maharashtra. This town lies more or less in the centre of the large drainage basin of the Bhima and upper Krishna rivers, which is bounded on the north by the long ranges of the Balaghats, on the west by the steep wall of the Sahyadri mountains, on the south by the Godavari range; and on the east it slopes into the low plains of the eastern coastline through several valleys. These valleys finally merge into the vast open plain around Pandharpur which forms the southern part of Maharashtra. The boundary line between the Marathi and Kannada languages passes not far to the east of the town of Pandharpur.

This geographical situation has given Pandharpur its importance. The town lies at the junction of several important lines of communication, where the roads coming from Ahmadnagar, Poona, Kolhapur, Bijapur, and Sholapur converge. The great railway line which connects Bombay and Madras runs some twenty miles to the east. There is, however, a small branch line from Kurduwadi Station on the Central Railway, which passes through the town of Pandharpur, connecting the Central and Southern Railways at Miraj. At times of pilgrimage there are bus services run by the government and private agencies throughout Maharashtra, and connecting with other regions.

From the agricultural point of view the region is not rich, although the soil in itself is fertile following good rain. The main crops are millet, known as *javār*, and *bājrā*. The *kuṇbī* or Maratha peasant has to toil hard to get his living. The country immediately surrounding Pandharpur is, however, relatively rich along the banks of the Bhima. Its deep, black soil is especially fine. Jowar covers nearly 70 percent of the tilled land. The Vārkarīs come mostly from the countryside, and most are farmers, brāhmaṇ landlords, or petty officers, craftsmen, or traders. Few of them are from towns, and these, although some wealthy townsmen are found among them, are mostly shopkeepers and traders from Bombay, Poona, and other such towns. Fewer still are drawn from the ranks of the middle class; there are some small businessmen or professionals such as teachers, professors, doctors, and lawyers. At the beginning the Vārkarī cult was looked upon as a popular religious movement of the country folk. Afterwards, under some great leaders, it slowly gained disciples among the intellectual class also.

Anybody who has a thirst for God can be a Vārkarī: there is no precondition that he or she should belong to a particular religion, caste, creed, or sex, or should be of particular poverty or wealth. Faith in the God of Pandharpur (Viṭhobā) is itself sufficient qualification. This faith is known in the Indian context as *śraddhā*.[2] The importance of the spirit of *śraddhā-bhakti*, or respectful dependence upon God, is that it is the devotee's first step in the system of the bhakti cult or doctrine of devotion. It should be kept in mind that any cult or religious group is the product of its time and environmental demands, and takes its own shape from the ideas and materials available, seeking to use these to create a harmony between nature and man, with the activities of human life and the local traditions of the groups concerned an aspect of that harmony. Thus within a cult, particularly in Indian culture, nature and environment are inseparable from human life.

Taking into consideration this human relation to environment, it is possible to analyse the function of the main implements or cult objects which the Vārkarī uses in his *sādhanā*. *Tulasīmālā, gopicandan, bukkā*, and *patākā* are the main cult objects. It is interesting to see what are the symbolic meanings and functions of these objects to the Vārkarī. Tulasī (*Basilicum sanctum*) is regarded as the favourite plant of Kṛṣṇa, hence to express the love of God a Mālkarī wears a tulasī garland; and by offering a garland of tulasī leaves he worships God (Viṭhobā). The tulasī plant, found in most parts of India, is three or four feet in height, and of two kinds, white and black. Its juice is used in many Āyurvedic medicines, for example, that of the black tulasī is used in treating typhoid patients, and tulasī seeds are used against dysentery and diarrhoea and in treating skin complaints. The tulasī plant is regarded as purifying the surrounding air and preventing disease.[3] The above functions are indicated already by Suśruta[4] and Caraka.[5]

Some traditional beliefs illustrating the place of the tulasī in Indian culture and Hindu religions are as follows:

1. A house surrounded by tulasī plants has the holiness of Ganges water, and the God of death is kept away from that house;
2. one who takes a false oath while holding tulasī leaves in his hand will go to hell and remain there for ever;
3. it is auspicious to see the tulasī plant, to touch it, to worship it, and to plant it; and to eat tulasī leaves regularly is to destroy sin for ever;
4. at the time of death of a Hindu tulasī leaves are placed in the mouth of the dead body, on its forehead and on both ears.[6]

From folk-tales in Maharashtra there is some information regarding the origin of the tulasī plant and its relation to the gods Kṛṣṇa and Viṣṇu.[7] Vṛndāvanī, Viśvapūjitā, Viśvapāvanī, Puṣpasara, Nandinī, and Kṛṣṇajīvanī are some of the names given to the plant:[8] each being explanatory of some attribute of it. Each part of the plant is respected in India either because of its medical qualities or for religious reasons. Hence the tulasī plant is the most important cult object for the Vārkarī in his devotion.[9]

The *tulasīmālā* is a rosary of tulasī beads prepared from wood of the plant. The Vārkarī uses this kind of rosary to honour God (Viṭhobā) and as an aid to devotion in muttering the name of God. The small beads of the rosary are separated from each other by a special kind of knot, called *brahmagranthi*, 'knot of creation'. The beads are strung on a strong cotton thread. Each rosary has an extra bead offset from the continuity of the main loop, called *sumeru*, which acts as reference point, so that the practitioner can know when he has completed a rotation of the rosary. The rosary is an essential part of most of the techniques of *jap* (muttering prayer). It serves mainly as a means to maintain awareness. While garlands are most commonly made from tulasī wood, sandalwood, *rudrākṣa*, China clay, or pieces of crystal, it is the *tulasīmālā* which is used most commonly in prayer. Tulasī is, as noted above, a highly venerated and sacred plant, and is regarded as having psychic and healing properties: a strong and purifying effect on the emotions and a soothing effect on the mind. The tulasī is in addition regarded as an incarnation of Lakṣmī, the wife of lord Viṣṇu (Viṭhobā). There are many interpretations of the significance of the number of beads (usually 108, sometimes 54 or 27) in the *tulasīmāla*. Three given below throw some light on the Vārkarī's understanding of this:

1. '1' represents the supreme consciousness; '8' the eight aspects of nature consisting of five fundamental elements, namely, earth, water, fire, and ether, plus *ahaṅkāra* (individuality), *manas* (mind), and *buddhi* (the

sense of intuitive perception); '0' represents the cosmos, the entire field of creation;

2. '0' represents Śiva, '8' Śakti, and '1' their union (*yoga*);[10]
3. according to the view that in the solar system there are twenty-seven constellations moving around the sun, each having four positions in its way through the cycle, there will be a total of 108 positions in all.[11]

The Vārkarī uses the fragrant and medicinal powder *bukkā* as a cult object in devotion. It seems that the word *bukkā* is not of Indo-Aryan origin although it is attested to in a Sanskrit source.[12] The Arabic word *abīr* is also used in Marathi as an equivalent to this term.

Abīr (bukkā) is to be offered to God at times of worship including times of *kīrtan* and *bhajan*, as well as *yātrā*. All devotees smear *bukkā* on their forehead, and devotees in the Vārkarī cult set importance on bringing *bukkā* as a divine gift from their holy places. *Bukkā* is used throughout India, and offered to God at Alandi, Pandharpur, and the other centres of the Bhāgvat Sampradāy in Maharashtra.[13] This substance is of two kinds, white and black. Black *bukkā* is made from coal, sandal, *nagarmoṭh* (a sweet-smelling grass), *bakul* flowers, *vāl* (redwood, *Adenanthera pavonina*), *davaṇā* (southernwood, *Artemisia abrotanum*), *maravā* (sweet marjoram), and other ingredients; white *bukkā* (used mainly in Bengal and among Jains) is made from camphor, sandal, *davaṇā, nācaṇī (Eleusine coracana), devadāru* (a species of pine), cloves, *velacī* (cardamom), etc.[14] Application of *bukkā* on the forehead etc. (see above) in accordance with yoga tradition is regarded as contributing to concentration and health of the mind. The Vārkarī cult and particularly Jñāndev inherit yoga traditions from the Nāth Sampradāy. *Gopicandan* is used in the same way as *bukkā*.

The last object used in *sādhanā* is *patākā*. This is prepared by dipping a white rough cloth in water of *gerū*, a kind of red ochre. It is also known as *guḍhī*. The Vārkarī carries a *patākā* on his shoulder to express his achievement in the field of devotion. It is a token of oneness with the supreme ultimate (*advaita*).

Although the Vārkarī cult has roots going far back into various earlier communities, such as those of the Nāths and of Rāmānuja, it has its own recognised identity. Yet the cult is not rigid in its practice of worship. The Vārkarī is mainly a devotee of Viṭhobā, but has no sense of alienation from other gods, such as Śiva, Rām, and Kṛṣṇa. He regards Viṭhobā as his father, mother, brother, and sister at one and the same time because Viṭhobā is all in all to him. His cult has accepted the Vedic teaching, that one supreme God is manifested in many, known by different names.

The cult requires, finally, no hard-and-fast rules of penance, ritual, or any special behaviour for *sādhanā* like various other cults. Rather, with easily available means, the devotee can approach God even while enjoying his worldly life: 'You can buy liberation there for nothing'.[15] Thus ease in practice encourages, rather than restricts, access by members of the Vārkarī cult to a wide range of religious traditions and cultural values.

NOTES

1. *BSK*, vol. viii, p. 607.
2. B. K. G. Shastri, *The Bhakti Cult in Ancient India*, Delhi, 1975, p. 4. *Śraddhā* is the embodied spirit or goddess at whom the whole course of devotion is aimed.
3. *BSK*, vol. iv, p. 156; Y. R. Dāte and C. G. Karve, *Sulabh viśvakoś*, Poona, 1950, vol. iii, p. 1098; G. R. Bhide, *Vyāvahārik jñānkoś*, Kolhapur, 1938, vol. iii; S. V. Ketkar, *Mahārāṣṭrīya jñānkoś*, Poona, 1925.
4. *Suśruta saṃhitā*, *c*. 1st cent. BC.
5. *Caraka saṃhitā*, *c*. 1st cent. AD.
6. *BSK*, vol. iv, p. 155.
7. Babar Sarojini, ed., *Nandadeep*, pp. 330–1, on the emergence of the tulasī plant after the churning of the ocean and on the mythology of princess Tulasī (who performed penance to obtain Viṣṇu as her husband, was loved by Kṛṣṇa, and elevated by Viṣṇu to the status of Rukmiṇī).
8. Ibid., p. 331.
9. *BSK*, p. 156.
10. Swami Satyananda Saraswati, *Bihar School of Yoga*, Monghyr, 1980, pp. 20–2.
11. S. S. Hanamante, *Saṅket-koś*, 2nd edn., Solapur, 1964, p. 404.
12. K. P. Kulkarni, *Marāṭhī vyutpatti koś*, Poona, 1964, p. 592; R. L. Turner, *A Comparative Dictionary of the Indo-Aryan Languages*, Oxford, 1966, s.v.
13. *BSK*, vol. i, p. 175.
14. *Marāṭhī viśvakoś*, vol. i, p. 310.
15. Tukārām: J. Fraser Nelson and J. F. Edwards, *The Life and Teaching of Tukārām*, Madras, 1922, p. 47.

Some particular expressions of the Ṣūfī presence in north India

The text of *Alakh Bānī*

S. C. R. WEIGHTMAN

In 1971 Bharat Prakashan Mandir published in Hindi a work entitled *Alakh Bani or Rushd Nama of Shaikh Abd-ul-Quddus Gangohi* with 'Introduction, translation, and annotation by Saiyid Athar Abbas Rizvi and Shailesh Zaidi'.[1] The importance of the *Rushd-nāmah*, which was probably written about AD 1480, derives from the fact that, although in all other respects it is a characteristic Persian *risālah* on the model of the *Lama'āt* of 'Irāqī and the *Lawā'ih* of 'Abd ar-Rahmān Jāmī, in one regard it is unique in that dispersed throughout its fairly modest compass there are some 250 lines of Hindi verse. Any authentic verses from the fifteenth century are important for the student of Hindi, but these verses have a further importance on account of their religious content and the use made of them by a middle-ranking but significant Ṣūfī shaikh. Since the *Alakh Bānī* of Rizvī and Zaidī is the first and only edition of these verses to appear in print since the publication of a lithographed edition of the *Rushd-nāmah* in Jhajjhar in 1896, it is now clearly time to examine carefully the text that the two authors offer of these important verses and their treatment of them. It is to this task that the present paper is addressed.

Alakh Bānī divides into two parts: the first half of the book is a lengthy introduction dealing with Sufism, the line of 'Abd al-Quddūs, his writings and the *Rushd-nāmah* in particular, and various aspects of the Hindi verses within it. The second half contains the Hindi translation of the Persian text with the Hindi verses, as the authors read them, occurring at their appropriate places usually without any attempt at interpretation, although translations are given of the marginal and interlinear glosses given in the Persian text. The introduction contains much of the necessary background information, and, taken together with Digby's full and perceptive analysis of the *Rushd-nāmah* and the attitudes of 'Abd al-Quddūs,[2] obviates the need to describe and discuss the work as a whole here. This permits attention to concentrate solely on the Hindi verses and matters relating to them, central to which are the sources used by the two authors in their establishment of the text.

Although the authors state that manuscripts of the work are numerous,[3] they have chosen themselves to make use of only two manuscripts, one from Aligarh and one from Berlin, in addition to the lithograph edition, which they rightly conclude is based on a manuscript similar to that at Aligarh. The Aligarh manuscript, which is in the Subhan collection in the University of Aligarh library, has a colophon dating it as AD 1676. The Berlin manuscript, which is in fact in the Universitätsbibliothek, Tübingen, has no colophon and no given date. The Aligarh manuscript has the commentary of the author's son, Shaikh Rukn al-dīn Quddūsī, written in the margin, some of which relates to the Hindi verses, and also between the lines there are sometimes glosses of either lines or words of the Hindi, and occasionally a Hindi line or word is vocalised. The Berlin manuscript has no commentary, gloss, or vocalisation. At some stage in its history the Aligarh manuscript was rebound and some pages were replaced in a different order from that of the Berlin manuscript. The authors have followed the Berlin order, which most accords with the demands of sense.

Even if all the manuscripts were to agree, and these two do not, there still remains the major problem of establishing the Hindi text, since the Arabic script is as ill suited to representing the phonology of Hindi as it is to Ottoman Turkish or even Persian. This complex task was apparently accomplished by Zaidī in just three or four days.[4] Although no details are given of the editorial procedures employed, and although the text is minimally critical in that only two of the available manuscripts have been utilised, this does not, of itself, mean that the readings are wrong, merely that they are unsafe. In order to take this investigation further, additional manuscripts will have to be used.

In addition to the Aligarh and Berlin manuscripts, and the lithograph, a copy of which is in the British Library, microfilms have been obtained of a manuscript in Princeton University Library (no. 113), one in the Anjuman-i Taraqqi-i Urdu, Karachi (catalogue entry 748), and two in the Sherani collection of the Punjab University Library, Lahore (catalogue entries 1246 and 1247). The Princeton manuscript has only some quarter of the Hindi verses written in the margin in the first segment of the work and no commentary or vocalisation. The manuscript is dated AD 1673. The Karachi manuscript is complete; it has the full commentary and interlinear glosses, and most of the Hindi is vocalised. It is dated AD 1724 and the scribe claims not only to have lavished great care on his work, but to have compared it with the 'original'. Of the Lahore manuscripts, the first is incomplete at the beginning but it contains some two-thirds of the work. It has the full commentary and interlinear glosses for the Hindi verses in it as well as being mainly vocalised. It is dated AD 1648. The second manuscript is complete but undated. It has less commentary and fewer glosses than the first, and there is little vocalisation.

With regard to the relationships between the manuscripts, it will be sufficient for present purposes to divide them into two groups on the basis of variation both in the Persian text and in the Hindi. The first group consists of the Aligarh manuscript, of which the lithograph is a copy, and the Princeton manuscript. The second group comprises the Karachi manuscript, the two in Lahore and the one in Berlin. The second group, although internally diverse, consistently offers the most probable readings for Hindi verses, but it must be said the pattern of relationship between the four manuscripts is too inconstant to allow for a coherent and mechanical doctrine of editorial preference. To illustrate this point and to make a start on this investigation of the *Alakh Bānī* text, it will be helpful to consider a three-lined *sabad* which occurs about a third of the way into the text. The microfilm of the Aligarh manuscript is missing this page, so the readings are those of the lithograph (A), the Karachi manuscript (C), the second Lahore manuscript (D), the first Lahore manuscript (E), of which this is the first poem due to the manuscript being damaged, and the Berlin manuscript (F). By this point in the work the Princeton manuscript has stopped showing the Hindi verses. The system of transliteration will be self-evident for those familiar with the Arabic script, although the use of 'ø' to represent *sukūn*, that is to indicate that the preceding consonant has no vowel, may be initially surprising. All head this poem *sabad.*

A	MRHW	PNDYT	MRNW	MYTHA
C	MaRaHu HuWø	PaNøDiYøTa	MaRaNu	MiYTHA
D	MRHW	PNDYT	MRN	MYTHA
E	MaRaHu HuWø	PaNøDiYøTa	MaRaNu	MiYøTaHaA
F	MRHW	PNDYT	MRN	MYTHA

A	JWN	MRNA	ShRY	GWRKH	DHYTHA
C	JaWø	MaRaNu	SuRiY	KuWøRaK2aH	DiYøTHaA
D	JW	MRNY	SRY	KWRKH	DYTHA
E	JuW	MaRaNu	SiRiYø	KuWøRaK2Hu	DiYøTaHaA
F	JW	MRN	SRY	KWRKH	DYTHA

A	MW'Y	TYN	JYW	JA'Y	JHAN
C	MuW'YN		JiYøWu	JaA'iY	JaHaAN
D	MW'YN		JYW	JAY	JHAN
E	MuWø'iYN		Ji'Yu	JaAY	JaHaANø
F	JW'Y		JYW	JAY	JHAN

A	JYWT	HY LY	RKHW	THAN
C	JiYaTaHiNø	JiYøRaA	DiYøHa	TaHaAN
D	JYTHYN	JYRA	DYNH	THAN
E	JiYaTaHiNø	JiYaRaA	DiYøHu	TaHaAN
F	JYTHN	JYRA	DYH	THAN

A	JYWTYN	CYRYN	JW	KWAW	MW'A
C	JiYaTiY	JiYaRiYøN	JaWø		MuWaA
D	JY'TYN	JYRY	JW		MWA
E	JiYaTiYNø	JiYaRiYøN	JuW		MuWaA
F	JYTYN	JYRYN	JW		MWA

A	SW'Y	KHYLY	PRM	NShNK	HWA
C	SuWø	KiHiYøLaYø	PiRaM	NiSaNøKa	HuWaA
D	SW	KHYLY	PRM	NSNK	HWA
E	SuWø	KiHYøLY	PiRaMa	NiShaNKa	HuWaA
F	SW	KHYLY	PRaM	NSNK	HWA

These then are the readings for these three lines in the four manuscripts and the lithograph. The text given in *Alakh Bānī* is as follows:[5]

सवद

मरिहौ पंडित मरनौ मोठा जौ मरना श्री गोरख धीठा ।।
मृए तें जिउ जाय जहाँ जीवत ही लै रखौ तहाँ ।
जिउ तें चीरें जो कोउ मुआ सोइ खेलैं परम निसंक हुआ ।।

It is clear from this that the text is, with certain unexplained modifications, the text of the lithograph – Aligarh manuscript (A). The text of the Berlin manuscript (F) is written in footnotes, again with unexplained renderings: मरिहौ पंडित मरन मीठा । जो मरन श्री गोरख डीठा ।। जोइ जीव जाय जहाँ । जियतैं जियरा देइ तहाँ ।। जियतै जियरें जे मुआ । सो खेलै परम निसंक हुआ ।। Not only then is there a failure to attempt to reconcile the two variant texts, but they are presented with modifications that obscure their original form so that the reader is unable to make the attempt himself. Given the various readings transliterated above most scholars would probably reconstruct the poem as follows:

मरहु हो पंडीत मरणु मीठा जो मरणु सिरी गोरक्ख दीठा ।
मूएँ जीउ जाय जहाँ जियतहि जियरा देहु तहाँ ।
जियतें जियरें जो मुआ सो खेलै पिरम निसंक हुआ ॥

The translation of these lines would be as follows:

Die, oh Pandit, [for] to die is sweet, [if it is the death] which Gorakh saw.
Where the spirit goes at death, place there the soul while still alive.
He who dies while his soul still lives sports in love having been freed from fear.

The total reliance on the Aligarh manuscript is not restricted to this verse but is common to all the verses. The text given throughout is that of the Aligarh manuscript as read by the editors, and the variants as read from the Berlin manuscript are sometimes given in full in the footnotes, sometimes in part, and sometimes not at all. Only in one verse is there an attempt to use the Berlin manuscript to help establish the text, and that is where the verse is particularly obscure due to being pseudo-Sanskrit. Not only then have the authors failed to use all the readily available sources, they have failed to make use of the second manuscript they do have. The problems the authors have created in consequence, however, derive not solely from defective editorial procedures, but also from the fact that the Aligarh manuscript when compared with all available manuscripts appears to be the most divergent and eccentric. This can be seen from the readings given above. A further example will reinforce the point:

A	Gur	HYRA KuR	CRA	KuDAR
B	KuR	HYRA KiRø	CRA	KuDAR
C	KuRu	BaYøRaAKuR	CiYøLaA	KuDaARa
D	KR	BYRAKR	CYLA	KDAR
F	KR	BYRAKR	CYLA	KDAR
G	KuRø	BaYøRAKR	CYLA	KWDAR

A	KHWDY	NKSY	HYRA	SAR
B	KHWDY	NKSY	HYRA	SAR
C	KuHuWDaYø	NiKRaYø	HiYøRaA	SaARu
D	KHWDY	NKRY	HYRA	SAR
F	KHWDY	TKRY	HYRA	SAR
G	KHWDY	NSRY	HYRA	SAR

This verse is not found in E, but is found in both the Aligarh manuscript (B) and the Princeton manuscript (G). The lithograph (A) follows B, of which it is a copy but has misread the sukūn, ø, in B and represented it as u between K and R in the first line. The verse has only eight words in it, but the Aligarh manuscript differs from the others in respect of three of them. Moreover, HYRAKiRø is a beautiful example of a scribe changing a word he does not know, बैरागर , into one he does know, हीरागिर , even though it would result in an unsatisfactory repetition of हीरा in both half lines. This shows very clearly how hazardous it is to rely solely on the Aligarh manuscript. The text given in *Alakh Bānī* slavishly follows the Aligarh manuscript:[6]

गृरू हीरागिर चिरा कुदार खोदे निकसै हीरा सार ।।

Out of the four variants between the Aligarh and the Berlin manuscripts, only one, चेला, is given in the footnotes. Given all the readings, a better text would be as below.

गृरू वेरागर चेला कुदार खोदै निकरै हीरा सार ।।

This would mean: 'The Guru is a mine of diamonds, the pupil a shovel; if he digs, there will emerge the essence of diamonds.'

The reliance on a single divergent manuscript, however, is not the only source of confusion: the opportunities offered by the Arabic script for the misreading of Hindi words are considerable, and such misreadings are well represented in the text of *Alakh Bānī*. Perhaps the most blatant example is the first line of a *dohrā* on p. 33. The readings are as follows:

A	JY	SWJHY	SHNS	HY
B	JY	SWJ(H)Y R	SHNS	HY
C	JiYø	SaWø JiYø Ri	SaHa(N)S2a	HaYø
D	JY	SW JY'RA	SHNS	HY
F	JY	SW JY R	SHNS	HY

A	SBHY	APN	SWY
B	SBHY	APN	SWY
C	SaB2HYø	AaPaYN	SuWø'iY
D	SBHY	APYN	SWY
F	SBHY	APYN	SWY

This is given as follows: जो सोझै रस हंस ही सबही आपन सोई । No variants are given from the Berlin manuscript, but, in order to help the reader, in the footnotes the following two phrases appear: 'जो शोध करे' । 'हदय में ब्रह्म को' । The footnotes compound the error of the reading. The line should in fact be read as follows:

जे सौ जे रि सहंस है सब्भी आपैं सोई ।

This means: 'If a hundred, if indeed a thousand, everything is he himself.' The certainty of this reading is established by a preceding Persian verse which translates as: 'If there are a hundred things, or if more than a hundred thousand, all are one if you see the reality.' Here the context should have prevented the swan of *rasa*'s descent into the text. Nothing, however, could have been expected to prevent the reading given for the first word, which is unaccountable, since it is not attested in any manuscript.

Should it be thought that, in this instance, a certain lack of clarity in the manuscripts excuses these misreadings, it must be said that there are numerous examples where this is not the case. In the verse given in *Alakh Bānī* as देखो री मन बूझो री देखो अंवं बानी ।[7] all the manuscripts agree in their readings of ANWN BANY, which most familiar with Hindi Ṣūfī literature would immediately recognise as अनवन बानी , where अनवन could also be read as अनवन, meaning 'different', 'various'. The whole line would then mean: 'Look , oh *man*, and understand, look at the different colours.' This is precisely what the Persian gloss requires it to be. But the reading given is inexplicable, and confusion is further confounded by the footnote, which glosses the final two words as अमृत वाणी . Another example is on p. 23, for which the various readings are as follows:

A	ANCL	KANTH	JW	ATPT	DYNY
B	ANCL	KANTH	JW	ATPT	DYNY
C	AaNøJaLa	KaANøTiHø	JuWø	AuTaPaTi	DiYøNHaY
D	ANCL	KANTH	JW	ATPT	DYNHY
F	ANJL	KANTH	JW	ATPT	DYNHY
G	ANCL	KANTH	JW	ATPT	DYNHYN

A	TW	HM	PYH	SWN	MAJA	KYNY
B	TW	HM	PH	SWN	BACA	KYNY
C	TaWø	HaMø	PiYa	SuWøN	BaAJaA	KiYøNHaY
D	TW	HM	PY	SWN	BACA	KYNHY
F	TW	HMN	PY	S(Y)WN	BACA	KYNHY
G	TW	HM	PY	SWN	BACA	KYNHYN

The text of this line is given as: अंजुलि गांथ जो उत्पति दीनी । तव हम पिय सों बाचा कीनी ।।. In the footnotes अंजुलि is glossed as अंजुरि, and गांथ as यश . As an additional help to the reader the two half lines are rendered into modern Hindi as follows: सृष्टि को उत्पन्न करते समय प्रदान किया । तव हमने ईश्वर से बातचीत की ।।. It must be said that such a degree of explanation is rare. Whether it makes things any clearer, however, is another matter. Since the context is concerned with the beginning of Creation, it seems probable that this line refers to the covenant made between God and man which is commonly mentioned in the Ṣūfī writings. The most likely reading of this line then would be as follows: अंचल गाँठि जो उत्पति दीन्ही । तौ हम पिय सूँ बाचा कीन्ही ।।. This would mean: 'When the knot was tied in the hem at the beginning of Creation, then we entered into a covenant with the Beloved.' It is, of course, only the first two words of the first half line that are in question here, but a correct reading of the Arabic characters as Hindi makes the difference between sense and obscurity.

There are, as has been said, a number of instances of obvious misreadings of the kind just discussed, that is to say, misreadings when the Aligarh manuscript is clear and not at great variance with the other manuscripts.[8] Presumably such mistakes arise from a basic lack of understanding of what the lines in question mean. Certainly those glosses designed to help the reader which have already been quoted would confirm such an incomprehension. Such glosses are rare, and, where they do occur, are not always obscure, but it is difficult sometimes to understand the thinking behind them. The very first verse contains the line क्यों नहि खेलूँ तुझ संग मीता । मुझ कारण तें इंता कीता ।।. This seems to be perfectly clear: 'Why should I not sport with you, oh friend? For my sake you have done so much.' But the word कीता is glossed as दुख, पीड़ा ।. No doubt the originator of this gloss had his own reasons for transforming a past participle into 'pain', but it would be idle to speculate on what they might have been. Curiously, this practice of giving strange glosses to words one does not understand is well in keeping with the tradition of the Aligarh manuscript. The scribe, puzzled by the word माई, 'mother', 'friend', which occurs at the end of one verse, clearly had recourse to an Arabic dictionary since he glosses it as 'water'.

Enough has already been said and demonstrated in this examination of the text of the Hindi verses in *Alakh Bānī* to conclude that it is thoroughly unsatisfactory. It is unsafe and uncritical because it makes use of only two of the available manuscripts, of which only one, the Aligarh manuscript, is used to establish the text, and that has been shown to be eccentric in its readings. It is furthermore unreliable because in a number of places the Hindi readings given of the Arabic letters are unsatisfactory and obscure. There is no doubt that this is a difficult text, but its difficulty is commensurate with its importance. It is a great pity that in a book that contains much that is interesting and well done, the Hindi text should be so bad. The actual translation from the Persian is both accurate and elegant, although there are places where a different text would have been preferred, and obscurities in the Persian and Arabic are sometimes matched by an equal obscurity in the Hindi rendering. There is now a need for a properly edited text of these important and interesting verses, and it is hoped that the forthcoming critical edition prepared by the present author will meet this need.

NOTES

1. अलख़बानी शेख अब्दुल कुद्दूस गंगोहीकृत रूश्दनामा का हिन्दी अनुवाद तथा संपादन.
2. S. Digby: 'Abd Al-Quddus Gangohi (1456–1537 AD): The Personality and Attitudes of a Medieval Indian Sufi', *Medieval India*, Aligarh: Aligarh Muslim University, 1975, vol. iii, pp. 1–66.
3. *Alakh Bānī*, Mandir, Aligarh, p. xiv.
4. डाक्टर ज़ैदी ने ३–४ दिन में ही समस्त दोहों इत्यादि का एक शुद्ध पाठ तैयार कर दिया । (ibid., p. xix).
5. Ibid., p. 40.
6. Ibid., p. 25.
7. Ibid., p. 18.
8. On p. 26, कोदा is read for कौड़ा, on p. 35, अर्वाहत is read for औहट (three and a half), on p. 37, कोद is read for गृद and सोद for सृद ; on p. 46, सृने दनक जे वाहरू is read for सृनी दंग जे पाहरू, on p. 48, होसै is read for होसी, on p. 51, एको काम न आव सवै जव परसै वेग is read for एको काम न आवसी जव पड़सी वेरा, on p. 57, गहे is read for गहै, and भुवनै is read for विहृनी, on p. 73, भै is read for भी, on p. 76, करौ is read for गुरू, and सुथ is read for सुठि. .

Kutuban's *Miragāvatī*: its content and interpretation

S. M. PANDEY

Kutuban's *Miragāvatī* is a Sūfī romance in Hindi which was composed in AH 909 (AD 1503), during the period of Husain Shāh Sharqī, an important king in the Jaunpur kingdom (AD 1394–1505). The poet describes the king, his generosity, and his kingly power, and he refers to the date of the composition of his work in the following words:

उन्ह के राज यह रे हम कही
नौ सै नौ जौ संबत अही ।।[1]

In his [Husain Shāh's] reign I narrated this poem. The year was nine hundred and nine.

At the end of the poem Kutuban also mentions the Hindu Vikrama year:

जहिआ पंद्रह सै हुत साठी
तहिआ यह चौपाइन्ह गाठीं ।।[2]

I composed these *caupāīs* when the year was 1560 [AD 1503].

Miragāvatī is, like the other Hindi Sūfī romances, an allegorical poem. The leading female character, Miragāvatī, represents divine beauty on earth, while a secondary heroine represents worldly love. The prince (the leading male character) is a seeker of love whose ultimate goal is Miragāvatī. On the Sūfī path of divine love a lover dedicates his life, suffers physically and mentally, and remembers God continually in order to achieve success. Forests, demons, sea journeys, crocodiles are all symbols representing hurdles on the Sūfī path that the hero has to overcome. Demons are evils on the path and ascetics are guides who lead the hero to success. According to Kutuban divine love is a gift of God; it is already assigned to the seeker's fate.

Kutuban's preamble

Praise of God

The poet begins with praise of God: the creator (*kartāra*), one (*ekaṃkāra*), invisible, dwelling in all the world; *alakhanirañjana*, the one that cannot be seen; existing in the form of light; causing the beholder to forget himself.[3] Following the Qur'ān, Kutuban then adds that God is neither in the form of man nor of woman; he has no father or mother, but is alone; no one else is equal to him; those who claim he has an equal go to hell (*naraka*) . . . All the birds twitter 'He is one, only one . . .' The paṇḍits have thought and said 'there is no peace in having two Gods'.[4]

Muhammad

Kutuban states that the creator first created the light of Muhammad and then for his sake manifested himself in the forms of Śiva and Śakti. He who does not repeat his name burns in the fire and cannot get salvation. He who remembers Him in his heart and utters words of prayer obtains salvation and goes to paradise (*indrāsana*) . . . 'He [Muhammad] is the king; he is the prince (*rāva*). For the sake of his love, God has created the whole world'[5]

The four friends of Muhammad

Kutuban, like all other Sūfī poets in Hindi, described the friends of the prophet: Abū-bakr, the first to accept Islam, who has magical powers (*siddhi*); Umar, who was famous for his justice; Usmān, who compiled the Qur'ān at the command of Muhammad; and Alī, the expert swordsman who conquered many forts thought to be impregnable.[6]

Kutuban's teacher

Following the Persian *masnavī* tradition Kutuban gives details of his teacher Shaikh Buḍhan:

Shaikh Buḍhan is a true teacher, by remembering whose name, the body (*śarīra*) is purified. He who touches his feet while recollecting his name is purified in the two worlds. He is a Suhrawardī; has destroyed all my sins, old and new; and has incarnated himself in a new form. Whomsoever he showed the path has reached the goal in a moment, provided he knew how to walk that path and could follow the path of truth.[7]

It is suggested that Kutuban was the disciple of Makhdūm Shaikh Buḍhan, who was in turn the disciple of Shaikh Muhammad Isā Tāj of Jaunpur, a distinguished Chistī. Buḍhan seems to have been initiated into both the Chistiyā and the Suhrawardiyā orders.[8] However, another Shaikh Buḍhan, a great musician, lived during the time of Husain Shāh Sharqī in Barnawa in the Meerut district near Delhi. The latter were both important Indian Muslim musicians of the day and the Shaikh's dwelling became a rendezvous for musicians from Delhi, the Deccan, and Jaunpur.[9] Although Shaikh Buḍhan was a Chistī like the other Buḍhan and his Suhrawardī connections are not very clear, it is most likely that Kutuban was a disciple of Shaikh Buḍhan of Barnawa. A Sūfī saint did sometimes have the authority to initiate his disciples into more than one sect, and it would not be surprising if we later discover that Buḍhan of Barnawa had this authority.

In a passage of *Miragāvatī*, moreover, Kutuban gives details of *rāgas* and *rāgiṇīs* in a very technical manner. This indicates that Kutuban was a musician himself, and encourages us to believe that Kutuban might have been a disciple of the musician saint Buḍhan of Barnawa.[10] (Barnawa became a centre of Muslim culture after Timur's invasion of Delhi in 1398, and was then named Mubārakābād.)

The contemporary king
Alluding to King Husain Shāh, Kutuban praises his greatness, learning, and deep study of the Qur'ān, his righteousness resembling that of Yudhiṣṭhira, his skill in languages, and his military prowess. At this point he also refers to his own composition (in two months and ten days) of *Miragāvatī*, a work requiring concentration of heart and mind to be fully understood.[11]

Kutuban clearly follows the Persian *masnavī* tradition in the verses of his preamble relating to God, Muhammad, the reigning king, etc. This can be illustrated from the compositions of Nizāmī (1141–1209: *Laylā-Majnūn, Shīrīn Khusrau*) and the Indian poet Amīr Khusrau (d. 1325).[12] The Hindi poets including Kutuban also follow Persian tradition in their references to their spiritual teachers; unlike the Persian or Turkish *masnavī* writers they do not, however, describe the prophet's heavenly journey (*Mirāj-i-Paighambar*) or their reasons for composing their works.

The Hindi Sūfī poet Maulānā Dāūd was the first poet to borrow these themes. In *Candāyan*, which was composed in 1379, Maulānā Dāūd dedicates the first seventeen verses to depicting God's excellence, the prophet's glory, the contemporary king Firozshāh Tughlaq, and his own teacher the Chistī saint Shaikh Zainuddīn. Candāyan set the example for Kutuban's *Miragāvatī* (which it also resembles in its *caupāī-dohā* structure and Avadhī language); and use of these introductory themes became an established tradition in Hindi *premākhyānas*.[12]

The narrative

Birth and childhood of the hero
The great king Gaṇapati Deva of Candragiri prayed continually to God for a son and eventually a son was born to him, as handsome as the full moon. The king invited priests to name his son and they chose the title Rājakuṁvara, consulting all the planets and checking the almanac; they told the king that everything would be well in his son's life except that he would suffer from *viraha*, the pain of separation from a woman.

It is significant to note here that the prince was predestined for pangs of separation and suffering in love. This governs the whole course of events in his life.[13]

The child is precocious and, given to the custody of nurses, starts to speak within a year. At five his education begins; he quickly learns to read the Qur'ān and becomes an expert in polo (*haiṅgarī*) and shooting (*bejha*).

Youth, the first glimpse of Miragāvatī, and the prince's suffering

When hunting, the prince beholds a hind having seven colours and a supernatural ability to assume many different forms; the hind is superbly beautiful and the prince falls in love with her. But the hind vanishes into a nearby lake. The prince's love is so profound that he forgets his own existence in the wish to see her. He enters the lake to search for her but cannot find her. He is distraught by love and will not leave the lakeside and its beautiful trees and gardens. He insists that the king build him a palace by the lake. A great palace of seven storeys is constructed and, in the upper storey, scenes from the *Rāmāyaṇā* such as the abduction of Sītā, the *līlā* of Kṛṣṇa with the milkmaids, and several other love stories are painted, together with portraits of Bhīma and Kīcaka, Bhartharī and Piṅgalā, Arjuna and Draupadī, Sahadeva with all the Vedas, and finally the hind.

The prince suffers throughout the three months of Bhādoṃ, Māgha, and Jeṭha, i.e. throughout the rainy, cold, and summer seasons. After one year a group of fairies appears, one of them being Miragāvatī in a second supernatural guise. Miragāvatī is conscious of a supernatural aspect of her love for the prince and his for her.

Miragāvatī's beauty and the prince as a yogi

The *nakhasikha* description of Miragāvatī is given; the prince steals Miragāvatī's clothes and thus stops her from flying away (in her guise as a fairy). Miragāvatī tells the prince that it was out of love for him that she had assumed first the form of a deer then that of a fairy. The couple now unite in love, but soon Miragāvatī finds her original clothes and flies away to her father's country, Kañcanapura, where after his death she becomes ruler of the country.

The prince assumes the guise of a yogi and goes in search of Miragāvatī from one forest to another and eventually reaches a city singing songs of *viraha*, where an ascetic (*jaṅgama*) tells him of the path to Kañcanapura. The prince sets out and begins the sea journey, but his ship is caught in a whirlpool for one month; he prays to God; he has other adventures while at sea, then eventually is able to get to the shore.

The prince reaches a grove of mangoes, where a beautiful princess, Rupamiṇī, has been made captive by a demon and enslaved. The prince kills the demon and frees Rupamiṇī. Rupamiṇī's father, the king of Subudhyā, gives his daughter to the prince in marriage. However, the prince cannot forget Miragāvatī and very soon abandons Subudhyā and goes in search of Miragāvatī in Kañcanapura. Before leaving Subudhyā he tells Rupamiṇī that he had started his journey from 'Gorakhapura' and that he is a disciple of yogi, Vṛṣanāthā.

The meeting with Miragāvatī

On his way to Kañcanapura the prince encounters and kills a fearsome man-eating demon who has taken the guise of a shepherd. Finally he meets Miragāvatī. Putting off his yogi guise he marries her and eventually becomes king of Kañcanapura. After an adventure with another demon, during which Miragāvatī suffers the pangs of *viraha*, the prince returns safely and he and Miragāvatī live together for some time. But meanwhile Rupamiṇī has sent her own message of *viraha* to the prince with a group of traders visiting Kañcanapura with their leader, who seems to be a brāhmaṇ. The prince now sets out for home, taking Miragāvatī with him.

The death of the prince and his two wives

The quarrels of the prince's wives and their pacification by their mother-in-law are described. Finally, the prince when hunting one day is killed by a lion. His dead body is brought home and his wives both commit satī on his funeral pyre.

Miragāvatī

Kutuban tells us in his introduction that God has created this world and displayed his *carita* (action), and we can see this as a picture, and search for the painter. In fact, Miragāvatī herself has been depicted as a *citra* (picture) in many verses, and, according to Kutuban, through her God can easily be seen.[14] This is the philosophy on which the whole symbolism of the text rests.

Miragāvatī's beauty is perfect, she is a Padmiṇī among women, and (as her *nakhasikha* description suggests) she represents divine beauty on earth and also the embodiment of love. She is the *kāraṇa bhūta* (means) through which God, who is beauty and light, can be seen easily. In one verse Kutuban calls her *bhāva*, which also means 'love' here. She has captured the prince's heart and is fixed in it; her eyebrows are like a bow, the same bow that was held by Rāma, Arjuna, and Paraśurāma. Her beauty is that of the autumn full moon and she possesses the full measure of the sixteen qualities and arts.[15]

Miragāvatī is, furthermore, *saddā suhāgina*, a woman eternally blessed by a husband's love.[16] Mīr Vāhid Bilgrāmī in his *Ḥaqā'iq-i-hindī* (AD 1566) explains how a reference in Hindavī texts to a *sadā suhāgin* is to be taken as suggesting the *insān-i-kāmil*, the perfect man, or one engrossed in *ma'rifat*, gnosis; God has created the world out of love for him.[17]

The prince

The prince's falling in love with such a being as Miragāvatī is no chance event; for (as Kutuban puts it), this love has been allowed by fate. The prince totally forgets himself but in his sense of *viraha* cannot forget Miragāvatī even for a moment. When he sets out to find Miragāvatī it is as a

Nāthapanthī yogi and he is then a *viyogī*, separated from his beloved, as was Bhartharī from Piṅgalā.[18] He grows matted hair (*jaṭā*), holds a *cakra* emblem, wears an earring (*mudrā*) and rosary (*japamālā*), and carries a staff (*ḍaṇḍā*), begging bowl (*khappar*), and tiger skin (*keharichālā*); he wears wooden sandals (*paṁvarī*), a sacrificial string or girdle (*mekhalā*), and a patch-cloth garment (*kanthā*), and has with him a *jogauṭā* or special cloth used during meditation.[19]

He also holds an *adhārī* (wooden stick) and *triśūla* (trident), a lute (*kiṅgarī*), *dhaṁdhārī* (an intricate iron or wooden stick), and *siṅgī* (horn). His body is smeared with ashes.[20] Yet he always remembers his love, and cannot forget Miragāvatī even for a moment. This is very significant: Nāthapanthī yogīs do not believe in the philosophy of love, being believers in Śiva and puritanical in their approach, but the prince, although he wears the garments of a Nāthayogī and carries all their emblems, is a *premayogī* (lover) in heart.

In the literature of the Nātha sect the meanings and function of these emblems are explained. The *Yogī-sampradāya-viṣkṛti* states that many cult objects used by the Nātha yogis were given by Śiva to Matsyendranātha, the teacher of Gorakhanātha. Thus the wearing of ashes indicates that the yogi is not affected by considerations of honour or insult, but is above them, and considers himself as the earth or the wood which has been burnt in the fire of knowledge, its hardness so being destroyed.[21] More recently Briggs has given the significance of the yogi emblems in detail. The wearing of earrings in the sect is referred to the practice of the great Yogi, Śiva, in wearing huge earrings. For any ceremony in the Nātha sect it is necessary that one is initiated and has earrings.[22] But why do the heroes in Hindi Sūfī texts undertake journeys as yogis? This is a very interesting question. Almost all the poets describe these lovers as *premayogīs*; nevertheless they all start their journeys as Nāthapanthī yogis. On the one hand at the level of contemporary realism it would have been easy for them to travel in this guise. More significantly, the contacts between yogis and Sūfīs that existed from the very beginning of the Sūfīs' settled residence in India contribute to the transformation of an original idea here, and an enlargement of the Nātha concept of 'dying to live'. Many emblems were common to yogis and Sūfīs, for example the patched frock (*k͟hirqa*) of the Sūfīs, much akin to the *kanthā* or *gudrī* of the yogis. Shaikh Shahābuddīn Suhrawardī (thirteenth century) explains the importance of this *k͟hirqa* to a seeker of God as follows:

the good news to the *murīd* is his acceptance by God . . . by putting on the *k͟hirqa* by the Shaikh possessed of love, the *murīd* knoweth that God hath accepted him; and his being united to the Shaikh (by the bond of sincerity, of desire and of acceptance) becometh a mirror wherein he seeth the beauty of his end.

The being united with the Shaikh is the result of the acquaintance of his soul with the Shaikh's soul which is the mark of kinship, as in Hadīs. Even so the *murīd*'s putting on of the *k͟hirqa* (by the Shaikh possessed of understanding) signifieth the *murīd*'s desire for the Shaikh and the Shaikh's love for the *murīd*.[23]

Siyaru'l Auliyā, a fourteenth-century compilation of the lives of the Chistī shaikhs, also emphasises the importance of the *khirqa*.

Such symbols as the *khirqa* and *gudrī* were, however, of Indian Nāthapanthī, rather than non-Indian, Sūfī, origin. Yet in Hindi Sūfī texts it remains the case that poets were able to take Nāthapanthī symbols and give them their own interpretations. These poets remind us again and again that although their heroes' outward guise is Nāthapanthī they are basically *premayogīs* (lovers). Their object is love and love only. Taking symbols from Hindu tradition and giving them an Islamic interpretation was not uncommon among Muslim scholars and Sūfīs in the late medieval period of India.[24]

Symbolism of the voyage

In Miragāvatī and other Hindi texts, the sea voyage is a standard symbol. This symbol has been referred to in classical Arabic Sūfī texts as well. Niffarī, a Sūfī theologian who appears to have flourished in the first half of the fourth century AH and who perhaps died in AH 354 (AD 956), gives an account of a sea journey stressing God's support for the voyager, the risk in sailing, and the need to risk, the possibility of salvation, and that only God can be a safe haven or support. If a man perishes other than in God, he belongs not to God but to that in which he has perished.

R. A. Nicholson describes the inner significance of the sea journey in Sūfism in his book *Mystics of Islam* as follows:

> The sea denotes the spiritual experiences through which the mystic passes in his journey to God. The point of issue is this: whether he should prefer the religious law or disinterested love? Hence he is warned not to rely on his good works which are no better than sinking ships and will never bring him safely to port. No, if he would attain God, he must rely on God alone. If he does not rely entirely on God but lets himself trust ever so little on anything else, he is still clinging to a plank. Though his trust in God is greater than before, it is not yet complete.[25]

Nicholson explains Niffarī's symbols in detail. One of his explanations is particularly important in the context of Miragāvatī, and deserves special mention here:

> Those beneath the waves are they who voyage in ships and consequently suffer shipwreck. Their reliance on secondary causes puts them ashore i.e. brings them back to the world of phenomena whereby they are veiled from God.[26]

Miragāvatī is the first Hindi Sūfī text to use the symbol of voyage and shipwreck. Some other Sūfī texts such as *Padmāvat, Madhumālatī*, and *Citrāvalī* also adopt it; while it is found in Dakkhinī Ghavvāsī's *Saiful-Mulūk Va Vadī'ul Jamāl* and Mulla Vajahī's *Kutub* [*Quṭb*]-*Mushtarī*.[27]

The prince, Miragāvatī and Rupamiṇī: various stages on the Sūfī path of love

In the course of his journey in search of Kañcanapura the prince tells Rupamiṇī cryptically that he is in love with a woman and therefore has assumed the guise of a yogi. He further states that he has started his journey from 'Gorakhapura'.[28] If 'Gorakhapura' is the start of his journey, its second stage is completed when he reaches 'Ayodhyā' and meets and stays with Rupamiṇī; while the third stage is gained at Kañcanapura, the city of Miragāvatī, who represents divine beauty on earth. These three cities are thus three stations of the prince's journey. Ayodhyā is the city where he finds profound worldly love, the love which leads to divine love.

Usmān, another Sūfī poet in Hindi, has expressed the characteristics of the Sūfī paths in some detail in his *Citrāvalī* (AD 1613):

> The first station on the path of love is called Bhogapura. Here a man remains engrossed in worldly affairs, the markets are filled with various worldly objects, and the man whose existence is transitory remains and is attracted to mundane things. Actually this is more or less the stage of *Nāsūt* in Sūfī theology. A person spends a normal life here. This is the lowest stage in human life.[29]

The second stage on the path is Gorakhapura, of which Usmān gives the details as follows:

> Here a person assumes the guise of a yogī, and we find yogīs and ascetics busy in meditation and remembering God. There are many cheats as well in this guise, and one who forgets himself in externals and does not open the eye of his heart cannot progress beyond here.[30]

Gorakhapura in Kutuban's *Miragāvatī* is the land where the prince takes on the guise of a yogi and fearlessly proceeds on in the search of Miragāvatī, learning eventually from the ascetic (*jaṅgama*) of the path to the city of Kañcanapura. This Gorakhapura resembles the Sūfīs' Malkūt, the divine world.[31]

Usmān again speaks of Nehanagara, 'city of love', where a traveller on the path arrives after leaving Gorakhapura. In Nehanagara the traveller forgets himself and falls in love with everything he beholds. A guide is needed here, for the seeker of love takes whatever he receives from others at this stage. A teacher and a religious scripture (the Qur'ān) is therefore necessary.[32] In the *Miragāvatī*, however, we do not find a symbol for the teacher or a guide. Of course the *jaṅgama* helps the prince in telling him the way to Kañcanapura. But most of the time the prince remembers God (*daiva*) and Miragāvatī's love directly:

> I pray and remember God and nobody else. Only he will help me. No one else will come to help. I remember the love of Miragāvatī. I have suffered the pains of heat and rains for her. The life of him who gives his life for a friend becomes holy (*pavīta*).[33]

If the prince has helpers at this stage, they are the principle of truth, with love itself. These protect him from the evil messenger (*durjana-dūta*), who is Satan in disguise; the prince constantly repeats the name of 'truth', which guides him in his later adventures. Finally he arrives in Miragāvatī's Kañcanapura, a city with all the perfection of outward beauty which its name symbolises, resembling the mythical Siṃhala-dvīpa which is the seeker's goal.[34] On beholding Miragāvatī the prince falls unconscious. Almost all the Sūfī texts in Hindi describe this state of ecstasy (*ḥāl*) when the hero meets the beloved.

We can compare Kañcanapura with *'Ālam-i-Jabarūt* of the Sūfīs, where a seeker of love surmounts all his difficulties and reaches the world of his beloved. Here there takes place the meeting with God, and only a few people reach this place. Usmān calls it 'Rūpanagara', a place where all external forms and guises are abandoned and the seeker of love becomes oblivious to his own existence. In Kañcanapura Miragāvatī and the prince live together. Their union thus follows much suffering on the way. The lover becomes a king now, giving up the guise of a yogi.

There is an additional aspect to the symbolism in Miragāvatī's love for the prince. During the last of his fights (with the demon at Kañcanapura) Miragāvatī sends the prince a message reminding him of their love. The wind (her messenger) tells the prince that she returns his love: for 'love between two human beings can be recognised only when both have the same kind of love (*rati*) as when bee and jasmine flower both have love for each other'.[35]

Thus love can not continue long without reciprocity. On the mystical path, God helps the devotee by bestowing his love upon him, and if this does not happen, love cannot stand on solid ground. Miragāvatī, however, fully responds to the love which the prince has shown for her in suffering so much on the path.

The prince has now achieved his true love, the demon's false love has been revealed for what it is and true love is shown victorious in the end. The prince now tells Miragāvatī:

> you are the monarch of the gods and the *gandharvas*, and the essence of the intoxication of the three worlds. Anyone who has sight in his eyes will forget himself at your sight. You control all beings by your magic power, and cause even the gods to love by you, what of human beings.[36]

We can find ambiguities in *Miragāvatī* and in other Hindi Sūfī *premākhyānas*, but generally these poems are clear in their symbols and suggestions. The poets express their deeper thoughts in many verses, explaining their inner significance in a subtle way. However, it will not be very fruitful if we look for symbols and suggestions in everything they say or narrate. At the end of *Miragāvatī* Kutuban repeats 'I have added to [the literal sense of] this text various meanings. He who wishes to understand them can do so if he is careful. I have explained all the meanings in it. Yoga, *sṛṅgāra* (erotic sentiment) and *vīra rasa* (heroic sentiments) are woven into it.'[37] It is only in this perspective that *Miragāvatī* can be well understood.

NOTES

1. *Miragāvatī*, ed. D. F. Plukker, Amsterdam, 1981, v. 11. 1. See also the edition of Mātāprasād Gupta, Agra, 1968, v. cit. References in this article, unless otherwise quoted, are from Plukker's edition.
2. v. 426. 4.
3. v. 1. 1–2.
4. v. 2. 3–7. Cf. A. J. Arberry, *The Koran Interpreted*, New York, 1955, vol. ii, p. 353.
5. v. 4. 3–7.
6. v. 5.
7. v. 6.
8. S. A. A. Rizvi, *A History of Sufism in India*, Delhi, vol. i, 1978, p. 367. Parameśvarīlāl Gupta refers to a Buḍhan who lived in Jafrābād near Jaunpur and was called Shamsuddīn. He was the son of Ruknuddīn and a grandson of Sadruddīn Chirāgh-i-Hind. Gupta refers to the Persian text *Tajjaliyāt-i-nūr*, which is a recent work and cannot be very much relied upon. Moreover, this text does not mention Kutuban or *Miragāvatī* or Husain Shāh in this context. P. L. Gupta, *Miragāvatī*, Varanasi, 1967, p. 116.
9. Śyāmmanohar Pāṇḍey, *Sūfī kāvya vimarśa*, Agra, 1968, introduction, p. 3. See also S. M. Ikram and A. T. Embree, *Muslim Civilization in India*, New York, 1964, p. 119.
10. vv. 246–53.
11. v. 7.
12. S. M. Pandey, 'Maulānā Dāūd and his Contributions to Hindi Sūfī Literature', *AION* 38, 1978, pp. 75–90; 'Some Problems in Studying *Candāyan*', *DLCR*, 1980, pp. 127–40; 'Love symbolism in *Candāyan*', *BCR*, pp. 269–93.
13. Cf. v. 288. 3.
14. Cf. v. 3. 2–3. S. M. Pāṇḍey, *Sūfī kāvya vimarśa*, Agra, 1968, p. 4, vv. 22. 4. *Miragāvatī*, 189. 1, 231. 5 (Gupta edn.).
15. vv. 11. 5, 22. 4.
16. v. 75.
17. Ch. 16. v. 59. 6–7. Mīr Wāhid Bilgrāmī, *Ḥaqā'iq-i-hindī*, trans. into Hindi from Persian by Atahar Abbās Rizvī, Varanasi, 1957, p. 55. The work was completed in AH 974 (AD 1566). The author was born in AH 915 (1509–10); Badāunī, a historian of Akbar's time, is said to have met him in Bilgrām (near Lucknow) in 1569–70. In this work more than 150 terms used in Hindī works of the late medieval period are discussed, and Islamic interpretations given. These terms include *nakhasikha* vocabulary, and many other Kṛṣṇaite words which were used in *dhrupada* singing.
18. Bhartharī (Bhartṛhari) was a king of Ujjain who according to legend became a

yogi. His love for his wife is celebrated in folk-songs of Bengal and Eastern Uttar Pradesh. Bhartharī is considered to be a great ascetic in the Nātha sect (Satyavrata Sinhā, *Bhojpurī lokagāthā*, Allahabad, 1957, pp. 180–90).

19. v. 106.
20. Ibid.
21. Hajārīprasād Dvivedī, *Nāth sampradāya*, Allahabad, 1981, pp. 15–21.
22. G. W. Briggs, *Gorakhnāth and the Kanphaṭā Yogīs*, first pub. Calcutta, 1938, repr. Delhi, 1973, pp. 6–7.
23. *'Awārifu'l ma'ārif*, trans. H. Wilberforce Clarke, first pub. Calcutta, 1891, repr. New York, 1970, pp. 38–9.
24. Cf. *Ḥaqā'iq-i-hindī.*
25. R. A. Nicholson, *The Mystics of Islam*, London, 1966, pp. 74–5.
26. p. 76.
27. Śyāmmanohar Pāṇḍey, *Madhyayugīn premākhyān*, Allahabad, 1982, pp. 209 f.
28. v. 131. 6–7.
29. Usmān, *Citrāvalī*, ed. Jagmohan Varmā, Banaras, 1912, v. 2.5.
30. vv. 207–8.
31. See *SEI*, pp. 78 f.
32. *Citrāvalī*, v. 211.
33. v. 173. 3–7.
34. v. 206.
35. v. 288.
36. v. 296.
37. v. 426.

Kṛṣṇaite and Nāth elements in the poetry of the eighteenth-century Panjabi Sūfī Bullhe Śāh

DENIS MATRINGE

Transferring themes and symbols from one religious sphere to another has long been a well-attested practice in South Asia.[1] In the Panjab, this phenomenon has been particularly exemplified by the Sikhs.[2] Concerning Islam, a sharp distinction must be made between the religious elite (*'ulamā* and most Persian-writing Sūfīs), which was always anxious to preserve the Muslim religion from contamination by Hindu practices and beliefs, and some Sūfīs more inclined to adjust Islam to its Indian environment.[3]

As a consequence, whereas throughout the period of the Muslim rule in the Panjab, and even later,[4] Persian remained the language of administration, 'orthodox' Islam, and 'higher' Sufism, there developed in some Sūfī circles a tradition of poetry in Panjabi, the first evidence of which goes back to the sixteenth century.[5] This poetry no doubt helped to bring so-called Hindu tribes into the Islamic sphere.[6] It has come down to us through an oral tradition which is still alive today, mostly in the performances of wandering bards (*ḍhāḍī*) and professional religious singers (*qavvāl*).[7]

In its formal aspects as well as in its symbols, Panjabi Sūfī poetry is deeply rooted in local culture. Some very common types of Sūfī poem are derived from folk-songs.[8] Similarly, activities of daily life, and love stories from the oral tradition, which are the theme of so many songs sung by women,[9] constitute for this poetry an inexhaustible thesaurus of symbols.[10] For example, the bride spinning cotton in order to accumulate a dowry acceptable to her future husband becomes a symbol for the Sūfī trying to follow a way of life that would please God.[11] In the same way, the Sūfīs quite often identify their soul with the heroine of a romance, whereas the hero for whom she is longing becomes a symbol of God.[12]

The popular culture from which Panjabi Sūfī poets drew many of their themes and symbols included a number of Hindu traditions.[13] Borrowings from that source are exemplified particularly in the poetry of Bullhe Śāh, the most famous Panjabi Sūfī poet, whose shrine in Qaṣūr is still a great centre of devotion.[14] This paper aims at studying the Kṛṣṇaite and Nāth elements in his poems.[15] Their presence, linked to the mystical theory of 'existential monism' (*waḥdat al wujūd*), according to which 'everything is He',[16] has led certain scholars to consider that he was more of an *advaita* Vedāntist than a

Sūfī,[17] while others would try to give a strict orthodox Muslim interpretation of his works.[18]

I shall first present here the Kṛṣṇaite and Nāth references found in Bullhe Śāh's poetry. I shall also explore their relationship with other symbolic material, and finally examine how they contribute to the formulation of the poet's mystical message.

Concerning the Kṛṣṇaite tradition, some verses of Bullhe Śāh advocate devotion to Kṛṣṇa as opposed to Vedic ritualism, thus indicating the superiority of inner faith to outward religious manifestations, and the self-evidence of God:

Hari pragaṭ pragaṭ hī dekho, kiā paṇḍit phir bed suṇāve.[19]
Look! Hari is manifest. Why then does the paṇḍit recite the Veda?[20]

Kṛṣṇa may be represented by his flute. Its music symbolizes the pervading immanence of God, and it provides an image for the merging of the devotee's soul into the Divinity (*fanā*', 'annihilation'):

bansī Kāhaṇa acaraja bajāī
. . .
bansī-vāliā cākā Rā̃jhā
terā sur hai sab nāl sā̃jhā
terīā̃ maujā̃ sāḍā mā̃jhā
sāḍī surtī̃ āp milāī.
bansī Kāhaṇ acaraj bajāī.[21]

Kāhaṇ[22] plays the flute wonderfully.
. . .
Flute-player, cowherd Rā̃jhā,[23]
Your melody unites with everything,
Your pleasures are in me,
Our appearances themselves have mingled.[24]
Kāhaṇ plays the flute wonderfully.

eh jo murlī Kāhaṇ vajāī
dil mere nū̃ coṭ lagāī.[25]

The melody played by Kāhaṇ on the flute
Has wounded my heart.

murlī bāj uṭṭhī aṇghātā̃
suṇ ke bhull gaīā̃ sab bātā̃.[26]

The song of the flute resounded suddenly,
And on hearing it, I forgot everything.

Even in poems where Kṛṣṇa is not named, the music of the flute is perceived as a divine call. In the following verses, Panjabi girls who had been fetching water and are now fully adorned behave just like the *gopīs*:

hatthī̃ mahindī pairī̃ mahindī
sar te dhaṛī gundāī
tel phulel pānā̃ dā bīṛā
dandī̃ missī lāī
koī jū sadd paio nẽ ḍāhḍī vissāriā ghar bār.[27]

They have put henna on their hands and feet,
They have plaited their hair,
They have anointed themselves with oil and perfume, and chewed betel,
They have put *missī* (manganese oxide) on their teeth.
When the call resounds, they forget house and home.[28]

Scandal is spreading:

'iśq dīvāne līkā̃ lāīā̃
ḍāhḍīā̃ ghaṇīā̃ satthā̃ pāīā̃.[29]

Mad love has disgraced me.
I am sued before the Council on serious grounds.

But the girls do not care. They go and dance with their beloved, just as a Sūfī 'outside the divine law' (*be-śar'*) like Bullhe Śāh gives free expression to his love for God:

jis tan laggiā 'iśq kamāl
nāce be-sur be tāl.[30]

Whoever is engaged in perfect love
Dances out of tune and rhythm.[31]

Or as Bullhe Śāh has put it in a *kāfī* usually sung with a very powerful drumbeat (*dhamāla*) on which so often fakīrs can be seen dancing to the point of ecstasy:

tere 'iśq ne nacāiā kar thayyā thayyā.[32]

Your love has made me dance, thayyā! thayyā![33]

Like Kṛṣṇa, Bullhe Śāh's God is mischievous: he hides himself in the way Kṛṣṇa did after dancing with the *gopīs*, until he was found again:

tusī̃ dil mere vicc vassde ho
aĩvẽ sāthõ dūr kiū̃ nassde ho
nāle ghatt jādū dil khassde ho
huṇ kit vall jāso nass kar jī
bass kar jī huṇ bass kar jī
ikk bāt asā̃ nāl hass kar jī.[34]

You dwell in my heart.
Why do you flee far away from me

And putting a spell on me snatch my heart?
Whither will you now run and go?
That's enough, now that's enough!
(Come), laugh and speak with me![35]

God is a hidden thief:

merī bukkal de vicc cor.[36]

There is a thief in the fold of my veil.

This '*ṭhag* of Lahore', as Bullhe Śāh calls him,[37] steals the heart of those who love him, and then disappears, as Kṛṣṇa did, leaving Gokul and Brindāban for Mathura, and abandoning the *gopīs*:

vekho nī kīh kar giā māhī
lai de ke dil ho giā rāhī.[38]

See what the cowherd did!
We exchanged our hearts, but then he set out on his way.[39]

Once the Beloved is gone, the mystic suffers the pangs of separation, and his poetry becomes a lament, here in Persianized style:

kīh bedardā̃ saṅg yārī
rovaṇ akkhīā̃ zāro zārī.
sānū̃ gae be-dardī chaḍḍ ke
hijre saṅg sīne vicc gaḍḍ ke
jismõ jind nū̃ lai gae kaḍḍh ke
eh gall kar gae haĩsiārī.[40]

See what the company of an indifferent one is, my friend!
My eyes weep away the time.
This indifferent one has gone abandoning me,
Piercing my breast with the dart of separation.
He snatched life away from my body and took it away.
That's what this cruel one did![41]

He would like his message of love to reach God and uses the symbol of the letter which Rādhā thinks of writing to Kṛṣṇa:

pattīā̃ likkhū̃gī maĩ Śām nū̃, piyā mainū̃ naẕar na āve.[42]

I shall write letters to Śām,[43] (because) my beloved does not come into sight.[44]

In despair, the seeker takes the garb of a yogini begging for a vision of the Lord:

ab kiū̃ sājan cir lāio re.
gal mirgānī sīs khaparīā̃
bhikh maṅgaṇ nū̃ ro ro phiriā̃
jogaṇ nām bhayyā liṭ dhariā̃
aṅg bibhūt ramāio re.
ab kiū̃ sājan cir lāio re.[45]

Why, my friend, are you delaying now?
A deer-skin to my neck, a begging bowl on my head [sic],
I wander begging in tears.
Yielding, I am called a yogini, brother.
Because of you, I have rubbed my body with ashes.
Why, my friend, are you delaying now?[46]

This opens the way to recurrent instances of Nāth symbols in Bullhe Śāh's poetry. In the poems where they appear, God is the supreme yogi whom the yogini is longing for, and the theme of departure comes to prominence:

maĩ vaisā̃ jogī de nāl matthe tilak lagā ke.[47]

I shall go with the yogi, having put a *tilak* on my forehead.[48]

This departure means renouncing the world for the sole quest of God, whose essence, in Bullhe Śāh's Sufism, is love.[49] So when God is identified with the yogi, the manifestations of love are described in terms which, although related to the Persian images of the 'fire of love',[50] are strongly reminiscent in that context of the terrible powers of the yogis:

jis ghar vicc terā pher hoiā
so jal bal koilā-ḍher hoiā
jad rākh uḍḍī tad ser hoiā.[51]

The house in which you came
Was burnt and turned into a heap of coal.
When the ashes blew away, you were satisfied.

As for the yogini, a similar imagery is used in the same poem for describing the drastic austerity she imposes upon herself:

tan bhaṭṭhī man āhiraṇ karīe
prem hathoṛā māran karīe
dil lohā agg pagāiā.[52]

Make your body a furnace and your mind an anvil!
Let the hammer of love beat
And let fire melt the iron of your heart!

This leads to considerable suffering, which Bullhe Śāh expresses through a striking contrast between the elevated Ṣūfī paradox of a love born on the first day of pre-eternity and the image from daily life of the frying-pan:

nī mainū̃ laggṛā 'iśq avval dā
avval dā roz azal dā.
vicc kaṛāhī tal tal jāve
taliā̃ nū̃ cā tal jāve.[53]

O, I have been in love since the first day,
Since the first day of pre-eternity!
Love fries me in a frying pan
And fries even those who are fried.

All these images are symbols for expressing the extreme hardship of the path which leads the mystic to God. All along her way, enduring the cruel torments of love and 'abstinence', the yogini is in a lamentable state:

khutthī mī̃ḍhī dast parā̃da
phirā̃ ujāṛ dā jāṛ.[54]

My plait is undone, I hold my *parā̃da*[55] in my hand.
I wander from desert to forest.

But 'suffering is the prerequisite of spiritual bliss',[56] and finally the yogi appears, divine grace thereby answering to the mystical quest after the trial:

Rā̃jhā jogīṛā baṇ āiā
vāh sā̃gī sā̃g racāiā.
es jogī de naiṇ kaṭore
bāzā̃ vā̃gū̃ laĩde ḍore
mukkh ḍiṭṭhīā̃ dukkh jāvaṇ jhore.
...
Rā̃jhā jogī te maĩ jogiāṇī
is dī xāṭir bharsā̃ pāṇī
aĩvẽ picchlī 'umar vihāṇī
es huṇ mainū̃ bharmāī.[57]

Rā̃jhā has come, having made himself a yogi,
The actor has played his role!
This yogi's eyes are cups,
They are as sharp as hawk's eyes.
When I saw his face, misery and the pangs of separation went away.
...
Rā̃jhā is the yogi and I am his yogini.
I shall fetch water for him.
I have wasted my past life,
But now he has enchanted me.

However, if Bullhe Śāh uses Nāth images here and there to express his own mystical path, there is nevertheless a fundamental difference between the Panjabi Ṣūfī's *kāfī* and, say, the *śabdī* of Gorakhnāth: namely the presence of loving devotion in Bullhe Śāh's poetry. Indeed, if Bullhe Śāh's poetry has the quest for divine union and certain symbols in common with the Nāth tradition, it is otherwise very far away from its aims and methods.[58] In his poetry, all that concerns the yogi is linked with a love relation alien to Nāth Śaivism.[59] Just as in the legend of Hīr and Rā̃jhā the young man makes it clear that the garb of a yogi is only a disguise for him, God manifests himself under the appearance of a yogi:

nī eh jogī nahī̃, koī rūp hai Rabb dā
bhes jogī dā is nū̃ phabb dā.[60]

O, this is not a yogi, but a manifestation of the Lord!
The garb of a yogi fits him well.

At the same time transcendent – he keeps *parda*[61] – and immanent, God can in fact be found everywhere and in everybody:

kiū̃ ohle bah bah jhākīdā
eh parda kis tõ rākhīdā.
kite rūmī ho kite śāmī ho
kite ṣāḥib kite ġulāmī ho
tusī̃ āpe āp tamāmī ho.[62]

Why do you sit peeping from behind a veil?
From whom do you keep this *parda*?
Here you are a Turk and there a Syrian,
Here a master and there a slave.
You are Yourself all that exists.

He can be Kṛṣṇa and the yogi, the thief and the banker, the mosque and the temple, the Muslim and the Hindu, the lover and the beloved, and so on. This perception of the 'uniqueness of being' leads Bullhe Śāh to reject the diversity of the constituted religions.[63] He proclaims:

hindū nā̃ nahī̃ musalmān.[64]

I am neither a Hindu nor a Muslim,

and thus takes a stand which reminds us of the Sants:

merī bukkal de vicc cor
nī merī bukkal de vicc cor.
kihnū̃ kūk suṇāvā̃ nī merī bukkal de vicc cor
corī corī nikal giā jagat vicc pai giā śor.
merī bukkal de vicc cor . . .
musalmān saṛne tõ ḍarde hindū ḍarde gor
dõvẽ ese vicc marde eho dū̃hā̃ dī khor.
merī bukkal de vicc cor . . .
kite Rāmdāṣ kite Fataḥ Muhammad eho qadīmī śor
miṭ giā dū̃hā̃ dā jhagṛā nikal piā kujh hor.
merī bukkal de vicc cor . . .[65]

There is a thief in the fold of my veil,
O, there is a thief in the fold of my veil!
To whom would I cry it, there is a thief in the fold of my veil!
He went out furtively and a tumult spread throughout the world.
There is a thief in the fold of my veil . . .
The Muslims fear the flame and the Hindus the tomb,
Both die in this fright, such is their hatred.

There is a thief in the fold of my veil . . .
Here was Rāmdās and there Fataḥ Muḥammad, what an ancient noise!
Their quarrel vanished, and Something New emerged!
There is a thief in the fold of my veil . . .[66]

This thief ravishes the 'self' of those who love him. He annihilates it and merges it within himself:

prem-nagar de ulṭe cāle
xūnī naiṇ hoe xwuśḥāle
āpe āp phase vicc jāle.
phas phas āp kūhāio re.[67]

In the city of love, everything is upside down,[68]
Reddened eyes become happy,
The 'self' gets caught in a net.
Once my 'self' was caught, you killed it.

So, Kṛṣṇaism and Nāth yoga provided Bullhe Śāh with an imagery from which he derived symbols to express the various states and emotions of his mystical experience: loving devotion (*'iśq, prem*) and renunciation (*zuhd, tyāga*) are as typical of Sufism as they are of Sant mysticism.

In the circles of the Persian-writing Sūfī elite of India, their similarities had been underlined long before Bullhe Śāh by Dārā Śikoh in his *Majma'ul baḥrain* ('The Mingling of the Two Oceans').[69] But as regards popular Sufism, even if Bullhe Śāh had such predecessors as Śāh Ḥusain of Lahore (1539–93/4),[70] no Panjabi Sūfī poet before him integrated Hindu elements to that extent in his poetry. Nor did any venture so far from Muslim orthodoxy in his religious construction.

We have noted the analogy between the mystical path followed by Bullhe Śāh and that of the Sants, in whose religion Kṛṣṇa bhakti and Nāth yoga, along with 'a marginal contribution' from Sufism, had been absorbed into a new synthesis.[71] In the case of Bullhe Śāh, the synthesis between Kṛṣṇaite and Nāth elements is chiefly operated through the poet's use of the legend of Hīr and Rā̃jhā, which is by far the main source of his allusions.

This legend is the dearest to the heart of all the Panjabi people, whatever their religion, and it is the subject of innumerable folk-songs. Bullhe Śāh largely resorted to the possibilities offered by the story for expressing his own relation with God, be it, for instance, his waiting for the coming of the Lord:

Bullhe Śāh ghar Rā̃jhā āve.[72]

Bullhe Śāh! May Rā̃jhā come to my house!

majjhī̃ āīā̃ Rā̃jhā yār na āiā.[73]

The buffaloes came, but my beloved Rā̃jhā didn't come.

or the final union:

Rā̃jhā Rā̃jhā kardī nī maĩ āpe Rā̃jhā hoī
saddo nī mainū̃ Dhīdo Rā̃jhā, Hīr na ākho koī.[74]

Repeating 'Rā̃jhā, Rā̃jhā', I have myself become Rā̃jhā.
Call me Dhīdo Rā̃jhā![75] Nobody should say Hīr anymore.

In the first part of the legend, Rā̃jhā, the charming flute-player, tending the buffaloes, in love with Hīr, and enjoying himself with her and her friends, is definitely a Kṛṣṇaite figure – whereas once Hīr has been married against her will to Saidā, Rā̃jhā is initiated by Balnāth and becomes, in the second part, a wandering Nāth yogi. When he meets Hīr again in the garb of a yogi, she elopes with him.

The legend thus offered an ideal repertory of both Kṛṣṇaite and Nāth symbols, as well as the allegorical framework of a mystical parable. That is why Bullhe Śāh could establish links between himself, Hīr, Rādhā, and the yogini on the one hand, and God, Rā̃jhā, Kṛṣṇa, and the yogi on the other.[76] In the same way, Bullhe Śāh composed mostly *kāfī*, formally identical to those Panjabi folk ballads whose protagonists are so often Hīr and Rā̃jhā.

The Kṛṣṇaite and Nāth elements found in the poetry of Bullhe Śāh, and their link in his *kāfī* with the story of Hīr and Rā̃jhā, reflect the composite and often syncretic nature of Panjabi popular culture.[77] Their symbolic use as mystical allegories by the poet indicates the attention he paid to the cultural universe of the common Panjabi people whom he addressed.

The great originality of Bullhe Śāh lies in his ability, starting from a Sūfī background, to combine these Panjabi symbols with others, taken from Arabic and Persian culture, in order to express his approach to that sublime point where all religions meet.

NOTES

1. e.g. borrowings from Viṣṇuism by Śivaism (Gonda 1965, pp. 92 f.), the influence of Hinduism on Buddhism (Snellgrove 1987, pp. 123 f., 128 f., etc.), the effects of Islam on Hinduism (Gonda 1965, pp. 129–31), the narration of Hindu parables by Indian Sūfīs (Ahmad 1964, pp. 135), etc.
2. Fundamentally, 'the cultural world of Guru Nanak was Hindu' (Cole 1984, p. 15), and it is not surprising to find in his poetry many allusions to Hindu mythology, notably to the story of Kṛṣṇa (Cole 1984, pp. 19 f.). More precisely, Nānak's religious conceptions derived mostly from the Sant tradition, which he reinterpreted in his own way. And thus, although Nānak rejected Nāth beliefs, early Sikhism incorporated Nāth elements remodelled within the Sant inheritance (McLeod 1968, pp. 151–8). It also made occasional borrowings from Islamic imagery (McLeod 1968, p. 160). Later on, while the Sikhs took refuge in the

Shivalik Hills, śakti symbols, such as the sword representing Kālī, made their way into their religion (see McLeod 1975, pp. 13 ff., and the passage from the *Dasam Granth*, trans. in Matringe 1986, p. 67).

3. See e.g. Eaton 1974, 1978, pp. 155–73; Schimmel 1982, pp. 135–69; Asani 1988.
4. Persian was the official language of the Sikh kingdom of the Panjab, and, after the British conquest, it kept that status, shared with English, in western Panjab (while Urdu became the official language of the eastern Panjab, along with English), see Singh 1977, pp. 93.
5. The poetry of Śaikh Farīd preserved in the *Ādi Granth* (references in Matringe 1988, p. 553).
6. For parallels, see e.g. Faruqi 1985.
7. On the problems resulting from this oral mode of transmission, see Matringe 1989, pp. 542–4.
8. The *kāfī*, analogous to the ballad (see Matringe 1989, pp. 533 f., nn.), the *aṭhvāra* (poem of the 'eight days'), the *bārāmāh* (poem of the 'twelve months', on which see Vaudeville 1965). Survey of these genres in Ramakrishna 1938, pp. xxii–xxv.
9. On the role of women in Indian popular Sufism, see Eaton 1974, pp. 119, 125 f.; 1978, pp. 157 f., 169–71.
10. See Ramakrishna 1938, pp. xxv–xxx.
11. Examples of Panjabi spinning-wheel songs with English trans. in Bedi 1971, pp. 130–1. On these symbols, see Matringe 1988*a*, pp. 214 f.
12. See Matringe 1988*a*, p. 24.
13. For parallels in Bengal, see Roy 1983, pp. 187–206.
14. There are no reliable records of Bullhe Śāh's life, but only traditional hagiographic accounts (*tazkira*), summarized in Usborne 1905; Ramakrishna 1938, pp. 40–9; Quddūsi 1962, pp. 157–63; Faqīr 1960, pp. i–xii; Gulzār n.d. The hereditary *qavvāl* of his shrine also relate countless anecdotes concerning his life. It is usually said that Bullhe Śāh was born into a sayyid family near Qaṣūr in 1680. After his studies, he went to Lahore, where he became a disciple of Śāh 'Ināyat Qādirī, to whose praise many of his poems are dedicated. He then came back to Qaṣūr where he died in 1758. He never married, and did not observe the religious law of Islam (*śar'*). He was a kind of ecstatic fakir and had to be buried clandestinely, at night, because the local mullahs refused him an Islamic funeral. The main source for the numerous editions of Bullhe Śāh's poetry published since the 1880s has been the *qavvāls*, especially those who hereditarily sing at his shrine in Qaṣūr. But for over 200 years, Bullhe Śāh's verses have been sung all over the Panjab and in Sind, transmitted orally from one generation of singers to the next, the written editions now interfering with the oral tradition. There are no old MSS either. Consequently, there cannot be any satisfactory philological edition, and we must consider that 'Bullhe Śāh' refers to the source of a coherent poetical tradition which did not vary much since the first editions, rather than to the author of an authentic set of poems. A convenient list of 'scholarly' editions can be found in Aḥmad 1982, pp. vii–x. The 'standard' edition to which I refer here is that published by Dr Faqīr Muḥammad Faqīr (Bullhe Śah, 1960: *KBS*); I also refer to a remarkable collection of *kāfīs* by Bullhe Śāh included in his *Qānūn-i 'iśq* (The Law of Love) (*QI*) by Anvar 'Alī Śāh (Bullhe Śah, 1905).
15. On Viṣṇusim in the Panjab, see Rose 1883, vol. i, pp. 366–90, and on Nāth yogis

Ibbetson 1916, pp. 76 f. and Briggs 1938, pp. 66, 71, 98–103. Indications can also be found in the Punjab District Gazetteers, e.g. in the *Shahpur District Gazetteer* (1917) on the Vaiṣṇavas (pp. 119 f.) and the Nāth yogis (p. 121); in the *Multan District Gazetteer* (1923–4) on the revival of Kṛṣṇaism in the 16th century (p. 122); in the *Jhang District Gazetteer* (1908, pp. 62 f.) and the *Gujranwala District Gazetteer* (1935, p. 92) on the Nāth yogis. On the link between Kṛṣṇaite elements and the use of 'Hindi' in certain poems of Bullhe Śāh, see Matringe 1989, pp. 544–7.

16. See Asani 1988, p. 90.
17. Ramakrishna 1938; Sharda 1974.
18. Bullhe Śāh 1905; Aḥmad 1982.
19. *KBS kāfī* 22, p. 35.
20. Cf. the poem of Sūrdās quoted below, n. 28.
21. *KBS kāfī* 28, p. 123, quoted below, p. 198.
22. i.e. Kṛṣṇa.
23. Hero of the most popular Panjabi romance. See Matringe 1988*a*, with detailed summary of the Vāris̤ Śāh version (1766–7), pp. 18–20.
24. *KBS kāfī* 110, p. 240.
25. *KBS kāfī* 44, p. 79.
26. *KBS kāfī* 110, p. 239.
27. *KBS kāfī* 34, p. 58.
28. Cf. Sūrdās 1972, no. 1618 (i. 481):

    जबहिं बन मुरली स्रवन परी
    चक्रित भईं गोपकन्या सब, काम धाम बिसरीं
    कुल मर्जाद बेद की आज्ञा, नैकहुँ नहीं डरीं
    स्याम सिंधु सरिता ललना गन जल की ढरनि धरीं
    अंग मरदन करिबे कौं लागीं, उबटन तेल धरी ।।

    As soon as the flute resounded in the forest,
    All in a flutter were all the cowherds' daughters; they forgot their work.
    They didn't care at all about family honour, nor about the injunctions of the Veda.
    Śyāma (i.e. Kṛṣṇa) is an ocean, and the women's party a river whose water flowed to him.
    They started anointing their body, applying balm and oil.

29. *KBS kāfī* 44, p. 79.
30. *KBS kāfī* 51, p. 97.
31. Cf. Sūrdās 1972, no. 153 (i. 42):

    अब मैं नाच्यौ बहुत गोपाल
    —
    भ्रम भोयौ मन भयौ पखावज, चलत असंगत चाल
    तृष्णा नाद घट भीतर, नाना विधि दै ताल ।।

    I have danced a lot now, Gopāl!
    . . .
    My mind is a tambourine sunk in confusion, it keeps a wrong tempo.
    Thirst resounds within my body, inducing beats of various sorts.

32. *KBS kāfī* 29, p. 49.
33. *Thayyā thayyā* is an onomatopoeia.
34. *KBS kāfī* 25, p. 40.
35. Cf. Sūrdās 1972, no. 1748 (i. 513):

    अँतर तैं हरि प्रगट भए
    रहत प्रेम के बस्य कन्हाई, जुवतिनि कौं मिलि हर्ष दए
    वैसोइ सुख सबकौ फिरि दीन्हौं, वहै भाव मानि लियौ
    वै जानति हरि संग तबहिं तैं, वहै बुद्धि सब वहै हियौ ।।

    Hari reappeared from among them.
    Kanhāī overpowered by love came back to give joy to the young ladies.
    He gave them all the same happiness again; he was welcomed with the same passion.
    They knew Hari had always been with them: the mind and heart of all of them had remained the same.

36. *KBS kāfī* 118, p. 260. See below, p. 196.
37. *KBS kāfī* 143, p. 310. On the *ṭhags* in the Panjab, see Matringe 1988*a*, p. 172.
38. *KBS kāfī* 148, p. 319.
39. Cf. e.g. Sūrdās 1972, no. 4026 (ii. 369):

    सबै सुख जु गए ब्रजनाथ
    —
    मदन गोपाल ठगौरी मेली कहत न आवै बात
    नंदनँदन जु विदेस गवन कियौ, वैसी मीँजति हाथ ।।

    The Lord of the Braj left, taking away all happiness.
    . . .
    How much Madan Gopāl acted as a ṭhag, I cannot say!
    Nandanand [i.e. Kṛṣṇa] has left for another place, and I twist my hands in grief.

40. *KBS kāfī* 96, p. 209.
41. Cf. e.g. Sūrdās 1972, no. 3906 (ii. 345):

    प्रीति करि काहू सुख न लह्यौ
    —
    सारंग प्रीति करी जु नाद सौं, सन्मुख बान सह्यौ
    हम जौ प्रीति करी माधव सौं, चलत न कछु कह्यौ
    सूरदास प्रभु बिनु दुख पावत, नैननि नीर बह्यौ ।।

    Making love never brought any happiness!
    . . .
    Enamoured with the song, the deer was struck by the arrow.
    We loved Mādhava [i.e. Kṛṣṇa], but he left without a word.
    Sūrdās! Without the Lord, we are unhappy and tears flow from our eyes.

42. *KBS kāfī* 35, p. 59.
43. Śām = Śyām, i.e. Kṛṣṇa.

44. Cf. Sūrdās 1972, no. 4000 (ii. 364):

    हरि परदेस बहुत दिन लाए
    —
    यह पाती हमारी लै दीजौ, जहाँ साँवरे छाए ।।

    Hari has been away for a long time.
    . . .
    Take this letter of mine to where my dark Lord resides!

45. *KBS kāfī* 2, pp. 2f.
46. A striking parallel in Sūrdās 1972, no. 3844 (ii. 333):

    गोपालहिं पावौं धौं किहिं देस
    सिंगी मुद्रा कर खप्पर लै, करिहौं जोगिनी भेस ।।

    In which country shall I now find my Gopāl?
    Taking the whistle, the ring and the begging bowl,
    I shall take the garb of a yogini.

47. *KBS kāfī* 136, p. 294.
48. A *tilak* is 'a sectarial mark . . . made with coloured eye-earths, sandal wood, or unguents upon the forehead and between the eyebrows' (Platts 1884), used notably as a sign of initiation.
49. *'isq Allāh dī zāt* (Love is the essence of Allāh), *KBS kāfī* 146, p. 315.
50. See Schimmel 1984, pp. 41, 72, 147, etc.
51. *KBS kāfī* 92, p. 199.
52. Ibid.
53. *KBS kāfī* 139, p. 302.
54. *QI kāfī* 67, p. 144.
55. Braided coloured yarn used by Panjabi women for tying up their plait.
56. Schimmel 1976, p. xii.
57. *KBS kāfī* 61, pp. 121–2.
58. See Briggs 1938, pp. 322–48.
59. For Sant parallels, see Schomer 1987, pp. 71–2.
60. Personal recording of *maĩ jānā̃ jogī de nāl* ('I shall go with the yogi'), a copy of which has been deposited in the library of the Institut de Civilisation Indienne, Collège de France, Paris.
61. The curtain which, in a traditional Muslim society, 'protects' the women from the sight of men.
62. *KBS kāfī* 95, p. 207.
63. See *QI kāfī* 58, p. 206:

    kahū̃ turk muṣalle paṛhte ho
    kahū̃ bhagat hindū jap karte ho
    . . .
    har ghar ghar lāḍ laḍāiā hai
    pāiā hai kuch pāiā hai
    sat gurū ne alakh lakhāiā hai

    Somewhere a Muslim, you say your prayers on a mat,
    Somewhere a Hindū bhakta, you do your meditations.
    . . .

In each and every house, he shows his love.
I have found, I have found something;
The True Gurū has made me see the Unseen!

And cf. Kabīr 1928, Śabda 10, p. 123:

हिंदू तुरक को एक राह है, सतगुरु इहै बताई ।।

For the Hindu and the Muslim, there is only one way, the one which the True Guru has indicated.

64. *KBS kāfī* 153, p. 328.
65. *KBS kāfī* 118, pp. 260 f.
66. See Kabīr 1928, Śabda 36, p. 165:

हरिठग जगत ठगौरी लाई, हरिबियोग कस जियहु रे भाई
—
ठगि ठगि मूल सभनि को लीन्हा, रामठगौरी काहुँ न चीन्हा
कहँहिं कबीर ठग सौं मन मान, गई ठगौरी जब ठग पहिचाना ।।

Hari the *ṭhag* has plundered the world, but without Hari, how would you live, brothers?
. . .
Having pillaged again and again, he robbed everybody, but none understood Rām's theft.
Says Kabīr: my soul has accepted the thief. The robbery ceases when one recognizes the *ṭhag*.

67. *KBS kāfī* 2, p. 3.
68. On this new order of things, cf. Kabīr 1928, Śabda 16, p. 131:

जागत-चोर मँदिल तह मुसैं, खसम अच्छत घर सूना
बिज बिनु अँकुल पेड़ बिनु तरिवर, बिनु फूले फलफरिया
बाँझ कि कोख पुत्र अवतरिया, बिनु पगु तरिवर चढ़िया ।।

The thief of the world entered the house; the spouse came, the house was empty.
Without seeds, there were sprouts, without trees, shrubby trees, without flowers, fruit.
The sterile woman gave birth to a son, somebody climbed a tree without feet.

69. The work was completed in 1655. For an analysis of its content, see Hasrat 1953, pp. 216–32.
70. On him, see Ramakrishna 1938, pp. 12–36.
71. McLeod 1968, pp. 151 f. See also Vaudeville 1959, pp. 23–5, 1974, pp. 89–110.
72. *KBS kāfī* 109, p. 238.
73. *KBS kāfī* 13, p. 24.
74. *KBS kāfī* 62, p. 123.
75. Rā̃jhā is the caste name by which the legendary character is called. Dhīdo is his given name.
76. On the assimilation of Rā̃jhā to Kṛṣṇa, see e.g. *KBS kāfī* 28, p. 46, quoted above p. 191. On Rā̃jhā as a yogi, see *KBS kāfī* 61, pp.121 ff., quoted above p. 195, etc.
77. One can get an idea of that syncretism by reading the initial invocation in the

story of 'The Marriage of Hīr and Rā̃jhā', collected by Sir Richard Temple (1884–1900, vol. ii, pp. 507 f.):

abbal nāũ Allāh dā lenā, dujā dos Muḥammad Mīrā̃
tījā nāũ mat pitā dā lenā, unhā̃ dā cungā dūdh sarīrā̃
cauthā nāũ an pānī dā lenā, jis khāve man banhe dhīrā̃
panjmā̃ nāũ Dhartī Mātā dā lenā, jis par qadam ṭakīmā̃
chevā̃ nāũ Xwājā Pīr dā lenā, jhul pilāve thaṇḍe nīrā̃
satvā̃ nāũ Gurū Gorakh dā lenā, patal pūje bhojan khīrā̃
aṭhvā̃ nāũ Lālā̃vāle dā lenā, bande bandā̃ de ṭore tabaq janjīrā̃.

Firstly, I take the name of God; secondly, of the Great Muhammad, the friend [of God]:
Thirdly, I take the name of father and mother, on whose milk my body throve:
Fourthly, I take the name of bread and water, from eating which my heart is gladdened:
Fifthly, I take the name of Mother Earth, on whom I place my feet:
Sixthly, I take the name of Kwājā [Khizar], the Saint, that gives me cold water to drink:
Seventhly, I take the name of Gurū Gorakh [Nāth], whom I worship with a platter of milk and rice.
Eighthly, I take the name of Lālā̃wālā, that breaketh the bonds and chains of the captives. (trans. R. Temple)

Concerning the existence of Muslim Nāth yogis, see Rose 1883, vol. ii, p. 408.

REFERENCES

Ahmad, Aziz (1964), *Studies in Islamic Culture in the Indian Environment*, Lahore and Karachi: Oxford University Press.

Aḥmad, Naẕīr, ed. (1982), *Kalām-i Bullhe Śāh*, Lahore: Packages Limited.

Asani, Ali S. (1988), 'Sufi Poetry in the Folk Tradition of Indo-Pakistan' *Religion and Literature*, 20, 1, pp. 81–94.

Bedi, Sohinder Singh (1971), *Folklore of the Punjab*, New Delhi: National Book Trust, India, 2nd edn., 1980.

Briggs, G. W. (1938), *Gorakhnāth and the Kānphaṭa Yogīs*, Calcutta: YMCA Publishing House, repr. Delhi: Motilal Banarsidass, 1973, 1982.

Bullhe Śāh (1905), *Qānūn-i-ʻiśq* (*QI*) by Anvar ʻAlī Śāh, 2 vols., Lahore: Faẓal Uddīn, repr. in 1 vol., Lahore: Allāhvale kī qaumī dukān, n.d.

——(1960), *Kulliyāt-i Bullhe Śāh* (*KBS*), ed. Faqīr Muḥammad Faqīr, 2nd edn., Lahore: Panjabi Academy, 1963.

Cole, W. O. (1984), *Sikhism and its Indian Context 1469–1708: The Attitude of Guru Nanak and Early Sikhism to Indian Religious Beliefs and Practices*, London: Darton, Longman & Todd.

Eaton, R. M., (1974), 'Sufi Folk Literature and the Expansion of Indian Islam', *History of Religions*, 14, 2, pp. 117–27.

——(1978), *Sufis of Bijapur 1300–1700: Social Roles of Sufis in Medieval India*, Princeton: NJ, Princeton University Press.

Faqīr (1963), see Bullhe Śāh (1960).

Faruqi, Khwaja Ahmad (1985), 'Impact of Hindu Society on Indian Muslims', in vol. in *Religion and Religious Education*, Islam in India: Studies and Commentaries, ed. C. W. Troll, New Delhi: Vikas Publishing House.

Gonda, J. (1965), 'L'Hindouisme récent', trans. L. Jospin, in J. Gonda (ed.), *Les Religions de l'Inde*, vol. ii, Paris: Payot.

Gujranwala District Gazetteer (1935), Punjab District Gazetteers, comp. and pub. under the authority of the Punjab Government, vol. xxiv A, Lahore: Government Printing, Punjab, 1936.

Gulzār, Muḥammad Śarīf (n.d.), *Bullhe Śāh*, Lahore: Ferozsons Limited.

Hasrat, Bikrama Jit (1953), *Dārā Shikūh: Life and Works*, Calcutta: Visvabharati.

Ibbetson, Sir Denzil (1916), *Panjab Castes*, Lahore: Government Printing, Punjab, repr. Lahore: Hafeez Press, 1974.

Jhang District Gazetteer (1908), Punjab District Gazetteers, comp. and pub. under the authority of the Punjab Government, vol. xxxii A, Lahore: The Civil and Military Gazette, 1910.

Kabīr (1928), *Bījak*, ed. Vicārdās Śāstrī, Allahabad: Rāmnarāyan Lāl.

McLeod, W. H. (1968), *Gurū Nānak and the Sikh Religion*, Oxford, Clarendon Press, repr. with corrections, Delhi: Oxford University Press, 1976, 1978.

——(1975), *The Evolution of the Sikh Community: Five Essays*, Delhi: Oxford University Press.

Matringe, D. (1986), 'Les Sikhs dans la société indienne', *Actes de la Recherche en Sciences Sociales*, 61, pp. 65–73.

——(1988), *Hīr Vāris̤ Śāh, poème panjabi du XVIII*[e] *siècle: Introduction, translittération, traduction et commentaire*, vol. i, Pondicherry: Institut Français d'Indologie.

——(1989), 'L'Utilisation littéraire des formes dialectales par les poètes musulmans du Panjab de la fin du XVIe au début du XIXe siècle', in C. Caillat, ed., *Dialectes en indo-aryen*, Paris: Publications de l'Institut de Civilisation Indienne, Collège de France, pp. 527–56.

Multan District Gazetteer (1923–4), Punjab District Gazetteers, comp. and pub. under the authority of the Punjab Government, vol. vii A, Lahore: Government Printing, Punjab, 1927.

Platts, J. T. (1884), *A Dictionary of Urdū, Classical Hindī, and English*, repr. 1930, 1974, London: Oxford University Press.

Quddūsī, I'jāz-ul-Ḥaqq (1962), *Taẕkira-i ṣūfīhā-i Panjāb*, Karachi: Salmān Academy.

Ramakrishna, Lajwanti (1938), *Pañjābī Sūfī Poets: A.D. 1460–1900*, repr. Karachi: Indus Publications, 1977.

Rose, H. A. (1883), *A Glossary of the Tribes and Castes of the Punjab and North-West Frontier Province*, 3 vols, Patiala: Languages Department, Punjab.

Roy, Asim (1983), *The Islamic Syncretistic Tradition in Bengal*. Princeton: Princeton University Press.

Schimmel, A. (1976), *Pain and Grace: A Study of Two Mystical Writers of Eighteenth-Century Muslim India*, Leiden: E. J. Brill.

——(1982), *As Through a Veil: Mystical Poetry in Islam*, New York: Columbia University Press.

——(1984), *Stern und Blume: Die Bilderwelt der persischen Poesie*, Wiesbaden: Otto Harrassowitz.

Schomer, K. (1987), 'The *Dohā* as a Vehicle of Sant Teachings', in K. Schomer and W. H. McLeod, eds., *The Sants*, Berkeley, Calif.: Berkeley Religious Studies Series, and Delhi: Motilal Banarsidass.

Shahpur District Gazetteer (1917), Punjab District Gazetteers, comp. and pub. under the authority of the Punjab Government, vol. XXX A, Lahore: Government Printing, Punjab, 1918.

Sharda, S. R. (1974), *Sufi Thought: Its Development in Panjab and its Impact on Panjabi Literature, from Baba Farid to 1850 AD*, New Delhi: Munshiram Manoharlal.

Singh, Khushwant (1977), *A History of the Sikhs*, 2 vols., 2nd edn., Delhi: Oxford University Press.

Snellgrove, D. (1987), *Indo-Tibetan Buddhism: Indian Buddhists and their Tibetan Successors*, London: Serindia Publications.

Sūrdās (1972 and 1976), *Sūrsāgar*, ed. Jagannāthdās 'Ratnākar', Varanasi: Nāgarī-pracāriṇī Sabhā.

Temple, Sir Richard (1884–1900), *The Legends of the Punjab*, 3 vols., repr. Islamabad: National Institute of Folk and Traditional Heritage, 1981.

Usborne, C. F. (1905), *Bullah Shāh, Sufi, Mystic and Poet of the Panjab*, Lahore: Rai Sahib Gulab Singh, repr. Lahore: Saadi Panjabi Academy, 1976.

Vaudeville, C. (1959), *Kabir: Au cabaret de l'amour*, Paris: Gallimard.

——(1965), *Bārahmāsā: Les Chansons des douze mois dans les littératures indo-aryennes*, Pondicherry: Institut Français d'Indologie.

——(1974), *Kabīr*, vol. i, London: Oxford University Press.

Some topics in the Kṛṣṇa poetry of north India

Three-three-two versus four-by-four: metrical frames for the *padas* of Sūrdās

K. E. BRYANT

The boundary solution

This paper addresses the question: What is the most useful way to describe the structure of medieval Hindi metres, and particularly the metres used in the *padas* of such bhakti poets as Sūrdās? Note that this is quite a different question from those which concern the prescriptive rules for such metres. The rules are more or less inflexible: they tell us what the poet *must* do if a poem is to be considered as conforming to metre *x*. What interests us here is less the regularity of metre 'by the rules' than those kinds of quasi-regularity which, while characteristic of a metre, and functional within the metre, are not matters of prescription.

While a description of metrical phenomena is the immediate goal, the eventual aim of this line of enquiry is a broader description of the composition process employed in Hindi bhakti poetry. It is common to think of *pada* literature as, at least in origin, an oral tradition; and we have come to expect of any oral tradition some degree of formularity – that is, some mechanism by which the poet, thinking on his feet, may conform what he has to say to the formal demands of his verse, without making superhuman demands on his ability to parse the line as he goes. Ordinarily we think of such formulas as time-honoured phrases of known metrical dimensions, ready to be plugged in where appropriate. This paper will make no claims for the existence of such a system within this tradition; it will, however, describe a metrical framework which appears to serve some of the same purposes: it provides the poet with a small and manageable repertoire of prefabricated slots for his words, while at the same time permitting great variety of rhythmic effect. Subsequent papers will examine the question of whether this framework is in fact the basis for a system of verbal formulas.

While we have said that prescriptive rules are not the issue here, it will be useful to review, very briefly, just what those rules are. The metres most commonly used in the Hindi *pada* are quantitative; in the mathematics of such metres, a short syllable counts as one *mātrā* and a long syllable counts as two. The rules for a particular metre prescribe the total number of *mātrās* which a line must contain; those rules do not, in the metres we are concerned with, prescribe any particular sequence of long and short syllables. If the rule calls for sixteen *mātrās*, this may in practice mean a line containing sixteen short syllables, or eight long syllables, or any intermediate combination, as long as it adds up to sixteen *mātrās*.

The choice of sixteen as example was not arbitrary: most *pada* metres are based on a cycle of sixteen, a fact which presumably reflects the pre-eminence of the sixteen-*mātrā* tāla cycle in Indian music.[1] Most such metres dictate a line of two unequal feet: a first foot containing a full cycle of sixteen *mātrās*, and a second foot containing a partial cycle, with an intervening caesura. The single most common metre, known as *sāra*, has an overall line length of twenty-eight *mātrās*, divided 16-12. Other common metres are divided 16-11, or 16-10, or 16-16.[2]

So much for the rules; and yet anyone who has worked with texts containing a large number of lines of *sāra* will have realized that the picture is more complicated than this: there are lines divided 16-12 which sound 'right' and others which sound 'wrong'; there are lines whose rhythm seems predictable, or hackneyed, and others whose rhythm surprises. Clearly, the *sāra* meter is characterized by something more than a caesura after the sixteenth *mātrā*. The terms often given to that mysterious 'something' are *laya* and *gati*. Maheshwari Sinha Mahesh calls *gati* 'the touchstone which determines whether a metre is wrong or right', but he adds: '*Gati* has no fixed rules.'[3]

A number of studies have suggested a further division of the sixteen-*mātrā* cycle into smaller segments. In the footnotes I have discussed several of these proposals: the most obvious division is one which reflects musical practice by dividing 16 into 4-4-4-4;[4] other divisions proposed have included 6-4-6, and 2-4-4-4-2.[5] But while each of these may satisfy a certain set of intuitions concerning the metre, none can be supported as having the status of a 'rule': that is, whenever a reasonable quantity of verse in the *sāra* metre is examined, numerous exceptions emerge to each of the hypotheses cited.

Most such studies, including a couple of my own, have asked the question: Are there points in the line at which divisions of some sort occur with enough regularity to be significant? In the present study, I've tried to ask the question in a different way, a way which requires the coining of one new term. The term is 'boundary pattern' – that is, a pattern of word boundaries; and it is best explained by example. Imagine a line of poetry, composed in *sāra* metre, in which the twenty-eight-*mātrā* length is filled by seven words of four *mātrās* each; the 'boundary pattern' of that line would be 4-4-4-4-4-4-4. If, in another line, the twenty-eight *mātrās* consist of words of four *mātrās* alternating with words of three *mātrās*, the 'boundary pattern' would be 4-3-4-3-4-3-4-3;[6] and so forth. The first question, then, is this: Are there some boundary patterns which are more popular than others?

A first approach to the question involved examining the 400 or so *padas* of Sūrdās which are included in a forthcoming critical edition;[7] the primary manuscript sources on which the readings are based are the Fatehpur manuscript, dated from the late sixteenth century,[8] and an early seventeenth-century manuscript from Bikaner.[9] Computer transcriptions of these poems were already available; several short programs were developed to perform metrical scansion, and to perform counts and tallies of various sorts. One of these was a program to tally boundary patterns. On a sample of about 400 lines of *sāra* metre,[10] the ten most frequent patterns were the following:[11]

(13) 3-3-2-3-3-2-3-3-2-4
(5) 3-3-2-3-5-3-3-2-4
(5) 2-2-3-3-2-4-3-3-2-4
(5) 2-2-3-3-4-2-3-3-2-4
(5) 2-2-3-3-4-2-2-2-3-5
(4) 3-3-2-3-3-2-4-3-5
(4) 4-3-3-2-4-4-3-5
(4) 4-3-3-2-4-2-4-2-4
(4) 4-3-3-4-2-3-3-2-4
(4) 3-3-4-2-4-3-3-2-4

The figures in parentheses indicate the number of times each pattern occurred, and it will be obvious at once that these numbers are too small to be terribly significant; even the most frequent pattern only occurred, out of 400 lines, a total of thirteen times. In a moment I'll talk about ways to extract more useful numbers from the same material; but there are two aspects of the present list on which I should like to dwell for a moment. First, there is the extraordinary regularity of that first, most frequent pattern: 3-3-2, 3-3-2, 3-3-2, 4. Secondly, it should be noted that the repeated unit in that pattern – the sequence 3-3-2 – is conspicuous throughout the other patterns as well; in fact, it occurs in all but one of the ten.

The 3-3-2 pattern has received notice in another north Indian literature. Nilratan Sen, in his book entitled *Early Eastern New Indo Aryan Versification*, has a good deal to say about what he calls a '3-3-2 moric pattern' in the *caryāgīti*. He contends that the metres of the *caryāgīti* are descendants of the Prakrit *pādākulaka, dohā*, and *caupaiā*. These Prakrit metres, he observes, are 'tetrarhythmic' – that is, based on a division of the line into four-*mātrā* units. In the Eastern Apabhraṃśas, he argues, this Prakrit division of a sixteen-*mātrā* line into four four-*mātrā* units was gradually overlaid with a 3-3-2 division, a division which he says better reflected the natural pattern of semantic pauses in late Prakrit, Apabhraṃśa, and Bengali.[12]

Our concerns here are not historical but synchronic, and of a sort that Sen does not address: What functional role does the pattern provide in Hindi verse? Whether or not Sen is right in portraying a progressive overlay of the 3-3-2 pattern on an older four-by-four division, how do the two systems of division interact? Does one dominate over the other? Would an answer to that question make any difference to our understanding of the structure of the verse?

Before returning to the realms of numbers, we should examine a line or two of the poetry the numbers are supposed to represent. What does a '3-3-2 boundary pattern' sound like? What, for that matter, does a 'tetrarhythmic' line sound like? Here are three examples. The first is the best specimen the data will produce of a 'tetrarhythmic' line – one that is divided simply 4-4-4-4, 4-4-4. I say the 'best specimen' because, in fact, there is no line in the corpus containing solely four-*mātrā* words. The second and third examples belong to the 'most frequent' pattern illustrated above – 3-3-2, 3-3-2, 3-3-2, 4.

First the 4-4-based line:

4 (3) (5) 4 4 4 4

– ᴗ ᴗ | – ᴗ | ᴗ – ᴗ ᴗ | – ᴗ ᴗ | – ᴗ ᴗ | – – | – –

मोह्न राग बजावत गावत आवत चारै धेनू ;[13]

then a 3-3-2-based line:

3 3 2 3 3 2 3 3 2 4

– ᴗ | ᴗ ᴗ ᴗ | ᴗ ᴗ | – ᴗ | – ᴗ | ᴗ ᴗ | ᴗ ᴗ ᴗ | ᴗ ᴗ ᴗ | ᴗ ᴗ | – –

कूप षनन जलआस सूर प्रभु भवन मदन दहि जैहै ;[14]

and finally a line in which the same sort of syncopation is further exaggerated by alliteration:

3 3 2 3 3 2 3 3 2 4

– ᴗ | – ᴗ | ᴗ ᴗ | – ᴗ | – ᴗ | ᴗ ᴗ | ᴗ ᴗ ᴗ | – ᴗ | – | – –

मेरु मूठि बर बालिबारि छबि बहुत बित्तकी लैनी .[15]

I hope the sound of those patterns will continue to echo in your ears for a few moments while we look at some more measures of the occurrence of the patterns. The small size of the numbers we had to deal with before – thirteen, remember, as the greatest frequency of any one pattern – stemmed from two sources: first, the relatively small number of lines of machine-scannable *sāra* metre available in the sample; secondly, the very large number of patterns possible in a line of twenty-eight *mātrās*. A way round both problems is to restrict our enquiry to the first foot of the line, the foot preceding the caesura. This gives us a single cycle of sixteen *mātrās*, with fewer patterns possible (although still a rather large number); it also allows us to expand our data-set to include, not only *sāra* metre (divided 16-12), but also those metres which, while showing the same sixteen-*mātrā* first foot, have second feet containing ten, eleven, or sixteen *mātrās*. From a sample of some 1,600 lines of assorted sixteen-based metres, then, these are the ten most frequent boundary patterns in the first foot:

(143) 3-3-2-3-3-2 (A)
(104) 4-3-3-2-4 (B)
(67) 4-3-3-4-2
(67) 2-2-3-3-2-4
(58) 2-2-3-3-4-2
(49) 3-3-2-3-5 (C)
(49) 2-4-2-3-3-2
(47) 3-3-4-2-4
(35) 4-3-4-3-2 (D)
(30) 3-3-2-2-2-4

I call your attention to the first two patterns on the list – let's call them pattern A and pattern B – accounting, between them, for about 250 of the 1,600 lines. Pattern A is simply two occurrences of 3-3-2, one after another. Pattern B has a single 3-3-2 sequence, sandwiched between the two four-*mātrā* words. Here are the first halves of six lines of verse, three illustrating each of these patterns:

A. 3-3-2 / 3-3-2:

सूर अधम की / होत कौन गति ...[16]

काम क्रोध मद / लोभ ग्रसित ह्वै...[17]

मुदित बदन अरु / उदित सदन तैं ...[18]

B. 4 / 3-3-2 / 4:

मागध / मथन हतन नृप / बंधन ...[19]

बेस्या / पुत्र सोभ नहि / पावै ...[20]

कंपित / त्रास सास अति / मुकुलित ...[21]

Sen describes the 3-3-2 sequence as an overlay on an older four-by-four system; I suggest that, in our patterns A and B, we can see two general principles by which the one system accommodates the other. The first principle is that the fundamental division is still 'tetrarhythmic': the easiest way to divide sixteen is still by four. The second principle is that this rhythmic structure, like any other, is only a norm against which to measure variation; and that the primary strategy for variation employed in Hindi metres – employed indeed with such frequency that it largely conceals the underlying four-by-four skeleton – is to take *any two adjacent fours* and weld them into an eight, with that eight displaying our familiar sequence: 3-3-2. Performing such a weld on the second and third four-*mātrā* units in the cycle produces pattern A; welding instead the first with the second, and the third with the fourth, produces pattern B:

Pattern A:	3 3 2		3 3 2	
'regular' line:	4	4	4	4
Pattern B:	4	3 3 2		4

These two somewhat obvious principles have several implications which may be less obvious. The first is that, according to such a rule, a sequence of 3-3-2 is restricted to certain positions in the line; we would not expect to find, for example, a line beginning with a two-*mātrā* word, followed immediately by a 3-3-2; and in fact such lines occur nowhere in the corpus. The 3-3-2s are confined, without a single exception in 1,600 lines, to three locations within a sixteen-*mātrā* cycle: they may occupy precisely the first half of the cycle, or precisely the second half; or – as in pattern B – they may begin with the fifth *mātrā* and straddle the centre.

The second implication, following from the first but ultimately much more important, is that there are only certain places in the line where the poet may place three-*mātrā* words; and certain others where four-*mātrā* words may be placed; and so on. To expand much further on this subject will require that we go beyond patterns A and B to their less frequent variations; it will also require going beyond first and second principles to some corollaries; but the examples seen so far are sufficient to establish the central point: there is a general framework, or rather there are a couple of alternative frameworks, on which the *pada* singer hangs his words.

Those words come in three main sizes, by the nature of the language: words of two, three, and four *mātrās* account for more than 90 per cent of the total words in our Sūrdās corpus, with two- and three-*mātrā* words each accounting for roughly a third of the total, and four-*mātrā* words for roughly a quarter. Given only the formal rules for the *sāra* metre, one might expect these two-, three-, and four-*mātrā* words to be strewn throughout the metrical line in sequences determined only by the sense of the line; in fact, the distribution of these three common lengths is closely regulated.

But just how closely? Our patterns A and B, while substantially more frequent than the others, still account for only 15 per cent of the total. Most of the remaining patterns are also studded with 3-3-2s; but how are we to measure the overall significance of that sequence? Another computer program illustrates one answer to the question. This program allows us to ask questions in the following format: Assume a poet who has begun his line with a word of *x mātrās*, or with a string of words having lengths *x, y*, and *z*; what does he do next? The program then examines the Sūrdās data and gives the frequency with which Sūrdās uses each possible solution in the same metrical context. For example, what does Sūr do after beginning a line with a three-*mātrā* word? In almost 80 per cent of such cases, he follows with a second three-*mātrā* word. Assume the poet takes this most travelled road and follows a three with a second three. We now have a line beginning with two three-*mātrā* words: what next? In that context, says the program, 66 per cent of the time Sūr uses a two-*mātrā* word. Our line has grown to 3-3-2: next? Next, says the program, another 3 (in 71 per cent of the cases); and then yet another 3 (70 per cent); and finally, of course, a 2.

The point of the exercise is this: If at each juncture we take the *most probable* branch, we arrive ultimately at that distinctive pattern: 3-3-2, 3-3-2. And how probable *is* the most probable branch in each case? At any sequential point in the construction of a line, the next word will in fact be of the length predicted by our 'two principles' about 70 per cent of the time.

What about the other 30 per cent? With one conspicuous exception, variations on this main line of development still conform recognizably to one or another of the two basic patterns already described. Five-*mātrā* words provide a case in point. While much less common than twos, threes, and fours, when they do appear it is in precisely those contexts where we would expect a 3 followed by a 2. The positions which permit the sequence 3-2 are extremely restricted: that sequence may begin only at the fourth, eighth, or twelfth *mātrā* of the cycle; and those same restrictions apply to words of five *mātrās*. Note that, of the ten most common boundary patterns mentioned earlier, only one – marked C – contains five-*mātrā* words; and the context here is readily recognizable: it is pattern A with this variation, that the second occurrence of 3-3-2 is replaced with a 3-5.

The stress solution

The conspicuous exception referred to – the one pattern, that is, which bears no visible relationship to patterns A or B – is that marked D in the list. '4-3-4-3-2': the theme here seems to be '4-3', almost as if this were a metre based on seven or fourteen rather than eight or sixteen. Either we must treat this as a flagrant violation, or our basic principles are themselves in need of revision.

The pursuit of this anomaly has, in very recent days, led this enquiry in quite a different direction. The point of departure was the observation that the thirty-five lines exhibiting pattern D share one other intriguing characteristic. In every one of the thirty-five, the third word of the line – the second four-*mātrā* word – has the same metrical pattern: short-long-short. This relatively uncommon pattern accounts for less than 15 per cent of all four-*mātrā* words; it seemed strange, then, that it should account for 100 per cent of the words in this particular context. In the following example the word in question is *cakora*, and in the discussion that follows I shall refer to words which exhibit this metrical pattern – short-long-short – as the *cakora* class:

4 3 4 3 2

– – | ⏑ ⏑ ⏑ | ⏑ – ⏑ | – ⏑ | ⏑ ⏑

धाए चतुर चकोर सूर सुनि...

The special role of the *cakora* class words is best explained, I now believe, in terms of word stress.

The possible significance of word stress in Hindi metre has been the subject of two recent papers by Constance Fairbanks, 'Stress and Metrical Rhythm in Hindi' and 'More on Stress and Metrical Rhythm'. I am going to give a very abridged summary of her argument here, focusing on those aspects germane to the present discussion. Let me begin with a quote which stakes out the ground:

While Hindi certainly has phonetic stress, it does not have phonemic stress to any significant extent. Furthermore, stress in Hindi seems to be much weaker than, for example, stress in English. For these two reasons the Hindi speaker tends to be less consciously aware of stress placement in Hindi than is the English speaker of English stress. Nonetheless, stress in Hindi is important in terms of speech rhythm, and as such plays an important role in creating the rhythms of poetry.[22]

Fairbanks reviews various hypotheses concerning the correct algorithm for assigning stress to Hindi words; she then sets out to test these hypotheses by examining Hindi poetry. She works with samples from the *caupāīs* of Tūlsīdās and Jāyasī, and from the Ālhā Khaṇḍ; both metres involved – the *caupāī* and the *ālhā* – are sixteen-based metres. Fairbanks assumes a four-by-four division of the sixteen-*mātrā* cycle, using musical practice as her guide; and, noting that the drummed accompaniment to musical performances of such poetry characteristically accents the first beat of each four-beat division, she assumes this as the primary accentual pattern for the metre. Her question then becomes: To what extent does word stress, as determined by each of the competing hypotheses, correspond with this pattern of metrical or musical ictus?

Her conclusion is that the most satisfactory algorithm for assigning word stress is that of G. A. Grierson in his 1895 article 'On the Stress Accent in the Modern Indo-Aryan Vernaculars'.[23] Specifically, she notes the following: in a sample of fifty lines of poetry from each of the three works, some 90 per cent of the metrical accents – that is, the first beat of each four-beat *gaṇa* – coincide with syllables which Grierson's rules predict as stressed.[24]

For our purposes, the intriguing aspect of this application of Grierson's stress rules is the special status those rules assign to words of the class here dubbed *cakora*. By Grierson's rules, all words of two, three, and four *mātrās, with the single exception of the* cakora *class*, are stressed on the first syllable;[25] *cakora*-class words are stressed on the second, long syllable. Both the rule (first-syllable stress) and the exception (*cakora* class) are significant here.

The significance of the rule is that there will be a general congruence between word boundary patterns, of the sort we have been examining, and what we must now dub 'stress patterns'. For example, a sixteen-*mātrā* foot containing only four-*mātrā* words would have the boundary pattern 4-4-4-4; it would also be likely to have a stress pattern 4-4-4-4, since each of those four-*mātrā* words (as long as they were not *cakora* class) would be stressed on the first syllable, producing a metronome-like, 'four-square' foot:

4 4 4 4

–́ ⏑ ⏑ | ⏑́ ⏑ – | –́ ⏑ ⏑ | –́ –

देषत अपनी आंषिनि ऊधौ ...

It is important to be sure that the notation used here for the two types of pattern is clear. To say that the boundary pattern for the example above is 4-4-4-4 means simply that the example contains four words of four *mātrās* each. To say that the stress pattern is 4-4-4-4 means that the intervals between consecutive stressed syllables are, in each case, four *mātrās*.

We're now ready to return to the matter of the *cakora*-class words, and to the pattern D, which appeared such an aberration in our original, boundary-based list of patterns. Whereas lines consisting of two-, three-, and four-*mātrā* words will, in general, display a stress-pattern identical to their boundary pattern, this is obviously not the case for lines containing *cakora*-class words, since such words carry the stress not on the first syllable, but on the second. If we return to our original example of a pattern D line and add word stress to the scansion, we find the following:

4 3 4 3 2

–́ – | ⏑́ ⏑ ⏑ | ⏑ –́ ⏑ | –́ ⏑ | ⏑́ ⏑

धाए चतुर चकोर सूर सुनि...

We may rewrite the line with syllables grouped by stress pattern, rather than word boundary:

4 4 3 3 2

–́ – | ⏑́ ⏑ ⏑ ⏑ | –́ ⏑ | –́ ⏑ | ⏑́ ⏑

धाए चतुर च - कोर सूर सुनि...

Whereas the boundary pattern was an uncharacteristic 4-3-4-3-2, the stress pattern is immediately recognizable: 4-4-3-3-2. In the terms of our previous analysis, the second half of the cycle has here been 'welded' into a single eight-*mātrā* unit, with stresses patterned 3-3-2. In fact, this proves to be the case for all thirty-five of the pattern D lines.

To think of such patterns in terms of Grierson's stress rules, rather than merely in terms of word boundary, thus accounted for the troublesome exception; it seemed worth while to explore stress patterning for the corpus as a whole. The metrical scansion programs were modified to incorporate Grierson's rules as well as the rules of Hindi metrical scansion; each line of the Sūr text was rescanned and marked for stressed syllables as well as for word boundaries and syllable lengths; and a list of 'most frequent stress patterns' was compiled along lines similar to those of the boundary patterns list. The ten most frequent stress patterns were the following:

(163) 3-3-2-3-3-2 (A)
(153) 4-3-3-2-4 (B)
(107) 4-3-3-4-2 (C)
(77) 4-4-3-3-2 (D)
(73) 3-3-2-4-4 (E)
(68) 2-2-3-3-2-4 (F)
(59) 2-2-3-3-4-2 (G)
(54) 4-4-4-4 (H)
(51) 3-3-4-2-4 (I)
(42) 4-3-3-2-2-2 (J)

The beginning of our list looks much as it did before – patterns A and B are unchanged, except that each now accounts for a larger fraction of the 1,600-line total. Our formerly aberrant pattern D is now a very mannerly pattern D, and the frequency of this pattern also shows a considerable increase. Perhaps the most interesting newcomer to the list of ten is pattern H: here, in eighth place, is the most straightforward pattern of all, an unadorned 4-4-4-4. One of the fifty-four lines exhibiting that pattern is, in fact, the line given earlier as an example of a 'nearly perfect' tetrarhythmic division; note that, when divided by stress rather than by boundary, its last 'imperfection' disappears:

4 4 4 4 4 4 4
–́ ⏑ ⏑ | –́ ⏑ ⏑ | –́ ⏑ ⏑ | –́ ⏑ ⏑ | –́ ⏑ ⏑ | –́ – | –́ –
मोहन राग ब-जावत गावत आवत चारे धेनू

Conclusions

The question which the paper set out to address was: What is the most useful way to describe the structure of medieval Hindi metres? In the case of those quantitative metres based on a cycle of sixteen, the answer suggested here is something like the following. First, the underlying norm should be seen as a simple division of the sixteen-*mātrā* foot into four *gaṇas* of four *mātrās* each; but a four-*mātrā gaṇa* represents the 'norm' for these metres only in the sense that a bar containing four quarter-notes (or crotchets) represents the norm for the 4/4 metre of Western music. No one would think of writing a musical piece containing only, or even primarily, quarter-notes arranged four by four. The most interesting rules of either system are those which regulate variations on the norm.

It may be useful to think of the system in generative terms, with the 4-4-4-4 pattern as the kernel, and the variations formed by a set of optional transformations. The set of rules needed will in fact be extremely small; while the analogy to Western musical rhythms may be instructive in some respects, the system of variations demonstrated in Hindi metres is incomparably less complex than that to be found in musical compositions. For the ten stress patterns listed – and these account for more than 50 per cent of the lines in the sample – only three 'transformation rules' are necessary. The first rule, and the most important, is one we have already discussed: this rule would allow any two adjacent four-*mātrā gaṇas* to be replaced by a 3-3-2 sequence. On our ten-pattern list, patterns B, D, and E each result from a single application of this rule: in the first half of the cycle for pattern E, the second half for D, and the middle for B. Pattern A, of course, is derived by applying the same rule to both first and second halves of the cycle:

Pattern H:	4	4	4	4
Pattern E:	4	4	3 3 2	
Pattern D:	3 3 2		4	4
Pattern A:	3 3 2		3 3 2	
Pattern B:	4	3 3 2		4

I have detailed in a footnote the other rules necessary to derive the other patterns.[26] The object here is not to arrive at a fully configured system of rules, but simply to suggest the general processes involved. Why bother to think in generative terms? What does such an approach imply, beyond descriptive convenience? It implies a possible algorithm for oral composition: a norm (4-4-4-4) with a few simple variations, a system which can produce a variety of rhythmic effects and accommodate words of a variety of shapes, while still employing a framework sufficiently simple to facilitate extemporaneous composition.

The above summary begs the question: Are the divisions – whether 4-4 or 3-3-2 – to be divisions marked by word boundary, or divisions marked by word stress? As we have seen, much of the time this will make little difference, simply because the most common classes of Hindi word carry – by Grierson's rules – first-syllable stress. The primary evidence given here in favour of the stress hypothesis is that certain classes of word which would have to be treated as exceptions in a boundary-based system are quite regular in a system based on stress; I have presented the example of four-*mātrā, cakora*-class words, but there are others equally dramatic among words of five *mātrās*. All in all, the system is much neater if stress is seen as the determinant; there are considerably fewer variations to be accounted for than in a boundary-based system. Whether conceived of in terms of boundary or stress, the 3-3-2 pattern is ubiquitous; by either reckoning, that sequence is, in the Sūrdās materials, more than twice as frequent as the simpler sequence 4-4.

There are at least two directions in which the further study of such patterns can usefully proceed. One of these is in the area of musical performance and practice. What is immediately evident is that the 3-3-2 sequence constitutes a very dramatic form of syncopation, a marked shift of accent from the underlying 4-4:

4-4:

| ⏑́ ⏑ ⏑ ⏑ | ⏑́ ⏑ ⏑ ⏑ |

3-3-2:

| ⏑́ ⏑ ⏑ ⏑́ | ⏑ ⏑ ⏑́ ⏑ |

It is also apparent that the alternation between 4-4 and 3-3-2 is a close cousin of a variety of phenomena in Western music, all of which involve playing off two against three, duple against triple, even against odd: phenomena such as compound metres like 6/8, in which a bar contains two major divisions, each divided into three; or the hemiola of baroque music, in which the underlying beat shifts in mid-composition from two to three, and then back again. (It might be noted that the specific rhythmic division in question – 3-3-2 – is best known in Western music as calypso rhythm!) I am sure that similar concepts must prevail in Indian theory (and indeed, my ears tell me that they prevail in Indian musical practice); further research in this direction will require someone with greater musical expertise.

The second direction which holds promise is an exploration of the notion of formulaic composition. I have attempted in this paper to set out the metrical framework into which words may be inserted; the next step is to essay, on the same data, an examination of the words which do in fact fill the slots. Certainly there are phrases in Sūr's poetry which take on the regularity of formula; it remains to be seen whether these are part of a larger system, and, if so, what role the metrical framework plays in that system. The database prepared for the Sūrdās critical edition provides a rich source of information potentially relevant to this enquiry. In particular, it seems desirable to look systematically at variants of individual lines, where these variants are clearly the product of oral improvisation rather than mere scribal error. In those many cases where half a line at a time has been rearranged, it should be instructive to see just how the rearrangement of words is constrained by the rules of metrical patterning.

Finally, it is necessary to extend this line of enquiry beyond the *sāra* metre and its cousins; I suspect that very similar principles may be at work in all medieval quantitative metres. I have in a very cursory way turned my programs loose on several hundred lines of Tulsī's *caupāī* metre, and several hundred lines of his *dohā*; and it is clear that, in these metres also, the primary alternation is between sequences of 4-4 and 3-3-2.[27]

NOTES

1. For a discussion of how metre is matched to tāla in one style of performance, see R. Snell, 'Metrical Forms in Braj Bhāṣā Verse: The *Caurāsī Pada* in Performance', in *BCR 1979–1982*, pp. 353–83.
2. As some indicator of the relative frequency of these metres, of the 400 *padas* by Sūrdās referred to below, 93% are in 16-based metres, of which the most common are 16-12 (24%), 16-11 (22%), 16-16 (16%), 16-10 (13%), 16-15 (6%), and 16-14 (5%). The only common metre not based on 16 is 14-10 (5%).
3. Maheshwari Sinha Mahesh, *The Historical Development of Mediaeval Hindi Prosody*, Bhagalpur: Bhagalpur University, 1964, p. 8.
4. A case for the 4-4-4-4 division will be discussed later; the argument is made for other 16-based metres in C. Fairbanks, 'Stress and Metrical Rhythm in Hindi', unpub. paper.
5. See K. E. Bryant, *Poems to the Child-God: Structures and Strategies in the Poetry of Surdas*, Berkeley: University of California Press, 1978, p. 132. The error lay in failing to disaggregate data. As will be argued later in this paper, there are several alternate divisions of the line; it is now evident that my earlier hypothesis rested on an averaging of these different divisions – not a very meaningful statistic!
6. The astute will have noticed that the latter pattern could not, in fact, represent a line of *sāra* at all: while it has the requisite 28 *mātrās*, it does not permit a caesura after 16. It is intended only to serve as an uncomplicated illustration of the notation.
7. The critical edition is the result of a joint project on which Jack Hawley and I have been working for a number of years. The project will appear in the Harvard Oriental Series in 2 vols., critical edn. Bryant, trans. Hawley.
8. MS no. 49 in the Reserved Collection, Maharaja Sawai Man Singh II Museum, City Palace, Jaipur; dated VS 1639 (AD 1582) at Fatehpur (Shekhavat). The MS is now available in a facsimile publication: *Pada sūrdāsjī kā*, ed. Gopal Narayan Bahura, with an introduction by K. E. Bryant, Jaipur: Maharaja Sawai Man Singh II Museum, 1984.
9. MS no. 157 in the Anup Sanskrit Library, Bikaner; dated VS 1681 (AD 1624) at Burhanpur.
10. The 400 lines used comprised all lines in the total corpus which the program scanned as 16-12. Note that the program was not instructed to attempt to make sense of lines in which one or another 'exception' must be introduced: for example, the program scanned the vowels 'e' and 'o' as long in all cases (although they may often be treated as short). To introduce scansion according to exception rules would increase the size of the sample, but it would also introduce a large element of subjectivity; someone must decide, in each line which does not fit the 'regular' paradigm, which of several possible syllables to treat as exceptional.
11. A comment is required on the definition of 'word'. The problem arises in the case of compounds: is the whole compound to be treated as 'word' or divided into its components? For the purposes of this exercise, all components which can stand as independent words (including postpositions) have been separated. Thus: *patita pāvana* as two words, but *adhikārī* as one.

12. Nilratan Sen, *Early Eastern NIA Versification*, Simla: Indian Institute of Advanced Study, 1973, pp. 5–25.
13. For a published version of this line, see *Sūrasāgar*, ed. Nandadulāre Vājpeyī *et al.*, Varanasi; Nāgarī Pracāriṇī Sabhā, 4th edn., 1972, *pada* 1995, line 2. I have in fact fudged the line to provide the clearest possible example of the 'theoretical' regular line; the last vowel is actually short, not long, so the line properly belongs to a 16-11, not a 16-12, metre.
14. For a published version see *Sūrasāgar*, ed. Vājpeyī *et al.*, *pada* 3198, line 6. It is interesting to note that, while the reading of this edition is greatly different from the one given here, the boundary pattern is the same in both:

    बरत भवन खनि कूप सूर त्यौं मदन अगिनि दहि जैहै

15. *Sūrasāgar*, ed. Vajpēyī, *pada* 455, line 5.
16. For a published version see ibid., *pada* 52 line 6.
17. For a published version see ibid., *pada* 111 line 8.
18. For a published version see ibid., *pada* 613 line 2.
19. For a published version see ibid., *pada* 17 line 5.
20. For a published version see ibid., *pada* 34 line 4.
21. For a published version see ibid., app. *pada* 94.
22. C. Fairbanks, 'More on Stress and Metrical Rhythm', unpub. paper, p. 1.
23. *JRAS* 3, 1895, pp. 139–47. Fairbanks provides a very practical summary of Grierson's algorithm: 'Assign stress to the penultimate syllable if it is heavy. If it is not, then keep moving backwards to a heavy syllable. If no heavy syllable is found, the stress is thrown back as far as possible, but no further than the fourth syllable from the end if the word ends in a light syllable, or the third syllable from the end if it ends in a heavy' ('Stress and Metrical Rhythm in Hindi', pp. 2–3). For this summary, and for a discussion of the various competing algorithms for assigning Hindi word stress, Fairbanks cites Manjari Ohala, 'Stress in Hindi', in L. M. Hyman, ed., *Studies in Stress and Accent*, Los Angeles: University of Southern California, 1977, pp. 327–8.
24. 'In my samples in Jaisi 91%, in Tulsi 90%, and in Alha 86% of the 400 ictus positions are filled by syllables which, according to Grierson, take word stress' (Fairbanks, 'Stress and Metrical Rhythm in Hindi', p. 3). These figures make the *caupāī* and *ālhā* metres seem very regular; but in fact they exaggerate the regularity considerably. The problem arises (in my opinion) from a major error in the way Fairbanks defines correspondence between stress and ictus. Stressed syllables are often long syllables – that is, syllables which cover two *mātrās* of the metrical cycle; Fairbanks counts these as coinciding with the 'ictus position' if *either half* of the long syllable overlaps the ictus position. Speaking of instances where a long syllable crosses the boundary of a four-*mātrā gaṇa*, Fairbanks says: 'While from a musical point of view these latter may be considered syncopation, from a metrical perspective one can say that the ictus falls on the syllable which contains the first of every four *mātrās*.' She provides the following example:

    ⏑́ – –́ ⏑

    कृपा सिंधु …

This she maps on to a pattern of four-*mātrā gaṇas* as shown below, with parentheses enclosing *gaṇas*:

(˘́ – *́ ˘ ...

In effect, this gives every long syllable *two* chances to correspond with a metrical ictus position; that is, by Fairbanks's reckoning, both of the following cases would count as 'ictus positions filled by stressed syllables':

(˘́ – ˘) (–́ ˘ ...

(˘́ – * ˘ ...

By my reckoning, only the first of the two shows a correspondence: that is, in the first, word stress is perceived at the same instant as metrical ictus is expected; in the second, word stress is perceived one *mātrā before* metrical ictus. Applying this reckoning to my own data, the 'regularity' of correspondence is much less dramatic, though still noteworthy: leaving aside the first word of the line (which begins with a stressed syllable in almost all cases), the correspondence between stressed syllables and the beginning of four-*mātrā gaṇas* is approximately 55%. While still significant, this leaves ample room for variation. Fairbanks's treatment of long syllables leads her to treat the two most common forms of three-*mātrā* word in two very different ways, even though (by Grierson's rules) both are stressed on the same syllable – the first. In two separate sections, she discusses lines beginning (*a*) *begi ānu* and (*b*) *gaṃga bacana*. The first she classes as an example of 'syncopation', and marks the result:

('More on Stress', p. 4)

(–́ ˘ *́ ˘ ...

The second she classes as an example of 'stress shift': 'the syllable filling the ictus position is given prominence in recitation even if that is not the syllable which would normally carry word stress' (p. 5). She marks the second example:

(–́ ˘ ˘) (˘́ ˘ ...

According to the hypothesis presented in this paper, both examples would show word stress at the same position, and both would be equally syncopated. Using my hypothesis but Fairbanks's notation, I would mark the two as follows:

(–́ ˘ * ˘ ...

(–́ ˘ ˘́) (˘ ˘ ...

25. Excluding, obviously, two-*mātrā* words consisting of a single long syllable.
26. *Patterns F and K*: these are equivalent to pattern B, except that F and K each substitute a sequence of 2-2 for one of the 4's in pattern B: in F it is the first four *mātrās* for which the substitution is made; in K it is the last (transformation 2).

Pattern B:	|	4	|	3 3 2	|	4	|			
Pattern F:	|	2	|	2	|	3 3 2	|	4	|	

Patterns C, G, and J: these each result from a somewhat more elaborate transformation: the final 2 of a 3-3-2 sequence is exchanged with a following 4-

mātrā unit. In the case of C, the 'parent' pattern is B; G is similarly 'descended' from F; and J from E (transformation 3).

Pattern B: | 4 | 3 3 2 | 4 |
Pattern C: | 4 | 3 3 4 2 |

We can summarize the three transformations necessary to produce all ten variations as:

Transformation 1: 4-4 → 3-3-2
Transformation 2: 4 → 2-2
Transformation 3: 3-3-2-4 → 3-3-4-2.

27. For the first (13-*mātrā*) foot of the *dohā*, there are two common stress patterns, each accounting for more than 20% of the total: 4-4-3-2 and 3-3-2-3-2. For the second (11-*mātrā*) foot there are, again, two common patterns; each accounts for more than 30%: 4-4-3 and 3-3-2-3. It is intriguing to note that the 24-*mātrā* total can be seen as three cycles of 8; and that we might divide the most common pattern this way: 3-3-2-(3-2) 3-3-2-(3). The elements in parentheses might be seen as the misordered bits of another 3-3-2; but I must admit I cannot conceive of any performance style that could stick the pieces together. The case with *caupāī* is more straightforward. Each foot is 16-*mātrās*; the three common stress patterns (each accounting for 10–15%) are: 3-3-2-4-4, 4-4-4-4, and 4-3-3-2-4. The rules governing the cadence of the *caupāī* preclude a pattern of 3-3-2-3-3-2.

Creative enumeration in the *vinaya* poetry of Sūrdās

JOHN STRATTON HAWLEY

In one of the most compelling sections of K. E. Bryant's *Poems to the Child-God: Structures and Strategies in the Poetry of Sūrdās*, he discusses what he calls 'frames for the icon'.[1] The icon is that of the child Kṛṣṇa, which serves as the focus for his study, and he goes on to describe these frames as 'paratactic' and 'sequential'. By pairing the two adjectives, Bryant is pointing to the particular finesse with which Sūr (using the name to refer to the collective author of poems in the Nāgarī Pracāriṇī Sabhā edition of the *Sūr-sāgar* (*SS*)) makes use of sheer enumeration in building his poems. It is not, Bryant says, that Sūr merely lists instances of a phenomenon to create a median section – a body – for a poem whose structure is 'thesis; examples; summation', but that he shapes this list of instances to form a sequence that will create the possibility of a tighter summary contract than the hearer can envision when the poem begins.[2]

With observations such as these Bryant, like A. K. Ramanujan, forces us to pull away from the notion that in the poetry of bhakti we have anything so simple and spontaneous as was thought to be the content of the Romantic *Erlebnislyrik*. First of all, it is clearly not raw experience that provides for a poem whatever structure it has.[3] And secondly, it is not necessarily the freshness or idiosyncracy of an experience that gives a poem its worth. The lists Sūr spins out are often conventional ones, and if one did not look too closely one might feel that the individual creativity and 'folkishness' that have often been taken as the hallmarks of bhakti verse had been altogether lost. The Hindi *pada*, which had seemed so well suited for its role as a vehicle of personal devotion, would then have been perverted in its function by the poet who is often considered to have used it best. As programmed by him it might turn out to be as crafted, as impersonal, and in the end as precious a medium as any other in the span of Indian literature.

To Sūr's enormous audience, for whom his verse has religious as well as literary import, such suppositions would seem to cut off the poetry from the poet's own experience, and in so doing fly in the face of a tradition that has always attempted to hold these two together. It has never taken long, in any language in which bhakti is expressed, for anthologies of devotional poems to be followed by anthologies of poets' lives: poetry and hagiography are twin garlands placed around the neck of the deity. Must we give up this close association?

In a certain sense, yes: the 'life' itself is a constructed one. As I have tried to show on earlier occasions, Sūr's biography reveals a craft less intricate but fully as intentional as his poetry.[4] But in another sense, no. The carefully classified lists that shape a number of Sūr's poems typically arrive at their point of summation just when the poet's signature – his 'own voice', in a sense we have yet to discover – enters his compositions. These lists and multiples, then, often turn out to have a personal reference that is distinctly appropriate to this genre, something more than the achievement of closure and the attainment of a successful poetic contract. Conventional lists that in some sense have first-person conclusions may seem strange beasts – telephone books that look you in the eye – but just such a phenomenon is part of the genius of Sūr's *padas*.

The purpose of this paper is to investigate several such lists as they occur in the *vinaya* sections of Sūr's poetry, that is, in poems that display what would seem to be a personal, petitionary stance on the part of the poet. The *vinaya* label, which was first applied to Sūr's poems a century after the poet's probable lifetime, is more than a little misleading, since the word means 'humility'. Many of these poems are anything but humble. Still, the *vinaya* categorisation has served the useful function of distinguishing between those poems in the Sūr corpus that involve the voice of a poetic 'I' and those in which the poet assumes the persona of one or another participant in the mythology of Kṛṣṇa or Rām. *Vinaya* poems are especially interesting for anyone asking the question whether there is such a thing as a 'poetics of bhakti' since they seem to involve the poet – the devotee, the bhakta – so directly.[5] The *vinaya* poems with which we will concern ourselves here are some of the oldest in the *Sūr-sāgar*. In fact, they were drawn together in Sūr manuscripts half a century before that title was applied to the collection as a whole. The sampling of 'lists' upon which we will draw takes us into the earliest strata of the *Sūr-sāgar* to which we have access – all of them are attested in the Fatehpur anthology dated to the equivalent of AD 1582 – and on that account, perhaps as close as we can come to the poet himself.[6]

Let us begin with a list that seems almost as simple in its design as the proverbial telephone book:

कहीयत राम त्यागी दानी
चारि पदारथ दिये सुदामहि अरु गुरु को सुत आनि
भिभीषन कों लंका दीन्ही पूरव ली पहिचानी
रावन के दास मस्तक छेदे कर गाह सारंग पानि
प्रहलाद की प्रतिग्या पूरै सुरपति कीन्हौ जानि
सूरदास को कहा निठुराई नैननि हू की हानि ।

(*SS* 135)

1. They say you're so giving, so self-denying, Rām,
2. That you offered Sudāmā the four fruits of life
   and to your guru you granted a son.
3. Vibhīṣaṇ: you gave him the land of Laṅkā
   to honour his early devotion to you.
4. Rāvaṇ: his were the ten heads you severed
   simply by reaching for your bow.
5. Prahlād: you fulfilled the vow he made;
   Indra, leader of the gods, you made a sage . . .

The structure of the poem is quite obvious in its critically edited form, although there are variants in which that structure is seriously compromised.[7] Clearly we are hearing a paean to the glories of Rām. The first word of the poem is *kahīyata*, 'They say', and the list that follows serves time and again to confirm that what people have always said is true. Rām is indeed *tyāgī dānī*, 'so giving, so self-denying': Sūr's cascades of examples proves it. The poet does not restrict himself to recalling incidents connected with Rām in the sense of Rāmacandra, either. Vibhīṣaṇ, an ally of Rāmacandra's, is on his list, but so is Sudāmā, the boyhood friend of Kṛṣṇa: so it is plain that Sūr is using the name Rām in the generic sense so frequent in north Indian bhakti poetry. Here Rām means 'God' in a sense at least wide enough to embrace these two aspects of Viṣṇu. The guru who was granted a son is again on Kṛṣṇa's side of the ledger: he restored to life the son of Kṛṣṇa's teacher Sāndīpani.

The examples of divine mercy that the poet calls to mind suggest breadth in another way, too. This time it is far more dramatic, for the next name on the list is that of Rāvaṇ. When we first hear it, our reflex is to understand it as having been introduced merely so that Sūr can explain how forceful was the Lord's intervention in wordly events on behalf of his devotee Vibhīṣaṇ: Rām took up his own bow to make Vibhīṣaṇ victorious over the brother from whom he had become estranged. Yet the positioning of Rāvaṇ's name at the beginning of the phrase it governs aligns it with the names of Vibhīṣaṇ and Kṛṣṇa's guru, suggesting that Rāvaṇ too ought to be understood as a recipient of divine grace. For indeed it is an article of Vaiṣṇava faith that the touch of the Lord, even a touch that brings death, is sufficient to redeem even the worst of his enemies.[8] This, then, is still more powerful evidence that what 'they say' is true: God saves both friend and foe.

In the next verse the poet makes this point yet again, as if to be sure we have understood. Here he lists two more targets of divine mercy, and they are again friend and foe. Prahlād is a willing devotee like Sudāmā, Sāndīpani, and Vibhīṣaṇ, while Indra resembles Rāvaṇ as one who struggled against the Lord. In the battle at Mount Govardhan, he acknowledged Kṛṣṇa as Lord only after an arduous, furious combat ended in defeat. This division of verse 5 into two parts – two more names on the list – recalls more than the typological division between Vibhīṣaṇ and Rāvaṇ. It also brings echoes of the second verse, which likewise served to list two names, and makes one wonder if the poet is moving in the direction of symmetry. If he were, this would be the penultimate verse, and its quickening of pace with reference to two preceding verses suggests this may be so. It is a sort of stretto, and the experienced listener knows that in a *pada* this often serves as a clue that closure is at hand.[9]

Sure enough, the next word we hear – the poet's name, his oral signature – confirms that this is so. In a great number of *padas* the signature comes at just this point, announcing, even without a verb to connect it to the rest of the syntax, that every other word in the poem is what Sūrdās says. Indeed, commentators usually supply the verb 'says' without a second thought. Here, however, there is something unusual. The name Sūrdās is followed by the postposition *ko*, forcing it into precisely the sort of grammatical connection with the rest of the phrase that is usually lacking. Sūr becomes himself some sort of object. The full phrase is: *sūra dāsa ko kahā niṭhurāī*, 'What is the cruelty pertaining to Sūrdās?' That is, 'Why this cruelty to Sūrdās?' And the final words of the poem explain what this cruelty is: *nainani hū kī hāni*, 'the lack of [his] very eyes', or to be more precise, 'an injury to the very eyes'.[10] The whole verse, then, can be translated:

6. Sūrdās: how could you be so harsh with him –
   leaving him without his very eyes?

Suddenly we see that this is not at all the sort of poem we thought. The ever-expanding catalogue of names that demonstrates the appropriateness of the title *tyāgī dānī* has come to a screeching halt, and precisely with the last name on the list. It is more than convenience and convention that has caused the poet to place his name at the beginning of this line: he wants it there so that it will take its place on the roster, right at the beginning of the phrase it introduces, just like the names of Sudāmā, the guru, Vibhīṣaṇ, Prahlād, and Indra before it. And that introduces a performative dimension. This is not mere accusation: the poet hopes that by putting his own name on the list – right here, in the most intensely lit spot in the poem – he can shame his Lord into granting him salvation like all the rest. 'It is not too late', he implies. 'Take away my blindness and you can still keep your record clean.'

So in the end this poem is not just a list – or rather, it is certainly not the sort of list one finds in a telephone book. It is a gauntlet thrown down, a challenge to God to act. The alternation between 'good guys' and 'bad guys' that develops as the list lengthens leaves the Lord no excuse: regardless of whether Sūr does or does not deserve salvation, there must be a place for him on the list. In fact, there is a certain peremptory sense in which, because the poem has now been constructed, he has already given himself such a place.

Here, then, is a variation of what Bryant calls a 'mythological sequence'.[11] Unlike the example he cites, one guided by the succession of Viṣṇu's avatārs, it does not proceed according to a fixed pattern. The poet does not make use of a definite sequence known to his audience. But he does choose from a range of very familiar examples, incidents in which Viṣṇu-Rām-Kṛṣṇa displayed mercy. The range is not broad enough, however. The poet avers that the net of rescue must be spread still wider if it is to catch him, and he manages such a suggestion merely by constructing a list – and not even a strictly sequential one at that.

A contrasting instance of the same type of poem is provided by *SS* 37, which begins, 'If Mohan adopts'. Here too the composition appears to be built on the recalling, one by one, of several well-known examples in the vast array of *magnalia dei* that the poet could potentially adduce as proof of God's protective power. We have Prahlād again (v. 5), and Indra, who is again called Surapati ('captain of the gods', v. 7), but this time it is not Indra's own salvation that is celebrated but the salvation of those upon whom he unleashed his rainy wrath: the people of Gokul and their leader Nanda, Kṛṣṇa's foster-father (v. 8). The new entries are Draupadī (vv. 3–4) and Dhruv (v. 6), both faithful devotees of Viṣṇu, as are all those featured in the list.

What is intriguing here is that, unlike the poem we have just considered, a scanning of the left-hand margin – or better, a recalling of the beginning of each phrase – would not enable one to construct the relevant list. It is woven into the syntax more delicately than that, and not merely because the position in which the names of the saved devotees are invoked has been changed from time to time. No, there is a definite principle of organisation, and the title line proclaims it: these are devotees each of whom has been linked with God by a process of adoption (*aṅga karai*). The Lord is here referred to as Mohan, 'the Beguiler', a title of Kṛṣṇa, and those he has saved are identified by means of the blood relationships that defined them before they were adopted into a new sort of family. Hence we meet Draupadī as 'Drupad's daughter' (v. 3); we hear of Dhruv as 'Uttānapād's son' (v. 6); and Hiraṇyakaśipu's name sets the stage for a mention of his son Prahlād (v. 5). Here is what happens as this list of adopted devotees grows:

जा कौ मोहन अंग करै
ता कौ केस षिसै नहीं सिर ते जो जग बैरु परै
राषि लाज द्रुपद तनया की को पट चीर हरै
दुरजोधन को मान भंग करि बसन प्रवाह् भरै
हिरनकसिप पचिहारि थक्यौ प्रह्लाद न रंच डरै
अजहूं लौ उत्तानपात सुत राज करत न टरै
जो सुरपति कोप्यो गोकुल परि क्रोधें कहा सरै
राषि लियौ ब्रज नंद के ठाकुर गिरिधर बिरदु फिरै

जा कौ बिरद है गर्ब प्रहारी सो क्यौं हित बिसरै
सूरदास भगवंत भजन तै सरन गए उबरै ।

(*SS* 37)

1. If Mohan adopts someone as his own,
2. Not a single hair on the head can be harmed
   even if the world is armed to oppose.
3. With him to guard the modesty of Drupad's daughter,
   who could steal away her clothes? –
4. He broke the proud plans of Duryodhan
   by covering her with streams of cloth.
5. Hiraṇyakaśipu went down in weary defeat
   while Prahlād felt no shred of fear;
6. And Uttānapād's son reigns unflinching to this day,
   shines with an unwavering light.
7. The captain of the gods aimed his rage at Gokul,
   but what could his fury command?
8. For Nanda's protector was the guardian of Braj
   and the Mountain-Lifter's honour filled the land:
9. Since he earns his fame by shattering pride,
   how could he fail to show the lowly his love?
10. Sūrdās says, by singing praises to that Lord
    one finds a place of refuge and is saved.

The final incident in the list of 'adoptions', the Govardhan episode (vv. 7–8), is (not unexpectedly) the most complicated of the set. This time it is the protector, not the protected, who is introduced in terms of his family ties – 'captain of the gods' – but, like the other guardian figures listed before him, he too attacks his charges. This happens when the cowherding people of Braj turn away from him who had formerly been their chosen deity, and begin to worship Kṛṣṇa by means of the mountain that represents him. For the first time since the title line, Kṛṣṇa is explicitly named as he comes on the scene – he is, of course, the Mountain-Lifter – but, like Indra, he is also designated by means of his relation to his wards. He is identified as Nanda's *ṭhākur*: 'Nanda's master' literally, but perhaps also Nanda's personal household god. In Brajbhāṣā this is a familiar, even affectionate, term of reference, since one tends one's family images, often called *ṭhākurs*, with a tenderness that frequently approximates the care that parents lavish on their children. And though Nanda's *ṭhākur* is his master, he is indeed also his son, since the Mountain-Lifter is Kṛṣṇa. This incident, then, both fits the paradigm established earlier and goes beyond it. Kṛṣṇa does intervene as a guardian when the old family relationships between gods and humans fall apart, but his intervention is from within: he is genuinely a member of the family he saves. Or so it appears. The truth is that the paradigm is fully apt and the list intact, since quite unknown to Nanda, Kṛṣṇa is not his natural but his adopted son.

Once again, then, the list that Sūr builds develops a density that goes much beyond parataxis. One associates the greatest extent of this density, as in the case of the stretto, with the penultimate line of the *pada*: the final line normally provides resolution and relaxation, as in music. But here we have not one line to go but two after this dense complication. The experienced listener will still expect a full couplet at the end of verse 8, since *padas* usually have an even number of verses even if, as here, the end-rhyme is constant throughout the poem. (When the rhyme varies from couplet to couplet, an even number of lines is absolutely required.) And if symmetry is again to prevail, as it did in the earlier poem, a two-verse 'summation' will be required to match the two-verse 'thesis' propounded at the beginning of the poem. The intervening verses are already well balanced, with two-line episodes occupying verses 3–4 and 7–8 and single verses inserted between them at the 'centre' of the poem (vv. 5–6), each relating a separate incident.

All this suggests that a couplet is still to come, but even so the poet keeps his listeners guessing. He first summarises with the words 'Since he earns his fame by shattering pride', and then asks a question: 'How could he fail to show the lowly his love?' (v. 9). The verb that ends the line, *bisarai*, which means in general 'forget' and is here translated 'fail', is one that Sūr frequently uses as the very last word in poems of this sort. It is the poet's eternal lament: 'how could he forget *me*?'[12] But a further verse is still to come: a disappointingly bland one, it seems, since it appears to dismiss the question that has just been raised as a merely rhetorical one. 'How could he fail to show the lowly his love?' He can't. Therefore the following affirmation:

> Sūrdās says, by singing praises to that Lord,
> one finds a place of refuge and is saved;

or alternatively,

> To sing the praises of Sūrdās's Lord
> is to find a place of refuge and be saved;

while there is still a third way of possibly understanding this verse:

> Sūrdās, singing praises to that Lord,
> has found a place of refuge and is saved.

The syntax of Brajbhāṣā poetry is sufficiently elastic to accommodate all three translations, and the last is perhaps most interesting. It raises the possibility, once again, that the poet himself is to be understood as the final cipher in the column, the last example on the list. The absence of definitive syntax governing the introduction of the poet's signature into his poem makes it possible to understand him not only as its narrator but as an important part of its subject-matter. And if there is performative utterance here, its effect is to bind the Lord into adopting the poet 'as his own' by declaring that the act of singing about him is what brings salvation. That, after all, is what Sūr has been doing, so it is unthinkable that he should not be the beneficiary of divine love. His stance is not combative this time – quite the contrary – but the effect is much the same. He smuggles his way to salvation by means of the list he has constructed; he adopts himself into the field of events that his own poem describes.

This, then, is a list of devotees who were saved – 'good guys'. Sūr insinuates himself into their number by adopting the devotee's stance: he sings his obedient song. We have also seen a list that combines these worthy recipients of salvation with a sprinkling of enemies redeemed to salvation by their very contact with God, even if in combat. Now let us look at a third type, equally common, in which Sūr builds a list exclusively constructed of 'bad guys' – reprobates who none the less became the recipients of divine attention.

The personalities involved in the next list are so well known in the literature of bhakti that there is no need for the poet to supply any narrative about them. Their names alone, even their occupational titles, are sufficient to establish their identities. This makes them the bane of a translator's existence, for they are as unfamiliar to English speakers as they are familiar to speakers of Indian languages. They are the stuff of which glossaries are made:

Ajāmil: the brāhmaṇ who deserted his family and ran off with a prostitute, but who happened to call out for help to his son Nārāyaṇ as he was dying and received instead the ministrations of his son's namesake, Viṣṇu (Nārāyaṇ) himself;

the hunter: Guha, who despite birth outside of caste and the nature of his livelihood, which required him to purchase his own survival at the expense of others, was drawn into the army that served Rām in his forest wanderings and became the recipient of his saving grace, even as an aboriginal;

the prostitute: Piṅgalā, who was accepted into Rām's fold when she reconsidered a life misspent, despite years of living in sin; or who, as another version has it, came to salvation only because she happened to teach her parrot the syllable 'Rām' (which meant that she pronounced the saving name frequently just to get the bird to speak); and

the vulture: Jaṭāyu, a member of the most heinous species of animals but a creature who was regarded by Rām as having leapt far above the deserts of his karma because he lost his life trying to save Sītā from being abducted by Rāvaṇ.

Note how these personalities are arrayed in the following poem:

जनु जिन के संग उर गायौ
तिन तुम पै गोबिंद गुसाई सबनि अपनपौ पायौ
सेवा यहै नाम सर औसर जा काहू कहि आयौ
कीयौ न विलंबु कबहू करुनामय सोइ सोइ निकट बुलायौ
अजामेल मुषि मित्र हमारौ सु मैं चलत समुझायौ
और कह लौं कहौ क्रिपन की काहु न श्रवन सुनायौ
ब्याध गिध गनिका जिहि कागर हौ तिहि चिठी चढायौ
मरियत लाज पांच पतितनि में सूर समै बिसरायौ ।

(*SS* 193)

1. Those others with whom my heart sang out for help
2. Have been redeemed by you, Govind Gosāin.
   You've taken them on as your own.
3. And this is how they served you: at some uncharted moment
   your name chanced to pass across their lips
4. And that would send you scurrying, merciful one,
   to summon each of them to your side.
5. Ajāmil – he's a great friend of mine.
   As he walked along, I talked with him,
6. Explained my case, and what did the miser do?
   He didn't even whisper a word of it to you.
7. Other names are also entered on your list –
   hunter, harlot, vulture – and I've added another:
8. One more sinner to make a Council of Five,
   but when his time came, you forgot Sūr.
   The shame of it — I could die!

This time the list is less constitutive of the structure of the poem than of its content, and even that is not entirely overt. We do not understand until the end – and with a surprise – that a list is being built, though the intriguing phrase with which the poem begins, 'Those others', suggests something is afoot. Another oddity is that the poet addresses himself to his Lord in the second line as Govind Gosāin, an appellation that is infrequent in the *Sūr-sāgar* and that increasingly suggests, as the poem proceeds, some landowner or petty monarch, someone who would customarily be known by a forename and surname, the latter indicating his station (Gosāin = Master). At first the poet relates himself to 'those others' with whom he ought to stand as a general group: others who have received favour while he, as we suspect from the beginning, has been passed over. It is particularly Ajāmil, the worst of the lot, that he claims as his close associate, and we hear him bluster and despair as things pass from an oral to a written medium (*kāgar, ciṭhī*, v. 7) and still he is not counted within the charmed circle of sinners whom Govind Gosāin has accepted. The penultimate line rises to a sudden stretto as three more names are added to the list.

In the last line the poet plays his final card. He says that he is dying of shame to have been excluded from the 'five sinners' (*pāṁca patitani*, v. 8), and we see that the group with which he has associated himself since the beginning forms a *pañcāyat* of sorts. Four have already been listed, both in the poem and in the document that is before Govind Gosāin (they are, in essence, the same) and as the poet reveals his own signature, we have the fifth. Thus in yet another way he seems to have forced his name into the magic ledger of salvation by enrolling himself in a poem of his own composition.

Of course, the person so enrolled is not a historical individual of the sort most easily conceived in the modern West. We are not talking about a 'personal' dimension that could be glossed as 'private'. We are not in the realm of individual autobiography here, perhaps not even in the poem that makes mention of blindness, Sūr's trademark. For the blindness he describes seems more an admission of spiritual deformity than physical, and that he shares with many of the rest of us.[13] No, the poet is using a generalised 'himself' precisely as an example of what must be true in some dimension for everyone. The signature required by a *pada* provides Sūr with a chance to inject into his poems an element of subjectivity or reflexivity – an 'I' – that is potentially inclusive of us all, all the people who are his audience. That is why he so often styles himself the worst of sinners: so that he, the speaker, may come to represent the limiting case that places all his hearers somewhere inside the pale of divine mercy at whose boundary he stands. The implication is that if Sūr can be saved, so can anyone. And the method by which this salvation occurs is the very singing of the poem, as he sometimes explicitly says.[14] This is how Sūr adds his name to the list of those who have experienced the divine presence, and it is the medium that he shares with his audience.

The function of the list in Sūr's *vinaya* poetry is not just to establish some genus of which the poet wants to be included as a member. It is also a self-distancing device. Unpoetic, even: it creates the impression that the poet is merely a receiver of what is given, a transmitter of tradition. He is just reporting what 'They say' (*kahīyata*). The passivity he projects has the effect of moving him in the direction of his hearers, for this, after all, is the position they occupy in relation to him. As the lists roll on, he seems to join his audience. The sense is that he too is merely taking it all in; they know the content of these lists as much as he does.

Once this bond of receptivity has been established, Sūr's exercise of the right to append his signature to a poem takes on a dramatic potential. When he speaks as 'Sūr' he is speaking not just for himself but for his whole audience: for anyone who has been listening to this extended, patterned recital. When he jumps back into the poem with his 'right of signature', he has the possibility of taking the rest of us with him. As he does so, he is speaking for himself not in some narrowly autobiographical sense but in a more broadly reflexive sense – for all our selves, for anyone who participates with him in achieving, by understanding, the closure of the poem he has created. His self – his reflexivity, the relentlessness with which he focuses the message on himself – becomes potentially the selfhood, reflexivity, and focus of every hearer.

Maybe this happens somehow in every poem, of whatever kind. Maybe poetry ultimately is religion. But it certainly makes sense in relation to that sort of engagement between self, others, and God that bhakti is said to describe. Like a poem – and really this is synecdoche more than simile – bhakti creates community as it emerges. One person's possession by God does not exclude others, it draws them in; yet the communality of devotion does not dilute it. The experience of bhakti is so intense as to seem more pointed than that of an individual ego, so although our experience of it has much to do with our sense of what it is to be an integer, a self, our language for it is appropriately displaced: we name it by the name of God. In so far as the peculiarly intense interaction between list and signature in Sūr's *vinaya* poems illuminates this dynamic, such a dialectic deserves to be seen as something that has especially to do with bhakti. I doubt that it has to do exclusively with bhakti, and it surely does not exhaust the field of bhakti poetics. But perhaps it highlights what must somehow be there for bhakti poetry to exist.

NOTES

I am grateful to the National Endowment for the Humanities for generous assistance provided to K. E. Bryant and myself in preparing a critical edition and verse translation of the *Sūr-sāgar*. This paper draws heavily upon research made possible by NEH. A version of it was presented to the conference on Indian literatures held at the University of Chicago in April 1986.

1. K. E. Bryant, *Poems to the Child-God*, Berkeley, Calif., 1978, p. 90.
2. Ibid., pp. 92, 94–105.
3. A. K. Ramanujan, *Speaking of Śiva*, Baltimore, Md., 1973, p. 38; cf. Ramanujan, *Hymns for the Drowning*, Princeton, NJ, 1981, pp. 164–6.
4. J. S. Hawley, *Sūr Dās: Poet, Singer, Saint*, Seattle and Delhi, 1984, pp. 14–22; Hawley, 'The Sectarian Logic of the *Sūr dās kī vārtā*', in *BCR 1979–1982*, pp. 157–69.
5. The question whether bhakti can claim a poetics specific to itself has been raised by Ramanujan in the context of Tamil poetry. See his *Hymns for the Drowning*, pp. 161–4, in particular his first and fourth points. Also relevant to the discussion are D. Shulman, 'From Author to Non-Author in Tamil Literary Legend', unpub. paper, 1984; N. Cutler, 'Biography and Interpretation in Tamil Hinduism: *Tiruvācakam* and the *Tiruvātavūrar Purāṇam*', Paper delivered to the

American Academy of Religion, Los Angeles, 1985; and J. S. Hawley 'Author and Authority in the *Bhakti* Poetry of North India', *JAS* 47, 1, 1988, pp. 269–90.

6. The translations of all poems discussed in this essay are based upon critical versions prepared by K. E. Bryant. The number assigned them in *SS* (vol. i, 1972) has been given in the text to facilitate their identification. For the Fatehpur version, see G. N. Bahura and K. E. Bryant, eds., *Pad Sūrdāsjī kā / The Padas of Surdas*, Jaipur, 1984. I am grateful to Mark Juergensmeyer for his critical review of my verse translations.
7. In certain MSS the line order varies, and in one version (A1, B3, V1, and therefore *SS*) v. 5 differs entirely from the lemma given here, which is based on J1 and related MSS. In that version the names of the dramatis personae are frequently displaced from the emphatic positions to which the poet seems originally to have assigned them.
8. See C. G. Hospital, 'The Enemy Transformed: Opponents of the Lord in the *Bhāgavata Purāṇa*', *JAAR* 46, 2, suppl., pp. 199–215.
9. Bryant, op. cit., pp. 99, 102–4.
10. On the ambiguity of this phrase, see Hawley, *Sūr Dās*, p. 31.
11. Bryant, op. cit. p. 95.
12. See the final lines of *SS* 158, 193, and 430 among poems included in J1 and parallels; also *SS* 42 and 235 in early MSS (trans. in Hawley, *Sūr Dās*, pp. 145, 165; cf. pp. 150–7 in general). Among J1 poems, the concluding verses of *SS* 133, 507, and 1271 display similar verbiage, but applied to interestingly different themes.
13. In regard to *SS* 135, see Hawley, *Sūr Dās*, p. 31; and in general pp. 29–33.
14. On this theme, see ibid., pp. 163–77. Peter Gaeffke has nicely compared this process with the classical 'act of truth' (*satyakriyā*) – adapted, of course, to the Kali age (Gaeffke, oral communication, Chicago, 19 Apr. 1986).

The *padas* attributed to Nanddās

R. S. McGREGOR

The poetic works of the nineteenth-century Brajbhāṣā poet called Nanddās are available for study in serviceable editions, but the many *padas* attributed to Nanddās have not received much attention. This is perhaps surprising. Nanddās' reputation is based today on his fine *prabandha* poems, but from Nābhādās' *Bhakt-māl* (a compendium of Vaiṣṇava biography and tradition which post-dates Nanddās by no more than a few decades) we can infer that Nanddās was originally as well known for songs (*padas*) on Kṛṣṇa's *līlā* as for his longer compositions.[1] In agreement with this, later sectarian tradition makes Nanddās a leading composer and singer of *padas* used in the Vallabhan cult at Govardhan, in the time of Viṭṭhalnāth, the second leader of the sect (d. 1585?).[2] If the Nanddās *padas* are not, today, much studied, the reason lies perhaps in the uncertain number, credentials, and availability of their extant sources, which consist of rather late MSS, and modern printed versions. A contributory factor may be that Nanddās' role in producing the early literature of the cult became obscured following the prolific growth of a body of cult verses assigned nominally to another of the poets of the sect, Parmānanddās.[3] Furthermore, the Nanddās verses were perhaps never much in circulation outside Vallabhan communities. They do not seem at least to have been generally identified outside the sect as a particular *pada* stock, as happened with the early Sūrdās *padas* and those attributed to Mīrābāī.

In this paper I attempt an outline interpretation of the character of the Nanddās *pada* material as far as it is known. I work chiefly from the two major editions of Nanddās, those of Umāśaṅkar Śukla (1942) and Vrajratnadās (1949).[4] I first refer to the nature of the materials, and the procedures of the two editors. I next discuss the content of that group of *padas* thought by Śukla most likely to be authentic, and compare this group with the other recorded *padas* in respect of content, readings, and to some extent style. The comparison allows some inferences about the structure of the Nanddās *pada* tradition, its likely early shape, and the nature of some later accretion to it.

The materials

Although MSS containing Nanddās' narrative poems date from 1700 onwards, the oldest dated manuscript which was known to Śukla to contain *padas* dates only from 1792. Śukla uses this manuscript, which contains seven Nanddās *padas*, and three or four[5] other manuscript sources containing up to about forty-five verses, of which only one is dated (1824). It is not clear that Vrajratnadās uses any manuscript unknown to Śukla. Of extant manuscripts not used by either editor, one found at Mathura is listed in the volume for 1932 of the Nāgarī Pracāriṇī Sabhā Search for Hindi Manuscripts (*Hastalikhit granthoṁ kī khoj*); the *pada* there excerpted does not seem to be represented by either editor.[6] Manuscripts of the anthology called *Padmuktāvalī* compiled by the Kṛṣṇa poet Nāgrīdās (1699–1764/5) should, to judge from the text of a printed edition, contain *padas* attributed to Nanddās.[7]

Of printed sources containing collections of the *padas*, the oldest is apparently the nineteenth-century anthology of songs in Hindi and other languages called *Rāgsāgarodbhab-rāg-kalpadrum*.[8] Some thirty Nanddās *padas* from the revised version of this source (1914–16) were printed in 1940 by Somnāth Gupta, unedited, in an anthology of Vallabhan poets' verses.[9] Most of these thirty *padas* are represented in appendices in Śukla's edition, and in Vrajratnadās' edition. Of other printed sources, *Śivsiṃh-saroj*,[10] the major nineteenth-century anthology of Brajbhāṣā verse, cites only one *pada* attributed to Nanddās: one which appears, moreover, unlikely to belong to an early stock as I shall indicate. By contrast, the voluminous *Kīrtan-saṅgrah* published at Ahmadabad in 1936 and much used in the modern Vallabhan cult includes a large number of *padas* on festivals and cult topics which are attributed to Nanddās. Some 180 of these are represented in Śukla, again in an appendix. A further printed source is Prabhudayāl Mītal's *Aṣṭchāp aur vallabh sampradāy*, a study and anthology of verses attributed to the major early Vallabhan poets. Of forty-six verses here printed, unedited, many are not represented in Śukla (whether in his text or the appendix) or in Vrajratnadās.[11]

Śukla in his editorial procedure gives weight in principle to *padas* found in manuscripts, as opposed to *padas* found only in printed sources. He relegates all the latter to the appendix of his edition. From the total of the *padas* found in manuscripts he removes those containing unsolvable textual confusions, and some which he judges to have been copied from the printed text of *Rāgsāgar-kalpadrum*. He is left with a total of thirty-five verses (i.e. separate *padas*). He does not consider the question of possible kinship between his manuscripts,[12] but does cite variants from within all his sources, and from these variants it is clear that his text is not based on the readings of any single source. Vrajratnadās presents about 190 verses in all. He does not describe his sources in any detail and cites only a very few textual variants. These do not accord in all cases with the variants noted by Śukla.

I turn first to the content of the thirty-five verses admitted by Śukla.

The verses admitted to Śukla's text

The thirty-five verses are arranged in sections dealing with eleven separate topics. Some of these topics are central themes of the Kṛṣṇa story, some pertain to Vallabhan cult worship or practice, and only one seems marginal to Vallabhan Kṛṣṇaism. Two of the topics fall within the field of the deeds of the child and youth Kṛṣṇa: those of the young child (which alone are classed as *bāl-kṛṣṇa* here) and those of Kṛṣṇa's dance (*rās*). The respective emphasis given these two topics is, to judge from their numbers, similar to what is found in early Sūrdās collections, where *rās* topics are not emphasised more than *bāl-kṛṣṇa* topics. I mention the point since it tends to confirm that the verses here given represent, for our period, an early Kṛṣṇaism consistent with early composition. The five *bāl-kṛṣṇa padas* are, however, even when counted with the *rās* poems, many fewer in number than those on festivals, which total fifteen. Of the latter *padas*, the largest subgroups are those on the topics of *holī* (six) and celebration (*badhāī*) of Kṛṣṇa's birth (five). Apart from the groups of *padas* on *bāl-kṛṣṇa* and on festivals, there are three other *pada* groups: one of five *padas* deals with devotion to the guru, a single verse deals with Kṛṣṇa's name, and finally there are two verses on Hanumān.

The style and texture of these verses I would describe as a combination of the popular and the artistic. The first *bāl-kṛṣṇa* verse describes Kṛṣṇa's being woken, to the sound of the birds' dawn chorus, by Yaśodā:

चिरैया चुहचुहानी सुनि चकई की बानी,
  कहति जसोदा रानी, जागौ मेरे लाला ।

The day's churning has already begun, the poet tells us, and Sudāmā is shown waiting, dressed in his best, for his friend Kṛṣṇa; then at the end of the verse, the world of Kṛṣṇa's Braj and that of the poet seem for an instant to merge, as Nanddās contrives to suggest that Sudāmā's devotion is the prototype or surrogate for his own. It is Sudāmā who gazes at the sleeping Kṛṣṇa, but Nanddās who calls out to him to wake. The style here is delicate, the mode one of understatement similar (we may note) to what is often found in verse known to be by Nanddās. Subjects of the other *bāl-līlā* poems include the nursing of Kṛṣṇa, the *dān-līlā*, and Kṛṣṇa's return from the day's herding. These poems seem not dissimilar in tone to that of the *pada* I have described. It may be worth mentioning that in none of these *padas*, whatever they show of popular and personal devotion, is the element of paradox and contrast between the child Kṛṣṇa's earthly state and divine majesty, which has been noted in early Sūrdās poems,[13] much emphasised. These are poems of a different mood.

Of the *rās padas*, a well-known and very expressive one deals with Kṛṣṇa as dancer (*nāgara naṭa*): a dancer both courtly, as the adjective indicates, and impassioned. In this *pada* as in the others on the dance, Rādhā is mentioned by name or by some title. These references mark out the *rās padas* as different in their approach from Nanddās' narrative poems based on the *Bhāgavata Purāṇa*, in which Nanddās proceeds more as poet-scholar than as popular hymnodist and follows his scriptural source in avoiding mention of Rādhā. By contrast the scriptural orientation of the *rās padas* (which are intended for use in cult observance) is minimal, and quite subordinate to their orientation towards a popular audience. In another poem on the dance the attitude of *sakhībhāva* is explicit. This attitude is, as is well known, usually more prominent where Kṛṣṇa's association is with Rādhā than where it is with the herdgirls generally. It may be worth anticipating, however, that the emphasis of Nanddās' *padas* on Rādhā, as given here by Śukla, falls short of an explicit Rādhā-Kṛṣṇa emphasis. The status of Rādhā does not seem to equal or exceed that of Kṛṣṇa. In this we see an aspect of earlier, rather than later Vallabhanism consonant with what would be expected in poetry of Nanddās' time.[14]

The *padas* on devotion to the guru deserve mention next, though they are placed last in order by Śukla.[15] These five verses deal with the context of daily worship, especially morning worship of the guru, the poet's hope or desire of audience with him, and his devotion through the guru to Kṛṣṇa. The guru is named as Viṭṭhalnāth, or referred to by patronymics such as *Vallabhasuta*, in almost all the verses. It is clear from two verses at least that Viṭṭhalnāth is referred to as alive and residing in Gokul. These verses should thus date from between about 1566, when Viṭṭhalnāth appears to have first moved to Gokul or Braj, and about 1585, the conjectured date of his death. They provide of course crucial evidence of Nanddās' period of activity. One of these verses contains an interesting historical detail in its reference to Viṭṭhalnāth as *pitā giridhara ādi*, 'the father of Giridhar and the others': Viṭṭhalnāth's eldest son Giridhar played only a minor role in the sect, however, and it is clear that he is mentioned here only as an aspect of his father's position. This reference further confirms that the verse in question is both contemporary with Viṭṭhalnāth, and was composed by someone close to him.

I turn to the *padas* on festivals. These are popular occasions and the poet often strikes a matching note of popular devotion. This note sometimes carries an overtone of the community's collective dependence on Kṛṣṇa, as in one delightful poem on the lifting of Govardhan Hill, which tells how the people of Braj ask Kṛṣṇa to put the hill down, in case he drop it: for they fear that they are in the double jeopardy of losing first their lives (in the accident) and then (as a result) the joy of consorting with him![16] A single illustration of the tone of these poems must suffice here. It is necessary now to refer to *pada* structure, and, specifically, to the length of the festival *padas*. The *padas* on two festival subjects, those of *holī* and *badhāī*, are found to include almost all those of Śukla's total selection, which are of more than eight or ten rhyming couplets. Conversely, the *padas* on these two topics are themselves almost all long: they average twice the length of the others. The reason for the extended treatment of *padas* on *holī* is surely to do with the sense of personal, uninhibited involvement that characterises that festival: the mood of excited celebration that *holī* evokes is rather different from what the devotee is likely to feel in contemplating the lifting of Govardhan Hill or the swinging of Kṛṣṇa (*jhūlā*), or in discharging the observances of *rakṣābandhan* or even *dīvālī*. A poet's dwelling at length on the *holī* theme may perhaps be seen as his attempt to mirror, in words and song, the well-known cumulative process whereby a *holī* gathering itself expands in size, as it rolls on its casual, unpredicted way through the village. The profusion of action and incident would itself invite the poet to linger, hoping to improve and then to improve further his picture of a mood of revelry. The procedure is descriptive, whether of scene or incident or participants' mood, the poet demonstrating skilled practice and craft rather than intimate involvement. The *badhāī* birth poems deal, in a way which has the same consequence for their length, with a joyful event of life; the focus of attention may here be a child who is divine as well as human, but the songs arising from it have lent themselves to extension beyond normal *pada* length for their human interest alone. It seems clear that this kind of extension is an organic process, one not pointing of itself to corruption in the Nanddās *pada* tradition.

Śukla includes one *pada* on the name of Kṛṣṇa. The herdgirls' intent devotion is the subject here, and the way they are forgetful of house and home and 'all ears' for Kṛṣṇa's name.

कृष्ण-नाम जब तें श्रवन सुन्यौ री आली,
  भूली री भवन हौं तौ बावरी री ।
  अंग अंग भई मैं तौ श्रवनमई री ।

The Hindi metaphor, less colloquial than its everyday English equivalent, is one made use of several times by Nanddās. This metaphor may well contain an overtone of the *Bhāgavata Purāṇa* injunction to *śravaṇa* as a means of cultivation of Kṛṣṇa devotion.[17] The name of Kṛṣṇa as referred to here is not, however, a symbol for the unknowable or indefinable aspects of the divine which are accommodated in the *Purāṇa*'s theology, and are more or less standard in Sant poetry. Here we are dealing with the same devotion for Kṛṣṇa as avatār (*mādhurī mūrati*) as is found generally in Brajbhāṣā Kṛṣṇa poetry: for instance, in Nanddās' own *Bhramargīt*.[18] The tone differs perceptibly from, for instance, that of a significant early Sūrdās poem on the name of Rām.[19]

The verses as given in Vrajratnadās' edition

Here I consider chiefly the emphasis given to particular topics, by comparison to what is found in the material derived solely from manuscripts admitted by Śukla; and I draw some inferences about the structure of the Nanddās *pada* tradition.

Just under 200 verses are presented by Vrajratnadās: more than five times the number of those admitted to Śukla's text, but fewer than the total number given in Śukla's appendix of verses collected from printed sources. The topics treated and sections to which they are assigned are not entirely the same as are found in Śukla: thus we have, again, sections of very different size devoted to the *bāl-līlā*, to the *rās*, to the guru, to festivals, and to Hanumān. One topic, that of the name of Kṛṣṇa, is not recognised by Vrajratnadās, although the verse representing it (the same one as given by Śukla) is cited under a new section title, that of *pūrvānurāg*.[20] There are other new section titles as well as new topics. A small but significant entirely new topic in the Vrajratnadās material is that of a pair of *padas* on joint devotion to Kṛṣṇa and Rām.

The proportional emphasis given to the *bāl-līlā padas* and to the festival *padas* taken as a group is roughly comparable in the two editions; within this composite group, Vrajratnadās gives proportionately rather fewer *bāl-līlā* poems and rather more festival poems than does Śukla. Among verses on the remaining topics, there are several distinguishable changes in content or emphasis.

1. Poems on the *rās* are proportionately fewer in Vrajratnadās' edition. However, if the poems dealing specifically with Kṛṣṇa and Rādhā's *prem-līlā* and with the associated subjects of the *sakhīs*' devotion and Rādhā's sulking (*mān*) are included with the poems on the *rās* to form a single topic (that is to say, the general topic of Kṛṣṇa's and Rādhā's love), this topic then bulks proportionately more than twice as large in Vrajratnadās as what is found on its components in Śukla.[21] We have in the Vrajratnadās material an increased Rādha–Kṛṣṇa, as opposed to Kṛṣṇa–Rādhā emphasis. This is in accord with what we would expect if the Vrajratnadās materials represented a later view of the Nanddās *pada* tradition than those of Śukla.

2. Vrajratnadās gives more poems on the guru than does Śukla.[22] But what is important is that the proportion of poems on the guru given by him is very much less than is found in Śukla's edition. The tenor of the additional poems is much the same as those admitted by Śukla. No new factual information or references seem to be present in them. As in the Śukla *padas*, Nanddās' guru is everywhere known to be Viṭṭhalnāth. There is no mention of the short-lived gurudom of Viṭṭhalnāth's successor Giridhar, or of that of Gokulnāth which ensued. We thus seem to have no Nanddās *padas* on guru-devotion, at least, which post-date Viṭṭhalnāth's death in or around 1585.

3. The impression given by the poems on joint devotion to Rām and Kṛṣṇa

is that they state, but hardly dwell upon, the complementarity of the two deities.[23] They seem to be descriptive in procedure and cumulative in intention, rather than expressive of inner conviction. There are references to acts or attributes of each deity in turn, but it is questionable if the nature of a relationship between the two has been very important for the poet concerned. If Rām is the bow-holder and lord of Avadh, Kṛṣṇa is the butter-stealer and life of Braj:

रामकृष्ण कहिये उठि भोर ।
ओहि अवधेश ओही ब्रज जीवन,
धनुषधरन अरु माखनचोर ।।[24]

It is unlikely that such aggregations of verses are by a gifted or sensitive poet such as Nanddās; and very probably they post-date Nanddās. Several traditions do exist, it is true, which associate Nanddās with Rām influences. I have described these elsewhere.[25] Most of these traditions seem exaggerated, and some are certainly spurious. It would be understandable in the light of such traditions, and with the ascendancy of modern Rāmaism from the time of Tulsīdās, if some revision had occasionally been sought for of the persona even of a poet of such strong Kṛṣṇa affiliation as the Vallabhan Nanddās. A long *pada* on the *svayaṃvara* of Sītā attributed to Nanddās in Nāgrīdās' *Padmuktāvalī*[26] illustrates the tendency from the eighteenth century; and the fact that the single Nanddās verse cited in *Śivsiṃh-saroj* (1878) is the very one referred to above, of all those we now know to be extant, illustrates it from the late nineteenth century. It would seem that by that time at least, Nanddās' verse cannot have been well known outside his community.

4. A few *padas* given in the Vrajratnadās edition deal with sacred places, chiefly the Yamunā.[27] One of these *padas* is cited in the *Do sau bāvan vaiṣṇavan kī vārtā*. Of two *padas* on the Braj region given by Vrajratnadās, one, to judge from its tone and structure, almost certainly long post-dates Nanddās.[28]

5. A few *padas* are presented as describing *nāyikās* from the viewpoint of categories of rhetoric: the *khaṇḍitā*, the *āgatapatikā*, and one or two others.[29] The technical titles are not used in the verses concerned, but are supplied by the editor as section titles. There do not seem to be any verbal echoes in these *padas* of the relevant sections of Nanddās' well-known adaptation of Bhānudatta's *Rasamañjarī*. Yet their treatment is interesting, their style varied. They seem to be more than a pedestrian attempt to create *ex post facto* a *pada* stock for a poet known for his interest in poetics, as well as for devotion. I am inclined to think they represent a further, secondary degree of adaptation of their subject-matter by Nanddās himself: just as the poet could treat the theme of Kṛṣṇa's dance in more scriptural, and more popular, ways, so he may have done with the subject of rhetoric.

In considering what deductions are legitimate from the comparisons I have made it is necessary of course to remember the character and status of the materials compared. There is no reason in theory why a smaller, earlier source for materials which typically receive accretions over time should be inherently preferable as a record to a later, larger source in respect of its size. The point is clear in practice, for example in the history of the Sūrdās tradition, which illustrates that the data of the very earliest manuscripts can be usefully supplemented from later MSS that are good;[30] likewise, some verses given by Vrajratnadās and absent from Śukla's edition (such as those on sacred sites, some of those on festivals, and perhaps those on rhetorical categories) can be assumed with more or less probability to go back to Nanddās. Small may be beautiful, but the Vrajratnadās sources are not invalidated by their late date alone, nor by the printed form of most of them. On the other hand, there *is* suspect material in the Vrajratnadās presentation (such as some Rādhā–Kṛṣṇa material, and the Rām–Kṛṣṇa material) which can be well explained as arising by accretion to an earlier, smaller nucleus. The reduced proportion of verses on the guru in the Vrajratnadās material also illustrates the converse, prevailing tendency in the material as a whole towards expansion with the passage of time. The community had enough sense of history, it may be inferred, not to tamper with the received tradition linking a respected poet and a revered guru, so that the stock of poems expressing this link was itself treated with respect; but new times did bring new needs, such as those of novelty or improvement in cult worship, and adjustment to the pressures from new attitudes in sectarian or popular religion. Adjustment to these needs was not confined to expansion of the Parmānanddās materials, and it is these needs that we see reflected or hinted at in the comparisons I have made.

Conclusions

The core of this *pada* tradition seems to consist of poems on *bāl-līlā, rās*, and festival topics, together with a small attached segment of personal utterance. Some innovation in the treatment of *bāl-līlā* and festival themes is assumed to take place over time. Some expansion is evident in the stock of *padas* on sacred sites. There is a much increased emphasis on the topics of *prem* and *mān*, and in this emphasis a Rādhā–Kṛṣṇa orientation (whether popular or specifically sectarian) is clear. Some measure of acceptance or tolerance of later Rāmaism is indicated. It is not clear whether this arises from conviction, or from a wish to conform with, or to pre-empt, attitudes of the seventeenth, eighteenth, or nineteenth centuries.

NOTES

1. *Bhakt-mal*, ed. Bhagvanprasād 'Rūpkalā', Lucknow, 5th edn., 1961, v. 696. On the Nanddās *pada* material, Dīndayāl Gupta, *Aṣṭchap aur vallabh sampradāy*, Allahabad, 1947, pp. 370 ff.; further Bhavānīdatt Upraiti, *Nanddās: jīvanī aur kāvya*, Pithauragarh, 1967, pp. 146 f; R. S. McGregor, *Hindi Literature from its Beginnings to the Nineteenth Century*, A History of Indian Literature, ed. J. Gonda, vol. viii. 6, Wiesbaden, 1984, pp. 84 f.
2. Vrajbhūṣaṇ Śarmā and Dvārkādās Parīkh, eds., *Do sau bāvan vaiṣṇavan kī vārtā*, Kankrauli, 1951–3, vol. iii, pp. 256 ff.
3. Govardhannāth Śukla, ed., *Parmānand-sāgar*, Aligarh, 1958. McGregor, loc. cit.
4. Umāśaṅkar Śukla, *Nanddās*, pts. 1 and 2, Allahabad, 1942; Vrajratnadās, *Nanddās granthāvalī*, Varanasi, 1949; 2nd edn., 1957.
5. Śukla, op. cit., pt. 1, p. 85.
6. p. 248.
7. Kiśorīlāl Gupta, ed., *Nāgrīdās*, vol. i, Varanasi, 1965. Of 18 *padas* attributed to Nanddās in this edition, 9 are represented in Śukla, and 13 in Vrajratnadās. For MSS of *Pad-muktāvalī* and the Nanddās verses likely to be involved, see this edn., pp. 107 ff., 541, and *Search for Hindi Manuscripts*, 1904, p. 186, Varanasi, 1912–14, p. 149.
8. Kṛṣṇānandvyās Deb, *Rāgsāgarodbhab-rāg-kalpadrum*, Calcutta, 1843; *Saṅgīt-rāg-kalpadrum*, 3 vols., Calcutta, 1914–16.
9. *Aṣṭchāp*, Lahore, 1940.
10. Śivsiṃh Seṅgar, *Śivsiṃh-saroj*, Lucknow, 1878.
11. 2nd edn., Mathura, 1949. As few as 8 of Mītal's verses are admitted to Śukla's text, and only 27 to that of Vrajratnadās.
12. The textural variants given imply overlaps, but not large overlaps, in the inventories of several MSS. Lack of material for comparison would have complicated the determination of kinship between MSS; and this process would have been all the more problematical, in so far as particular songs might have been written down from memory rather than copied from written sources. Another complication in determining MS kinship would have been that the MSS in question contain verses by several poets.
13. K. E. Bryant, *Poems to the Child-God*, Berkeley, Calif., 1978, pp. 35 ff.
14. M. Corcoran, 'Vrndavana in Vaisnava Braj Literature', University of London Ph.D. thesis, 1980, pp. 85–103, 123–35.
15. With this positioning cf. the position in MSS containing Sūrdās *padas* or *padas* expressing personal devotion and entreaty (*vinay*) to Kṛṣṇa: these, in earlier MSS, follow rather than precede *padas* dealing with topics of the Kṛṣṇa *līlā*. J. S. Hawley, 'The Early Sūr Sāgar and the Growth of the Sūr Tradition', *JAOS* 99, 1979, p. 66. Śukla's editorial arrangement of his Nanddās *padas* thus follows an earlier, rather than a later, pattern of arrangement. Vrajratnadās by contrast follows the later pattern in presenting the *padas* in question almost at the beginning of his text.
16. Cf. *Sūr-sāgar*, ed. Nanddulāre Vājpeyī, Varanasi, 4th edn., 1964, vv. 1491–2

(where the people simply ask Kṛṣṇa gratefully not to drop the hill), v. 1494 (where the herdsmen prop the hill up).

17. vii. 5. 23–4.
18. v. 3.
19. ed. cit., v. 351.
20. v. 54.
21. vv. 62–73, 74–90, 127–40.
22. vv. 5–13.
23. vv. 2–4.
24. v. 3.
25. *The Round Dance of Krishna and Uddhav's Message*, London, 1973, pp. 33 f.
26. ed. cit., pp. 67 ff.
27. vv. 14–17, 21–2.
28. v. 22.
29. vv. 91–102, 104–6.
30. Hawley, loc. cit.

Synoptic and sectarian bhakti in the poetry of Dhruvdās

RUPERT SNELL

Most traditions with Vaiṣṇavism develop their own theologies: whether as a natural working-out of religious ideas latent in the perceptions of their teachers, or whether as an *ex post facto* attempt to establish a claim to orthodoxy *vis-à-vis* other codes, there is a strong tendency for any *sampradāy* to present itself as a rational system capable of being understood through the accepted language of religious structures. The Caitanya tradition has prodigious theologians and rhetoricians; the Puṣṭi Mārg has Vallabha's own philosophical elaboration of the *Bhāgavata Purāṇa*; and the literary canons of other traditions likewise put great emphasis on the elucidation of philosophical and religious matters. The case of the Rādhāvallabh *sampradāy* is rather different: here the emphasis is on the production and enjoyment of devotional sentiment, *rasa*, and the complexities of theological debate are regarded as an unwelcome distraction from that total absorption in the *līlā* of Rādhā and Kṛṣṇa which should constitute the main preoccupation of the true devotee. This paper looks at aspects of the *rasik* poetry of Dhruvdās, a sixteenth- to seventeenth-century Brajbhāṣā poet who continues the Rādhāvallabhī devotional tradition instigated by Hit Harivaṃś (*c.* 1502–52);[1] typical themes in the poetry are discussed with a view to finding an answer to the question of the extent to which a poet such as Dhruvdās should be seen as a primarily 'sectarian' poet.

Following Rādhāvallabhī priorities, Dhruvdās is principally concerned to describe the *nikuñj-vihār* of Rādhā and Kṛṣṇa. Based on the principles and rhetoric of a style established earlier by Hit Harivaṃś in his *Caurāsī pad* and both refined and redefined by the *Caurāsī pad*'s successive commentators, this theme emphasises the unique benefits of concentration upon the eternal *līlā*. While Rādhāvallabhīs share with their Vaiṣṇava co-religionists a great regard for the *Bhāgavata Purāṇa* as the most authoritative expression of bhakti attitudes, many elements of the Kṛṣṇa narrative elaborated in the *Bhāgavata* – such as the entire *bāl-līlā*, the Mathura and Dwarka episodes, the manner of *virah* depicted in the *gopīs*' lament to Uddhav, or the raising of Govardhan Hill – do not feature at all in the deliberately narrowed focus of the Rādhāvallabhī perspective. Instead, emphasis is placed on the sweet *rasa* which can be relished in the ethereal and transcendental *līlā*, in which the purāṇic *gopīs* are translated into *sakhīs* of Rādhā and as such take a vicarious enjoyment in promoting (but not participating in) amorous and sentimental situations of the kind portrayed in Jayadeva's *Gītagovinda*.

Dhruvdās is surrounded by that historical obscurity which typically attends the faithful bhakta: his dates are uncertain, and the few facts which can be construed about his life shed little light on his poetry.[2] He was born into a kāyasth family in 'Dev-van', that is Deoband, a place revered inside the Rādhāvallabhī fold as the birthplace of Harivaṃś himself (and celebrated more generally as the location of the Dār-al 'Ulūm seminary). His father was one Śyāmdās; his grandfather (or great-uncle: the genealogy is unclear) was Viṭṭhaldās, a major figure in the *sampradāy*'s history; more significantly, Dhruvdās was the disciple of Gopīnāth, the third son of Harivaṃś. He belongs to that generation of sectarian writers who are typically the first to formalise the raw religious insights of the spiritual masters from whom a sectarian tradition stems; and in this regard he stands in relation to Hit Harivaṃś as Bihārindās does, for example, to Svāmī Haridās. According to a legend retailed by an early seventeenth-century hagiography, Bhagvat Mudit's *Rasik-ananya-māl*, Dhruvdās came to live in Vrindaban but was unable to express in verse his devotional sentiments and aspirations; he lay for three days and nights without food on a *rāsmaṇḍal* which to this day forms a centre for sectarian activity, and eventually came to the notice of Rādhā, who took pity on him and showed her grace in the novel manner of giving him a kick on the head while performing her nightly dance.[3]

These or perhaps more conventional circumstances started a literary career which was to produce a total of forty-two short works[4] together with a hundred or so *padas*. Best known outside the Rādhāvallabh sect is the hagiology *Bhakta-nāmāvalī*, undated but certainly not very many decades younger than Nābhādās' more famous work and therefore an early example of the 'Bhakta-māl' genre; the text shares two conspicuous qualities of its forebear, namely a catholicity of coverage (despite a preliminary sectarian dedication) and a tantalising unconcern with the actual data of narrative biography, the throw-away reference always being preferred to the hard historical fact. After briefly dispatching such early bhaktas as Prahlād and Uddhav, Dhruvdās moves on to those of historical times, beginning with Jayadeva and then progressing to nearer contemporaries of the fifteenth and sixteenth centuries. Haridās, Vallabh, and Viṭṭhalnāth, and Caitanya and his disciples (who abandoned their homes and hastened to Vrindavan 'like the flood-waters of Sāvan') are all included, and numerous bhaktas from other traditions are alluded to in respect of their appetite for *rasa* and, frequently, their consummate skill in poetry. Some episodes from the lives of devotees, such as the famous attempted poisoning of Mīrā, are briefly alluded to. Poets of the *nirguṇ* tendency are not forgotten, and the high panegyrical tone is maintained consistently, regardless of sectarian affiliations. Acknowledgement is made of the superior qualities of the hagiology's antecedent written by Nābhādās (here referred to as 'Nārāyan').

Vaidyak-jñān-līlā: a devotional electuary

The largely non-sectarian nature of the *Bhakta-nāmāvalī* hagiology characterises other texts also. Remarkable for its use of an extended metaphor is the *Vaidyak-jñān-līlā* (*VJL*), a brief parable in sixty couplets which prescribes an electuary for the holy life. The narrative tells how a learned Vaidya, advertising a panacea for all ills, is approached by a man suffering from an advanced case of worldliness: with 'venery's vile venom' (*viṣay viṣam viṣ*) coursing through his body he is spurned by family and friends and is afflicted by the cruel irony that his desires continue unabated though his physical faculties decline with the approach of old age. The Vaidya prescribes dietary treatment, advising abstinence from 'the tamarind of the female sex', 'the sour taste of greed', 'the sweetness of infatuation', and 'the curd of anger'. But even this regimen fails to bring an end to the patient's sensual torment, and the balance of *guṇas* in his make-up is gravely impaired. He begs for a more potent cure, which the Vaidya then proposes in the following words[5] (with a modicum of licence here for the sake of the English):

Take the root of the tree of asceticism, and mix with the dry ginger of contentment;
Let the pungent chilli of compassion be blended with the peepul berry of friendship free from desire.
Take the creeper of gentleness and mix all the ingredients with the honey of sacred utterance;
Add the myrobylan and mango of purity and kindness – through these the body will be purified.
Take the *asagandh* herb and sit in steady posture: let mind's jewel overcome care;
Be confident in the medicinal herb of cognizance, in the fennel of contemplation, in the aromatic of adoration and the cummin of concentration.
Add the clove of truth to the alchemist's potion of tranquillity, without which happiness can never be found;
Take all the mineral elements of divine faith and season with the elixir of the holy Name.
Blend together all these medicines and pound them in the mortar of knowledge;
Pour into the crucible of the heart and set to boil over the fire of sentience.
Cover with the lid of absence-of-envy, stirring the while with the ladle of faithfulness;
Once the manual preparation is done, and if ever you attain the company of saintly folk,
Then pour the draught into the chalice of love, and set it down on the ground of poverty;
Drink with the water of strength in the dawn of compassionate grace: your affliction will leave you and you will live from age to age.

Few of the ingredients in this prescription would prove indigestible to Vaiṣṇavas of any persuasion. Other of Dhruvdās' poems maintain this synoptic vision, addressing the Vaiṣṇava everyman with universalised homilies. In particular, Dhruvdās is fond of warning of the dangers of worldliness, pride, calumny, and of course sensuality, and he speaks of lives wasted in the pursuit of creature comforts and the pleasures of the flesh; he who is infatuated with his livelihood or with wife and home is an object of derision, at the whim of his desires like a dancing monkey (*Jīv-daśā-līlā*). The defeat of worldliness is through devotion, and salvation is obtainable through the power of the divine Name. The benefits of bhakti extend to the eschatological sphere: he who has the treasure of *bhakti-rasa* is untouched by the winds of death and illusion (*Khyāl-hulās-līlā*). Taking up a rhetorical style suggestive of the *nirguṇ* poets, Dhruvdās explains that single-mindedness of devotion, *rasik-ananyatā*, is a difficult path to follow: stray from it by the slightest degree and the whole is lost (*Man-śikṣā-līlā*); the path of love is as difficult as walking through fire, and it is contrary, making renown offensive and abuse sweet to hear (*Khyāl-hulās-līlā*). The worshipper must be as valiant as a warrior in battle, who fights on even when his body is torn apart (*Man-śikṣā-līlā*). Homiletics of this kind might be found in almost any devotional work; but Dhruvdās argues against association with those who follow a broadly defined creed, as it is essential to stay close to those whose devotion is reserved for the groves of Vṛndāban.[6]

Dhruvdās' accommodation of other systems is perhaps little more than nominal. It conforms with the principle that personal *sādhanā* is as much a matter of choice as is the selection of a personal deity (*iṣṭadev*); but in matters close to the heart Dhruvdās shows little real enthusiasm for anything other than the priorities of Rādhāvallabhī bhakti. The path of knowledge (*jñāna*) can rival bhakti no more effectively than a collection of lamps could hope to rival the light of the sun; and the fluttering banner of Rādhāvallabh declares victory over Vaiṣṇava orthodoxy, the so-called *Bhagavat-dharm* (*Bhajan-kuṇḍaliyā-līlā*). The appearance of a title such as *Braj-līlā* amongst his forty-two texts might seem to suggest a venturing into the broader canvas of *Bhāgavata*-based Kṛṣṇa narrative: but in fact this text too is restricted to the Rādhā–Kṛṣṇa theme, the 'Braj' reference referring merely to the fact that here the protagonists appear as the adolescent offspring of Vṛṣabhānu and Nanda respectively. Not altogether following his own definition of *virah* as given, for example, in the *Siddhānt-vicār-līlā* discussed below, he describes Kṛṣṇa's captivation by his first glance of Rādhā, 'as though all the enchantresses and charmers of the three worlds were brought together in one place'.[7]

A state of longing is a speciality of Dhruvdās' description of divine love: it is a state alluded to by images of succulence and savoury qualities, words like *rasa, lāvanyatā*, and *caṭpaṭā* featuring prominently in his imagery, a further source of metaphor being drawn from words depicting brilliance and lustre – *chaṭā, chabi, joti, ujjval.*

The chronological development of poetic style

With Dhruvdās, as with pre-modern literature generally, a dated text is a rare luxury: only five of the forty-two *līlās* bear dates (all five being plainly stated with versified numerals, the ambiguities of the cryptic chronogram being for once avoided here). The earliest and the latest of these five texts are separated by a full forty-eight years, a period which is surely likely to represent the major part of the poet's *floruit: Rasānand-līlā* is dated VS 1650 (AD 1593), and *Rahasya-mañjarī-līlā* VS 1698 (AD 1641). A distinct development of style and presentation can be observed between the two extremes of this half-century.

The 185 verses of *Rasānand-līlā* (*RL*) include a number of successive narrative contexts, all of course pertaining in some way to the expected theme of *nikuñj-vihār* and held together by a unity of sentiment, but oddly disparate in terms of actual thematic composition. Descriptions are quite literal and relate largely to physical appearances, adding detail to successive detail in a serial fashion and with little expansion or commentary. After a conventional *maṅgalācaraṇ* (stanzas 1–14) comes a celebration of the *rasa* available in Vṛndāvan (15–25) and a description of Rādhā and Kṛṣṇa (26–58). The *sakhīs*, 'tendrils in love's garden', are described in the context of the servile role allocated to them in the Rādhāvallabhī system (59–83), the eight principals being named and details of the actuality of their *sevā* being described. A reference to *nikuñj-vihār* (84) introduces the theme of a game of dice (*caupar*, 85–94) in which garments, ornaments, and souls are successively forfeit in a kind of sublimated 'strip poker'. A *ban-bihār* theme then signals a return to the describing of Vṛndāvan (95–106) and leads directly into a *phāg/holī* context (107–14), succeeded in turn by a sequence of verses based on the swing motif (*hĩḍorā*) and a generalised eulogistic description of Rādhā and Kṛṣṇa watched by the *sakhīs* (115–34). Then, somewhat unexpectedly, and suggesting that the poet intends nothing less than a complete run-through of the favoured Rādhāvallabhī themes within this single poem, comes an account of the *rās* dance (133–55): here, in the competitive artistry transferred to such *rās* descriptions from the innately oppositional performance style of Kathak and other dances, Rādhā's performance is of course easily able to outdo Kṛṣṇa's. The 'water-games' which *Bhāgavata Purāṇa* convention makes follow the exertions of the *rās* are here located in the sectarian site of Mansarovar, a pleasant oasis-like pond across the river from modern Vrindaban, this account being interwoven with further *nikuñj* description and the popular 'exchange of clothes' motif (156–75). The remaining lines form a brief concluding section (176–85).

The later poem, *Rahasya-mañjarī-līlā* (*RML*), has the pronouncedly more metaphysical character suggested by its title. The reduced importance of a narrative framework means that the poem does not lend itself to the serial description given for *RL* above: as though by default, the context is that of *nikuñj-vihār*, and the relating of successive incidents is dictated by that motif. Though this kind of distinction might be expected to exist between two qualitatively different themes as a matter of course, an overall shift in rhetorical emphasis suggests that what we are seeing here may be a reordering of priorities over the half-century of Dhruvdās' literary career. The restless and fickle switching seen in the *RL* between tenuously connected motifs has given way to a more stable and perhaps more mature concentration on a restricted subject-matter; descriptions are markedly more allusive and make Vṛndāvan an unequivocal paradise – with jewelled gold much in evidence, for example, and a hundred love-gods in constant attendance. An increased tendency towards the use of symbolism makes the Yamuna a 'stream of bliss' (v. 10); everything is ethereal, with emotional states featuring much more prominently than descriptions of *sevā* or other ritualistic activity. The love which exists between Rādhā and Kṛṣṇa is constantly described as wondrous and ineffable (26) and beyond ordinary comprehension: the key adjective *adbhut* occurs many times throughout the poem. Explicit reference is made to the subtle nature of *virah*, which in the sectarian conception exists simultaneously with *saṃjog* (29). Hazarding an evaluation of poetic quality, it might be said that the style of *RML* is less transparently imitative of Hit Harivaṃś' *Caurāsī-pad* than is the *RL*, which has barely digested the massive influence of its illustrious forebear. This influence marks the majority of Dhruvdās' poetry. The second of the five dated texts, *Premāvalī-līlā* (*PL*), for example, borrows many a phrase from the *Caurāsī-pad* and tends towards the formulaic in its composition generally (which Braj poet has *not* likened the Yamuna to a garland put on by Vṛndāban?); but still its descriptions of the *nikuñj-vihār* and the so-called 'post-coital lustre' (*suratānt-chabi*), another favourite theme, have an undoubted power of their own.

Siddhānt-vicār-līlā: a prose manual of Rādhāvallabhī bhakti

The undated *Siddhānt-vicār-līlā* (*SVL*) is a rarity among original devotional texts (as opposed to textual commentaries), being written mainly in prose.[8] The purpose of the text is not to expound a complete system of devotional thought *ab initio*, far less to propose an autonomous sectarian theology, but rather to elucidate the rhetoric of Rādhāvallabhī bhakti for the convenience of the devotee. That a sectarian primer such as this represents a novelty of a kind not generally available at the time of Dhruvdās' writing (with the single exception of the *Sevak-vāṇī* of Dāmodardās) is suggested by his own statement that he wrote the *SVL* partly in order to better his own understanding.[9] Being an explanation and expansion of concepts deriving from Rādhāvallabhī texts generally, rather than a commentary on any one specific poem, the *SVL* is able to concentrate on straightforward exegesis without recourse to the devious etymological games that the *ṭīkākār* so often loves to play with the text he has chosen as his victim. Only once does the *SVL* resort to the techniques of creative philology, when in his discussion of the concept of *āsaktatā* he ventures a mischievous definition: *āsakta kahā? sakti rahit āsakta.*

Through the means of a *praśnottar* format, the *SVL* discusses Rādhāvallabhī interpretations of the concepts *prem, nem, mān*, and *virah*, and is at pains to distinguish these interpretations from those current among the generality of devotional systems. Also emphasised are the importance of single-mindedness (*ananyatā*) as a means of ensuring a properly focused devotional attitude, and the appropriate nature of the devotee (*rasik*) as one for whom no consideration other than absorption in the eternal *līlā* has any lasting appeal.

Dhruvdās explains divine love, *prem*, as being characterised by such features as tenderness, savour, ever-newness, and as having neither beginning nor end; this is contrasted with *nem*, the finite manifestations of *prem*, varied in kind and including laughter, loving speech, *mān*, and all those aspects of love-making whose existence is subject to the ordinance of time. The constant, eternal quality of *prem* is unaffected by the temporary manifestations of various *nem*, just as the quality of gold survives its moulding into the specific form of a particular ornament; but in another analogy a more interdependent status is suggested for *prem* and *nem*, mutually complementary 'like the warp and the woof of the thread [in cloth]'.[10] In answering his own question about what becomes of *nem* when *prem* is produced, Dhruvdās distinguishes further between those *nem* which are of their very nature distinct from *prem*, and which fall away, and those which are linked (*jantrit*) to it and therefore endure by being assimilated into *prem* and partaking of its nature. A parallel is drawn with the progression from the nine limited and finite aspects of devotion constituting *navadhā* bhakti to the *prem-lakṣanā* bhakti which succeeds it and supersedes it.[11] The *prem/nem* opposition is also used to elucidate the distinction between *prem* and *kām: kām* is secondary and finite, because it only endures so long as pleasure (*sukh*) lasts;[12] the pleasures of *kām* are therefore to be classified alongside *nem*. True *prem* is transcendental (*adbhut*), and is not to be confused with physical pleasure: and the selfish pursuit of pleasure for oneself is an indication not of *prem* but of 'ordinary physical enjoyment' (*sādhāraṇ sukh-bhog*). Constant selfless love is found only in Rādhā and Kṛṣṇa: their passion (*kām*), sung of by the *rasiks*, is not base (*prākṛt*) but is infused with love (*prem-maī*).

The concepts of *mān* and *virah* are redefined *vis-à-vis* their conventional values. A state of *mān* is produced not in the usual 'lover's tiff' narrative context, but rather in a spontaneous manner when Rādhā momentarily fails to pay full attention to Kṛṣṇa, at which point his dependency on her becomes as complete as the dependency of a fish on water. For Dhruvdās, the concept of *mān* on the model of the *Gītagovinda* (or, for that matter, the *Caurāsī-pad*) is hardly admissible, since it presupposes an actual and literal separation of

Rādhā from Kṛṣṇa. Here, any separations are fleeting and spontaneous and are to be distinguished from the other sort as 'subtle' (*sūkṣma*) versus 'gross' (*sthūl*). *Sūkṣma virah* is exemplified by the moment when the blinking eyelids obscure a view of the beloved, or when there is so much as a consciousness in the lover of a distinctness between the two bodies.[13] *Adbhut prem* is a subtle state to which all other varieties of *virah* are inappropriate: it is unjust to threaten with a sword one who withers at the sight of a flower-garland.[14]

Dhruvdās is plainly conscious that his definitions of these concepts are out of line with accepted norms, an objection he anticipates by explaining that the forms of *mān virah* described by the divines (*mahāpuruṣ*) are mere conventions meant only as a preliminary stage of spiritual instruction.[15] The revelation of the superior stage of spiritual endeavour described here by Dhruvdās is naturally ascribed to Hit Harivaṃś, referred to by the conventional honorific *śrījī* in the following statement of sectarian principle:

> Before this great love, all other forms of *prem* and *nem* are mere means: know this with certitude. Rādhā and Kṛṣṇa are resplendent in the transcendental joy of love of the bower-sport, which is eternal, continuous, constant, innate, devoid of purpose, sweet beyond all things. There is no higher sentiment, no other pleasure, no other love. Lalitā, Viśākhā and the other *sakhīs* are deeply absorbed in the essence of the sentiment which derives from it. This mode of devotion of the love of transcendental sentiment, essence of essences, the delight of love, has been made manifest by Śrījī, dauntlessly, for the well-being of all; hold it firm, should it enter your heart.[16]

Dhruvdās steers a careful course between the exclusivity of a narrowly defined sectarian teaching and respect for the broader context of Vaiṣṇavism to which he also adheres; and while underlining the superiority of the Rādhāvallabhī system he is quick to maintain respect for the followers of other paths. Yet the Rādhāvallabhī path is clearly to be seen as *primus inter pares*, and the status of its teaching is elevated in such a way that its purity becomes susceptible to the polluting influence of alien contact: matters of sectarian principle are not to be raised with outsiders who neither understand nor appreciate them. Dhruvdās' use of the word *vijātī* to designate those with whom this *rasa* must not be shared suggests that this prohibition is not merely conventional (though the usual advantages of *satsaṅg* are indeed given due prominence) but actually implies a sectarian social restriction of some kind.[17]

A further characteristically Rādhāvallabhī attitude is the limited stress on the role of prescribed ritual activity: concomitant with the emphasis placed upon the appreciation of *rasa* is a lack of interest in the procedural niceties of complex rites of service and worship. Dhruvdās maintains that excessive ordinances harden the heart and make it ill suited for appreciating the delicate nature of devotional love. The minimal amount of observances which will satisfy Vaiṣṇava norms of behaviour are sufficient, and even these should not be attributed with any great significance; the service of Rādhāvallabh is infinitely preferable to other more general ritual.[18] This theoretical position is confirmed by a recommendation of *sevā* practice in *Bhajan-sat-līlā* (vv. 4 ff.), where the instructions for ritual bathing and the applying of a *tilak* are followed not by further such physical rituals but by the assumption of appropriate mental attitudes.

Perhaps the most unequivocal statement on sectarian identity is that found in the dedications to Hit Harivaṃś made so frequently throughout the forty-two texts. Though appearing in the formulaic contexts of *maṅgalācaraṇ* and the like, these encomiums are not themselves mere empty formulas but explicit statements of Harivaṃś' role both as 'revealer' of the sectarian path and as the incarnate form of divine love itself:

Taking the form of love manifest, the exalted Hit Harivaṃś
made manifest the quintessence of Śrī Rādhāvallabh-lāl.[19]

Thus the Rādhāvallabhī poisition is parallel to that of the Gauḍīya and other traditions in that it establishes the fount of sectarian wisdom – that figure for which the beguilingly convenient designation 'founder' is so difficult to displace – not only as a means to the realisation of *rasa* but also as a component part of the divine essence itself.

As mentioned earlier, Dhruvdās was descended from the Rādhāvallabhī Viṭṭhaldās. An incident from the life of the latter as told in Bhagvat Mudit's *Rasik-ananya-māl* has a symbolic bearing on Dhruvdās' devotional attitude and is summarised here:

Viṭṭhaldās was appointed subedar of Junagarh. When the court visited Dwarka, all members of the court and the army were expected to take *darśan* of Raṇchoṛ [the presiding deity there]. Viṭṭhaldās failed to comply, causing a scandal which reached the king. The king [whose identity is not given] summoned Viṭṭhaldās and bade him explain in a plenary session of the court why he had started up a 'separate tradition' (*nyārau mat*). His reply affirmed his total commitment of 'the two-armed Rādhikā-vallabh', with Harivaṃś his *guru* and Vṛndāvan his *dhām*, there being no room in his heart for 'the four-armed form [Raṇchoṛ]'; and he maintained that the delights of the *rās* were manifest in every hair of his body. The king, furious at such an indulgent statement, had him stripped of his clothing: the literal truth of Viṭṭhaldās's claim then became apparent, every hair on his body being composed of the flourishing trees, creepers and flowers [of Vṛndāvan] and resonant with the musical sound of cymbals, drums and dancers' anklets and Kṛṣṇa's flute. The king repented and fell at Viṭṭhaldās's feet, praising him for his single-mindedness of purpose and seeking his grace.[20]

The parable is unintentionally symbolic of the position held by a *rasik* poet such as Dhruvdās on the continuum between a broadly defined normative Vaiṣṇavism on the one hand and a precisely delineated sectarian mode of religion on the other. Dhruvdās' verse constantly (if not consistently) emphasises the particularity of the bhakti promulgated by Hit Harivaṃś, in which *nikuñj-vihār* represents the quintessence of devotional love and the sole provider of the *rasa* on which the devotee depends; yet many of his devotional and religious attitudes are indistinguishable from those accepted by a broad spectrum of the Hindu religious tradition. In the Dwarka episode, Viṭṭhaldās was challenged and vilified for his seeming rejection of the path accepted by other Hindus: but his apparent unorthodoxy, and his determined pursuit of a distinct path, turned out on closer examination to be no unorthodoxy at all but rather a distillation of the elements of devotional religion, one which both typifies and transcends the general attitudes of Vaiṣṇava bhakti. So too Dhruvdās is able to operate on either the general or the specific plane without fear of contradiction, the wide-angle and the close-up lenses both fitting equally well into the camera of his devotional perception.

Synoptic and sectarian bhakti resolved

This paper has tried to show how Dhruvdās' poetry represents a diversity of bhakti positions, both assimilating the general tenets of Vaiṣṇavism and establishing a distinct and particular mode of secular devotion. The ease with whch Dhruvdās moves between different points on the spectrum between the broadly *Bhāgavata*-based devotion on the one hand and the *rasik* sectarianism on the other is perhaps surprising given the seemingly vehement conviction of the sectarian attitude: but in fact the two positions are not so much mutually exclusive theological systems as mutually complementary aspects of Kṛṣṇaism. The formal opposition between them provides an area of discourse which is part of the rhetoric of the statement of bhakti; it is in many ways analogous to that laboured opposition of *saguṇ* and *nirguṇ*, categories which the student of religion with his love of rational taxonomy would like to allocate to safely watertight compartments, but which the devotee in his wisdom perceives as equally valid if partial descriptions of the mystery of God.

NOTES

1. The poetry of Hit Harivaṃś is treated in R. Snell, *The Eighty-Four Hymns of Hita Harivaṃśa: An Edition of the Caurāsī Pada*, Delhi, 1991.
2. Data relating to Dhruvdās' biography is discussed at considerable length in Kedārnāth Dvivedī 'Yatīndra', *Śrīhit Dhruvdās aur unkā sāhitya*, Dehradun, 1971, pp. 51–97.
3. L. P. Purohit, ed., *Rasik-ananya-māl*, Vrindaban, n.d., p. 78:

   खांन पानं तजि मण्डल परयौ । देख्यौ गुन बरनौं हठ करयौ ॥

दिन द्वै गये तीसरौ आयौ । तब राधे कौ हिय अकुलायौ ।
आधी रात लात सिर दई । चौंकि परचौ नूपुर धुनि भई ॥
वानी भई जु चाहत कियौ । उठि सो वर तोकौं सब दियौ ॥
एसे कहि अंतरहित भई । ध्रुव कौं रति मति वानी दई ॥

4. Whether any numerological significance attaches to the number 42 I am not sure; but it is, of course, the precise half of 84, which, in addition to its own auspicious quality, appears in the title and composition of the *Caurāsī-pad* of Harivaṃś. The text on which the present discussion is based is *BLP*.
5. *BLP*, p. 6:

जड़ वैराग वृक्ष की लावहु । सोंठ सँतोषहि आनि मिलावहु ॥
मिरच तीतिक्षन करुना चीता । निस्पृह पीपर मिलवहु मीता ॥
कोमलता सब सौंज गिलोई । मधुवानी सों लेहु समोई ॥
हरर आमरे शुचि अरु दाया । तातें निर्मल ह्वैहै काया ॥
असगँध आसन दृढ़ कै करौ । चिंतामनि चिंता परिहरौ ॥
मुसलि सौंफ अजवाइन जीरा । ज्ञान ध्यान जप जोग में धीरा ॥
सांत मृगांग बिना सुख नाहीं । साँच लौंग मिलवहु ता माहीं ॥
भगवत धर्म धातु सब लीजै । नाम सुधारस की पुट दीजै ॥
ये औषधि सब आनि मिलावौ । ग्यान ओखली माहिं कुटावौ ॥
हिय हांडी में आनि चढ़ावौ । चेतन वह्नी करि औटावौ ॥
निर्मत्सर चपनी ढकि लैयै । श्रद्धा करछी फेरत जैयै ॥
हस्त क्रिया जबहीं बनि आवै । जो कबहूँ सत्संगति पावै ॥
पुनि लै प्रेम चखक में करै । भूमि गरीबी में लै धरै ॥
प्रात कृपा बल जल सों पीवै । रोग जाइ अरु जुग जुग जीवै ॥

6. Loc. cit.:

बहुत भाँति के मत जहाँ तिनिहि न समुझै संग ।
नव किशोरता माधुरी बिना न अपनो रंग ॥ ३८ ॥
देखो प्रेम बिलास वृन्दावन घन कुंज में ।
जिनकै यहै उपास ऐसो संग जु कीजिये ॥ ३९ ॥

7. *BLP*, p. 256 (Kṛṣṇa speaking):

ललिता एक किशोरी देखी । मानौं रूप की सींवा पेखी ॥ ११५ ॥
कौन भांति मुख की छबि कहियै । चितवत सखी चित्र ह्वै रहियै ॥ ११६ ॥
कहा कहौं अंग अंग निकाई । छिनक माहिं लियौ चित्त चुराई ॥ ११७ ॥
मनौ मोहनी और ठगोरी । तीन लोककी करि इकठोरी ॥ ११८ ॥

8. Another of the 42 texts, *Priyā jī kī nāmāvalī*, is also technically a 'prose' work, being an unstructured litany of 100 of the names of Rādhā; but it hardly qualifies as a piece of connected prose writing in any meaningful sense.
9. *BLP*, p. 53: या रस कौ बिचार अपने मन समुझाइवे कौं कै जिनकौ मन या रस में होइ तिन के हेत कह्यौ ।
10. *BLP*, p. 47: प्रेम नेम जैसे तंतु का ताना बाना, न्यारौ कोई नाहीं । और सोना है ताते भूषन करचौ सो नेम भयो । सोना एकरस है सो प्रेम है ।

11. *BLP*, p. 44: जे नेम प्रेम तें न्यारे हैं ते जाँइ, जे नेम प्रेम सौं जंत्रित हैं ते कैसे जाँइ। नवधा भक्ति हूं नेम है, जब प्रेम लच्छिना उपजै तहां प्रेम में लीन ह्वै रहै। ताकौ दृष्टांत, जैसे स्वेत वस्त्र लाल रँग्यो तब वह लाल भयौ वस्त्र कहूँ नाहीं गयौ।
12. *BLP*, p. 45: एक ने कही प्रेम में अरु काम में कहा भेद है सो कहो, समुझाइ देहु। तातें जैसी यथामति उपजी तैसी कही। और जहां तांई सुख हैं तिनपर काम रस अधिक है यापर और नाहिं।
13. *BLP*, p. 49: जो कोऊ कहै स्थूल कहा सूक्ष्म कहा। सूक्ष्म प्रेम यासौं कहिये जो एक सेज पर रूप देखत चन्द चकोर ज्यों नैनांचल ओट भये महा कठिन दशा होइ। अरु देह हूँ अपनी न्यारी नाहीं सहि सकत, यह भी बिरह मानत हैं।
14. Loc. cit.: ऐसे अद्‌भुत प्रेम में और भांति को विरह न संभवै। जो फूलनि की माला देखें कुम्हिलाइ ताकौं असिवार कौ दिखाइवो अनीत है।
15. Loc. cit.: जो कोउ कहै कि मान बिरह महापुरुष गायौ है सो सदाचार के लिये। औरनि के समुझाइबे कौं कह्यौ है। पहिले स्थूल प्रेम समझै तब आगे चलै।
16. *BLP*, p. 50: और सब प्रेम-नेम या नित्य महाप्रेम रस के आगे साधन हैं, यह निर्धार जानिबौ। नित्य अखंडित एकरस सहज निमित्य रहित महामाधुरी निकुंज केलि अद्‌भुत रसिकानन्द दोऊ बिलसत हैं। या पर न और रस न और सुख न और प्रेम। तहां कौ जु रससार तामें सखी ललिता विसाखादि आसक्त हैं। सार कौ सार प्रेम सुख यह अद्‌भुत महारस प्रेम की उपासना श्री जू प्रगट कर दई है निश्शंक सबके कल्याणार्थ। जो उर में आवै ठहराय।
17. Loc. cit.: जिन यह रस समुझ्यो नाहीं तासों रस की बात करनी उचित नाहीं। जो कहै तो आपतें जाइ, अन्तर परै निस्संदेह। ताते मौन होइ रहनौ बहुत भलौ है। विजाती सों मिलबौ भलौ नाही। बिन सजाती सौं मिलि बात न चलावै। अनेक भांति भक्ति भेदनि के भेद तेसेई भक्त हैं। जैसौ जाकौ भाव है तैसो सिद्ध होइ। ताते ओरनि सों प्रयोजन नाहीं।
18. *BLP*, p. 51: तब एक ने कही आचार न करै। थोरौ बहुत करै सदाचार के लिये। . . . वैष्णव सदाचार के लिये आचार करै। मन में विश्वास न धरै कि याही तें कारज सिद्ध होइगौ। शुद्धता के लिये करै। श्रीजी की टहल कोटि कोटि आचार कौ स्वरूप है। बहुत आचार तें हियौ अति कठोर होइ जाय है। यह भजन अति कोमल है, कोमल कठोर एक संग न बनै।
19. *BLP*, p. 169 (*Premāvalī-līlā*):
    प्रगट प्रेम कौ रूप धरि श्री हृतिबंश उदार।
    श्रीराधाबल्लभ लाल कौ प्रगट कियो रस सार ॥ १ ॥
20. Purohit, ed., op. cit., p. 13.

Discussions of the Rāma tradition in north and north-east India

Taraṇisena: a parochialised devotional motif

W. L. SMITH

In the story of Taraṇisena, writes D. C. Sen, 'the Bengali genius found a proper field, however strange it may appear to us, for introducing the spirit of devotion'.[1] 'This curious adversary of Rāma'[2] is, like his father Vibhīṣaṇa, a devotee of Rāma, but while the father deserts Laṅkā to join Rāma's forces, the son chooses to remain behind, for his goal is to be slain by Rāma and thereby be purged of his sins, freed of his demon body and to obtain instant bliss. As the war for Laṅkā approaches its climax, Taraṇisena enters the battlefield with the name of Rāma decorating his chariot, emblazoned on his banners, and painted on his very body, and then, after some difficulties, he manœuvres the object of his devotion into killing him.

While the story of Taraṇisena is a comparatively recent contribution to Rāma lore, the basic motif is much older and already appears in Bhāsa's play, the *Bālacarita* (second to fourth centuries), in which the bull-demon Ariṣṭa resolves to fight Kṛṣṇa in order to be killed by him and thus gain heaven.[3] The germ of the belief that any contact with the deity, even hostile contact, was beneficial[4] reaches full development in the *Bhāgavatapurāṇa* in the figures of Kaṃsa and Śiśupāla. Kaṃsa is so terrified of Kṛṣṇa that he sees him everywhere and, when killed, is saved to the consternation of the gods, while Śiśupāla, who was slain by avatārs of Viṣṇu in two previous lives and hence so obsessed with hate for Kṛṣṇa that he can think of nothing else, is similarly rewarded when the same fate befalls him. Here it is not merely the physical contact with the deity which is decisive; the two demons are saved because of their obsession with Kṛṣṇa, and the motives behind their concentration on him are not important; what is is the fact that they do, indeed, whole-heartedly concentrate on their divine foe.[5] This mode of bhakti is known as 'hate-devotion', *dveṣa-bhakti*.[6]

Later the motif was adopted in Rāmāyaṇa literature, where the figure chosen to play the role of the demon devotee is king Rāvaṇa. This happened despite the fact that the *Bhāgavatapurāṇa* points out that Rāvaṇa's concentration on Rāma was imperfect since he was preoccupied by thoughts of Sītā.[7] Later, Bengali theologians drew attention to another, quite obvious, point: the Rāma avatār, unlike that of Kṛṣṇa, did not have the power of granting salvation since Rāvaṇa, though slain by Rāma's hand, was after all condemned to suffer rebirth as Śiśupāla.[8] Descriptions of Rāvaṇa's new role already appear in the north-western and eastern recensions of Vālmīki. According to the former, Rāvaṇa once met Sanatkumāra, the son of Prajāpati, and asked him the fate of the demons slain by Viṣṇu. Sanatkumāra replied that they go to Viṣṇu's heaven, thus causing Rāvaṇa to wonder how he might become the enemy of the god and so ensure his own death by his hand. Sanatkumāra then informed the demon that Viṣṇu would be born in a future incarnation as king Rāma and exiled to the forest with his wife Sītā; if Rāvaṇa would kidnap Sītā, Sanatkumāra suggested, he would arouse the wrath of the god. Rāvana decided to follow his suggestion.[9] In the eastern recension of Vālmīki Rāvaṇa tells his brother Kumbhakarṇa that he is well aware that Rāma is the avatār of Viṣṇu and Sītā that of Lakṣmī, and explains that he did not kidnap Sītā for the sake of revenge or because of lust, but solely in order to make Rāma his implacable enemy.[10] A passage very similar to the above appears in the *Adhyātmarāmāyaṇa*, a later work which had enormous influence on many of the Rāmāyaṇas written in NIA languages, though here, as in the Vālmīkian interpolation, it is peripheral. The night before his final confrontation with Rāma, Rāvaṇa explains to his wife Mandodarī, in words very much like those spoken to Kumbhakarṇa in Vālmīki, that he knows Rāma's true identity, and that the abduction was intended solely to infuriate Rāma.[11] In none of these passages is there any mention of Rāvaṇa's being possessed by hate for or fear of Rāma or, for that matter, devotion. He is aware of Rāma's true identity and uses that knowledge for his own advantage. Commentaries on the *Adhyātmarāmāyaṇa* claim, however, that Rāvaṇa, like Kaṃsa, saw the universe pervaded by Rāma and was filled with hate and fear of him.[12] Nevertheless, the text itself does not support this and the passage, like those in Vālmīki, seems an afterthought.

Much later the theme is taken up in the Bengali *Rāmāyaṇa of* Kṛttibāsa. This work, perhaps written in the last quarter of the fifteenth century, is a problematic one since it has undergone such great changes during the course of its transmission that the 'original version' is extremely difficult, if not impossible, to reconstruct.[13] Although it is difficult to say to what degree bhakti ideas influenced the original version of the poem, it is clear that as the centuries passed it was increasingly coloured by devotional attitudes. Several late manuscripts of Kṛttibāsa describe Rāvaṇa acting the devotee and here his motives are even more ambiguous than in the Sanskrit versions.

According to these texts Rāvaṇa's transformation into a devotee takes place during the final confrontation between him and Rāma. In one version their duel is inconclusive until Rāma's charioteer Mātali suggests that he use the *brahma* weapon against Rāvaṇa. When Rāvaṇa sees this terrible projectile capable of destroying the three worlds hurtling at him, he begs for mercy, announces that he will immediately return Sītā, and addresses a long *stuti* to Rāma. When Rāma hears this, impressed with the demon's devotion, he dismounts from his chariot, throws his bow to the ground, and embraces Rāvaṇa. The war, he declares, is over. Relieved, Rāvaṇa sets off for Laṅkā to fetch Sītā. The gods, however, have no desire to see their mortal enemy escape with his life. Extremely upset by this abrupt turn-about, they decide to take matters into their own hands and so order the wind-god, Vāyu, to possess the demon. Vāyu does as ordered, causing the deluded Ravaṇa to turn around, march back to Rāma, and boast that he will now kill him and so be able to enjoy Sītā to his heart's content. When Rāma hears this, he picks up his bow, remounts his chariot, and shoots the demon dead.[14]

In another account Rāvaṇa is suddenly converted when he sees the entire universe pervaded by Rāma. He then addresses a long *stuti* to Rāma causing him again to throw down his bow and announce an end to the war, and Rāvaṇa returns to Laṅkā to bring back Sītā. Here, while on his way, Rāvaṇa suddenly realises that he is in a situation in which he cannot possibly lose: if he fights Rāma and wins, he will be able to possess Sītā unimpeded; if Rāma kills him, he will immediately be transported to the heaven of Viṣṇu. Meanwhile Rāma too has been having second thoughts and suspects that Rāvaṇa has been playing the role of devotee in order to save his own skin. When the demon suddenly returns to taunt and insult him, his suspicions seem confirmed and he kills Rāvaṇa.[15]

The motif takes a similar turn in the story of Taraṇisena, an apocryphal nephew of Rāvaṇa who apparently appears only in Bengali Rāmāyaṇa literature. The episode is associated with Kṛttibāsa and is often considered to be representative of his work, as for the last century or so it has been a standard feature of the numerous popular printings or bazaar editions of his poem. D. C. Sen, who bases his remarks on a version of the tale from such an edition, suggests that it might have been borrowed from a later poet, Śaṅkara Kabicandra,[16] whose version of the epic was written in 1702.[17] There are also independent retellings of the episode, usually with the title *Taraṇisener yuddha*, 'Taraṇisena's Fight', still in manuscript, and these bear the signatures of Dvija Daẏārāma, Rāmaśaṅkara, and 'Kṛttibāsa'.[18] The last is dated 1698, making it older than the full Rāmāyaṇa of Kabicandra. The Taraṇisena story, however, is not found in older Kṛttibāsa manuscripts or in the two relatively reliable printed editions of his poem (both based on eighteenth-century manuscripts); it was interpolated into bazaar printings and late manuscripts in deference to the custom of ascribing all sorts of apocryphal episodes to Bengal's first Rāmāyaṇa poet. Śaṅkara Kabicandra was very fond of the episode since he reduplicates it in the nearly identical stories of the demon devotees Subāhu, Araṇi, Atikāya, and Bīrabāhu. The story of the last demon was also interpolated into the *Jagamohana Ramāyaṇa* of the Oriya poet Baḷarāmadāsa.[19]

In Śaṅkara Kabicandra's Rāmāyaṇa the story runs as follows. After all the other *rākṣasa* leaders have fallen in battle, Taraṇisena goes to his uncle and volunteers to fight Rāma. Rāvaṇa is naturally somewhat sceptical and suspects that Taraṇisena will take advantage of the opportunity to desert to the enemy just as his father had done. When Taraṇisena insists that he is sincere and vows to kill Rāma and Lakṣmaṇa and bring back his father as a prisoner, Rāvaṇa, feeling he has nothing to lose, grants his permission. Taraṇi then sets off with 60 lakhs of chariots, 80 lakhs of elephants, and 100 crores of horses, stopping on the way to say goodbye to his mother, Śaramā, who asks him to convey her greetings to Rāma. As soon as he enters the battlefield, Taraṇi proclaims his devotion to Rāma and asks the monkey warriors he encounters where he might find him. Hanumān and his fellows, suspecting that this is a demon trick, attack him, but in short order Taraṇi defeats Aṅgada, Hanumān, and Lakṣmaṇa. When Rāma himself enters the lists, Taraṇisena flings himself to the ground, grasps his feet, and gives him a *stuti.* Moved by his devotion, Rāma advises him to leave the battlefield, but with apologies Taraṇi explains that he is a warrior and that it is his *kṣatriya dharma* to fight, and tells Rāma that he will parry every one of Rāma's arrows with his own. The apparent arrogance of the last remark infuriates Rāma and battle is joined. It is Taraṇisena's great devotion which makes him such a formidable opponent: each time Rāma knocks him down, he murmurs the *rāma-nāma* and immediately revives; over each arrow he fires he invokes the mantra of Rāma's name and even the arrows themselves have appropriate names, as the *bhakti-bāṇa* and *biṣṇu-bāṇa.* Finally, to his consternation, he succeeds in striking down the object of his devotion. Fortunately Rāma recovers and Taraṇisena attains his goal when he cleaves an arrow fired by Rāma and one of the halves unexpectedly decapitates him. The demon's severed head then rolls across the battlefield singing Rāma's praises and Rāma takes it into his arms and weeps, distressed that he has slain such a devotee for the sake of the insignificant (*tuccha*) Sītā. His entire army is moved to tears as well. When Vibhīṣaṇa appears to inform Rāma that Taraṇisena is his son, Rāma is astonished; had he known that he would not have fought him. Then, when Vibhīṣaṇa attempts to take his son's head into his arms, it protests: it is Rāma Taraṇisena prefers. In the end Śiva takes Taraṇi's head to Mount Kailāsa and Hanumān takes his body to Prayāg while Rāma stands alongside his friend Vibhīṣaṇa, greatly embarrassed (*rāmera lajjā adhika haila*).[20]

In other versions of the tale considerable guile has to be exercised to ensure that Rāma slays his bhakta. According to a version of the episode in a bazaar edition, when faced with Taraṇi's devotion, Rāma refuses to fight him and announces that he will abandon the siege of Laṅkā, forget Sītā, and retire to the forest. This causes Taraṇi, like Rāvaṇa in the story described earlier, to change tactics: he accuses Rāma of being a coward, taunts him for allowing himself to be exiled from the kingdom that was rightfully his, and boasts that he will seat Sītā on Rāvaṇa's lap himself. Unfortunately this insolent speech enrages Lakṣmaṇa instead of Rāma and it is Lakṣmaṇa who challenges the demon to fight. Vibhīṣaṇa, seeing the disappointment on his face, saves the situation by urging Rāma to kill the 'wicked demon' and, when Rāma has difficulties doing so, suggests to him that he use his *brahma*-weapon and with this the demon is decapitated. The weeping Vibhīṣaṇa then reveals his victim's identity and when Rāma reproaches him for not mentioning it, Vibhīṣaṇa points out that he has really done his son a favour, freeing him of his demon body and granting him nirvāṇa. His own tears, he tells Rāma, are not for Taraṇi, but for himself, for he cannot enjoy the same favour but must remain behind alive.[21]

Episodes featuring other demon devotees, such as the story of Bīrabāhu which appears in both the Bengali and the Oriya versions, follow the same pattern. When Bīrabāhu, a son of Rāvaṇa, enters the battlefield he falls at the feet of Vibhīṣaṇa and asks to be taken to Rāma. Again Hanumān, Lakṣmaṇa, and the other leaders in Rāma's camp suspect duplicity, oppose him, and are quickly and easily overcome. When Bīrabāhu comes face to face with Rāma, praises pour forth from his lips and Rāma, disarmed in the face of such devotion, announces that he will abandon the war. Frustrated, Bīrabāhu declares that if Rāma will not fight him, he will kill everyone in Rāma's army. The perplexed Rāma then turns to Vibhīṣaṇa for advice and his adviser, quite aware of Bīrabāhu's real intentions, tells Rāma that this is demon trickery and urges Rāma to kill him; but when Rāma attempts to do so, he is immediately knocked unconscious by the demon. Bīrabāhu apologises, rushes to his prostrate body, and sits holding Rāma's hand until he recovers. When he revives, Rāma offers the demon a boon, but the boon that Bīrabāhu asks is that Rāma cut off his head, and this Rāma cannot grant. Rāma announces his retirement a second time and Bīrabāhu finds himself in the same quandary again. This time he is saved (so to speak) by the gods: afraid he will escape, the gods order Sarasvatī and Khaḷa[22] to possess him, and, as soon as this is done, *stutis* are replaced by insults, and Rāma, presuming he has been duped, kills Bīrabāhu with an arrow selected by Vibhīṣaṇa. Bīrabāhu is then transported to heaven in a celestial car.[23]

The pattern, then, is a common one. The devotee vows (falsely) to Rāvaṇa that he will slay Rāma and Lakṣmaṇa, offers battle, and easily defeats all opposition including Rāma himself. Touched by his devotion, Rāma declines combat, but is lured into it when the devotee either feigns hostility or is possessed by the gods. All the while Vibhiṣaṇa, who knows the true state of affairs, keeps Rāma in the dark and co-operates with the devotee.

In these vernacular tales the motif is taken to a logical extreme: since death at Rāma's hands confers immediate salvation, any means to achieve that goal, even deceiving Rāma himself, seems legitimate. Otherwise than in *dveṣa-bhakti*, a concept refined by generations of theologians, here we have the motif as seen from the other end of the social spectrum, i.e. as devised for and presented to a mass audience. Many of the elements in these scenes, as D. C. Sen notes,[24] border on the farcical; devotion seems almost parodied. It is suggestive that in the poems themselves the monkeys in Rāma's army are described as bursting into laughter when they see Taraṇisena decked out in the name of Rāma,[25] and their response is the same when Bīrabāhu suddenly switches from eulogy to invective.[26] Though it is difficult to gauge the intentions of the poets, it is clear that they were very far from being bhaktas of the level of Tulsīdās or Eknāth. They were professional singers who earned their livings by composing and performing narratives on popular themes. Śaṅkara Kabicandra, besides his *Rāmāyaṇa*, wrote a *Śiva Maṅgal*, a *Dharma Maṅgal*, and a version of the *Bhāgavatapurāṇa*. As a professional he was careful to include episodes which had audience appeal; he certainly felt that this was such an episode since he included no fewer than five different and relatively lengthy versions of it in his rather concise *Rāmāyaṇa*.

Śaṅkara and the other poets were part of a regional folk tradition which, once it had absorbed the Rāma theme, transformed it along popular lines. What is perhaps most striking here is Rāma's fallibility, a characteristic he shares with Dharma, Manasā, and other local deities. This is in absolute contrast to many other *Rāmāyaṇa* versions in other NIA languages where Rāma is the all-knowing, imperturbable avatār consciously acting out his *līlā*. Here, instead, he is the victim rather than the master of events, and easily manipulated by those around him: when a demon abruptly addresses a *stuti* to him, Rāma is immediately impressed and ready to quit the war; moments later, when the same demon begins taunting him, he is instantly enraged. Vibhīṣaṇa is, like the satellite gods advising Dharma and Manasā, far more perspicacious than his master. He is careful not to mention to the unknowing Rāma that Taraṇi is his son, he plays along with Bīrabāhu, and even selects the weapons with which Rāma slays his devotees. It is he who controls the situation. Rāma has to be tricked into killing his devotees, by the demons' play-acting, by the manœuvres of Vibhīṣaṇa and by the intervention of the minor gods. Rāma becomes less the end of devotion than the malleable instrument by which instant felicity can be obtained.

NOTES

1. *The Bengali Ramayanas*, Calcutta, 1920, p. 106.
2. Ibid., p. 103.
3. F. Hardy, *Viraha Bhakti: The Early History of Kṛṣṇa Devotion in South India*, Delhi, 1983, p. 85.
4. W. D. O'Flaherty, *The Origins of Evil in Hindu Mythology*, Berkeley, Calif., 1976, p. 308.
5. N. Sheth, *The Divinity of Krishna*, New Delhi, 1984, p. 147 ff.
6. O'Flaherty, op. cit.
7. Sheth, op. cit.

8. S. K. De, *Early History of the Vaisnava Faith and Movement in Bengal*, repr. Calcutta, 1961, p. 245.
9. R. Antoine, *Rāma and the Bards: Epic Memory in the Ramayana*, Calcutta, 1975, p. 100 ff.
10. Goressio's edn., 6. 41. 24–5.
11. Gītā Press edn., 6. 10. 57–8.
12. Cf. *The Adhyātma Ramayana*, trans. L. B. Nath, repr. New Delhi, 1979, p. 168 n.
13. A. K. Banerjee, ed., *The Ramayana in Eastern India*, Calcutta, 1983, p. 136 ff.
14. *Rāmāyaṇa*, ed. S. Mukhopādhyāẏa, Calcutta, 1981, p. 292 ff.
15. Serampore edn., 1802–3, vol. vi, p. 409.
16. Sen, op. cit., p. 99.
17. A. K. Bandyopādhyāẏa, *Bāṁlā sāhityer itibṛtti*, vol. iii, Calcutta, 1966, p. 1046.
18. S. Sen, *Bāṅgālā sāhityer itihās*, vol. ii, Calcutta, 1965, p. 407.
19. K. C. Sahoo, *Rama Sahitya: A Study of the Ramayana Tradition in Oriya*, Ph.D. thesis, Ranchi, 1965, p. 419.
20. Śaṅkara Kabicandra, *Biṣṇupurī Rāmāẏaṇa*, ed. Citrā Deb, Calcutta, BE 1386, p. 181 ff.
21. *Kṛttibāsi Rāmāẏaṇa*, ed. A. Bhaṭṭācārya, Calcutta, n.d., p. 369 ff.
22. *Khaḷa*, lit. 'wicked', is in Oriya Rāma literature a celestial being whom the gods employ as an instrument of possession.
23. Baḷarāmadāsa, *Ḍāṇḍi* (*Jagamohana*) *Rāmāyaṇa*, ed. Gobinda Ratha, Cuttack, 1913, vol. vi, p. 251 ff.
24. Op. cit., p. 103.
25. Ibid.
26. Baḷarāmadāsa, op. cit., p. 267.

Tulsīdās and Confucius

JIN DINGHAN

Tulsīdās (AD 1532–1623) was India's greatest religious reformer and poet during the Middle Ages. His epic *Rām-carit-mānas* has spread far and wide among Indian people over the centuries. The behaviour and activities of Rām and Sītā in *Rām-carit-mānas* are considered to be the highest model of ethics and morality. Rām's kingdom is a utopia for Indian people, and Rām is synonymous with God.

Confucius (551–479 BC) was the greatest ideologist, philosopher, and educator in ancient China. He was the founder of Confucianism and his *Analects* is the first classical work of Confucianism. His ideology was developed by Mencius (372–289 BC) and others, and became a complete system of ethics and education. During the following two millennia, it was popularized by the emperors of many dynasties and became the ruling ideology of the feudal society. For this reason, it has had a tremendous influence on Chinese society.

India and China are two ancient countries with large populations. They both have long histories and vibrant cultures. A comparison of Tulsīdās and Confucius therefore possesses great significance for studies of Indian culture and Chinese culture, and also for studies of world cultures.

World outlook

Tulsīdās believed in God. He held that the supreme God is Brahma, Brahma is Viṣṇu, and Rām is the incarnation of Viṣṇu. He said:

एक अनीह अरूप अनामा । अज सच्चिदानन्द परधामा ।।
ब्यापक बिस्वरूप भगवान ।दृ तेहि धरि देह चरित कृत नाना ।।

(*Rām-carit-mānas, Bāl-kāṇḍ*)

There is only one God, who is free from desire, form, name, and birth. He is true, happy, and has profound knowledge. He lives in Heaven, but is omnipresent in the world. He has many incarnations to guide and serve the people in all aspects of life.

He also said:

बंदउं राम नाम रघुबर को । हेतु कृसानु भानु हिमकर को ।।
बिधि हरिहरमय बेद प्रान सो । अगुन अनूपम गुन निधान सो ।। (ibid.)

I salute the name of Rām, who is the source of fire, sun, and moon. He is Brahma, Viṣṇu, and Śiva – three in one. He is the life of the Veda. He is incomparable. He is either without qualities or a treasure-house of good qualities.

Confucius also accepted the existence of destiny. He said:

bù zhī mìng, wú yǐ wéi jūn zǐ yě. (*Analects*, 20)

He who does not understand the will of Heaven cannot be regarded as a gentleman.

But he doubted the existence of God or spirits:

zǐ bù yǔ guài, lì, luàn, shén (ibid., 7)

He never talked of prodigies, feats of strength, disorders, or spirits.

wèi zhī shēng, yān zhī sǐ? (ibid., 11)

Until you know about the living, how are you to know about the dead?

wèi néng shì rén, yān néng shì guěi? (ibid., 11)

Until you have learnt to serve men, how can you serve spirits?

jìng guěi shén ér yuǎn zhī. (ibid., 6)

Have respect for the spirits, but keep them at a distance.

The differences between these two ideas of God and spirits reflect the differences between the national characters of the Indian and Chinese peoples. At this level Indian people can be said to favour imagination, while the Chinese people prefer practice. This is the reason why many religions were founded in India, Hinduism, Buddhism, Jainism, and Sikhism prominent among them. But in China, only Taoism has been founded, and Taoism has been deeply influenced by Buddhism in the history of its development. These ideas also shaped the different attitudes of Indians and Chinese toward religion. In India, people often regard religion as the totality of all things (*tvam eva sarvam mama devadevā*). But in China, people regard religion only as a kind of belief. A person can believe this religion or that religion, or even no religion. In this field, he or she is free.

Ethics and morality

Tulsīdās has established a systematic scheme of ethics and morality. Rām is a model son, brother, husband, and king. Sītā is a model wife, daughter-in-law, and queen. Daśrath is a model father and Kauśalyā is a model mother. Bharat and Lakṣmaṇ are model brothers ... All the persons Tulsīdās portrayed are model types.

On the other hand, Tulsīdās denounced the violation of ethics and morality. He said:

सोचिअ बिप्र जो बेद बिहीना । तजि निज धरमु बिषय लयलीना ।।
सोचिअ नृपति जो नीति न जाना । जेहि न प्रजा प्रिय प्रान समाना ।।

(*Rām-carit-mānas, Ayodhyā-kāṇḍ*)

We must denounce that brāhmaṇ who doesn't know the Veda and wallows in sensual pleasures. We must denounce that king who neither knows politics, nor loves the people as his own life.

सोचिअ बयस कृपन धनवानू । जो न अतिथि सिव भगति सुजानू ।।
सोचिअ सूद्र बिप्र अवमानी । मखरु मानप्रिय ग्यान गुमानी ।।

(ibid.)

We must denounce that vaiśya who is very miserly. He neither entertains guests, nor piously worships Śiva, although he is very rich. We must denounce that śūdra who insults brāhmaṇs. He is fond of the limelight and shows off his knowledge.

सोचिअ पुनि पति बंचक नारी । कुटिल कलहप्रिय इच्छाचारी ।।

(ibid.)

We must denounce that woman who betrays her husband. She is a wilful shrew.

सब बिधि सोचिअ परपकारी । निज तनु पोषक निरदय भारी ।।
सोचनीय सबहीं बिधि सोई । जो न छांड़ि छल हरि जन होई ।।

(ibid.)

We must denounce that person who harms others and only pays attention to his own body. He is very cruel, he does not give up cheating and swindling, and he is not devoted to God.

Thus Tulsīdās made a systematic exposition of ethics and morality.

The kernel of Confucius' system of ethics and morality is 'Ren'. Confucius said:

dì zǐ rù zé xiào, chū zě dì, jǐn ér xìn, fàn ài zhòng, ér qīn rén. (*Analects*, 1)

A young man's duty is to behave well to his parents at home and to his elders abroad, to be cautious in giving promises and punctual in keeping them, to have kindly feelings towards everyone, but seek the intimacy of Ren.

fú rén zhě, jǐ yù lì ér lì rén, jǐ yù dá ér dá rén. (ibid., 6)

As for Ren, you yourself desire rank and standing; then help others to get rank and standing. You want to turn your own merits to account; then help others to turn theirs to account.

jǐ suǒ bù yù, wù shī yú rén. (ibid., 12)

Do not do to others what you would not like yourself.

Fán Chí wèn rén, Zǐ yuē: 'ài rén.' (ibid., 12)

When his disciple Fan Chi asked about the Ren, he answered: 'He loves men'.

From these, we know that the basis of Ren is love. The thought of Ren was developed into a perfect system of ethics and morality by Confucius' disciples. For more than 2,000 years, this ideology has dominated the Chinese people. It has influenced Chinese society so deeply that no one can understand Chinese society without knowing Ren.

Comparing Confucius' Ren with Tulsīdās' ideology, we will find that they share a common foundation.

In *Rām-carit-mānas*, Rām is considered as *kṛpāsindhu* (ocean of benevolence) and *kṛpānidhi* (treasure of benevolence). He is benevolent to the people and the people are devoted to him. And the basis of benevolence and devotion is also 'love'.

From this, we know that these two ideologies are based on love. This is the reason why the ideology of *Rām-carit-mānas* is not unfamiliar to the Chinese people.

Confucius advocated trustworthiness. His wishes are:

lǎo zhě ān zhī, péng yǒu xìn zhī, shào zhě huái zhī. (*Analects*, 5)

In dealing with the aged, to be of comfort to them; in dealing with friends, to be of good faith with them; in dealing with the young, to cherish them.

He also said:

rén ér wú xìn, bù zhī qí kě yě, dà chē wú ní, xiǎo chē wú yuè, qí hé yǐ xíng zhī zāi! (ibid., 2)

I do not see what use a man can be put to whose word cannot be trusted. How can a wagon be made to go if it has no yoke-bar, or a carriage if it has no collar-bar!

Zǐ Gòng wèn zhèng. Zǐ yuē: 'zú shí, zú bīng, mín xìn zhī yǐ'. Zǐ Gòng yuē: 'bì bù dé yǐ ér qù, yú sī sān zhě hé xīan?' yuē: 'qù bīng.' Zǐ Gòng yuē: 'bì bù dé yǐ ér qù, yú sī èr zhě hé xīan?' yuē: 'qù shí. zì gǔ jīe yǒu sǐ, mǐn wú xìn bù lì.' (ibid., 12)

When his Disciple Zi Gong asked about government, he said: 'sufficient food, sufficient weapons, and the confidence of the common people'. Then Zi Gong asked: 'Suppose you had no choice but to dispense with one of these three, which would you forgo?' He said: 'weapons'. Then, Zi Gong asked: 'Suppose you were forced to dispense with one of the two that were left, which would you forgo?' He said: 'Food. For from ancient times, death has been the lot of all men; but a people that no longer trusts its rulers is lost indeed.'

The supreme expression of trust is in the keeping of one's pledge. Tulsīdās considered this to be the highest morality, in accordance with the tradition of Hinduism. He expressed this idea by means of King Daśrath's words:

रघुकुल रीति सदा चलि आई । प्रान जाहुं बरु बचनु न जाई ।।

(*Rām-carit-mānas, Ayodhyā-kāṇḍ*)

In our Raghu Family, the custom is to never break a promise, even if we must give up our life.

नहिं असत्य सम पातक पुंजा । गिरि सम होहिं कि कोटिक गुंजा ।।
सत्यमूल सब सुकृत सुहाये । बेद पुरान बिदित मनु गाये ।।

(ibid.)

Many other sins considered together are not equal to the one sin of breaking one's promise. Could ten million seeds of the Ghuṅghucī creeper be equal to a mountain? Being true to one's word is the origin of all good activities. This is a very famous view in the Veda and Purāṇas, and is also explained by Manu.

तनु तिय तनय धाम धनु धरनी । सत्यसंध कहं तृन सम बरनी ।।

(ibid.)

A man who keeps his word regards his body, wife, son, home, property, or land as no more than some blades of grass.

King Daśrath so loves Rām that he cannot expel Rām to the forest. But he must keep his word. He has an intense ideological struggle. Finally, he makes the painful choice. Thus, by keeping his word, he becomes a model of proper behaviour. I think that in the view of Confucius also this choice would be worthy of praise.

Tulsīdās and Confucius had the same attitude toward women. Tulsīdās said:

बिधिहु न नारि हृदय गति जानी । सकल कपट अघ अवगुन खानी ।।

(ibid.)

Even God could not learn the way of a woman's heart. A woman's heart is a mine of tricks, sins and shortcomings.

While Confucius said:

wéi nǚ zǐ yǔ xiǎo rén wéi nán yǎng yě, jìn zhī zé bù xùn, yuǎn zhī zé yuàn. (*Analects*, 17)

Women and people of low birth are very hard to deal with. If you are friendly with them they get out of hand, and if you keep your distance they resent it.

This is a feudal ideology, and has a tremendous influence on both Indian and Chinese society.

Educational ideology

Tulsīdās and Confucius both stress the importance of educating the young. Tulsīdās said:

सोचिअ बटु निज ब्रतु परिहरई । जो नहिं गुर आयसु अनुसरई ।।

(*Rām-carit-mānas, Ayodhyā-kāṇḍ*)

We must denounce the brahmacārī who does not keep celibate and does not act in accordance with his teacher's dictates.

In his opinion, every young man must have education. Even Rām could not be an exception.

For young men, Confucius said:

yǒu jiào wú lèi. (*Analects*, 15)

There is a difference in instruction, but none in kind.

xìng xiāng jìn yě, xí xiāng yuǎn yě. (ibid., 17)

By nature, near together; by practice, far apart.

cháng dú lì, lǐ qū ér guò tíng. yuē: 'xué shī hū?' duì yuē: 'wèi yě.' 'bù xué shī wú yǐ yán.' lǐ tuì ér xué shī. tā rì yòu dú lì, lǐ qū ér guò tíng. yuē: 'xué lǐ hū?' duì yuē: 'wèi yě.' 'bù xué lǐ, wú yǐ lì.' lǐ tuì ér xué lǐ. (ibid., 16)

Once when Confucius was standing alone and his son was hurrying past him across the courtyard, he said: 'Have you studied the Songs?' His son replied: 'No.' He said. 'If you do not study the Songs, you will find yourself at a loss in conversation.' So his son retired and studied the Songs. Another day he was again standing alone, and his son hurried across the courtyard, he said: 'Have you studied the Rituals?' His son replied: 'No.' He said: 'If you do not study the Rituals, you will find yourself at a loss how to take your stand.' Then his son retired and studied the Rituals.

Both Tulsīdās and Confucius advocated education, rather than punishment. Confucius said:

dào zhī yǐ zhèng, qí zhī yǐ xǐng, mín miǎn ér wú chǐ. dào zhī yǐ dé, qí zhī yǐ lǐ, yǒu chǐ qiě gé. (ibid., 2)

Govern the people by regulations, keep order among them by chastisement, and they will flee from you, and lose all self-respect. Govern them by moral force, keep order among them by ritual and they will keep their self-respect and come to you of their own accord.

While Tulsīdās' ideal is:

दण्ड जतिन्ह कर भेद जहं नर्त्तक नृत्य समाज ।।

(*Rām-carit-mānas, Uttar-kāṇḍ*)

(In Rām's kingdom) there is no punishment but sticks in ascetics' hands; there is no discrimination but between different kinds of dance.

A society free from punishment is, indeed, a very good ideal. The problem is how to realize it.

Tulsīdās and Confucius both divided man's life into several stages, the first stage being for education.

Tulsīdās divided life into four stages in accordance with Hindu tradition. The first stage (*āśram*) is that of *brahmacarya*, in which young men are unmarried and receiving education.

Confucius offered his own experiences as an example of six stages of life. He said:

wú shí yǒu wǔ ér zhì yú xué, sān shí ér lì, sì shí ér bù huò, wǔ shí ér zhī tiān mìng, liù shí ér ěr shùn, qī shí ér cóng xīn suǒ yù, bù yú jǔ. (*Analects*, 2)

At fifteen, I set my heart upon learning. At thirty, I had planted my feet firm upon the ground. At forty, I no longer suffered from perplexities. At fifty, I knew what the biddings of Heaven were. At sixty, I heard them with docile ear. At seventy, I could follow the dictates of my own heart; for what I desired no longer overstepped the boundaries of right.

Here also, the first stage is for education.

Tulsīdās and Confucius both stressed the importance of having good friends and associates. Tulsīdās said:

प्रथम भगति संतन्ह कर संगा । दूसरि रति मम कथा प्रसंगा । ।

(*Rām-carit-mānas, Āraṇya-kāṇḍ*)

The first devotion is in keeping company with ascetics, and the second devotion is in love of the subject of my story.

He also said:

हानि कुसंग सुसंगति लाहू । लोकहु बेद बिदित सब काहू । ।

(ibid., *Bāl-kāṇḍ*)

Intercourse with bad friends is harmful, while with good friends it is beneficial. Both cases happen very often, and are explained in the Veda. All the people know this.

गगन छढ़ै रज पवन प्रसंगा । कीचहि मिलै नीच जल संगा । ।
साधु असाधु सदन सुक सारी । सुमिरहिं रामु देहिं गनि गारी । ।

(ibid.)

In company with wind, the dust can fly in the sky; while in company with water below, it will become dirty mud. The parrot and myna can speak Rām's name in a holy man's home, but they can only shout abuse when fed in a scoundrel's home.

Confucius said:

lè duō xián yǒu, yì yǐ. (*Analects*, 16)

The pleasure of having many wise friends is profitable.

wù yǒu bù rú jǐ zhě. (ibid., 1)

Refuse the friendship of all who are not like you.

yì zhě sān yǒu, sǔn zhě sān yǒu. yǒu zhí, yǒu liàng, yǒu duō wén, yì yǐ. yǒu biàn pì, yǒu shàn róu, yǒu biàn nìng, sǔn yǐ. (ibid., 16)

There are three sorts of friends that are profitable and three sorts that are harmful. Friendship with the upright, with the true-unto-death, and with those who have heard much is profitable. Friendship with the obsequious, with those who are good at accommodating their principles, and with those who are clever at talk is harmful.

Tulsīdās is also similar to Confucius in his view on the proper method of learning. He stressed the importance of reading and listening to *Rām-carit-mānas* regularly, so as to get *mokṣa*, release.

Confucius said:

wēn gù ér zhī xīn, kě yǐ wéi shī yǐ. (ibid., 2)

He who by reanimating the old can gain knowledge of the new is fit to be a teacher.

xué ér shí xí zhī, bù yì yuè hū? (ibid., 1)

To learn and at due times to repeat what one has learnt: is that not after all a pleasure?

Whom shall we learn from? On this question, Tulsīdās and Confucius have different ideas. Tulsīdās stressed the importance of learning from brāhmaṇs, and a guru. He said:

वंदे बोधमयं नित्यं गुरुं शंकररूपिणं ।
यमाश्रितो हि वक्रोपि चंद्रः सर्वत्र वंद्यते ।।

(*Rām-carit-mānas, Bāl-kāṇḍ*)

I salute the Guru, who has profound knowledge, who is eternal, who is an appearance of Śaṅkara, who makes the lowly respected.

बंदउं गुरु पदकंज कृपासिंधु नररूपहरि ।
महा मोह तम पुंज जासु बचन रविकर निकर ।।

(ibid.)

Salute to the Guru's lotus-like feet, which are oceans of benevolence, which are Hari (God) in human form, which are sunshine in the darkness of ignorance.

बंदउं प्रथम महीसुर चरना । मोह जनित संसय् सब हरना ।।

(ibid.)

Firstly, I salute brāhmaṇs, gods on earth, who dispel the doubts that emerge from ignorance.

But Confucius stressed learning from everyone who can teach. He said:

mǐn ér hào xué, bù chǐ xià wèn, shì yǐ wèi zhī wén yě. (*Analects*, 5)

He was diligent and so fond of learning that he was not ashamed to pick up knowledge even from his inferiors.

sān rén xíng, bì yǒu wǒ shī yān, zé qí shàn zhě ér cóng zhī, qí bù shàn zhě ér gǎi zhī. (ibid., 7)

Even when walking in a party of no more than three, I can always be certain of learning from those I am with. There will be good qualities that I can select for imitation and bad ones that will teach me what requires correction in myself.

Fán Chí qǐng xué jià, zǐ yuē: 'wú bù rú lǎo nóng.' qǐng xué wéi pǔ, yuē: 'wú bù rú lǎo pǔ.' (ibid., 13)

When Fan Chi [his disciple] asked him to teach him farming, he said: 'You had much better consult some old farmer.' And when Fan Chi asked him to teach him gardening, he said: 'You had better go to some old vegetable-gardener.'

These two ideas reflect the different traditions in Indian culture and Chinese culture. In the former, a brāhmaṇ can be regarded as a deputy of God, thus having a very high position; whereas in China, the order of positions is 'God, Emperor, parents, and teacher.' Perhaps this is why the teacher's position is not so high in China.

Ideal society

Both Confucius and Tulsīdās put forward their idea of society. They both described the political system of ancient times as a model on which to reform the modern systems. Confucius regarded four ancient kings – Yu, Tang, Wen, and Wu – as models, while Tulsīdās proposed Rām as a model king.

Confucius described a Society of Great Harmony. He said:

dà dào zhī xíng yě, tiān xià wéi gōng, xuǎn xián yǔ néng, jiǎng xìn xiū mù, gù rén bù dú qīn qí qīn, bù dú zǐ qí zǐ, shǐ lǎo yǒu suǒ zhōng, zhuàng yǒu suǒ yòng, yòu yǒu suǒ zhǎng, guān guǎ gū dú fèi jí zhě jiē yǒu suǒ yǎng, nán yǒu fèn, nǚ yǒu guī, huò wù qí qì yú dì yě, bù bì cáng yú jǐ, lì wù qí bù chū yú shēn yě, bù bì wèi jǐ. shì gù bì ér bù xīng, dào qiè luàn zéi ér bù zuò, gù wài hù ér bù bì, shì wèi dà tóng. (*Book of Rites, Li Yun*, 1)

The greatest doctrine is that of absence of selfishness in the world. Virtuous and able persons are appointed as officers. People trust each other and live in harmony, loving one another's parents and children as their own. The old men die a natural death. The adults have their own jobs. The children grow smoothly. Widowers, widows, orphans, the childless and the handicapped can be cared for. The men are dutiful. The women are married. People like to give their own possessions to others, instead of wasting them. They use their physical strength to serve others without stinting. As a result, there are no cheaters or swindlers, no thieves or robbers. People shut their doors without bolting them at night. This is called the Society of Great Harmony.[1]

Tulsīdās depicted his ideal society comprehensively, saying:

दैहिक दैबिक भौतिक तापा । राम राज नहिं काहुहि व्यापा ।।
सब नर करहिं परसपर प्रीति । चलहिं स्वधर्म निरत श्रुति नीती ।।

चारिउ चरन धर्म जग माहीं । पूरि रहा सपनेहु अघ नाहीं ।।
राम भगति रत नर अरु नारी । सकल परम गति के अधिकारी ।।

अल्प मृत्यु नहिं कवनिउ पीरा । सब सुंदर सब बिरुज सरीरा ।।
नहिं दरिद्र कोउ दुखी न दीना । नहिं कोउ अबुध न लच्छन हीना ।।

सब निर्दंभ धर्मरत पुनी । नर अरु नारी चतुर सब गुनी ।।
सब गुनग्य पंडित सब ग्यानी । सब कृतग्य नहिं कपट सयानी...

(*Rām-carit-mānas, Uttar-kāṇḍ*)

In Rām's kingdom, there are no physical, mental or material sorrows. All the people love one another. They observe the regulations of Veda and Dharma.

The world is full of the four activities of religion. No sins can be found, even in dreams. Men and women all devote themselves to the worship of Rām. Everyone has the right to attain to *mokṣa*.

No one dies young. There is no grief. All persons are beautiful and healthy. There is neither pain nor poverty, neither fools nor ill luck.

There is no cheating. People are kind and devoted to religion. All the men and women are clever and noble. They acknowledge all good qualities. They respect paṇḍits and respond to kindness with their own good deeds. There is no deceit.

Tulsīdās' ideal and Confucius' ideal have a common ground – noble mental civilization and lofty morality. Confucius' Society of Great Harmony and Doctrine of No Selfishness have influenced the Chinese people far and wide during the last 2,000 years. Even in the early part of this century the greatest Chinese revolutionary, Dr Sun Yat-sen, took this ideal as his own purpose. And as for Tulsīdās, we know that his Rāmrāj has been the Indian people's ideal society during the last several centuries.

From the above comparison we learn that Tulsīdās and Confucius are similar in many respects. This is why the Chinese people have high regard for Tulsīdās, and feel that the verses of *Rām-carit-mānas* touch their hearts.

NOTE

1. It is considered that these words were not uttered by Confucius himself, but by his disciples. But this thought became the ideal of Confucianism, and has had great influence on Chinese society.

Modernisation in the nineteenth and twentieth centuries

Hariścandra of Banaras and the reassessment of Vaiṣṇava bhakti in the late nineteenth century

VASUDHA DALMIA-LÜDERITZ

I

Hariścandra of Banaras (1850–85) was known to his countrymen as 'Bhāratendu', the Moon of India. In a short life span of thirty-five years he created a body of literature which, while reconfirming the continuity of a major area of tradition – Vaiṣṇava bhakti – found also a new language of legitimisation for this tradition. It became possible thereby to establish links with the body of knowledge about India which was being generated by European orientalists, who in their turn were necessarily linked with the European political presence in India.

The first part of this paper reviews the cultural and political configurations in nineteenth-century north India. It is from this perspective that the significance of Hariścandra's work is surveyed. In the second part I discuss the nature of the authority Hariścandra inherited and embodied, the social formations in Banaras and their interest in invoking tradition. In the third section, finally, there is an analysis of Hariścandra's literary works, and their relationship to the tradition of Vaiṣṇava bhakti and the means of its perpetuation; in short, of how in his time Hariścandra sought to mediate between tradition and change.

Apart from coming to terms with the European orientalists' concern with the ancient past, traditional religious discourse had primarily to contend with the challenge posed by Christianity. The missionary denigration of Hinduism was at its most vociferous in the first half of the nineteenth century.[1] Missionary tracts began often with what seemed to be a genuine attempt to argue the merits of Christianity in an open-minded comparison with the Indian religions, but the conclusions reached were manifestly foregone, and the attempt to establish common ground for discussion a ruse for finding within native discourse concepts and terminology which could be used, in fact, to explicate the tenets of Christianity to the unwary. The most notorious attempt from the Hindu viewpoint had been made by James Ballantyne, Professor of Moral Philosophy and Principal of the Government College at Banaras in *Christianity contrasted with Hindu Philosophy: An Essay in Five Books, Sanskrit and English. With Practical Suggestions Tendered to the*

Missionary among the Hindus (1859). The book was dedicated to the Lieutenant-Governor of the North-Western Provinces.[2] It concluded with a challenge which summarised the contemporary theological convictions:

> The conclusion reached by Natural Theology compels the thinking mind to ask the question, 'Has the God of nature anywhere, except in nature, revealed himself to man?' The answer to this question we offer to the Hindu in our Scriptures. But his compatriots, he replies, have scriptures of their own. True, we rejoin; but scriptures resting their claims only on the futile ground of self-assertion. Of our own, we tender him the evidences, historical and internal.[3]

And if the Hindus noted the premisses of the challenge – the need to provide internal, historical evidence – but continued to be wary, there were other indirect modes of operation, with effects that were more enduring.

The missionaries were also pioneers in education. M. A. Sherring, of the London Missionary Society, long stationed in Banaras, a sympathetic observer of the Indian scene well acquainted with Hariścandra, with numerous books to his credit, stated quite clearly: 'Let it be well understood, that education de-hinduizes the Hindu, breaks down idolatry, and inspires him with a distaste for it, and a latent desire to be free from it.'[4] Two great movements in response to the growing need to redefine contemporary tradition within this new political, cultural, and social context, the Brāhma Samāj and the Ārya Samāj, made scant progress in the North-Western Provinces, especially in the eastern region. Banaras had ancient claims to respect as a centre of traditional learning and stronghold of orthodoxy, claims which had received considerable support and reinforcement from the Marathas in the eighteenth century.[5] The Brāhma Samāj, heretical in its outright rejection of ritual, in its universalism and eclecticism, and in its 'arid intellectualism'[6] was too closely connected with a Western life-style and Western outlook to be immediately comprehensible. For if Western education had become accessible, there was little to no private social contact with the British.[7] The Ārya Samāj, by tracing its source back to the Veda and disconnecting itself from later tradition, made a break too radical for most to follow with any degree of comfort, and its founder, Dayānand Sarasvatī, was twice humiliated in Banaras.[8]

And yet tradition also needed to reassert itself, to find a new voice, to reactivate what seemed in danger of becoming 'residual'. For 'at a deeper level the hegemonic sense of tradition is always the most active: a deliberately selective and connecting process which offers a historical and cultural ratification of a contemporary order. It is a very powerful process, since it is tied to many practical continuities – families, places, institutions, a language – which are directly experienced.'[9] This hegemonic sense of tradition, far from remaining inert, itself underwent change and reorganisation under colonial rule.[10]

Hariścandra of Banaras, in reconfirming Vaiṣṇava bhakti, both as a poet and as a leading figure in the cultural life of the city, could fulfil a task he was eminently suited to perform. It was a reconfirmation not as spectacular as the faith propagated by the Brāhma Samāj, nor as radical and aggressive as the Ārya Samāj. Though it also involved selection and shift of emphasis, it pleaded for continuity and a tradition which had known no break. And if Hariścandra could do this with an easy assurance from within the fold of the Vallabhans, it was no coincidence. For in his person he embodied continuities, reassembled to be sure, and always in some form linked with the ruling power, but all three continuities – family, institutions, and the place, Banaras – were powerful agents of authority. It is a short survey of these agents of authority and their interaction that I focus on next, before going on, in the final section, to a consideration of the means with which Hariścandra secured this cultural and historical ratification.

II

By the end of the eighteenth century, Banaras had established its position as one of the most important trading and banking centres in northern India.[11] Hariścandra belonged to the city's commercial aristocracy, the Naupaṭṭī Mahājans, bankers who rose to prominence in the troubled period before the collapse of the Awadh *nawābī* and the formal takeover of the province by the East India Company.[12] They had been instrumental in the installation of a Hindu king instead of the Muslim military commander Mir Rustam Ali, who had been appointed by the Nawab of Awadh and had served also as the revenue and administrative head of the region. The interests of the Naupaṭṭī Mahājans were closely linked, though not always identical, with those of the Raja and the Company. Hariścandra's family were relative newcomers on the scene. They had had connections with the Delhi Mughal court and had moved with the Mughal *Sūbedār* of the province to Bengal, first to Rajmahal and then to Murshidabad. They had had dealings with the East India Company and stakes in their fortunes, but after a disastrous collision with Robert Clive, Fatahcand, the son of the offender Amīncand and Hariścandra's great-grandfather, had moved to Banaras. Here he had married into a Naupaṭṭī Mahājan family and, as the only surviving heir of this family, had inherited the power, prestige, and status of the Naupaṭṭīs. If on the one hand the Naupaṭṭīs were arbitrators in disputes within the merchant classes, they also mediated between the British and the people of the city. Fatahcand had supported Governor-General Warren Hastings in the campaign to oust Raja Chait Singh of Banaras, one-time fledgling of the Company who had incurred the wrath of Hastings. Fatahcand further distinguished himself by co-operating with Jonathan Duncan, the British Resident – who in effect ruled the city – in administrative, revenue, and judicial matters. His son Harakhcand set forth the tradition of his ancestors. He was particularly remembered for the courtly splendour of his life-style. He maintained close relations with the Mahārājā and contributed greatly to the festive and ritual life of the city. Of his part in the establishment of the Gopāl Mandir, the great Vallabha temple of the city, more later. His son Gopālcand, the poet's father, had sheltered the British during the troubled months of 1857. In addition to their political and social activities, both Harakhcand and, more prominently, Gopālcand found the leisure to become bhāṣā poets of some repute.

Hariścandra himself was an honorary magistrate of the city until his voluntary resignation. He was on terms of easy friendship with the Mahārājā and it is said that he contributed greatly to the expansion of the Rāmlīlā of Rāmnagar by devising the dialogues of the Līlā. He took a leading role in the cultural life of the city, and there are accounts of the gatherings of poets and of the musical evenings which he organised.[13] He was not only in contact with the local British officials and orientalists, he also maintained relations with the Asiatic Society of Bengal in Calcutta, kept track of their publications, and knew and corresponded with the Society's secretary, Rājendralāl Mitra, a venerable scholar and ardent Vaiṣṇava. This in addition to the societies and the school he founded, and the three journals he edited.

Just as Rammohan Roy before him, Hariścandra in his turn made full use of the two modes of establishing communication and community: the association or society, and the Press. The Vaiṣṇava association which he founded, Tadīya Samāj (1873), seems to have been one of several of its kind – associations which sprang up spontaneously in response to the need to define a social–religious identity, only to subside just as suddenly into mainstream community life.

The city's Gopāl Mandir had been established by the rebel Raja Chait Singh in 1777. But it had first come into prominence through the services of the charismatic Girdharjī Mahārāj, who traced his genealogy to Yadunāth, the youngest son of Viṭṭhal. He was known in Banaras for his high learning and piety. On the strength of this high learning he had persuaded Dāujī Mahārāj of Nathdvara to part with a *svarūpa* of Śrīnāthjī, no easy task but carried out with great strength and tenacity of purpose. The image, Mukundrāyjī, though not one of the *satsvarūpa*, was reputed to have been one of the two additional images originally in the possession of Vallabhācārya himself. In 1827 Mukundrāyjī travelled with much pomp from Nathdvara to Banaras, in a great train of attendants and bhaktas, accompanied for protection on the way by a caprāsī provided kindly by the British Resident in Udaipur.

Near Banaras, on the outskirts of the city, Mukundrāyjī was received by Harakhcand (the poet's grandfather), who then not only saw to the immediate arrangements for the deity, but also contributed substantially to the funding and maintenance of the temple complex, which was ready two years later, in 1829. The details of the whole transaction are preserved in the Brajbhāṣā *Mukundrāyjī kī vārtā* (first published in book form in 1923),[14] with much information on matters of the devotional ritual, the elaborate attention paid to maintain aesthetic harmony in the celebration of divine love.

It was through the grace of Girdharjī Mahārāj that Harakhcand's only son Gopālcand was born. Gopālcand proved to be equally devoted; his *chāp*, pen-name, Girdhardās, bears testimony to this attachment. The images of all the other gods and goddesses were removed from the family shrine, and, according to the testimony of Hariścandra himself, from now on strict monotheism prevailed. Thus the connection of the family to the renewed establishment of the faith of Vallabha in the city of Śiva, which Hariścandra has duly commemorated in his verse: *Kāśī meṁ gokula kari dīnho*[15] and *Brindāvana ko anubhava kāśi pragati dikhāyo.*[16] Not only was the city transformed into the landscape of Braj, the spiritual experience of this landscape became accessible in Kāśī. The new merchants had connected themselves to the propagation of a faith which was undergoing reinvigoration in the city of Banaras.

What I have tried to demonstrate then is:

1. The social formations in Banaras. Hariścandra's family had become part of the Naupaṭṭī Mahājans as relative newcomers. The Mahārājās of Banaras had, within a short period, twice to adjust their lineage to maintain the political approval and support of the British. The temple derived its authority from the prestige of Nathdvara, yet in Banaras it could be considered freshly arrived. All three, Mahājan, Mahārājā, and Mandir, were interlinked and largely supported one anothers' religious and cultural activities.

2. The link with the British as imperial masters, and as financial, judicial, and revenue administrators was evident; even Mukundrāyjī had sought the protection of the British Resident in Udaipur. But there was also the necessity of establishing some kind of equivalence with the British in their capacity as generators of a new body of knowledge about the country. Hariścandra's contact with the Asiatic Society testified not only to his intellectual curiosity but was also exemplary of the need to take cognisance of this new seat of learning.

3. Hence the authority which emanated from the above social formations – all relatively newly established and therefore all the more interested in harking back to an older tradition and their modes of perception – as powerful agents in providing the sense of continuity as well as future perspective.

III

In this section I deal with three aspects of Hariścandra's explicitly Vaiṣṇava literature: the first, his establishing himself as a Vaiṣṇava poet in the drama *Candrāvalī* (1876), thereby making the Brajbhāṣā *rāslīlā* accessible in modern

Hindi; the second, his locating himself and other contemporary poets within the traditional hagiographical accounts of Vaiṣṇava bhaktas in the long poem *Uttarārdha-bhaktamāl* (1876), which also encompasses Vaiṣṇava *sampradāyas* other than his own; and finally his attempt to locate Vaiṣṇavism in history as well as in the contemporary social–political scene, in the essay 'Vaiṣṇavata aur bhāratvarṣ' (1884), here incorporating the terminology and, to some extent, the approach of Western scholars.[17]

Candrāvalī, along with Lalitā, has a place of some importance in the Vallabha pantheon; in Nathdvara her birthday is celebrated two days before Rādhā's, on *bhādra śukla ṣaṣṭhamī*.[18] The play is a celebration of the traditional *sakhya bhāva*: it is with her love for Kṛṣṇa that Hariścandra identifies himself as a bhakta. Candrāvalī in the play signs her love-letter by making the sign of the sickle moon, a signature Hariścandra was known to use himself.[19] In fact the play constantly evokes the androgynous nature of the *sakhya bhāva*, making possible the interchangeability of gender, since both seem to be inherent in either lover. Candrāvalī identifies herself as Kṛṣṇa, when in her lovelorn state she is asked who she is. Kṛṣṇa appears as a yogini, beautiful even in disguise and radiating such a profound resemblance to Kṛṣṇa that Candrāvalī is instantly struck by the possibility that the yogini is in fact Kṛṣṇa. And, in the final act, Kṛṣṇa can maintain that whereas actually she is within him, as he is within her, *viraha*, the pain of separation, is also *līlā*, since the bhaktas seem to love *viraha* more than they love him.

The body of the play, consisting of four short *aṅkas*, or acts, in Hindi prose interspersed with Brajbhāṣā verse, is enframed within the conventions of classical Sanskrit drama. The play begins with a *prastāvanā*, a prologue, which serves primarily to introduce the playwright. Asked by the *pāripārśvika*, assistant manager, why the play of such a raw beginner has been chosen for performance, the *sūtradhāra* can explain:

परम प्रेमनिधि रसिक बर, अति आदर गुन खान ।
जग जन रंजन आशु कवि, को हरिचंद समान ।।

(p. 440)

Abode of love, best of all the *rasikas*, a mine of virtue worthy of the highest respect, who in all the world can equal Hariścandra as spontaneous poet, when it comes to delighting people?

The two vacate the stage to make way for Śukadeva. The *viṣkambhaka*, introductory scene, consists of a dialogue between Śukadeva and Nārada, the two heavenly bhaktas, who yet view the love of the *gopīs* as more elevated than theirs. Of these *gopīs*, Candrāvalī has attained the most advanced state of love. Although for reasons of love Rādhā has become two, it is she who prevents the union of the two lovers. The two bhaktas, caught in the remembrance of Braj, unable to bear the pain of separation, need only hear the sound of the flute to rush away to witness the *līlā*. By using these introductory devices, the play is effectively set within a context whereby Candrāvalī's love is not to be mistaken for earthly passion, but to be seen rather as the most elevated form of bhakti.

The whole range of emotions possible in the state of separation is depicted in the body of the play. In the second *aṅka*, Candrāvalī's long soliloquy is interrupted by the Devī of the forest, and by Sandhyā and Varṣā, personifications of evening and rain respectively, who tease and provoke her out of her wits. Gay, mischievous, and mournful, the scene rushes through a whole variety of moods: Candrāvalī runs to trees to ask them of Kṛṣṇa, mistakes the moon for the sun, night for day, herself for Kṛṣṇa, and runs finally into the dark of the forest to falter and lose her way. She despairs and faints, to be rescued by the three who have after all followed her. Hariścandra's lively use of Khaṛībolī, teasing, provocative, wild, melancholy, and tragic by turns, makes accessible the ten well-known stages of *viraha*, with the exception of the last, *maraṇa*, death, as being inappropriate and inauspicious.[20] It is Candrāvalī then who speaks the *bharatavākya*, the closing aphorism of the play:

यह रत्नदीप हरिप्रेम को सदा प्रकाशित रहे ।।

(p. 460)

May the jewel-lamp of the love of Hari keep the world lighted for ever.

This was a successful incorporation into the literary canon, which Hariścandra was in the process of establishing, of the traditional *rāsalīlā*, which in its turn was fast acquiring the status of a 'folk' form.[21] The plot of the play corresponds to the typical *nikuñjalīlā*, the largest class of *līlās*.[22] In creating drama in modern Hindi, Hariścandra then appropriates two models, the *rāsalīlā* and Sanskrit drama: and the latter, in providing the initiatory and other structural conventions, raises the whole as it were to a 'classical' status. He is then free, at appropriate moments, to introduce 'folk' lyric, as when Kṛṣṇa disguised as a yogini sings a *lāvaṇī*:

सांची जोगिन पिय बिना बियोगिन नारी ।।

(p. 457)

Only in a woman pining without her beloved, is a true yogini found.

Hariścandra is indulging in something more than a merely repetitive exercise in piety. He ensures continuity in that he innovates, not only formally, but most of all in the use of a language which was only then beginning to achieve literary flexibility. If earlier critics tended to magnify the qualities of the play,[23] a later more puritanical age reacted with some discomfort and made efforts to marginalise it, since the play ill befitted the image of a poet who had himself been canonised as the father of modern secular Hindi literature.[24] Yet it had been Hariścandra's effort to perpetuate Kṛṣṇa bhakti, and reacting either celebratively or dismissively clearly implies a failure to take into account that it is *this* bhakti, emotionally experienced, rooted in the Vallabha tradition, that Hariścandra refers to in his essayistic work, and not an abstract internalised devotion, puritanically cleansed of its erotic associations.[25]

The *Uttarārdha-bhaktamāl*, written in the same year, 1876, and published in instalments in Hariścandra's journal *Hariścandracandrikā*, begins with his own religious experience, his own sense of the urgency of his calling as a *bhakta-kavi*, and his own biography seen as hagiography, before going on to the lives of traditional Vaiṣṇava bhaktas.

Even though the poet was an utter rascal, not worthy of compassion and forgiveness, Kṛṣṇa had taken pity on him. He had appeared to the Kṣatrāṇī in a dream – a reference to his companion Mādhavī, one-time Rājpūt turned Muslim in the courtesan profession – and it was he who had told her that she should view the poet as a Sant, a bhakta.[26]

It is with this personal prologue that Hariścandra proceeds to enumerate the bhaktas of the Vaiṣṇava tradition, commencing with the *parama guru*, Śiva, Nārada, Vyāsa, Viṣṇuswāmī, Gopīnātha, the seven gurus up to Bilvamaṅgala and finally Vallabha, his *vaṃśa*, his followers, and then all the devotees, *premījan*, who follow the ways of Hari: a catalogue having a certain open-endedness. The poem is to be understood as the posterior half of the seventeenth-century *Bhaktamāl*, since it also incorporates accounts of later poets.

The poet includes a short history of his own family, going back to the Mughal times: his grandfather Harakhcand, who had introduced *sevā* in the family, his father, Gopālcand, who had gone yet further and removed all the other images from the house, finally Hariścandra, who composed these verses by the grace of Vallabha.

He refers also to the four great Vaiṣṇava *sampradāyas*, to focus then upon Vallabha and his descendants Viṭṭhalnāth and his seven *svarūpas*; further upon Harirāyjī, who had celebrated the great feast of Annakūṭa, and Ācārya Girdhar, by whose grace Kāśī was honoured by the presence of Mukundrāyjī; and finally upon Girdharjī's daughter Śyāmābeṭījī, the present incumbent of this, the sixth pīṭha of Śrināthjī.

The eight *sakhās*, the eight poets of the *aṣṭachāp*, are then celebrated, after which there is a *chappay* each for the rest of the eighty-four bhaktas of the *Caurāsī vaiṣṇavan kī vārtā*. This is the most substantial portion of the poem; it forms the core of the Vaiṣṇava tradition as depicted here, making thereby key incidents in the lives of these bhaktas accessible to contemporary readers. Following these, Hariścandra incorporates many of the bhaktas of the subsequent *Do sau bāvan vaiṣṇavan kī vārtā*; some are just listed as names, without further details of their lives as bhaktas.

He goes beyond these, however, gathering up the many strands of bhakti and including bhaktas from different regions of the subcontinent – from

Bengal, Panjab, the south, Muslim bhaktas, Raskhān, Kabīr, culminating in the famous line:

इन मुसलमान हरिजनन पै कोटिन हिन्दुन वारियै ।।

(p. 80)

sacrifice crores of Hindus for these Muslim men of Hari.

Somewhere, wedged in between the bhaktas from Lucknow and Panjab, a place is also reserved for the poet's father as well as for Hariścandra himself:

नित श्याम-सखी सम नेह, नव श्याम-सखी हरि सुजस कवि ।।

(p. 81)

the renowned poet Hariścandra, who loves as the sakhī of Śyāma, as the ninth or the new friend of Śyāma.

Thus the extension of the *aṣṭachāp* by a ninth poet, by no means perfect, filled with doubt, devoted to women, arrogant, but a devoted bhakta all the same, seeking the protection of Vallabha and Kṛṣṇa.

With this poem, then, Hariścandra locates himself within the lineage of Vaiṣṇava poets as a *navasakhā*, and spreads the net of bhaktas over time and space, subsuming thereby a number of traditions within the fold of Vaiṣṇava bhakti.

By 1884, when he came to write the essay *Vaiṣṇavatā aur bhāratvarṣ*, Hariścandra had evolved a theology of Vaiṣṇavism which, while forming the core of a Hinduism with national dimensions, reached out at the same time to establish equations with the world religions, Christianity and Islam. In order to achieve these ends effectively, Vaiṣṇavism needed both to locate itself historically, and to clarify its claims to genuine monotheism. All along, Hariścandra had been aware of the need to rest on historical foundations.[27] His friend the Revd M. A. Sherring had – as many others before and after him – deplored the lack of historical sense among the Hindus, a people, he allowed, otherwise endowed with the capacity to think most intricately and even precisely. Their ancient records were so interwoven with legend and fantasy

that the finest microscopic intellects of Europe, after patient and long-continued examination, have been well nigh baffled in the attempt to discover what is fiction and what is fact.[28]

Thus Sherring in the introduction to his well-known book on Banaras. Hariścandra made selective use of the body of historical knowledge which carried with it the claim to objectivity. Max Mueller had already established the 'instinctive monotheism of the Aryans' as the natural religion of this race in his *History of Ancient Sanskrit Literature* (1859).[29] His ideas were further popularised in India by Rājendralāl Mitra, who, as the Secretary of the

Asiatic Society of Bengal, was particularly effective in communicating the findings of this scholarship to his countrymen. For Hariścandra, it was a question of finding historical legitimisation while remaining firmly rooted in his own faith, as well as of forging new alliances and opening up new perspectives.

The essay *Vaiṣṇavatā aur bhāratvarṣ*, published in the last year of his life, in 1884, is an ambitious attempt to gather and weave into one the diverse threads which go to the making of Vaiṣṇavism, and to present them as an intrinsically coherent historical continuum.

Hariścandra begins his exposition with the proclamation that India's oldest faith is Vaiṣṇavism. For the Aryan people were the first to embrace civilisation and they were the teachers of the world in *dharma* and *nīti*, state polity. In this first period, understanding the sun to be the most beneficial and life-generating of the elements of nature, the Aryans first worshipped him as Sūrya-Nārayaṇa and knew just this one God. The counter-image of the sun on earth is fire, fire is *yajña*, and the deity of *yajña* is Rudra; so there came into being a duo of gods, which further multiplied with time. But the problem of polytheism is discussed later.

Hariścandra first deals with Viṣṇu's claim to supremacy as against Rudra. According to Hariścandra, European orientalists view Rudra as a non-Aryan deity, for which they bring forward eight reasons, which he proceeds to enumerate. Mueller's *History* is often invoked as testimony. A great deal of the evidence thus cited consists of taking stock of the uncouth nature of Rudra, also in the associated manifestations of Bhairava and Kālī. The evidence is undisguisedly discriminatory, but Hariścandra treads cautiously in that he maintains that he is merely citing the view taken by Western orientalists, which is of no concern to Indians. But of course by quoting thus extensively without actually contesting them, he is endorsing these views, while apparently maintaining a certain distance.

His next concern is to demonstrate the continuity of the *prakṛt mat*, the natural religion.[30] The Aryans had known Viṣṇu in their original abode in Central Asia, he tells us, before parting ways with the Iranians. Rājendralāl Mitra had divided the evolution of Vaiṣṇavism into five stages, which Hariścandra classifies as follows:

1. The Age of the Vedas. Viṣṇu as the All-God. Fire, Wind, and Sun as manifestations of Viṣṇu, thence the anthropomorphic form of the trinity: Brahmā, Śiva, and Viṣṇu.

2. The Age of the Brāhmaṇas. Viṣṇu is viewed as separate from the Sun.

3. The Age of Pāṇini. Knowledge of the Kṛṣṇa-incarnation, its worship, and bhakti become widespread. In fact, they ante-date Pāṇinī. Even at this stage, however, bhakti is considered the most beneficial of all forms of worship.

4. The Age of the Purāṇas. Even though Vaiṣṇavism remains primary, a host of other connected faiths spring up.

5. The Present Age, which is heir to these developments. Hariścandra does not elaborate further.

He then considers the reasons for this polytheistic proliferation.

Apparently, he tells us, apprehension of the 'unknown Great Cause' was followed by further speculation. Here Hariścandra begins to follow Mitra so closely that it seems appropriate to quote directly from Mitra's essay 'The Primitive Aryans':

But when the religious faculty is once quickened, the human mind cannot rest satisfied with the idea of the elements themselves being the end it sought . . . he [the primitive observer] vivifies the sun, the moon and the stars, the trees of the forest and the waters of the sea, the earth he inhabits and the sky over his head, each with a separate vital spark . . . next comes the deification of the poetical imagery, or the individualisation of metaphors and allegories, and lastly the apotheosis of heroes and patriarchs, completing the galaxy of the spiritual pantheon.[31]

Now Rājendralāl Mitra considered that primitive polytheism had *preceded* 'Vedic monotheism'. Unlike Max Mueller, he seemed willing to concede that the ancient Aryans had initially known a primitive, tribal form of worship, that they vivified the elements and deified poetic imagery, and worshipped the sun as part of just this intuitive process of deifying the elements. Hariścandra uses this argument to explain the diversification which *followed* 'Vedic monotheism', for, as he sees it, man did not rest content with just perceiving the one Sun-God, Sūrya-Nārāyaṇa; he continued to diversify, in that he continued to vivify the elements.

It was a question then, of showing how the recognition of the one, personal godhead had still been possible. If, entrapped in the snares of ritual, polytheism prospered, man's thinking did not stop there. The natural faculty of reason speculated further: an omnipresent, omnipotent creator must regulate the cosmic order. At this stage, it was possible to discard polytheism, for this line of reasoning could further lead either to atheism or to *upāsanā*, devotion, and within this latter, either to the worship of a formless, abstract All-God or to an anthropomorphic godhead, so that, by a natural process of reasoning, man arrived once again at the instinctive monotheism of the Aryans and Vaiṣṇavas. Thus in India the orientation provided by the Vaiṣṇava faith was the most spontaneous and natural one (*prakṛt mat*), just as, all over the world, the devotional is the primary path, as for instance in the Christian and Muslim faiths. The deeds (*caritra*) of Jesus are much like Kṛṣṇa's, though Buddhism in emphasising asceticism, penance, and the performance of meritorious deeds is much more akin to the *smārta* tradition within Vaiṣṇavism. Hariścandra's universalism, then, does not seek to absorb all other possibilities: it primarily postulates correspondences while allowing for differences.

Hariścandra emphasises that the root portion of Vaiṣṇava devotionalism has come down to present times in an unbroken historical tradition from the most ancient period – here the difference from the Brāhmo and Ārya Samāj becomes obvious – and this lends the tradition a certain inherent stability. With this in mind it is, according to Hariścandra, not difficult to face the changes that are inevitable, for these can be in the spirit of what the great teachers of the faith had themselves propagated: that men of all castes join the ranks of the Vaiṣṇavas, that gurus retain their position of respect, not by virtue of position but by earning merit in the eyes of their followers, that the Vallabha order be cleansed of promiscuity, that the love play of Kṛṣṇa be explained for its symbolic significance and that too only to the most devoted followers.[32] If this faith were progressive, then men of the other faiths, Sikhs and Kabīrpanthīs, would join in, and this would be further evidence that Vaiṣṇavism was the natural religion of the country. It was not the time to insist on outward compliance; much rather, a progressive, internally felt bhakti filled with love was to be propagated.

In his concluding paragraph, having arrived at contemporary social issues, Hariścandra has no compunction about switching over from speaking of the Vaiṣṇava faith to the Hindu faith.[33] The alliances have been forged, the historical course charted. Within a colonial context it is a question of solidarity at different levels, and realignment. Here it is a question of nationalism based on economic deprivation, directed initially against the colonial power, but also in unmistakable competition with other groups, defined and distinguished increasingly by their belonging to specific religious communities. In the struggle for professional employment, all the positions not occupied by the British themselves are being taken by men of other faiths: Muslims, Parsis, Christians are forging ahead. In order to fulfil the dharma of all mankind – filling one's stomach – there would have to be a unity motivated by togetherness on the part of the Aryan community (*ārya jāti*). All those who bear the name of Hindu, whatever their inner differences, must unite, dropping all the denominations with which they designate their faith, and must participate in the progress of the natural religion. Here Vaiṣṇavism is once again reinforced without being explicitly named, for Hariścandra has variously proved that it is the *prakṛt mat* of the country.

The categories he employs have more or less clear functions: Aryans, whenever the ancient heritage is invoked; Hindus as descendants of these and reared on Hindu milk – a cultural–political category which could in principle include men of other faiths;[34] and finally, within the diversity of faiths which proliferated on Indian soil, unbroken in its tradition and yet capable of change, that inner core, that path of love, Vaiṣṇavism.

It was a constituting and constitutive process, whereby the Vaiṣṇava community was preserved intact, with a progressive outlook and with possibilities of opening up its ranks, in fact with clearly national aspirations.[35] The way into the past was cleared, and a broad framework established within which present issues could be tackled. If the finest intellects of Europe had applied themselves to the task of reconstructing ancient Indian history, the tradition as it emerged in the late nineteenth century could appropriate the fruits of their labour for its own ends, while claiming an equal measure of 'objectivity'.

If, on the one hand, Hariścandra could elaborate with easy facility on a classical theme in bhakti poetry and celebrate the *sakhya bhāva* in *Candrāvalī*, and in the *Uttarārdha-bhaktamāl* could integrate his own perception of himself as a bhakta within the larger tradition of Vaiṣṇava bhaktas, he could, on the other hand, with the same easy assurance, adopt the mode of discourse of Western orientalists for propagating the continuity of tradition. I have tried here to trace the interaction of the social forces which made this range of authority possible: the literary text, then, as embedded in and emerging from within a complex arrangement, the dynamic interrelationships between groups functioning as powerful agents of authority: Mahājan, Mahārāj, Mandir – family, institutions, place – interrelationships further constrained in the colonial context to accommodate the dominant orientalist discourse.

NOTES

1. Ingham, in his study of missionary efforts in the first half of the 19th century characterises the general attitude of the missionaries as follows: 'Though relatively few in number the missionaries' abilities were exceptional and their enthusiasm never flagged. Because their main object was evangelisation they could not remain aloofly uncritical of the Hindu religion and the social system which it engendered. Not only considerations of humanity but the very progress of the Christian gospel demanded that Indian society should be *purged* and *renovated.* This spirit generated in the missionaries a *violent* sense of urgency' (1956, p. 4, my italics). The first mission in Banaras was established in 1807. By the 1840s there were 11 missionaries in the city. The situation and official attitudes had changed radically in the intervening decades and the Company's officials had themselves become committed to the missionary cause. Cf. Cohn 1961–2, p. 196.
2. Ballantyne was Principal of the Benares Sanskrit College. His was a decidedly more belligerent approach than his predecessor's: 'he insisted that the Sanskrit Courses in the College "should pay tribute instead of scowling defiance"' (Young, 1981, p. 55).
3. p. 235. Ballantyne's publications aroused much hostility in literate circles in Banaras. Hariścandra's grandson and biographer, Brajratnadās (1962, p. 190), cites the call of the Hindi paper *Sudhākar* (1848) to his countrymen to disprove Ballantyne's assertions.
4. Sherring 1868, p. 350.
5. For the most extensive and lucid account of Maratha connections with and

activities in the city, following the decline of the Mughal empire, see Motīcandra 1985, pp. 277–86.

6. Ghose 1978, p. xvi.
7. 'In addition to their personal servants and their Indian subordinates, the British had contacts with Indians usually described as "respectable gentlemen", i.e. the leading merchants of the town, the local chiefs and rajas, and the big landholders. With these men, social relations were usually restricted to the most formal occasions – a *darbār* (audience), a celebration of a holiday or a festival, or a big party for an important visitor. The English tended to view the "respectable native" with a mixture of contempt and curiosity' (Cohn 1961–2, p. 187). Similarly, Marshall (1989) on the paucity of social contact.
8. See Jordens 1978, pp. 67–9, for an account of the debate between Dayānand and the Banaras pandits. For Dayānand's impact on the Banaras pandits, see Vyās 1901, pp. 18–20. For providing me with a copy of Vyās I am grateful to Dr Dhirendranath Singh of Banaras. Hariścandra's reaction to the tenets of the Ārya Samāj is recorded in his 'Dūṣaṇamālikā' (first pub. 1870).
9. Williams 1978, p. 116.
10. Cf. Bipan Chandra 1970, p. 6.
11. Cf. Motīcandra 1985, ch. 8: 'Banāras ke mahājan', pp. 313–30; Bayly 1978, pp. 181–2.
12. There are various stories associated with the rise and formation of this group of banker-merchants. Motīcandra 1985, pp. 410–12, provides a list of their names as available in a contemporary document. See also Sahay 1975, p. 18; Bayly 1983, pp. 177 ff., as also Brajratnadās 1962, p. 31, which provides also the most detailed account of Hariścandra's forebears (pp. 17–61).
13. For a graphic account of one such gathering see Vyās 1901, pp. 7 ff.
14. I am grateful to Dr Kalyan Krishna of the Banaras Hindu University for drawing my attention to the *Vārtā*.
15. *Śrīgirdharjī kī badhāī*, p. 146.
16. *Uttarārdhabhaktamāl*, p. 70.
17. All quotations from Hariścandra's works are from the edition of his collected works in a single volume: Hariścandra 1987.
18. Cf. Vairāgī 1977, p. 43. Hariścandra was almost certainly acquainted with Rūpa Gosvāmī's play *Vidagdhamādhava*, where Candrāvalī in her love for Kṛṣṇa is Rādhā's chief rival. Cf. Wulff 1982.
19. Śarmā 1984, p. 126.
20. Brajratnadās 1962, p. 282, enumerates the ten well-known stages of *vipralambha śṛṅgāra*, as also, following him, Tripāṭhī 1986, pp. 107–15.
21. By Hariścandra's own estimation, the *rās* was to be considered *bhraṣṭa*, corrupt, 'jis meṁ nāṭaktā śeṣ nahīṁ rah gayī hai', 'wherein no dramatic quality has survived' – this as against the classical Sanskrit dramatic forms. See the essay 'Nāṭak' (p. 1014). This estimation corresponds to H. H. Wilson's categorisation of these forms as of 'inferior description' in the introductory essay to his influential *Select Specimens of the Theatre of the Hindus* (1835, p. xv).
22. Cf. Hein 1972, pp. 163–78.
23. Sahāy 1975, pp. 183–8, Brajratnadās 1962, pp. 161–2, Vārṣṇey 1974, pp. 93–4. As Vārṣṇey points out, in addition to the conventions of Sanskrit drama, Hariścan-

dra seems also to have made a successful attempt to maintain here the three unities of Western drama.

24. So, for instance, the discomfiture of Śarmā (1984, p. 114) and the relatively distanced interpretation by Tanejā (1976, pp. 74–80), who views the play as lacking in internal and external conflict and the erotic element as disturbing the dramatic quality of the play.
25. As, for instance, in Lütt (1970, p. 92) in his interpretation of Hariścandra's bhakti concept, mistaking thereby the criticism, which Hariścandra certainly expressed, as central to his devotional attitude. This was to remain firmly rooted in the Puṣṭimārg to the end of his days.
26. Later information supports the significance of this incident, the dream was to be taken as a signal for Mādhavī to reconvert to Hinduism. Cf. Rāykṛṣṇadās 1976, p. 43.
27. Thus, for instance, in the opening lines of his brief survey of the history of Kashmir, to the effect that 'there is no glimpse of the moon of history in the lucid sky of India, since along with the ancient sciences of India, history has also disappeared' (ed. cit., p. 708).
28. Sherring 1868, p. 4.
29. For the significance of this work in establishing the Aryan past of the Indo-Germanic peoples see my article (1987).
30. For a discussion of the nineteenth-century conceptualisation of 'natural religion', particularly as envisaged by Max Mueller, see Kohl 1985.
31. Mitra 1969, p. 446.
32. Apparently a defensive reference to the Maharaj Libel Case, which had caused such public scandal about the practices of the Puṣṭimārg in the Bombay Presidency in 1862.
33. Cf. Sudhir Chandra (1984).
34. '*Hama hindū, hindū ke beṭā, hinduhi ko paya pāna kiyo*' (p. 39), as Hariścandra himself defined it in his poem entitled 'Jain kautūhal' (1873), which was written in order to defend himself when the visit to a Jain temple led to a public outcry.
35. Which is not to say that the ranks could not close just as suddenly in a given political constellation. Anderson (1983, p. 133) has commented on the apparently contradictory nature of nationalism whereby, once embedded in 'history', 'the nation presents itself as simultaneously open and closed'.

REFERENCES

Anderson, B. (1983), *Imagined Communities: Reflections on the Origin and Spread of Nationalism*, London: Verso.

Ballantyne, J. R. (1859), *Christianity Contrasted with Hindu Philosophy: An Essay in Five Books, Sanskrit and English, with Practical Suggestions Tendered to the Missionary among the Hindus*, London: James Madden.

Bayly, C. A. (1973), 'Patrons and Politics in Northern India', in J. Gallagher, G. Johnson, and A. Seal, eds., *Locality, Province and Nation: Essays on Indian Politics 1870 to 1940*, Cambridge: Cambridge University Press.

——(1978), 'Indian Merchants in a Traditional Setting, Benares 1780–1830', in C. Dewey and A. G. Hopkins, eds., *The Imperial Impact: Studies in the Economic History of Africa and India*, London: Institute of Commonwealth Studies.

——(1983), *Rulers, Townsmen and Bazaars: North Indian Society in the Age of British Expansion, 1770–1870*, Cambridge: Cambridge University Press.

Brajratnadās (1962), *Bhāratendu hariścandra*, Allahabad: Hindustānī akādemī.

Chandra, Bipan (1970), 'Colonialism and Modernization in the Study of Modern Indian History', Presidential Address, *Indian History Congress, Proceedings of the Thirty-Second Session, Jabalpur*, vol. ii, pp. 1–31.

Cohn, B. (1961–2), 'The British in Benares: A Nineteenth Century Colonial Society', *CSSH* 4, pp. 169–99.

Dalmia-Lüderitz, V. (1987), 'Die Aneignung der vedischen Vergangenheit: Aspekte der frühen deutschen Indien-Forschung', *Zeitschrift für Kulturaustausch. Utopie – Projektion – Gegenbild, Indien in Deutschland*, 37, 3, pp. 434–43.

Ghose, Benoy, ed. (1978), *Selections from English Periodicals*, vol. vii: *1878–80, Brahmo Public Opinion*, Calcutta: Papyrus.

Hariścandra (1987), *Bhāratendu samagra*, ed. Hemant Śarmā, Vārāṇasī: Hindī pracārak saṃsthān.

Hein, N. (1972), *The Miracle Plays of Mathura*, Delhi: Oxford University Press.

Ingham, K. (1956), *Reformers in India 1793–1833: An Account of the Work of Christian Missionaries on Behalf of Social Reform*, Cambridge: Cambridge University Press.

Jordens, J. (1978), *Dayānanda Sarasvatī: His Life and Ideas*, Delhi.

Kohl, K.-H. (1985), 'Naturreligion: Zur Transformationsgeschichte eines Begriffs', in R. Faber and R. Schlesier, eds., *Die Restauration der Götter: Antike Religion und Neo-Paganismus*, Würzburg: Königshausen und Neumann.

Lütt, J. (1970), *Hindu Nationalismus in Uttar Pradeś 1867–1900*, Stuttgart: Ernst Klett.

Marshall, P. (1989), 'The British Community in Nineteenth Century India', Paper presented at the India International Centre, Delhi, 27 Mar.

Mitra, Rājendralāl (1969), 'The Primitive Aryans', *Indo-Aryans: Contributions towards the Elucidation of their Ancient and Medieval History*, vol. ii, first pub. 1881, repr. Delhi and Varanasi: Indological Book House.

Motīcandra (1985), *Kāśī kā itihās: vaidik kāl se arvācīn yug tak kā rājnaitik-sāṃskṛtik sarvekṣaṇ*, first pub. 1962, repr. Vārāṇasī: Viśvavidyālaya prakāśan.

Mueller, F. M. (1968), *A History of Ancient Sanskrit Literature, so far as it Illustrates the Primitive Religion of the Brahmans*, first pub. 1859, repr. Varanasi: Chowkhamba.

Rāykṛṣṇadās (1976), 'Neh kā divānā', *Dharmayug*, Bombay, 17 Oct., pp. 40–3.

Śarmā, Rāmvilās (1984), *Bhāratendu hariścandra aur hindī navajāgaraṇ kī samasyāeṁ*, first pub. 1953, repr. New Delhi and Patna: Rājkamal prakāśan.

Śāstrī, Pt. Rāmnāthjī, ed. (vs 2041), *Śrīmukundrāyjī kī vārtā tathā śrīgopāllāljī kī vārtā*, first pub. vs 1980, repr. Varanasi: Rāmdās Agravāl.

Sherring, M. A. (1868), *The Sacred City of the Hindus: An Account of Benares in Ancient and Modern Times*, London: Trübner.

——(1875), *The History of the Protestant Missions in India from their Commencement in 1706 to 1871*, London: Trübner.

Sudhir, Chandra (1984), 'Communal Elements in Late Nineteenth Century Hindi Literature', *Journal of Arts & Ideas*, Delhi, Jan.–Mar., pp. 5–18.

Tanejā, Satyendrakumār (1976), *Nāṭakkār bhāratendu kī raṅgparikalpanā*, Delhi: Bhāratī bhāṣā prakāśan.

Tripāṭhī, Rāmmūrtī (1986), 'Bhāratendu kā bhaktiparak sāhitya', *Bhāratendu aur bhāratīya navajāgaraṇ*, ed. Aśok Jośī Śambhunāth, Calcutta: Ānevālā kal prakāśan.

Vairāgī, Prabhudās (1977), *Śrināthdvārā kā sāṃskṛtik itihās*, Aligarh: Bhārat prakā-śan mandir.

Vārṣṇey, Lakṣmīsāgar (1974), *Bhāratendu hariścandra*, Allahabad: Sāhitya bhavan.

Vyās, Ambikādatt (1901), *Nijavṛttānt*, Bānkipur: Khaḍgavilās pres.

Williams, R. (1978), *Marxism and Literature*, Oxford: Oxford University Press.

Wilson, H. H. (1835), *Select Specimens of the Theatre of the Hindus*, transl. from the original Sanskrit, vol. i, London: Parbury, Allen.

Wulff, D. M. (1982), 'A Sanskrit Portrait: Rādha in the Plays of Rūpa Gosvāmi', in J. S. Hawley and D. M. Wulff, eds., *The Divine Consort: Radha and the Goddesses of India*, Berkeley, Calif., Berkeley Religious Studies Series.

Young, R. F. (1981), *Resistant Hinduism: Sanskrit Sources on Anti-Christian Apologetics in Early Nineteenth-Century India*, Vienna: Publications of the De Nobili Research Library.

A reinterpretation of bhakti theology: from the *Puṣṭimārg* to the Brahma Kumaris

R. K. BARZ

Two of the Hindu movements that have been most successful in moving into the world at large, the International Society for Krishna Consciousness (the Hare Krishnas), and the Brahma Kumaris World Spiritual University[1] (the Brahma Kumaris) are bhakti groups. In addition to their bhakti orientation and international extent, the Hare Krishnas and the Brahma Kumaris share some other characteristics. Both require their fully committed members to adopt a diet that is strictly defined and rigidly vegetarian, encourage them to wear an Indian costume of distinctive colour, and expect them to live together in communal establishments where possible. Furthermore, the attraction of new members is a major concern for both organisations and both take great pains to present themselves and their message to the public, making particular use of fairs, festivals, and other occasions at which large crowds gather. Finally, non-Indian Hare Krishnas and Brahma Kumaris both recognise India as their spiritual homeland and try to visit their centres in India as often as possible.

There are differences between the two groups as well. Hare Krishnas lavish a great deal of attention on temple worship with divine images and elaborate ritual while the Brahma Kumaris have no temples or divine images as such and only vestiges of ritual. The orientation of the Hare Krishna movement toward masculine authority and male dominance contrasts with the active role for women and female leadership in the Brahma Kumari organisation. In terms of external impact, the Hare Krishnas, though they had in 1978 only 'some 4,500 members in all scattered in some hundred temples throughout the world'[2] have been the object of a good deal of publicity, while the Brahma Kumaris, despite the 167,885 members associated with 421 centres in India and 145 abroad which they claimed in 1986[3] and their affiliation to the Department of Public Information of the United Nations, have been much less in the public eye. As a result, the Hare Krishnas have received considerable scholarly attention,[4] but, as far as I know, the Brahma Kumaris have been the subject of only two academic studies.[5]

From the point of view of those interested in modern Hinduism, the most striking difference between the International Society for Krishna Consciousness and the Brahma Kumaris World Spiritual University is that the former stresses its bhakti heritage by proudly proclaiming its descent from the Caitanya sect (*Caitanya sampradāy* or *Gauḍīya sampradāy*) founded in the sixteenth century by the Bengali Vaiṣṇava leader Caitanya, while the latter does not associate itself with any earlier Hindu movement, bhakti or otherwise. None the less, there is a link between the Brahma Kumaris and the Hindu bhakti tradition. The founder of the Brahma Kumaris World Spiritual University, Lekhraj Kriplani (Lekhrāj Kṛpalānī), was born in a family owing allegiance to the Vallabha sect (*Vallabh sampradāy*). The Vallabha sect was established by Vallabhācārya about the same time that Caitanya's sect was taking shape and the two groups have been the leading bhakti sects in northern India for the past 300 years. The Vallabha and Caitanya sects both developed major centres in the Mathura area of modern Uttar Pradesh, where they came into such intimate, though not always friendly, contact with each other that their bhakti doctrines have come to have much in common. Though not acknowledged by either group, the Hare Krishnas and the Brahma Kumaris thus have at least a tenuous genetic connection with one another.

Although Lekhraj Kriplani would have had an understanding from his childhood of the sort of bhakti practised by followers of Vallabhācārya, I have never come across any indication by Brahma Kumaris either in writing or in speech that the doctrines of the Vallabha sect have had any influence on the Brahma Kumaris World Spiritual University. It is certainly not the intention here to suggest that the Brahma Kumaris are in any sense an offshoot of the Vallabha sect in the way that the Hare Krishnas are an outgrowth of the Caitanya sect. Nevertheless, there are many fascinating parallels between Raja Yoga (*rāj yog*, 'regal yoga'), the term used by Brahma Kumaris to describe their system of beliefs and spiritual practice, and Vallabhācārya's *Puṣṭimārg* 'way of nurturing [grace]' method of devotion. The extent to which these parallels are evidence of a reworking of a bhakti theology like that of the Vallabha sect within the Brahma Kumaris World Spiritual University is the theme of this paper.

The Brahma Kumaris and Hindu bhakti

At the very beginning it would be well to ask how the Brahma Kumaris see their relations with Hinduism. Do they see their movement as a part of Hinduism? As far as the term 'Hinduism' is concerned, their opinion is very clear. They say that 5,000 years ago the Supreme Being himself established the Adi Sanatan Devi Devata Dharma (*Ādi Sanātan Devī Devtā Dharm*, 'primordial eternal religion of goddesses and gods'), which they describe in English as the Ancient Original Religion of Deities, but that through complete forgetfulness and decadence the adherents of this religion came to misapply a geographical term, 'Hindu', as the name of the religion. At last, in our day, the Supreme Being incarnated himself to resuscitate and re-establish the Adi Sanatan Devi Devata Dharma.[6]

As to the question whether or not the Brahma Kumaris World Spiritual University falls within this Adi Sanatan Devi Devata Dharma, the Brahma Kumari reply is more than a little equivocal. On the one hand, in addition to founding their organisation Lekhraj Kriplani was also the individual whom the Brahma Kumaris say the Supreme Being chose for the incarnation through which the Adi Sanatan Devi Devata Dharma would be reformed and reconstituted. On the other hand, after establishing the Brahma Kumaris World Spiritual University, Lekhraj advocated communication with the Supreme Being through meditation rather than by worship of the deities of the Adi Sanatan Devi Devata Dharma. In the words of a Brahma Kumari publication, 'the priests and pujaris (worshippers), who had continued to beat the drums of old rituals and of idol worship' were called upon by Lekhraj 'to break their age-old shackles of blind faith and superstition and meaningless rituals and to take to Life of Brahmcharya [i.e. celibacy], Purity and Meditation on one Incorporeal God'.[7] In fact, the Brahma Kumaris never state plainly that their Raja Yoga does or does not come within the Adi Sanatan Devi Devata Dharma.

With regard to bhakti the situation is much clearer. Within carefully defined parameters, the Brahma Kumaris consider their movement to be an expression of bhakti. These parameters are described in the following passage from a book by a Brahma Kumari theologian:

> If the meaning of 'bhakti' can be taken to be 'limitless love of the Supreme Soul (*paramātmā*)' and 'unbroken faith', then this [Raja] Yoga can also be called bhakti yoga . . . but if the meaning of bhakti is *pūjā* ['ritual worship'] then we cannot call it bhakti yoga . . .[8]

In addition to their own self-definition, both the outward conduct and system of beliefs of the Brahma Kumaris place their movement firmly within the bhakti tradition. The following two examples illustrate this.

In terms of behaviour, Brahma Kumaris are neither unemotional nor unappreciative of the need for music and drama in religion. They value cheerfulness and often bring humour and lightheartedness into their meetings. Taped spiritual music is employed to assist in their meditation and programmes of live devotional music or skits on religious themes are sometimes presented at their gatherings. At the same time, Brahma Kumaris keep the overall atmosphere of their meetings calm and dignified and centre them on the stillness of a period of meditation. There is normally little scope for the communal devotional singing (*kīrtan*) and its accompanying fervour and outpouring of emotion so essential to just about every variety of Hindu bhakti. None the less, an emotional approach typical of the bhakti spirit and what seems very much like *kīrtan* does occur at some Brahma Kumari functions. An instance of this is the following description in an official

Brahma Kumari publication of one of the assemblies at which the Supreme Being speaks through a Brahma Kumari trance medium: 'and they were singing songs of love, hoping that Baba would stay and Baba responds as follows: BapDada is the Ocean of Love, and yet is also the One who is detached ... By all means, enjoy everything: celebrate, eat and drink and dance, but let it be constantly. Just as now, all of you are merged in love, always remain merged in this way. BapDada constantly listens to the songs from the hearts of all the children and today the songs through the lips have also been heard.'[9]

As for doctrine, if there is any philosophical idea that one would expect to find in every bhakti school it is that human emotions are not to be denied or suppressed but are to be focused on the divine through love. For example, the sixty-fifth *sūtra* of the *Nārada Bhakti-sūtras* states that one who has given all of his actions to the Supreme Being as a part of his devotion should include in his offering his lust, anger, pride, and other such emotions.[10] In other words, if a devotee happens to be a hot-headed, contentious person he (or she) is expected to concentrate on opening himself to the flow of divine love rather than to do battle directly against the defects of his own personality. As this love permeates his soul it is assumed that such a devotee will be purified of selfishness and negativity, though his bhakti may retain something of a truculent cast.[11] In standard Hindu bhakti thought this preference for the transmutation rather than denial of emotion expresses itself in the five ways that a devotee, in accordance with personal temperament, can love the divine: either with the affection of a friend for a friend (*sakhya bhakti*), or with the passion of two lovers (*mādhurya bhakti*), or as a parent loves a child (*vātsalya bhakti*), or as a servant is devoted to a master (*dāsya bhakti*), or even in dispassionate quietude (*śānta bhakti*). Here Brahma Kumari theology is in harmony with mainstream bhakti thought. Instead of trying to destroy negative emotions, Brahma Kumaris are advised in the following passage to recognise such feelings and to turn them into benign helpers on the spiritual quest:

There are 5 vices .... 'The soul that stays in spiritual intoxication is the one who can transform ... all the vices. The vice of lust is transformed into pure desire, elevated good wishes, and so is used in service .... The fire of anger should be transformed into the fire of yoga. In the same way, the vice of greed ... should change and become pure desires .... Everyone also has a great deal of attachment! All of you have attachment to BapDada, don't you? There is the feeling that you don't want to be separated for even one second and so, this is attachment .... And so, even the vice of attachment can be used for service .... The same applies ... to ego .... From body-consciousness, let there be soul-consciousness and the pure arrogance, that is, 'I have become a special soul' ...[12]

Lekhraj Kriplani and the Vallabha sect

Guruship in the Vallabha sect passes down through the agnate line from Vallabhācārya through the descendants of his eight grandsons, with each of these descendants being entitled to attract his own following and set up his own temple. Because of this form of organisation, together with the fact that from the beginning the majority of its members have been engaged in business, the sect was able to spread widely from its original stronghold near Mathura throughout Rajasthan, Gujarat, and eventually cities and towns all over India. The eighth grandson, for instance, migrated to western Panjab and settled at Dera Ghazi Khan, where he built a temple. Later, one of his sons moved further north to Dera Ismail Khan and established another temple there. This section of the Vallabha sect in the course of time throve to such an extent in this region that, before the mass exodus of Hindus from Pakistan after 1947, its members, along with those associated with other branches of the sect, had come to make up a substantial and influential part of the Hindu merchant community from Sindh north along the Indus River.[13]

It was in this area, near the city of Hyderabad (Sindh), that Lekhraj Kriplani was born in 1876. Since the family into which he was born was a Sindhi family of mercantile background associated with the Vallabha sect, it is tempting from the above survey to assume that it was attached to the eighth branch of the sect. Unfortunately, Lekhraj's biography[14] gives no information that would allow anything to be said about his family's exact intrasectarian affiliation. It cannot even be determined from the biography if Lekhraj himself was a fervent or merely nominal adherent of the Vallabha sect, nor is there any way of knowing from it whether or not he had any sort of instruction in the sect's *Puṣṭimārg* philosophy. About Lekhraj's own religious preferences the biography tells us only that he felt special reverence for the Hindu god Nārāyaṇ and would make almost any sacrifice for his personal guru. Though not a deity given prominence in the Vallabha sect, Nārāyaṇ is a form of Viṣṇu and so it would not be very odd for a member of the Vaiṣṇava Vallabha sect to choose him as his personal deity. It is true that the hereditary leaders of the Vallabha sect received and still receive today extreme veneration from many of their followers, but this proves only that nothing in Lekhraj's behaviour is inconsistent with his guru's having been a Vallabha sectarian leader.

The only information linking Lekhraj directly with the Vallabha sect in adulthood is presented differently in the various versions of his biography. According to the Hindi version of the biography,[15] Lekhraj's wife and other family members took the opportunity of a visit to the Maharaja of Udaipur to go to pay homage to Śrī Nāthjī at the town of Nathdwara in Udaipur District, Rajasthan. As Śrī Nāthjī is the image of Kṛṣṇa worshipped at the primary centre of the Vallabha sect's senior branch at Nathdwara, this would imply at least the possibility of a strong association of Lekhraj and his wife with the sect. Inexplicably, in the first of the two English versions of the biography[16] the king being visited has become the ruler of Valaipur instead of Udaipur and Śrī Nāthjī is described as 'a visiting saint' and not as a divine image. The second English version[17] relates that Lekhrāj 'was very staunch in his religious beliefs and practices' so that once, immediately after arriving at the palace of the Maharaja of Udaipur on a visit, 'he went to the Nathdwara temple to pay his respects to the deity'.

This is the extent of the overt evidence for Lekhraj's contact with the Vallabha sect. Although it is circumstantial, vague and very meagre, it does confirm that Lekhraj Kriplani must have had some degree of familiarity with the type of bhakti taught and practised by Vallabhācārya and his followers. In any case, there is nowhere any indication that Lekhraj had as much contact with any group or school of thought as he did with the Vallabha sect. That sect and the *Puṣṭimārg* system of bhakti promulgated within it is the most likely source of any outside theological influences that may have acted upon Lekhraj as he laid the foundations for the Raja Yoga of the Brahma Kumaris World Spiritual University.

Some differences and congruences between the *Puṣṭimārg* and Raja Yoga

While there is at least a modicum of proof that Lekhraj had had some contact with the Vallabha sect, the results of a search for signs of theological influence from Vallabhācārya's *Puṣṭimārg* on Lekhraj's Raja Yoga are at first disappointing. It is true that both systems agree that the Supreme Being loves human souls, that human souls are distinct from and dependent upon the Supreme Being, and that the Supreme Being has revealed divine truth through the *Bhagavadgītā*. Such premisses are, however, a part of a great many formulations of Hindu bhakti and cannot show that these two have a particularly close relationship. Moreover, when the three premisses are examined in detail as they appear in the *Puṣṭimārg* and Raja Yoga, so many fundamental dissimilarities appear that the two systems seem to be basically different.

For instance, there is the nature of the Supreme Being. On the basis of material in a Brahma Kumari catechism[18] and in a Brahma Kumari theological exposition,[19] the following sketch can be drawn of the Supreme Being in Raja Yoga. Because the Supreme Being is the benefactor, he is called 'Shiva' (*śiva*, 'benign') and because he is the supreme soul and the father of all souls his titles are *Paramātmā*, 'Highest Soul', and *Parampitā*, 'Highest Father'. The title *Bhagavān*, 'Lord', is also sometimes used for the Supreme Being in Brahma Kumari literature. In substance he is a point of light. He is called the formless (*nirākār*), the indestructible and conscious seed of the tree of the universe and the creator of Brahmā, Viṣṇu and Śaṅkar. He is unborn and does not die. He is free of all physical qualities, an ocean of delight, and omnipotent. He is not, however, omnipresent because it is inconceivable in the Raja Yoga system that the Supreme Being could pervade despicable and filthy things. Most emphatically, he is not Kṛṣṇa or any of the other Hindu gods. The Brahma Kumaris do recognise Kṛṣṇa, but for them Kṛṣṇa is Lekhraj Kriplani reborn at the beginning of the Golden Age (*sat yug*) and not the Supreme Being.

While in Raja Yoga the Supreme Being is called 'Shiva', Vallabhācārya refers to the Supreme Being in his writings by the title *Bhagavān* or with Vaiṣṇava names like Hari, Viṣṇu and Kṛṣṇa. But whatever name he might employ, in the fourth verse of the first part of his *Tattvārthadīpanibandha* he makes it clear that for him 'the one god is [Kṛṣṇa] the son of Devakī'.[20] This does not mean that he denies sanctity to Śiva. Rather, as he states in the eleventh and seventeenth verses of his *Bālabodhaḥ*,[21] he feels that Viṣṇu and Śiva are the two benefactors of the universe but that Śiva grants temporal satisfaction (*bhoga*) while Viṣṇu offers final liberation (*mokṣa*). The *Puṣṭimārgī* view of the Supreme Being is put very well in the twenty-third and sixty-fifth verses of the first part of the *Tattvārthadīpanibandha*, where Vallabhācārya maintains that the universe is the work of the Lord and describes him as omnipresent, imperishable, omnipotent, and devoid of physical qualities, and as consisting of being, consciousness, and delight. Vallabhācārya sees two aspects to the Supreme Being: one being Kṛṣṇa, the saviour, and the other being *brahman*, the impersonal ground of existence. The former includes the latter within himself.[22] Setting aside such expected attributes of a Supreme Being as omnipotence, indestructibility, and benevolence, the description of *Parampitā paramātma* Śiva as a disembodied point of light that is not all-pervasive bears very little resemblance to the portrayal of Kṛṣṇa as an omnipresent, anthropomorphic deity.

Turning to the treatment of authoritative scripture in Raja Yoga and the *Puṣṭimārg* one will find no more similitude between the two systems than was apparent in their concepts of the Supreme Being. The basic variance between the two does not lie in any difference of opinion about which scripture is sacred. Both are in harmony in exalting the *Bhagavadgītā* as divinely revealed scripture. The discrepancy arises over the question of the extent to which the *Bhagavadgītā* as we have it today is the same document that was given by the Supreme Being. Vallabhācārya's opinion on this point is quite straightforward. In the same verse cited above from the first part of the *Tattvārthadīpanibandha*, in which he hailed Kṛṣṇa as the one god, Vallabhācārya also proclaimed that 'the one scripture is the [*Bhagavad*] *Gītā* of the son of Devakī'. Three verses further on he qualifies this by giving particular recognition to, in addition to some other scriptures, 'the words of Kṛṣṇa (*śrīkṛṣṇavākyāni*)'. This is generally taken to mean those verses in the *Bhagavadgītā* which are actually spoken by Kṛṣṇa. For Vallabhācārya and the followers of his *Puṣṭimārg* the *Bhagavadgītā* has perfectly preserved the teachings of Kṛṣṇa. The situation is completely different in Raja Yoga. The

Bhagavadgītā is, indeed, considered in Raja Yoga to contain truth revealed by *Paramātmā* Śiva himself. This truth is called *Gītā*-knowledge (*Gītā-jñāna*) and is the essence of all the Vedas and *śāstras*. It is recognised as the knowledge that is the foundation of Raja Yoga. It does not follow, however, that the *Bhagavadgītā* is considered to have survived intact from the time it was divinely revealed to the present day. Quite to the contrary, Brahma Kumaris believe that it has suffered such major distortion in its passage through time that much of the text as it exists today is unreliable. Consequently, most Brahma Kumaris rely on practice of Raja Yoga to give them access to the *Gītā*-knowledge rather than on study of the *Bhagavadgītā*.

Raja Yoga and the *Puṣṭimārg* differ in their ideas about the human soul, but the gap between the two systems in this matter is not so great as it was with regard to the Supreme Being and authoritative scripture. In fact, it is in doctrines about the soul that the first glimmerings of a theological congruity between the teachings of the Vallabha sect and the Brahma Kumaris World Spiritual University first begin to appear. The differences, being more apparent than the congruities, should be taken up first. To begin with, in Raja Yoga the soul, which is called the *ātmā*, is a single, indivisible being, while Vallabhācārya, who terms it the *jīva*, sees it as having another entity within it. This second entity, which he calls the *antaryāmin*, 'inner controller', is the manifestation of the Supreme Being. Its function is to experience the actions of the *jīva* without being affected by them. The idea that the soul is intrinsically unaffected by actions performed in mundane life is not at all alien to Raja Yoga. The *ātmā* in one Raja Yoga text[23] is specifically described as being the *draṣṭā*, 'observer'. That is, it is able to watch the actions of the body without being influenced by them. This observer is, however, not the same as *Paramātmā* Śiva. In Raja Yoga the *ātmās* are distinct from the Supreme Being and are inferior to him in knowledge, peace, delight, love, and power. Any notion that the *ātmā* shares the identity of *Paramātmā* Śiva in the way that the *antaryāmin* in the *Puṣṭimārg* participates in the identity of Kṛṣṇa would be contrary to Raja Yoga. Another point at which the Raja Yoga conception of the *ātmā* disagrees with the *Puṣṭimārgī* view of the *jīva* concerns the relationship that is posited in the two systems between the soul and the material world. According to Vallabhācārya the physical world is the expression of the *sat*, 'existence', aspect of Kṛṣṇa. Since the *jīva* also partakes of the *sat* aspect, there is a sense in which, in the *Puṣṭimārg*, the *jīva* and the world spring from the same source. This would be completely impossible in Raja Yoga since a basic tenet of that system is that the *ātmā* is the antithesis of the world.

In their visualisation of the form of the soul, Raja Yoga and the *Puṣṭimārg* come close to one another. In Raja Yoga the *ātmā* is described as an exceedingly fine, conscious point of light, and in verses 53 and 55 of the first part of his *Tattvārthadīpanibandha* Vallabhācārya says that the *jīva* is as minute as the point of an awl but the light of its consciousness fills the body in which it resides. In addition to resembling one another in form, the Raja Yoga *ātmā* and the *Puṣṭimārgī jīva* also have a similar character as emanations of the Supreme Being. Vallabhācārya, in verses 27 to 30 of the first part of his *Tattvārthadīpanibandha*, states that the *jīvas* came out of the Supreme Being like sparks from fire and that they share in his being and consciousness but not in his delight. In other words, in the *Puṣṭimārg* the *jīvas* are not, as the *antaryāmin* is, identical with Kṛṣṇa but they do proceed from Kṛṣṇa's essence. They differ from him in degree but not in kind. This is exactly the way in which the *ātmās* in Brahma Kumari thought are related to *Paramātmā* Śiva. They and he have the same subtle form as points of light. Although it is nowhere in Raja Yoga literature explained exactly how or why the *ātmās* come into being, they evidently somehow arise from the essence of *Paramātmā* Śiva as they are called his offspring (*Parampitā paramātmā kī santān*).[24] They are said to descend from his unmanifest world (*parama dhām*, 'Highest Abode') to take up human bodies and repeated births in this world.[25] The agreement of the two systems in seeing the human soul as having been produced from the Supreme Being is the basis for a very important theological correspondence between them in the matter of the predicament of the human soul in the world.

The predicament of the soul in the *Puṣṭimārg* and Raja Yoga

Both the *Puṣṭimārg* and Raja Yoga teach that human souls, as children of *Paramātmā* Śiva in the one case and as sparks from the essence of the divine in the other, are inherently pure. But, according to both systems, in becoming embodied beings the souls have forgotten their true nature as subordinate associates of the divine and have fallen prey to the delusion that they are autonomous creatures who move through *saṃsār*, the cycle of repeated births and deaths. They are, in this way, innately sullied by the sin of egotism (*ahaṅkār*). A Raja Yoga book[26] puts the situation this way:

> This *ātmā* is pure (*pavitra*) in its original nature but when it enters the body it is gradually corrupted by pride in the body. That is why the Lord said [at *Bhagavadgītā* 13: 19] that 'corruption (*vikārāṃś*) is produced in the soul by contact with the material world'. The sense of this is that in the course of time the *ātmā* forgets the knowledge of the body and the soul . . . and considers itself a father, son, mother, husband, wife and so on. This is the pride in the body by which the *ātmā*'s natural virtue of love is changed into attachment, greed or lust. The result of this is sorrow.

In *Tattvārthadīpanibandha* 1. 31–33a Vallabhācārya phrases it differently but with the same import:

> Knowledge and ignorance are the powers of Hari, they are produced by *māyā*,
> They belong to the *jīva* and to no other and they cause it sorrow and helplessness (*anīśatā*).

The four impositions [on the *jīva*] – that of the body, that of the senses, that of life and that of the mind – together with ignorance of the true nature,
These are the five knots of ignorance; tied up in them [the *jīva*] moves in the round of rebirth.

Though they come to the same conclusion that the result of the soul's slide into ignorance of its real nature is sorrow, the two statements differ in one interesting detail. Vallabhācārya explains why the soul comes to be involved in *saṃsār*. According to him Kṛṣṇa, as a part of the mystery of his divine play (*līlā*), has exercised his own *māyā* energy to produce the interaction of knowledge and ignorance that causes the *jīvas* to forget their true state. In contrast, Raja Yoga teaches only that it is the soul itself that loses memory of its true state and imagines itself to be an ego identified with a body. Nothing is said about whether this forgetfulness is in accordance with the will of *Paramātmā* Śiva or is the result of the inexorable law of karma and unconnected with him.

There is an antidote to the ignorance of the soul: knowledge. The soul must recover from its state of spiritual amnesia by realising that it is a soul and not an ego or a body. In the words of Vallabhācārya at *Tattvārthadīpanibandha* 1. 33b, 'with the removal of ignorance by knowledge the *jīva* will be freed (*vidyayā vidyānāśe tu jīvo mukto bhaviṣyati*)' and, as put in Raja Yoga, 'remembering *Paramātmā* is the means of gaining freedom from the karma of past births'.[27] The predicament of the soul according to both Raja Yoga and the *Puṣṭimārg* is that, though the antidote is at hand, it is impossible for the soul to perceive it. The soul wants to escape from the unhappiness of embodied, egotistical life but is prevented by its own egotistical nature from doing so. The heart of this predicament is a paradox. From the *Puṣṭimārgī* point of view, being inherently pure, the *jīvas* are in truth neither egos nor, since *saṃsār* is a figment of their own ignorant imagination and has no existence in reality, in *saṃsār* at all. But, since they are innately polluted by imagining themselves to be egos in *saṃsār*, they cannot realise their own divinely related true nature. In Raja Yoga, because the ideal is not to finish with *saṃsār* but to experience it in perfection in the coming Golden Age, the same paradox is present but is conceived of in a slightly different manner. From the Raja Yoga standpoint, the paradox is that the *ātmās*, being inherently pure, disembodied spirit, are the masters of their bodies but imagine themselves to be the same as their bodies. They cannot free their consciousness from the body and its physical needs because they cannot see themselves as separate from their bodies. In either case, the more the *jīvas* and *ātmās* try to free themselves by their own efforts from the false state of being in which they imagine themselves to be, the more they reinforce their belief in the reality of that state and enmesh themselves in it. It is plainly futile for an imaginary being to try to escape its own imagination by efforts that are, as the product of that imagination, themselves imaginary.

If the Supreme Being had no compassion, the predicament of the soul would be insurmountable. As one would expect of bhakti systems, both Raja Yoga and the *Puṣṭimārg* postulate a compassionate supreme deity. In a Raja Yoga book[28] the compassion of *Paramātmā* Śiva is expressed in these words: '*Paramātmā* observes his duty to make the miserable world (*saṃsār*) happy and to destroy anti-dharma and re-establish true dharma and to make humanity again divine.' In *Tattvārthadīpanibandha* 1. 48 Vallabhācārya puts it this way: 'From time to time and place to place Kṛṣṇa grants liberation (*mocayet*) to his devotees.' The difficulty then lies with the soul and not with any lack of compassion on the Supreme Being's part. Because of the ignorance that contaminates both the *jīva* and the *ātmā*, the compassion of Kṛṣṇa and *Paramātmā* cannot be directly received. An intermediary that is neither fully human and polluted nor completely divine and pure is needed. Both *Puṣṭimārg* and Raja Yoga supply this intermediary in the same way: the Supreme Being incarnates himself in a human being and, teaching through that human being, accomplishes the deliverance of souls.

Divine incarnation in Raja Yoga and the *Puṣṭimārg*

Within the Vallabha sect Vallabhācārya is revered as the incarnation of the *mukhārvind*, 'lotus mouth', of Kṛṣṇa. As the incarnation of the divine mouth he could transmit the method of salvation, the *Puṣṭimārg*. Since the divine mouth is the source of cleansing sacred fire, Vallabhācārya also was able to burn away the sins of his followers in order to restore them to the purity necessary for travel along the *Puṣṭimārg* to receive the grace of Kṛṣṇa. Because Vallabhācārya was the incarnation of the divine mouth from birth, there is no record of the exact moment of incarnation. There is, however, an account of the occasion on which Kṛṣṇa appeared to Vallabhācārya and revealed to him the *Brahmasambandha* 'connection with Brahman' mantra by which human souls can be cleansed of their impurity. On the testimony of the *Caurāsī vaiṣṇavan kī vārtā*,[29] a hagiography belonging to the Vallabha sect, this happened at Govind Ghāṭ near Mathura at midnight on the eleventh day of the light half of the month of Śrāvaṇ (August–September) in the year 1494.

Unlike Vallabhācārya, Lekhraj Kriplani was not born a divine incarnation. Rather, Brahma Kumari literature asserts, as in the following statement,[30] that *Paramātmā* Śiva descended into him when he was past middle age: '[*Paramātmā* Śiva] in order to give knowledge and to carry on the battle against *māyā*[31] entered an elderly human body . . . He came [into that body] in order to make humanity glorious, wise, righteous, and prosperous through instruction in [Raja] Yoga.' In a way that is reminiscent of Vallabhācārya's status as the *mukhārvind* of Kṛṣṇa, Lekhraj, after he had received *Paramātmā* Śiva into his body, is referred to as conveying the divine knowledge through his *mukhārvind*: '[*Paramātmā* Śiva] imparted instruction in natural Raja

Yoga and the *Gītā*-knowledge through his [i.e. Lekhraj's] lotus mouth (*mukhārvind*) for the benefit of all.[32] Moreover, just as Vallabhācārya as the divine mouth was able to purify those whom he took into his spiritual protection, so is Lekhraj, whom *Paramātmā* Śiva had renamed *Prajāpitā*[33] *Brahmā*, through his lotus mouth able to transform his followers into 'brāhmaṇs in the lineage of the mouth' of Brahmā and grant them entrance to the Golden Age.[34] Furthermore, again like Vallabhācārya, Lekhraj performs this purification through the holy fire that will burn away the impurities of his followers: 'By the fire of that divine knowledge which *Parampitā paramātmā* [Śiva] bestows through *Prajāpitā Brahmā* the vices (*vikarm*) of human souls are burnt away. In this way, the seed of the sorrow of the human soul is obliterated and the soul is purified.'[35]

The appearance of Kṛṣṇa to Vallabhācārya at Govind Ghāṭ did not take place in secret, but was observed by his companion Dāmodardās and has been recorded in writing. There was likewise an eyewitness to the initial descent of *Paramātmā* Śiva into Lekhraj. A daughter-in-law named Brijindra (Bṛj Indrā) gave the following description of the event:

I noticed that Dada's, that is, Baba's, eyes were so red that it was as if a red light bulb were burning in them. His face also was entirely red and the room was filled with light. I seemed to have lost awareness of my body, it was as if I were out of my body. Meanwhile, a voice seemed to be coming from above, as if someone else were speaking from Dada's mouth. At first the voice was soft but then gradually became louder. This was what it said [in Sanskrit]:

निजानन्द स्वरूपं शिवोऽहम् शिवोऽम्
ज्ञानस्वरूपं शिवोऽहम् शिवोऽहम् । प्रकाश स्वरूपं शिवोऽम् शिवोऽहम् ।।

I am Shiva, I am Shiva, the essence of innate joy,
I am Shiva, I am Shiva, the essence of knowledge,
I am Shiva, I am Shiva, the essence of light.

Then Dada's eyes closed. To this very day I have never forgotten either that wonderful scene or that voice. The whole atmosphere was memorable and I will always remember that feeling of being disembodied. Dada's eyes opened and he gazed all around the room with wonder. He was absorbed in what he had just seen. I asked, 'Baba, what were you looking at'. He replied, 'Who was it? It was a light, a power. It was a new world . . . . A light and a power said, "It is this sort of world that you must make". But it didn't say how I was to make it.'[36]

Although at first Lekhraj did not know what it was that had entered him at the time of this experience, after reflection he concluded that it could only have been *Parampitā paramātmā* Śiva. As the first step in the foundation of the new world of his vision, he brought the Brahma Kumaris World Spiritual University into being.

For those who practised the *Puṣṭimārg* and Rāja Yoga during the lifetimes of their founders, there was no problem about recovering the state of purity requisite for deliverance. But both Vallabhācārya and Lekhraj had human bodies that would have to die. In 1531 Vallabhācārya passed away and in 1969 Lekhraj's earthly life came to an end. How would those who joined the Vallabha sect or the Brahma Kumaris World Spiritual University after those dates be purified without the divine incarnation? The problem for both groups was somehow to preserve contact with the founder after his death. The two groups solved this problem differently but equally successfully.

In the course of one of his pilgrimages Vallabhācārya visited the city of Pandharpur in Maharashtra. There the form of Viṣṇu worshipped at the main temple had decided to incarnate himself as Vallabhācārya's son. He appeared to Vallabhācārya and instructed him to marry so that the incarnation might take place. As a result of this second incarnation, all of the direct male descendants of Vallabhācārya's son were accepted by their followers as incarnations of Kṛṣṇa. This belief can still be attested for the mid-nineteenth century[37] but nowadays members, including leaders, of the Vallabha sect are much more circumspect about it.[38] For those that continue to believe that the descendants of Vallabhācārya are, like him, incarnations of Kṛṣṇa, Vallabhācārya and his spiritual function will be present as long as his biological line lasts.

Although Lekhraj had children, the requirement that all who practise Raja Yoga be celibate makes it impossible for the divine incarnation to pass down through his descendants. Another solution had to be found. Even before Lekhraj's death, some Brahma Kumaris were able to go into trance and receive communications direct from *Paramātmā* Śiva.[39] After Lekhraj's passing, this ability was confined to a single woman in the movement.[40] At the present time this 'trance messenger' receives the teachings, called *murlīs*, 'flutes', of *Paramātmā* Śiva given though Lekhraj, who is in the Subtle Angelic World (*Sūkṣam devtāõ kā lok*, 'World of subtle deities').[41] In this way, Lekhraj remains always with the members of the Brahma Kumaris World Spiritual University and will be able to serve as intermediary between them and *Paramātmā* Śiva for an unlimited length of time.

Raja Yoga as a reinterpretation of bhakti theology

Though Brahma Kumaris recognise a quiescent state for the *ātmā* in the *parama dhām* world of *Paramātmā* Śiva, that is not the goal toward which they are striving. Instead, through the practice of Raja Yoga, they expect to be translated from this world of evil and error doomed to imminent destruction to the perfect Golden Age to be established on an earth new and reconstituted. Such a goal is millennial in character. Millenarianism is, as Babb[42] has pointed out, rather unusual but by no means unknown in the Indian context. In this regard, though, the Brahma Kumaris World Spiritual University does bring to mind a Christian millennial Church like that of the

Shakers in the United States[43] more than a bhakti movement like the Vallabha sect, with its goal of salvation in Kṛṣṇa's unearthly *Golok* 'Cow-world' paradise. It may be that this resemblance to millenarian Christianity, even if only superficial, has been instrumental in making Raja Yoga attractive in countries with a European heritage.

The millennial character of the Brahma Kumaris World Spiritual University is framed in a Hindu bhakti cultural milieu. Specifically, it is Vallabhācārya's variety of Hindu bhakti that seems to have provided the Brahma Kumaris with their theological vocabulary. In the preceding pages I have shown how a few items of this vocabulary have been adopted into Raja Yoga but at the same time adapted in meaning to fit into the millennial goal of that system.

NOTES

I owe a debt of gratitude to members of the Brahma Kumaris World Spiritual University in Australia, Germany, and India, who have welcomed me to their meetings and have discussed their theology with me. I have also benefited from the comments of Jonathan Bader of the Australian National University on an early draft of this paper.

1. The name of the organisation in English is derived from its Hindi name, *Prajāpitā brahmākumārī īśvarīya viśva-vidyālay*. *Prajāpitā Brahmā*, 'Father of Mankind, Brahmā', is a title of the founder of the organisation (see n. 33 below). *Kumārī* is the word for 'maiden' in Hindi. The masculine equivalent is *kumār*. The followers of *Prajāpitā Brahmā* call themselves *brahmākumār* and *brahmākumārī* (Brahma Kumars and Brahma Kumaris in English), 'the pure sons and daughters of Brahmā' (Jagdish Chander, *Adi Dev, the First Man*, Mt. Abu, Rajasthan, 1983, p. 49). By convention the followers collectively refer to themselves as Brahma Kumaris.
2. A. Burr, *I Am Not My Body: A Study of the International Hare Krishna Sect*, New Delhi, 1984, p. 3.
3. *Prajapita Brahma Kumaris Ishwariya Vishwa Vidyalaya: Introduction and Addresses of Some of the Centres in India and Overseas*, Mt. Abu, Rajasthan, [1986], p. 2.
4. R. Hummel, *Indische Mission und neue Frömmigkeit im Westen*, Stuttgart, 1980, pp. 49, 258.
5. H. Streitfeld, *A Psychologist Reports on the International Brahma Kumaris Movement*, San Francisco, 1982, and L. A. Babb, *Redemptive Encounters*, Delhi, 1987, pp. 93–155.
6. J. C. Sanjoy, ed., *Godly Truth and Wisdom in the Auspicious Real Gita*, Mt. Abu, Rajasthan, [1960], pp. 43–54, and Chander, op. cit., pp. 25–6.
7. Jagdish Chander, *A Brief Biography of Brahma Baba*, Mt. Abu, Rajasthan, 1984, p. 52.
8. Jagdish Chander, *Mahābhārat aur Gītā kā saccā svarūp aur sār*, Mt. Abu,

Rajasthan, 1977, pp. 521–2. As with all translations from Hindi or Sanskrit in this paper the English version of the passage quoted is, unless otherwise stated, mine.

9. *Avyakt Bapdada: God the Supreme Speaking with the Angel Brahma to his Brahmin Children during 1984–85*, Sydney, n.d., pp. 62–3. BapDada (*Bāpdādā*, 'Father Grandfather') is a composite term used to indicate the Supreme Being (= Bāp) speaking through Lekhraj's (i.e. Dādā's) incorporeal form. Lekhraj is also called Baba (*bābā*, 'Father').
10. Tyāgīśānanda, *Aphorisms on the Gospel of Divine Love or* Nārada Bhakti Sūtras, Madras, 1955, p. 19.
11. R. K. Barz, 'Kṛṣṇadās Adhikārī: an Irascible Devotee's Approach to the Divine', *JCSR* 14, pp. 35–54.
12. *Avyakt Bapdada*, pp. 60–2.
13. A. W. Entwistle, *The* Rāsa Māna ke Pada *of Kevalarāma*, Groningen, 1983, pp. 54–70, 84–92.
14. For my information on the life of Lekhraj I have relied upon three biographies, all published by the Brahma Kumaris World Spiritual University and all evidently by the same author. The first of these (Jagdish Chander (Jagdīś Candra), *Jīvan ko palṭānevālī ek adbhut jīvan kahānī*, Mt. Abu, n.d.) is in Hindi, the second (Jagdish Chander, *Adi Dev*, 1983) seems to be an English version of the first and the third (Jagdish Chander, *A Brief Biography*, 1984) is probably an abridgement of the second. In spite of being so closely interconnected each of these books differs occasionally from the other two in detail.
15. Chander, *Jīvan ko palṭānevālī. . . kahānī*, pp. 13–14.
16. Chander, *Adi Dev*, p. 27.
17. Chander, *A Brief Biography*, p. 12.
18. Jagdish Chander, *Sāptāhik pāṭhyakram*, Mt. Abu, Rajasthan, 1975, pp. 40, 45, 60–1.
19. Chander, *Mahābhārat aur Gītā*, pp. 190, 285–6, 463–6, 478.
20. Verses cited in the following pages from the first part of Vallabhācārya's *Tattvārthadīpanibandha* are from the text edited, with English and Gujarati translations, by Harishankar Onkarji Shastri under the title *Saprakāśastattvārthadīpanibandhaḥ tasya prathamaṃ śāstrārthaprakaraṇam* (Bombay, 1943).
21. Sītārām Caturvedī, *Mahāprabhu śrīmadvallabhācārya aur puṣṭimārg*, Varanasi, 1966, pp. 279–80.
22. R. K. Barz, *The Bhakti Sect of Vallabhācārya*, Faridabad, Haryana, 1976, pp. 66–7.
23. Chander, *Mahābhārat aur Gītā*, p. 447.
24. Chander, *Sāptāhik pāṭhyakram*, p. 28.
25. Chander, *Mahābhārat aur Gītā*, pp. 467–8.
26. Ibid., p. 447.
27. Chander, *Sāptāhik pāṭhyakram*, pp. 163–4.
28. Ibid., pp. 80–1.
29. Dvārikādās Parīkh, *Caurāsī vaiṣṇavan kī vārtā: tīn janm kī līlā bhāvanā vālī*, Mathura, 1970, pp. 4–5. An English version of this passage is given in Shyam Das, *Eighty-four Vaishnavas*, Baroda, 1985, pp. 17–18.
30. Chander, *Mahābhārat aur Gītā*, p. 191.
31. *Māyā* in Raja Yoga is the false, imaginary view of the soul as part of the physical world. It is not, as it is in the *Puṣṭimārg*, a power of the Supreme Being.

32. Ibid., p. 226.
33. Originally, as in a set of Brahma Kumari circulars in Hindi dated Feb., June, and July 1942, the title seems to have been *Prajāpati*, 'Lord of mankind' (*Vartmān mahābhārī mahābhārat laṛāī aur unkā pariṇām*, vol. xvi, Karachi, 1942, p. 1). Monika Thiel-Horstmann drew my attention to these circulars.
34. Chander, *Mahābhārat aur Gītā*, p. 226.
35. Ibid., p. 478.
36. Chander, *Jīvan ko palṭānevālī . . . kahānī*, pp. 25–6.
37. *Report of the Maharaj Libel Case and of the Bhattia Conspiracy Case Connected with it*, Bombay, 1862, p. 133.
38. P. Brent, *Godmen of India*, Harmondsworth, 1973, pp. 178–9, 191–3.
39. Sanjoy, *Godly Truth and Wisdom*, p. vi.
40. Babb, *Redemptive Encounters*, p. 106.
41. Chander, *Adi dev*, pp. 167–71, and Chander, *Sāptāhik pāṭhyakram*, p. 24.
42. Babb, *Redemptive Encounters*, pp. 107–9.
43. Like the Brahma Kumaris the Shakers saw themselves as being at the dawning of an age of spiritual perfection. They were also similar to the Brahma Kumaris in many other ways, among which are: the acceptance of women as leaders, the utter rejection of sexual relations as impure, and the recognition of the divine spirit manifested in their founder (M. Melcher, *The Shaker Adventure*, Cleveland, Ohio, 1960, pp. 10–11, 111, 155).

INDEX

UNIVERSITY OF CAMBRIDGE
ORIENTAL PUBLICATIONS PUBLISHED FOR THE
FACULTY OF ORIENTAL STUDIES

1 *Averroes' Commentary on Plato's Republic*, edited and translated by E. I. J. Rosenthal
2 *Fitzgerald's 'Salámán and Absál'*, edited by A. J. Arberry
3 *Ihara Saikaku: The Japanese Family Storehouse*, translated and edited by G. W. Sargent
4 *The Avestan Hymn to Mithra*, edited and translated by Ilya Gershevitch
5 *The Fuṣūl al-Madani of al-Fārābi*, edited and translated by D. M. Dunlop (out of print)
6 *Dun Karm, Poet of Malta*, texts chosen and translated by A. J. Arberry; introduction, notes and glossary by P. Grech
7 *The Political Writings of Ogyú Sorai*, by J. R. McEwan
8 *Financial Administration under the T'ang Dynasty*, by D. C. Twitchett
9 *Neolithic Cattle-Keepers of South India: A Study of the Deccan Ashmounds*, by F. R. Allchin
10 *The Japanese Enlightenment: A Study of the Writings of Fukuzawa Yukichi*, by Carmen Blacker
11 *Records of Han Administration*, vol. i: *Historical Assessment*, by M. Loewe
12 *Records of Han Administration*, vol. ii: *Documents*, by M. Loewe
13 *The Language of Indrafit of Orchā: A Study of Early Braj Bhāṣā Prose*, by R. S. McGregor
14 *Japan's First General Election*, 1890, by R. H. P. Mason
15 *A Collection of Tales from Uji: A Study and Translation of 'Uji Shūi Monogatari'*, by D. E. Mills
16 *Studia Semitica*, vol. i: *Jewish Themes*, by E. I. J. Rosenthal
17 *Studia Semitica*, vol. ii: *Islamic Themes*, by E. I. J. Rosenthal
18 *A Nestorian Collection of Christological Texts*, vol. i: *Syriac Text*, by Luise Abramowski and Alan E. Goodman
19 *A Nestorian Collection of Christological Texts*, vol. ii: *Introduction, Translation, Indexes*, by Luise Abramowski and Alan E. Goodman
20 *The Syriac Version of the Pseudo-Nonnos Mythological Scholia*, by Sebastian Brock
21 *Water Rights and Irrigation Practices in Lahj*, by A. M. A. Maktari
22 *The Commentary of Rabbi David Kimhi on Psalms cxx–cl*, edited and translated by Joshua Baker and Ernest W. Nicholson
23 *Jalāl al-dīn al-Suyūṭī*, vol. i: *Biography and Background*, by E. M. Sartain

24 *Jalāl al-dīn al-Suyūṭī*, vol. ii: 'Al-Tahadduth bini'mat allah', Arabic text by E. M. Sartain
25 *Origen and the Jews: Studies in Jewish–Christian Relations in Third Century Palestine*, by N. R. M. de Lange
26 *The* 'Visaladevarāsa': *A restoration of the text*, by John D. Smith
27 *Shabbetha Sofer and his Prayer-Book*, by Stefan C. Reif
28 *Mori Ogai and the Modernization of Japanese Culture*, by Richard John Bowring
29 *The Rebel Lands: An Investigation into Origins of Early Mesopotamian Mythology*, by J. V. Kinnier Wilson
30 *Saladin: The Politics of the Holy War*, by Malcolm Cameron Lyons and David Jackson
31 *Khotanese Buddhist Texts*, revised edition, edited by H. W. Bailey
32 *Interpreting the Hebrew Bible: Essays in Honour of E. I. J. Rosenthal*, edited by J. A. Emerton and S. C. Reif
33 *The Traditional Interpretation of the Apocalypse of St John in the Ethiopian Orthodox Church*, by Roger W. Cowley
34 *South Asian Archaeology 1981: Proceedings of the Sixth International Conference of South Asian Archaeologists in Western Europe*, edited by Bridget Allchin (with assistance from Raymond Allchin and Miriam Sidell)
35 *God's Conflict with the Dragon and the Sea; Echoes of a Canaanite Myth in the Old Testament*, by John Day
36 *Land and Sovereignty in India: Agrarian Society and Politics under the Eighteenth-Century Maratha Svarājya*, by André Wink
37 *God's Caliph: Religious Authority in the First Centuries of Islam*, by Patricia Crone and Martin Hinds
38 *Ethiopian Biblical Interpretation: A Study in Exegetical Tradition and Hermeneutics*, by Roger W. Cowley
39 *Monk and Mason on the Tigris Frontier: The Early History of Ṭur 'Abdin*, by Andrew Palmer
40 *Early Japanese Books in Cambridge University Library: A Catalogue of the Aston, Satow and Von Siebold Collections*, by Nozomu Hayashi and Peter Kornicki
41 *Molech: A God of Human Sacrifice in the Old Testament*, by John Day
42 *Arabian Studies*, edited by R. B. Serjeant and R. L. Bidwell
43 *Naukar, Rajput and Sepoy: The Ethnohistory of the Military Labour Market in Hindustan, 1450–1850*, by Dirk H. A. Kolff
44 *The Epic of Pābūjī: A Study, Transcription and Translation*, by John D. Smith
45 *Anti-Christian Polemic in Early Islam: Abū 'Īsā al-Warrāq's 'Against the Trinity'*, by David Thomas
46 *Devotional Literature in South Asia: Current Research 1985–1988. Papers of the Fourth Conference on Devotional Literature in New Indo-Aryan Languages*, edited by R. S. McGregor
47 *Genizah Research after Ninety Years: The Case of Judaeo-Arabic. Papers read at the Third Congress of the Society for Judaeo-Arabic Studies*, edited by Joshua Blau and Stefan C. Reif